Documentary Problems in Canadian History

Volume I
Pre-Confederation

Documentary Problems in Canadian History

Volume I
Pre-Confederation

Edited By

J. M. Bumsted, Ph.D.

Assistant Professor of History
McMaster University
Hamilton, Ontario

1969

Irwin-Dorsey Limited, Georgetown, Ontario

First Printing, May, 1969

The front and back cover pictures are used courtesy of Manitoba Archives (for Fort Garry, and the early construction of the Canadian Pacific Railway) and of Historical Pictures Service, Chicago (for Lieutenant-Governor Simcoe opening the Legislative Assembly of Upper Canada, the charge of the British Highlanders at Quebec, a voyageur on a Canadian stream, the citadel of Quebec, and a fur train from the far north).

Library of Congress Catalog Card No. 79–85480

Printed in Canada

Preface

I have designed this two-volume work with the collaboration of 23 leading scholars in Canadian history in the hope it will prove useful as a textbook principally for those who teach Canadian history at the university level. It has long seemed to me (and to the contributors) that there has been a shortage of readily available material beyond the standard textbook for use in the classroom. This lack was not so readily apparent a few years ago, when most courses in most universities were taught solely in large lecture halls with little or no opportunity for exchange of views between teacher and student. But the introduction of the seminar, tutorial, and discussion group into even survey courses in Canadian history and certainly into advanced courses has greatly altered the needs of both teacher and student. Most of us have discovered—as we began to meet regularly with students in small groups—that the old reading lists were greatly inadequate and the library not able to take up the slack. Regular discussion requires something to talk about—not simply information, but concepts, ideas, issues, and problems. All students must do the same basic reading, more written work is frequently required, and all of this entails new approaches to classroom material.

One way to respond to the new teaching situation is by employing thematic "problems." Assuming the validity of this approach, the next question arises over both subject and content. The problems may well be the traditional ones within the field, emphasizing historiography and retrospection. Several quite useful works within this context have appeared since I began editing this one, which is based upon quite different principles. I have asked some of the leading specialists in a number of areas of Canadian history to produce what seems to them to be a significant and representative problem within their own specialized field by making available to the student some of the documentary evidence which would be employed by them—as specialists—in considering this problem. As I had hoped, the response has been to develop problems which reflect on-going work in Canadian history rather than the issues of the past. I think the student who uses this collection will have a good idea of where research in Canadian history is heading, and perhaps will even be stimulated to become involved in this himself.

Although the content of the problems is largely composed of documents (with careful introductions by the specialist to sketch necessary background and suggest meaningful questions), the framework is quite different from the bits and pieces of unfocused documents which up to now have been most common in collections of primary sources. Documents here are not illustrations of the findings of other historians, but the raw material of history which require the student to come to grips with the historical process. It should therefore be possible for the interchange between teachers and students employing these problems as a basis for discussion to be concerned not only with the conclusions of historians but with their methods as well.

Dundas, Ontario
April, 1969

J. M. BUMSTED

Table of Contents

PROBLEM 1

The Indian Problem in the 17th Century

CORNELIUS J. JAENEN,
University of Ottawa

Among the several consequential problems raised by the contact of the French and the Amerindians was that of the Frenchification or assimilation of the latter. The French who came to North America were sustained by an idea of order, based as they thought on eternal and immutable religious principles. They found not an empty continent but an inhabited hemisphere, and this posed a problem which was at once practical and theoretical. Practically, they had to overcome or dominate this natural man, they had to integrate him into their commercial, political, and cultural aspirations, and, not least, they had to live with him. Theoretically, they had to understand this natural man, this savage. The French brought with them a pattern of culture, an idea of order, in which theory and practice were taken to be identical.

In a sense New France was a new found chaos. Natural wealth, such as cod, furs, and lumber, was there for the taking. But what about the natural men? Frenchmen were extremely conscious of their civilized heritage, and in their colony they found not only an uncivilized environment but also uncivilized men or natural men living in a natural world. There was a challenge in this to elevate brutish savages to civilized men, that is, to men refined in manners and improved in arts and learning above their natural state.

It was not thought possible to civilize men without also Christianizing them. Indians assimilated into a French cultural pattern would necessarily venerate the God made in the French image. Henry IV issued a mandate to evangelize the North American tribes and assimilate them into French colonial life. The task of assimilating the aborigines was soon left to the Catholic missionaries, although the state continued to make civilization of the tribemen part of its ill-defined colonial policy. The missionaries did not distinguish between Christianization or evangelization on the one hand, and Frenchification or civilization on the other hand. By 1627 a baptized Indian was reputed a citizen, and by 1663 Indians were declared subject to the laws of France, although they were not accorded the same rights and privileges as Europeans. Champlain's dream of a French Indian Catholic empire gave way to the concept of a biracial colony of Europeans and civilized

Indians, which in turn was replaced by the less ambitious and idealistic royal province containing a few segregated communities of converted natives.

The missionary problem initially was one of finding suitable vehicles of expression for conveying the concepts of Christianity. This was soon compounded by the cultural clash which grew out of the commercial contact of a sophisticated European group, significant numbers of which did not practice the virtues extolled by the missionaries or who practiced a deviant Protestant form thereof, with a semi-nomadic assortment of tribesmen who while possessing no concepts of personal property and personal salvation were nevertheless admirably well adjusted to their environment. State officials, for political purposes and economic gain, pressed the ideal of assimilation by means of religious conversion, integrated education, racial intermarriage and equal legal status. Was this policy realistic?

The documents which follow are designed to indicate first of all the impressions of the first Europeans to settle in Canada concerning the aboriginal population. These impressions are usually closely related to aspirations—political, economic, and religious. Allied to imperialistic dreams and hopes of commercial exploitation were visions conjured by Catholic apocalypticalism—an Indian Israel, the millenial kingdom, the Third Age of the Holy Ghost—and the evangelical zeal of early 17th-century French *dévotisme*. The French were certain that man could realize his highest potentialities only in that kind of society which they possessed in the motherland. Added to the challenge of civilizing the American man was that of realizing the pure and ideal European Christian society. Did practice always bear out theory? What evidence is there that the Indians were sometimes destroyed, not civilized? From the idea of the natural savage, how did the impression change to one of bloodthirsty, filthy, and depraved barbarians? Why did the Jesuit missionaries and the hospital and teaching sisters who came to Canada seeking sacrifice and suffering also expect martyrdom?

When it was found that many Frenchmen who came into contact with the Indians actually adopted the Indian way of life, and that the tendency to "Americanization" was indeed one of progressive barbarization, the foremost cultural ambassadors, the missionaries, had recourse to the segregationist scheme of the Franciscan missionary, Geronimo de Mendieta, so successfully adopted by the Jesuits in South America as *reducciones*. The reserve at Sillery in 1637 was the first Canadian version of this approach. Why has it continued to be the mainstay of Indian policy? When drunkenness developed into the chief social problem of the areas of contact between Europeans and Amerindians, prohibition legislation was drafted. Why has it remained an important feature of the Indian question? Was there a significant difference between French and English attitudes toward the Indians? How did the Indian regard the various groups of European intruders? Is there any evidence that the Indian was prejudicially discriminated against in New France?

Two opposing interpretations of this period of Canadian history have been advanced. One argues that the heavy hand of royal authority, trade monopolies, and clerical and seigneurial supervision drove men to the forests in search of freedom and in defiance of the regulations. The other sees the problems arising rather out of the lack of adequate social controls, the absence of an effective police power, and clerical and secular inability to enforce regulations over a vast and sparsely populated colony. Was the phenomenon of the *coureurs-de-bois*, an important link between Indians and Europeans, merely a defiance of royal and ecclesiastical policy? Or was it, at the practical level, a means of supplementing family income and perhaps the real means of subsistence for immigrant families? Did the presence of large numbers of *coureurs-de-bois* indicate that the French— as a minority group dispersed over a large territory and less well adapted to the environment than the Indian in several respects—were being assimilated all too frequently into Indian society?

Were assimilation and evangelization necessarily complementary efforts? Did the religious deliberately confuse the two ideals? Why did the secular authorities adopt the policy formulated by the missionaries for the realization of their objectives? What does the 17th-century experience of the French in Canada indicate to us concerning acculturation and assimilation? The evaluations made in the 17th century of the contact between the two cultures must be considered. But it should be remembered that we have no detailed Indian exposition of native beliefs and attitudes, and no Indian account of the results of the cultural clash. This is a very unfortunate and irreparable lacuna. The reader is invited to give some thought to the subsequent developments in the role of the Indian in Canada and to current theories of assimilation and acculturation.

The best general work on Canadian Indians is still Diamond Jenness, *The Indians of Canada* (1963). The work of the missionaries is recounted in R. G. Thwaites (ed.), *The Jesuit Relations and Allied Documents* (73 vols., Cleveland, 1896–1901); O. M. Jouve, *Les Franciscains et le Canada* (1915); and Joyce Marshall (ed.), *Word from New France* (1967). For an account of all aspects of Indian life, R. Douville and J. D. Casanova, *La Vie quotidienne des Indiens du Canada à l'époque de la colonisation française* (1967) is recommended. Of direct bearing on this topic, the following are suggested for further reading: Alfred G. Bailey, *The Conflict of European and Eastern Algonkian Cultures, 1504–1700* (1937); R. H. Pearce, *The Savages of America. A Study of the Indian and the Idea of Civilization* (1953); Gilbert Chinard, *L'Amérique et le rêve exotique dans la littérature française au XVIIe et XVIIIe siècles* (1917); Frank C. Hibben, *L'Homme primitif américain* (1953). The editor of this problem has in preparation a full-length study of relations between church and state in New France, in which the problem of Frenchification of the Indians will be dealt with exhaustively, to be published by the University of Ottawa Press.

A. European Impressions and Aspirations

Document A–1

D'AVITY—THE NATURAL SAVAGE

(Pierre d'Avity, *Description Générale de l'Amérique, troisième partie du Monde* [Paris, 1637], pp. 30–31.)

The view of the "natural savage," a savage who was a fit subject for conversion and assimilation into French life, but who remained nevertheless a savage, an untutored, uncultured, unsophisticated aborigine, was basically optimistic. It should *be contrasted with another European view that the Indians deserved to be cruelly subjugated and enslaved in punishment for their idolatry, their barbaric customs, and their paganism. The Spanish jurist, Juan Ginés de Sepúlveda, had advanced such a thesis on the basis of the Aristotelian theory that the imperfect must be subject to the perfect and that the superior must rule the inferior. Were French attitudes influenced by arguments of natural inequality or by views such as Montaigne's that the "duty" of colonizing nations was to "gently polish and cultivate" the indigenous peoples and enlist their collaboration "inasmuch as they are equals being human beings"?*

The inhabitants of these countries are of medium height, well proportioned, oily-skinned or well tanned, not dark by birth: but being naked most of the time, they rub themselves with oils against flies, besides they lie on the ground, and are exposed to heat and wind. Nearly all of them have dark hair, except a few who are chestnut, but there are no blonds or redheads among them. As for the beard, they have all the hair removed, and there are only the Sagamos for the most part who have some beard. Most have dark eyes, not blue or green. Moreover, they are as handsome young men and beautiful young women as may be seen in France. They are great runners and swimmers, and the women too have a marvellous disposition. They are usually more slim and nimbler than we, and one finds none who are paunchy, hunchbacked, deformed, niggardly, gouty or stony among them. They are moreover most skilful in wrestling.

They take very little care for the future, as all other Americans; to the extent that when they have something they celebrate and make a perpetual feast with songs, dances and harangues and to constrain them to restrain themselves when they are not at war is to speak of sedition. It is true that the women are thrifty and if one wishes to believe them they make provisions for winter of cured meats, of some

roots, peas, beans, acorns and prunes, putting these in sacks which they hang in the branches of trees so that neither the humidity of the ground nor the rats will despoil them. They do not steal from one another, although the Armouchiquois incidentally are clever robbers. They do not fight one another, are naturally fearful and cowardly, although they boast they are brave, and try by all means to be esteemed as such, because valour among them is regarded as the perfection of virtue. The majority of them are not at all malicious, but liberal, have a good mind and a clear one in so far as discerning common and sensible matters, deducing their reasons with gracefulness, always employing some pleasing comparison. They have a very good memory for material matters, such as having seen you, the qualities of a place where they have been, or what one did in their presence some twenty or thirty years ago; but it is impossible for them to learn by heart the sequel of a discourse. They mock at the defects or deformities of body of others, they have the word of command when in private, and although they lack police, power, letters, arts, wealth and other things, they despise other nations and esteem themselves highly. They are in no wise ungrateful, but give each other everything without ever daring to refuse their companions, or to eat without sharing with them what they have. They are of fairly gay humour while being somewhat dreamy, and they speak very precisely as if to make themselves well heard. The Armouchiquois must be treated with terror because if one fondles them they immediately scheme some surprise. They do not lack wit, but are also very cunning and treacherous. The Iroquois are very similar in temper and manners.

They occupy themselves for the most part with hunting and fishing inasmuch as they do not concern themselves with ploughing. The girls practice dancing; but the women work more than the men, be it fishing, be it something else, without being forced to do so. They are not present nevertheless at the *Tabagies* or feasts of the menfolk, nor at their council meetings. They go with their prisoners to gather wood, make mats of reeds with which they garnish their cabins or use to sit upon. They trim and render supple beaver skins, moosehides and pelts of other animals and sew them together neatly, if required, make baskets of reeds, shells, bark of trees for drinking and storing their meats, and work at their scarves, necklaces or bracelets, called Matachia, or at their canoes and small boats, or plough the ground in the countries where agriculture is practiced, while the men amuse themselves only with hunting and warfare. . . .

Document A–2

LAMOTHE CADILLAC—THE LOST TRIBES

(Milton Quaife [ed.], *The Western Country in the 17th Century. The Memoirs of Antoine Lamothe Cadillac and Pierre Liette* [New York, 1962], pp. 53–58.)

Catholic apocalypticalism and the evangelical zeal of the various reformist mystical circles characteristic of the early 17th-century religious revival in France were responsible for the dream of creating a New Israel in the New World. Though few entertained for long the hypothesis that the Indians were descendants of the 10 lost tribes of Israel, many continued to draw comparisons between Indian and Hebrew cultures thus reinforcing speculation concerning the advent of the millenial kingdom, or the spiritual church of the mystics as opposed to the institutional church of the papacy. In a sense, the discovery of the New World could be equated with the imminent end of the world. To what extent do the memoirs of Antoine Lamothe Cadillac—a fur trader and soldier—embody this particular strain of thought?

If the statements set forth in this chapter are considered attentively the reader may think, as I do, that all these tribes are descended from the Hebrews and were originally Jews, which may also be observed from the terms they use in conversation and in their speeches and customs.

The Jews formerly called one another brothers and companions; the Indians do the same. The Jews annointed and perfumed their hair; the Indians oil and grease theirs. The Jews fought desperately and in an undisciplined manner to preserve their liberty, preferring to kill their parents and their wives and children and themselves rather than to fall into the hands of their enemies alive. The Indians are so jealous of their liberty that they defend it to the death, and think there is nothing in the world so shameful to a man as slavery. For this reason they never leave anything in the hands of their prisoners which could aid in their destruction, for they kill themselves at the first opportunity: and when they are in the midst of torture, they display a degree of fortitude which amazes their tormentors. The Jews were uneasy, restless, seditious, jealous of the prosperity of their neighbors, even when they were of the same race as themselves and this is the real character of the Indians also.

The Jews were fond of war, assemblies, councils, and speeches, and under some fine pretext they were always indulging in acts of perfidy, treasons, and horrible massacres. The Indians cannot live without frequent feasting; councils and assemblies are their daily bread; and while they are pretending to be negotiating for friendships and alliances, whether with friends or enemies, they watch for an opportunity of making a good stroke as they call it, that is, of destroying them utterly in their characteristic fashion.

The Jews believed in dreams and visions, and the Indians believe that in their sleep a guardian spirit shows them their destiny, and especially what is to happen to them on their war forays. . . .

The Jews married several wives, and put them away whenever they pleased; the Indians follow the same practice. . . . The Jews paid the greatest honor to their dead and were most careful as to the right of burial; the Indians hold nothing so precious as the bones of their dead, and preserve them as relics. The Jews held feasts and made prayers to God, interceding for those who were dead; and the Indians hold feasts and festivals and make presents and sacrifices to the Sun and Moon for the souls of their relatives.

The Jews prayed to God to take the souls of their relatives to Eden, that is, to the garden or paradise of delight. The Indians pray to the Sun to guide and light the spirits of their tribe during their journey until they reach the happy dwelling-place of their ancestors.

The sect of the Essenes among the Jews believed that souls, on quitting their bodies, crossed the western sea and went to dwell in islands of delight, where sugar and all sorts of pleasant things abounded, where the air was soft and mild and exceedingly pure, and that they were exempt there from all the woes met with in the present life; and the Indians believe that their souls go to a region towards the east, where they have everything in abundance, where it is never cold nor hot, a country carpeted with the skins of martens and all kinds of furs.

The sect of the Sadduces among the Jews denied that souls were either tor-tured or honored, as well as denying the resurrection; and the Indians will not even listen to a word of the pains of hell, and say that such statements are lies invented to inspire fear, for they cannot understand that one who is dead can rise and live again. The Jews spoke in parables and metaphysically, and the Indians scarcely ever talk in any other way.

Finally, while it is from the Jews that we learn how the Deluge came, we see that the Indians also know about it. Nor is there any occasion for surprise at their fictions on this and so many other subjects; for if the Jews, who were so near to God and concerned for their history went astray, and if so many other peoples who have had the resource of writing to supply any defect of memory have plunged into an abyss of legends, how could the Indians, who know nothing of reading and writing, have retained what so many centuries have effaced? So I believe, from the observations I have just set forth that many people will be convinced that they are descended from the Jewish race, since their manners, customs, and ceremonies resemble those of the Jews more closely than any other nation. We shall see, also, in various passages of this Memoir, other details which will confirm the preceding ones and will complete, as far as possible, the proof of my theory; but to find out by what route the tribes have spread into the New World — that is the secret.

Document A–3

LE CLERCQ—EARLIER CHRISTIAN CONTACT

(Chrestien Le Clercq, *Nouvelle Relation de la Gaspesie, qui contient les Moeurs & la Religion des Sauvages Gaspesiens* [Paris, 1691], pp. 268–75.)

There was some speculation in the 17th century that Christianity had been introduced to the North American tribes before the arrival of the French but that the faith had degenerated until only a few vestiges, such as the usage of the cross, remained. In some recent historical writing, the Irish monks have been credited with planting Christianity in North America, and there is accumulating evidence of Norse Christian settlement. The presence off the coasts of fishermen who sometimes landed to trade, among other activities, also could explain the practices which interested Chrestien Le Clercq. The important matter raised by Le Clercq, however, is the question of how to facilitate accommodation and assimilation. What solutions does he offer?

The use of the Cross, and the honour which our Gaspesians rendered to this sacred sign of our salvation, gave me the very subject for explaining to them the holy mysteries of which in the darkness of their errors and blindness they were ignorant. Thus I had them conceive that this Cross, which they shared with others through the singular favour of Heaven, should bring them to the worship and adoration of the One who had taken it to himself because of His love for us: that they had even more pressing obligations than the other Nations of New France to profess the Faith of JESUS-CHRIST; and that to this end they must leave their erroneous ways and receive Baptism, without which they cannot be saved. They seemed very pleased and satisfied with this discourse, and promised me they would follow exactly the charitable advice I gave them; all of them protested publicly that they were very sorry that their ancestors had for so long neglected the worship of the God of the Cross: they offered me their small children, asking me to baptize them in the interval that they themselves be instructed sufficiently to receive it. . . .

I leave to the Reader the freedom to judge as he pleases the origin of the cult of the Cross among this Pagan Nation; since I have no more solid basis for persuading the reader of this truth than the testimony of the older Indians and of the French, confirmed by the Relation made of it by Monseigneur de Saint Vallier, presently Bishop of Quebec. . . .

Here, in any case, in abridged form, are some of the main reasons which oblige me to believe that the Cross had been venerated among these Barbarians before the first arrival of the French in this country; because as I attempted one day to have them admit that the missionaries who preceded me had taught them the manner in which they ought to revere the Cross, the Chief said to me,

Well, come now, you are an Elder; you want us to believe all you propose but you do not want to believe what we tell you. You are not yet forty years old and you have lived with the Savages for only two years, and still you pretend to know our maxims, our traditions and our customs better than our ancestors who taught them to us. Do you not see here every day the aged Quioudo, who is more than one hundred and twenty years old? He saw the first ship which reached our Country; he has repeated so often to you that the Indians of Mizamichis did not receive from Strangers the use of the Cross; and that what he knows about it himself he learnt from the tradition of his forefathers who lived at least as long as he has. So you can deduce whether we received it before the French came to our coasts. . . .

If the Cross is the sacred mark which distinguishes Christians from Infidels, as you teach, tell us why the Elders would have given us the usage of it in preference to our brothers of Restigouche which they baptized, and who nevertheless have not always held this sign of Christianity in veneration as our ancestors who never received baptism did? You see clearly then that it is not from the missionaries that we have the mystery of the Cross.

This reasoning will be called savage; I admit it is so; but for all that it is neither less persuasive nor less convincing; Because it is true that the Savages of Restigouche are baptized, and that they do not wear the Cross. . . .

That is all I have been able to discover about the origin of the Cross, and all that we have done to procure its re-establishment among those People, who have never had the perfect knowledge of any Divinity, having been always in the past, as most of them today, indifferent in the matter of Religion. . . .

Document A—4

RADISSON—INDIAN BARBARITY

(Arthur T. Adams [ed.], The Explorations of Pierre Esprit Radisson [Minneapolis, 1961], pp. 19–21.)

There is a growing body of evidence that the practice of intensive torture, as described by Radisson, the coureur-de-bois, in the passage which follows, was a late development in Iroquoian culture intensified by the desire, when subjected to pressure by rival tribes and the Dutch and French, to obtain victory by the use of terror. The Algonkian tribes probably began to torture as a retaliatory measure. In any case, by the end of the 17th century all the tribes in contact with Europeans, except those of the Far West, engaged in it. Also, it is noteworthy that nomadic Indians avoided scalping, just as they avoided corpses and burial grounds, at the time of contact with Europeans, whereas the sedentary Indians regarded scalps as a proof of courage. It is now believed that the Iroquois introduced scalping to the Algonkians and that the introduction of firearms encouraged its practice.

Even if platform torture originated in human sacrifice to the sun or war god, and scalping in the cult of the skull, the whole question of Indian cruelty and barbarity remains important. There are those who point out that European warfare and judicial proceedings at the time were no less ghastly and that French officials and missionaries did not prevent the torture of captives by Indian allies and converts. Why has much of the literature on the Indian since colonial times stressed this quality of barbarism? Was it a barrier to civilization and assimilation?

They made me go up the scaffold, where were five men, three women, and two children captives. I made the eleventh. There were several scaffolds nigh one another, where were these wretches, who with a doleful singings replenished the heavens with their cries.
. . .

. . . They tie the prisoners to a post by their hands, their backs turned towards the hangman, who hath a burning fire of dry wood and rind of trees, which doth not quench easily. They put into this fire hatchets, swords, and such like instruments of iron. They take these and quench them on human flesh. They pluck out their nails for the most part in this sort: they put a red coal of fire upon it and, when it's swollen, bits it out with their teeth; after, they stop the blood with a brand, which by little and little draws the veins the one after another from off the fingers, and when they draw all as much as they can they cut it with pieces of red hot iron; they squeeze the fingers between two stones and so draw the marrow out of the bones, and when the flesh is all taken away, they put it [the fingers] in a dish full of burning sand. After, they tie the wrist with a cord, putting two for this effect, one drawing him one way, another of another way. If the sinews be not cut with a stick, putting it through and turning it, they make them come as fast as they can and cut them in the same way as the others. Some others cuts pieces of flesh from all parts of the body and broil them, gets you to eat it, thrusting them into your mouth, putting into it a stick of fire. They break your teeth with a stone or clubs. [They] uses the handle of a kettle, and upon this do hang five or six hatchets red hot, which they hang about their [victim's] neck. [They] roast your legs with brands of fire, and thrusting into it some sticks pointed, wherein they put a lead melted and gunpowder, and [they] then give it fire like unto artificial fire and make the patient gather it by the stumps of his remaining fingers.

. . . In the next place, they clothe you with a suit made of rind of a tree, and this they make burn out on your body. They cut off your stones, and the women play with them as with balls. When they see the miserable die, they open him and pluck out his heart. They drink some of his blood and wash the children's heads with the rest to make them valiant.

That day they plucked four nails out of my fingers and made me sing, though I had no mind at that time, I became speechless oftentimes; then they gave me water wherein they boiled a certain herb that the gunsmiths use to polish their arms. That liquor brought me to my speech again. The night being come, they made me come down all naked as I was and brought [me] to a strange cottage. (I wished heartily it had been that of my parents.) They tied me to a post, where I stayed a full hour without the least molestation. A woman came there with her boy, enticed him to cut off one of my fingers with a flint stone. The boy was not four years old. This [child] takes my finger and begins to work, but in vain because he had not the strength to break my fingers; so my poor finger escaped, having no other hurt done to it but the flesh cut round about it. His mother made him suck the very blood that runned from my finger. I had no other torment all that day. At night I could not sleep because of the great pain. I did eat a little and drunk much water by reason of a fever I caught by the cruel torments I suffered.

Document A—5

COBES—READY FOR EVANGELIZATION

(Sieur de Cobes, Coppie d'une Lettre Envoyée de la Nouvelle-France, ou Canada, par le Sieur de Cobes, Gentilhomme Poictevin, à un sien amy [Lyon, 1609], pp. 13–14)

As early as 1508 some Indians were brought to Rouen where they were the objects of much curiosity. Jacques Cartier in a letter to Francis I broached the missionary possibilities of winning "savage peoples living without a knowledge of God and without the use of reason." There was no following to this suggestion (perhaps insincere) until Henry IV commissioned de Monts in 1603 to arouse the Indians "to the knowledge of God and to the light of the Christian faith and religion." The following excerpt, which evokes the missionary motivation, is taken from a letter sent on February 13, 1608, by the Sieur de Cobes, who visited Canada in 1605. What other motivations were operative?

Now to describe the nature of those who inhabit it, you should know that they are very handsome men, white as snow, who let their hair grow down to their waists (both men and women), with high foreheads, eyes burning like candles, strong in body and well proportioned. The women too are very beautiful and graceful, well formed and dainty, so much so that given the fashion of their clothes which is somewhat strange one would say they were Nymphs or some goddesses, very charming and tractable, but apart from that prepared to be massacred rather than consent to their dishonour, or have knowledge of any other man besides their husbands. Apart from that, in their manner of living they are very brutish, but they are beginning to become civilized and to take on our manners and our ways. They are easily instructed in the Christian religion and are not too opinionated in their Paganism, to the extent that if Preachers went down to them I believe that in a short time the whole country would give in to the Christian faith without being otherwise constrained, and that by this means the way would be opened in the whole of the remainder of America for the conquest of souls, which is greater than all the lands one could ever conquer.

Now you must know that we possess a great expanse of country in the name of the French and have undertaken the conquest of the Atars, which is one of the richest countries of the whole land of Canada, and where there are mines of gold and silver in great abundance, which are very productive, and even all along the rivers one finds sometimes pebbles as it were of fine gold, many precious stones, diamonds, and other riches. That people is cruel and bellicose, so much so that they give us much trouble, and we shall well require succour from France, as I believe Monsieur du Dongeon has written to the King, and I promise you that if we are aided we will overcome and will accomplish things the renown of which shall be memorable to all posterity, and will have the glory of the French live forever in the whole of America.

Document A—6

LE FEVRE—LIMITED OPTIMISM

(Thomas Le Fevre, *Discours sommaire de la Navigation et du Commerce* [Rouen, 1650] pp. 207–8.)

Le Fevre's impressions, which he attributed to interviews with several sea captains who knew the New World well, indicate a desire on the part of Europeans to find some common ground between natural religion as practiced by the Amerindians and revealed religion as professed by Europeans. How serious were such problems as diversity of languages, intertribal rivalries, nomadism, and primitivism?

Several of these peoples of Canada already believe there is a God the Father, a mother, an immortal soul, a son and Sun which is the author or preserver of all things, that the Father is above all, that since he has had to be stern with mankind the mother devours them but the Sun is good to them, preserves them and gives them life. They believe strongly in their dreams and certain men whom they call Pilotois who visibly communicate with the Devil. These men and their womenfolk are physically well formed, of good stature, nevertheless quite dark-skinned because of the dyes with which they adorn themselves. They dress in hides and marry, making love to the girls who reach the age of 14 or 15. Five or six years later after having enjoyed the favours of several men, those girls who wish to marry choose the lover that pleased them most and henceforward cease to give themselves to any other. If they bear no children the husband may marry another. When they die they bury their dogs, kettles, pots, axes, arrows, bows, robes and furs, with all their dearest possessions, with them, believing that in passing from this world to the next they go to rejoice with their friends.

These peoples number as many as forty nations speaking diverse languages, living under different laws and diverse customs, most of them waging cruel warfare on one another, some being sedentary and settled in villages and others nomadic and wandering from one country to another like migratory birds. Some live in warmer climes than others, regions which are better populated and where there is more hope of conversion and settlement than elsewhere.

Document A—7

MARIE DE L'INCARNATION—A WOMAN'S VIEWPOINT

(Joyce Marshall [ed.], *Word from New France. The Selected Letters of Marie de l'Incarnation* [Toronto, 1967], pp. 75–76.)

The Ursuline Superior at Quebec belonged to a cloistered order, but her knowledge of the colonial world was vast and her zeal was unlimited. Why did this mystic lose her original optimism? She wrote in 1640 that the state officials were ignorant of the problems those who lived and labored on the frontier encountered. Before her death she spoke of hundreds of Indian children who had passed through their hands, but said, "We have civilized scarcely one." Why were service and sacrifice so poorly rewarded?

It is a singular consolation to us to deprive ourselves of all that is most necessary in order to win souls to Jesus Christ, and we would prefer to lack everything rather than leave our girls in the unbearable filth they bring from their cabins. When they are given to us, they are naked as worms and must be washed from head to foot because of the grease their parents rub all over their bodies; and whatever diligence we use and however often their linen and clothing is changed, we cannot rid them for a long time of the vermin caused by this abundance of grease. A Sister employs part of each day at this. It is an office that everyone eagerly covets. Whoever obtains it considers herself rich in such a happy lot and those that are deprived of it consider themselves undeserving of it and dwell in humility. Madame our foundress performed this service almost all year; today it is Mother Marie de Saint-Joseph that enjoys this good fortune.

Besides the Savage women and girls, whom we receive in the house, the men visit us in the parlour, where we try to give them the same charity we do their women, and it is a very sensible consolation to us to take bread from our mouths to give it to these poor people, in order to inspire them with love for Our Lord and for his holy Faith.

But after all it is a very special providence of this great God that we are able to have girls after the great number of them that died last year. This malady, which is smallpox, being universal among the Savages, it spread to our seminary, which in a very few days resembled a hospital. All our girls suffered this malady three times and four of them died from it. We all expected to fall sick, because the malady was a veritable contagion, and also because we were day and night succouring them and the small space we had forced us to be continually together. But Our Lord aided us so powerfully that none of us was indisposed.

The Savages that are not Christians hold the delusion that it is baptism, instruction, and dwelling among the French that was the cause of this mortality, which made us believe we would not be given any more girls and that those we had would be taken from us. God's providence provided so benevolently against this that the Savages themselves begged us to take their daughters, so that if we had food and clothing we would be able to admit a very great number, though we are exceedingly pressed for buildings. If God touches the hearts of some saintly souls, so that they will help us build close to the Savages as we have the design to do, we will have a great many girls. We are longing for that hour to arrive, so that we will be more perfectly able to do the things for which Our Lord sent us to this blessed country. . . .

B. The Policy of Frenchification

The stated objective of Frenchification of the Indians was to be achieved by means of evangelization, segregated settlement of the converted tribesmen on reserves, integrated education, and racial intermarriage.

Document B–1

SAGARD—SEGREGATION

(Gabriel Sagard-Théodat, *Le Grand Voyage du Pays des Hurons* [Paris, 1632], pp. 175–78, 183–87.)

Brother Gabriel Sagard, a Recollet friar, was one of the first to record his fear of the cultural clash that would result from the meeting of a commercial Catholic European civilization with a primitive, communal, semi-nomadic Indian culture. How did the few months he spent among the Hurons in 1623–24 convince him that the natives should be isolated from the European traders and settlers? Would segregation preserve the best elements of their own culture and facilitate their assimilation into a controlled cultural pattern? What opinion did the Indians have of themselves? How would this affect attempts to assimilate them?

We had commenced to teach them their letters, but as they are libertine and want only to play and have a good time, as I said, they forgot in three days what we had taken four days to teach them because of the lack of continued application and the failure to come back to us at the times appointed; and they cleared themselves by telling us they had been prevented because of a game. Also it was not à propos to be harsh with them or correct them otherwise than gently, and in an affable way admonishing them to acquire more knowledge which could profit them so much and bring contentment in time to come. . . .

The women compete with each other as to who will have the most lovers . . . and there are pimps and wicked people in the towns and villages who engage in no other occupation than offering and presenting these creatures to the men who want them. I thank God that they took our reprimands quite well, and eventually began to have more modesty and some shame of their dissoluteness daring, only very rarely, to employ impertinent words in our company, and on learning from us of the propriety of the girls in France admired it, which gave us hope of a great amendment in their way of living in a short time, if the Frenchmen who came up with us (for the most part) had not told them the opposite in order to enjoy their sensual pleasures like brute beasts without restraint and in this lust they wallowed to the extent of keeping in several places harems of these wicked women, so that those who should have backed up our teaching by being good examples to these people were themselves those who went about destroying and obstructing the good that we were establishing for the salvation of these peoples and for the advancement of the glory of God. There were, nevertheless, a few good men, honest and clean living, with whom we were very pleased and by whom we were much edified, just as on the contrary by these other brutal, atheistic and carnal fellows who hindered the conversion and reformation of these poor people we were troubled. . . .

. . . these people esteem us to possess little intelligence in comparison to themselves . . . they used to say the same to us missionaries but now they hold us in higher esteem saying we have a great deal of sense and the Hurons have none . . . that we are people who know things from above and supernatural but did not have this opinion or belief concerning other Frenchmen in comparison with whom they estimated their own children wiser and more intelligent, so good an opinion have they of themselves and so little esteem for others.

. . . To say what I think about some of them, which ones are the happiest or most wretched, I consider the Hurons and other Sedentary tribes as the nobility, the Algonquin Nations as the bourgeoisie, and the other Savages nearer us, such as the Montagnais and Canadiens, the villagers and poor people of the country. . . .

All the Savages in general have a very good mind and fairly good understanding, and they are not so uncouth and stupid as we in France imagine. They are of quite cheerful and contented disposition, yet a bit inclined to melancholy. They speak very composedly, as if they wanted to be understood, and suddenly stop to think for a long interval, then resume their speech, and this restraint is the reason they call our Frenchmen women because they are too hasty and turbulent in their actions, they all speak at once and interrupt each other. They fear dishonour and reproach, and are stimulated to do good for honour's sake. . . . As for liberality, our Savages are praiseworthy in the exercise of this virtue in proportion to their poverty . . . they also show kindness and mercy in victory towards the wives and little children of their enemies, whose lives they spare, although these remain prisoners to serve them.

Document B–2

de SESMAISONS—MISCEGENATION

(This document is found in *Archives of Society of Jesus, Rome*, Gallia 110, 111, fols. 356–57. Also was published in *Nova Francia*, Vol. IV, No. 3 [1929], pp. 143–45.)

Champlain told the Hurons that if they would accept the Catholic religion brought by the Recollet missionaries, the French would come to live among them in their villages, would marry their daughters, and would teach them their arts and trades. The pious founders of Montreal repeated, in 1642, the hope that intermarriage would result in mass conversion, a marked increase in the colonial population, and a rapid development of the agricultural potential of the St. Lawrence lowlands. What do the arguments of Pierre de Sesmaisons tell us about response to these hopes?

Reasons which can induce His Holiness to permit Frenchmen inhabiting New France to Marry Savage Girls although not Baptized nor as yet much Instructed in the Christian Faith.

The First is that they are imbued with no religion contrary to the Catholic Apostolic and Roman faith,

That every Frenchman who will want to take to wife a savage girl will take her young for fear that she be corrupted and she will be no older than twelve years of age, which is a tender age to be instructed in what we wish and there is a chance even that those who are to be married to Frenchmen will be taken from among the savages before this age to give them some inkling of our religion.

That being under the care of their husbands and attached to them they will be close not only to the French to be instructed by their example but also to the Jesuit Fathers who are in each *habitation* and from whom they can receive instruction and baptism in time.

And that these women having young relations very often destitute of father and mother will be able to draw them near to them to cultivate the soil through necessity because it is the greatest happiness for savages to know they will not go hungry, and thus it will be easy to instruct them when they are near to the French.

That it is a means of diminishing the numbers of savages and of augmenting that of the Christians inasmuch as all their children will be baptized whereas *if* these women remain uncivilized the children will be savages.

That these women recounting their happiness to their relations will be able to attract some to a settled life like ours without which little advance is made in the faith among Vagabonds who spend only three or four months in proximity of the French, and not a fortnight in any one place, so that whatever has been shown them in such a short time leaves them when they move away from the French and so they return to their licentiousness.

If these marriages are not permitted in the Christian church it is out of fear that one of the partners defile the other, or else the fear that the children be not raised and instructed in the true religion. But in this permission neither one nor the other danger is to be feared because as for defilement it cannot come from the husband who is a Catholic nor yet less from the wife inasmuch as having no religion and having knowledge of none other than our own she can in no wise incite her husband to pervert it. As for the education of the children it is not to be presumed that the mother will prevent them being well instructed since the savages so approve our approach that several have already given their children to be educated to the Reverend Jesuit Fathers and others to some of our Frenchmen.

That from the pleasantness which they will experience in this kind of life, coming from one as miserable as their own, they will have such esteem for their husbands so that they will naturally do whatever pleases them. The wives of the savages are very obliging and obedient to their husbands suffering all imaginable fatigue in the misery of their condition.

That this will oblige all the savages to love the French as brothers. They testify that they passionately desire this because they are never more pleased with our discourses than when we promise them we will take their daughters in marriage and after such discourses they applaud us greatly.

They tell us that when we will enter into these marriages they will consider us as belonging to their nation accounting descent and relationship of their families through the women and not the men, inasmuch as they say that one can know assuredly who is the mother of the child but not be assured of who is the father.

That the savages take ten times more account of a girl than of a boy inasmuch as she can produce many warriors for them and so they esteem that the children procreated of such marriages would assist them in their wars and all their needs as their brothers and blood relatives.

That they will undertake no attempts on Frenchmen except the relatives of women married to Frenchmen give them some warning.

That these women having aged relatives will with the help of the French and of their husbands draw some close to themselves and thus provide them the means of instruction and dying in the Christian faith.

These marriages will greatly advance the populating of this large country where God is not served because our Frenchmen marrying here will be retained by the sacred bonds of marriage and will not return to France as they do now to take a wife who soon prevents them from returning, also several young bachelors will plan to go it being possible to marry there.

The location and nature of this country seem to require this permission for as it is overseas it is very difficult, not to say impossible, to find girls (at least in sufficient numbers) who possess the courage to expose themselves to the dangers of the ocean crossing, nevertheless it is necessary to have some if one wishes to augment the Christian faith.

The Doctors seem to favour this request for, after having demonstrated that His Holiness may grant a dispensation because in this case there is a reasonable cause, they cite the example of the Indies where there being hope of conversion and a shortage of Christian girls it is easier (so they say) to obtain this permission.

Finally, these marriages can produce no harmful results for never will the savage women seduce their husbands to live miserably in the forests as do the peoples of New France and the children of these unions can only be Christians nourished and raised among the French as they will be, also that there is no indication, judging from the docility of these people imbued with no other religion, that the women once married will not readily be influenced to follow the religion of her husband which, when she considers the differences in manner of life, will be like partaking of the life of the angels compared to the misery of other savage women.

These reasons seem to me to be sufficiently pressing to induce His Holiness to permit the French who inhabit New France to marry the savage girls although the latter are neither baptized nor yet much instructed.

Pierre de Sesmaisons

Document B–4

LE JEUNE—INTEGRATION

(R. G. Thwaites [ed.], *The Jesuit Relations and Allied Documents* [Cleveland, 1896–1901], Vol. XIV, pp. 190–94.)

What problems did racial intermarriage pose for the missionaries? Why did the Indians consider it a proper matter for negotiation? Was integration adopted as part of French colonial policy?

On the 17th, I again accompanied the Father Superior to Iahenhouton, where resides the chief of the council of this place. The object of this journey was to make them 3 propositions: 1st, whether they had not at last resolved to believe what we taught, and to embrace the faith; 2nd, whether it would be acceptable to them that some of our Frenchmen should marry in their country as soon as possible; 3rd, whether there was any probability of a reunion between them and the people of *Ossosané* and some of the surrounding villages. Your Reverence knows the cause of their division; we wrote to you about it fully last year, on the occasion of their feast of the Dead. As regards the first proposition, we did not gain all the satisfaction possible; this Captain is not one of the most intelligent men in the world, at least outside the little perplexities of their affairs; as for the second and third, they approved of them heartily, and assured us that they were under a great obligation to us for this so close alliance that we wished to make with them, and for our great interest in the welfare of the country. . . . And thereupon, as the Father declared that he greatly desired to have these matters proposed in a general assembly, he replied that the thing was not impossible, that they would confer about it among themselves and give us their opinion afterward; however, concerning the marriages, it was not necessary to go through so many ceremonies,—that those Frenchmen who had resolved to marry were free to take wives where it seemed good to them. . . .

Document B–5

LOUIS XIV—INTEGRATION & EDUCATION

(This document is found in *Public Archives of Canada, Series B, Vol. I, Louis XIV to Bouteroue,* 1668, pp. 76ff.)

After the Recollets, then the Jesuits, and finally Bishop Laval had abandoned hope of mass conversions of the Indians and their assimilation into a French way of life, the state officials continued to press for the policy of integration and education which the missionaries, as the first cultural ambassadors of Europe to the native encampments, had originally suggested and supported. Louis XIV's instructions to the Intendant, Bouteroue, leaving for his posting in Quebec in 1668, give the official view that the missionaries had not applied themselves wholeheartedly to the realization of the ideal and that state pressure would have to be exerted in order to achieve the objectives stated. How fair a judgment was this?

INSTRUCTIONS TO SIEUR BOUTEROUE

. . . It appears that up to the present time the maxim of the Jesuits has been not to call the natives of the country into community of life with the French, either by giving them common lands and dwellings, or by the education of their children and by marriages. Their reason has been that they have thought to preserve more perfectly the principles of the holiness of our Religion by holding the converted savages to their ordinary form of life rather than by calling them to live among the French.

As it is all too easy to recognize how far removed this maxim is from all good conduct, as well for Religion as for the State, it is necessary to act gently to have them change it, and to employ all the temporal authority to draw the said savages among the French, which may be accomplished through marriage and the education of their children.

The trade in wine and brandies with the savages, which is called the liquor traffic, has been a subject of perpetual contest between the Bishop of Petrae and the Jesuits and the principal inhabitants and those who trade in that country. The Bishop and the Jesuits have contended that these alcoholic beverages made the savages drunk, that they were unable to consume it in moderation, that drunkenness made them slothful in the hunt, and that it gave them all kinds of bad habits, as well for Religion as for the State. The principal inhabitants and the traders, on the contrary, contend that the desire to have alcoholic beverages, which are traded at high prices, obliged the savages to go hunting with more application.

It is necessary to examine carefully these two opinions and for the Intendant to give his considered advice to the King.

C. The Problems of Contact

The efforts to Frenchify the Indians were plagued by several problems. There was some misunderstanding of the role played by the environment. Why did evangelization progress more rapidly among the tribes which were both sedentary and agricultural and which possessed a complex social and religious organization than among semi-nomadic primitive hunters? Was the Indian a relatively well-adjusted man in the North American environment? The role of the enigmatic missionary needs to be reconsidered—his doctrine, his way of life, his motivations were neither understood nor trusted. To what extent was he a political agent? An underminer of established society? Did the missionaries tend to become religious chiefs among their converts, sharing their food, their villages, their language, their customs, and even some of their values and ways of thinking? What did this indicate about assimilation trends?

What consequences might result from the demographic weakness of the French? The Indians outnumbered the French, and the latter depended on the Indians for the supply of furs, for allies in wartime, and for their own safety and convenience. It is commonly stated that assimilation is facilitated for a minority group dispersed throughout a majoritarian sector and possessing an inferior culture. Did the Indians constitute such a minority group in the 17th century? Was a campaign of assimilation involving sufficient money, men, and materials even conceivable at that period?

Document C–1

D'ASSELINE DE RONUAL—INDIAN RELIGION

(P.A.C., Series J, "Journal en abrégé des voyages de Mons. d'Asseline de Ronual tant par terre que par mer, avec plusieurs Remarques, circonstances et aventures très curieuses" [1662], pp. 34–36.)

The following prayer of the "upper country" Indians to the Great Spirit, while couched in the terminology of the European traveler, is revealing, nevertheless, of certain Indian religious concepts. What do these seem to emphasize?

Great Spirit, master of our lives, Great Spirit master of things visible and invisible, Great Spirit master of all other spirits both good and evil, command the good spirits to be favourable to your children the Otaouis, Algonquins and Hurons. Command the evil spirits to depart from them.

O, Great Spirit, preserve the strength and courage of our warriors so they may resist the fury of our enemies, preserve our old men whose bodies are not yet completely worn out so they may give counsel to the Youth. Preserve our children, augment their numbers; deliver them from the evil spirits and from the hand of evil men so that in our old age they may keep us alive and cause us to rejoice. Preserve our houses and our animals if you wish us not to starve; guard our villages and our hunters in their chase; deliver us from deadly ambush when you cease to give us the light of sun which bespeaks your greatness and power. Warn us by the spirit of dreams what you wish us to do or not to do. When it pleases you that our lives come to an end send us to the great land of souls where are those of our fathers and our mothers, of our wives, of our children, and of all others our parents.

O, Great Spirit, Great Spirit, hearken to all your children and remember them at all times.

Document C–2

LE JEUNE—MISSIONARY METHODS

(Reprinted from R. G. Thwaites [ed.], *The Jesuit Relations and Allied Documents* [Cleveland, 1896–1901], Vol. XIV, pp. 2–4.)

Among the clearest expressions of means employed by the missionaries to assimilate the Indians into French cultural patterns was Father Le Jeune's Relation of 1638.

Superstition, error, barbarism, and consequently, sin, are as if in their empire here. We employ four great contrivances to overthrow them. First, we make expeditions to go and attack the enemy upon their own ground, with their own weapons,—that is to say, by a knowledge of the Montagnais, Algonquin, and Huron tongues. When the doors shall be opened to us in nations still more remote, we will enter there if God lend us his help. Now I will say upon this point, in passing, that many did not expect anything from the old Savage stocks, all hope being placed only in the young; but experience teaches us that there is no wood so dry that God cannot make it become green again, when it pleases him. We begin to see in the Huron country, and among the Montagnais and Algonquins, a few families publicly professing the Faith and frequenting the Sacraments, with a devotion and modesty which have nothing of the Savage except the dress. This low opinion that people had of our poor wandering Savages must be changed into thanksgivings and blessings, as we shall see hereafter.

Secondly, as these peoples are attacked by serious diseases, we are obtaining for them the erection of a hospital. The men are now hard at work thereon, so far as the conditions of the country allow. Madame the Duchesse d'Aiguillon, who laid the foundations of this great work, can after this year enjoy the fruits of her liberality. For the men who are working here to carry out her plan, having given assistance this winter to some poor forlorn Savages, God so touched them that in truth I would desire a death similar to that which he has granted to two of these Barbarians, who became children of God in the blood of Jesus Christ.

In the third place, we are endeavoring to begin Huron, Algonquin, and Montagnais Seminaries. We have them now at Kebec, of these three kinds. . . .

In the fourth place, we are trying to fix the wandering Savages. I confess that golden chains are needed for this purpose; but their souls are more precious than gold and pearls, and it is an advantageous exchange to win them by this allurement. A person of great virtue has begun to lay this snare for them, having hired some men to aid these poor Barbarians to build for themselves, and to cultivate the land. At the first setting of this divine trap, he caught two families, composed of about twenty persons. I am mistaken,—he caught more; for although only these two families have yet been lodged, there are many others that have been gained by this miracle of charity. It is a blessing to see these poor Savages become children of God,—some, indeed, by means of holy Baptism, the others through desire and good will; we will speak of these more fully, in the proper place. . . .

Document C–3

BIGOT—THE BRANDY TRAFFIC

(R. G. Thwaites [ed.], *The Jesuit Relations and Allied Documents* [Cleveland, 1896–1901], Vol. LXIII, pp. 101–13, 131–35.)

There was much argument about the validity of segregation as opposed to integration. However much the brandy trade was deplored, most colonials had to admit that it was a central feature of the staple trade underpinning the economy of the overseas outpost. How could it be controlled? Father Jacques Bigot, in a letter dated November 8, 1685, from Sillery, described conditions in the first segregated settlement of converted natives.

A wish has been expressed to me that, in addition to the short relation that I send to you this year regarding the present state of our mission, I should write a special account of what has passed here during the past two months when the Sillery Savages, in the most agreeable manner in the world, wholly abandoned intemperance. This has caused very special pleasure to Monseigneur Our Bishop and to Monsieur our Governor; and it happened thus. A wretched Algonquin, who had been here for some days, came back from Quebek, on sunday night, in a state of intoxication. He brought a bottle filled with brandy, and intoxicated his brother, who had also been here for some days. The Algonquin caused a great disturbance during the night; for he seized burning firebrands wherewith to strike those who were in his cabin, and nearly set fire to it. As his Cabin was near mine I immediately heard the cries of those whom the drunkard was tormenting. I go to the Cabin; I call for assistance; I cause the drunken man to be bound, and carried to a cellar where there is nothing to drink or to seize. On the following day, I send Secretly for archers to remove the wretch to prison. Monsieur our Governor had already informed me of his intention to prevent the evils of intemperance, as far as lay in his power, and to secure the observance of the orders that he found we had already given here to check such disorderly conduct. Accordingly, after assembling all our Savages, I made him speak to them, which he did, in an admirable manner, in regard to the disturbance caused in our mission by the drunkard of whom I have just spoken, who was at the same time expelled from this mission. You see all the Pious juggleries which I employed to inspire terror in the others, especially in those who are here only for a time, and whose sole object in coming seems to be to disturb the piety and fervor of all the good christians who properly compose this mission. Orders had already been sent to Quebek to imprison the Savages who might be found intoxicated there; but no heed was paid to those orders, and most of the Savages who became drunk escaped from Quebek with-

out being taken. To obviate this, I told all the Savages that the Great Captain had heard that many Savages who became intoxicated in Quebek were not imprisoned there, in Accordance with the orders issued against the drunkards; and that he Insisted upon my promptly informing him if any one returned to Sillery in a state of intoxication after escaping from Quebek without being imprisoned. In such a case, he would at once send archers for him, in order that the drunkard might, by the hardships of the prison, make reparation to God for his sin. I told them that, in doing this, the Great Captain wished to show Holy compassion for all the christians of this mission, and, by that order, prevent them from casting themselves into the dungeons of hell. I added that, for the better observance of his orders, he Desired that I should, with a Holy audacity, take away from every Savage whom I found intoxicated some petty effects belonging to his Cabin, in order that the effects so taken might Serve to pay the Archers who would come to put that drunken Savage in prison. This has been called here, during the past two months, "the Holy pillage"—that is to say, as I made them understand, a pillage that is effected for the purpose of obeying God and of establishing prayer. . . . Three days after this 1st exhortation, a Savage came back from Quebek in a state of intoxication. I heard his voice; I went to his Cabin and plundered him for the holy purpose—as I had asserted I would do, the first time any one should come back intoxicated. I contented myself with saying to that Savage: "Let me take this; I shall talk to thee when thou Becomest sober." The Savage's Sister, who is a very good Christian and who was extremely unhappy at seeing her brother drunk, said to him: "Why art thou astonished that our Father should take this in thy Cabin? Knowest thou not that he told us that he would piously plunder those who became intoxicated?" Such are the expressions she used. When the Savage had somewhat recovered from his intoxication, he withdrew Secretly from the fort. The Archers who came to take him searched for him everywhere in the fort; I had thoroughly instructed them in the part that they had to play in order to impress the imaginations of the Savages. They went to search for him in the Vicinity. Upon his return, he came to me to protest that he had not fled in earnest, and that he was not rebellious to the orders of the great Captain, but was ready to do whatever he wished; and that he would make reparation to God for his sin, in whatever manner we might order. He said all this to me in the presence of a very great number of our savages. I told him that the great Captain would be well pleased to see him in that disposition; that I would speak in his favor and that I hoped to obtain His pardon, although he Knew the penalty enacted against those who fled when persons were sent to arrest them—namely, twelve days' imprisonment. I had authority to represent monsieur the Governor as saying whatever I liked, and, in his name, to proclaim all the punishments that I might think suitable for producing a good effect. It was not difficult to obtain this savage's pardon, as you may imagine; but I caused it to be granted in such a way as to inspire all our other Savages with still greater dread of drunkenness. It would take too long were I to relate all the Holy juggleries of which I made use. I seemed to take our savages' part, while I was doing whatever I could against them. All had compassion on me, and thanked me for the trouble that I took for them. Monseigneur the Bishop and Monsieur the Marquis have taken special pleasure in making me relate all the petty stratagems which I employed in maintaining order among our savages, and in keeping them from getting drunk. Although all the most inveterate drunkards among our savages were here at the time when I established everything that I desired, in less that eight days I issued

all the orders that I wished for the suppression of intemperance. In all, I had only four imprisoned—two Etchemin men, an Etchemin woman, and a Soquoqui woman. . . . The Soquoqui woman, however, fell once more into the same sin, ten days afterward. When she recovered from her intoxication, in the middle of the night, her relative informed her that I had gone into her Cabin while she was sleeping; and they exhorted her to accept imprisonment as a punishment for her offence. . . . I also caused a telling fine to be imposed upon the frenchman who had made her drunk, and who continually did the same with others. This showed our savages that the wicked french are punished equally with the wicked savages. I have entered into all these petty details to prove that, if we choose to display a little firmness in repressing the evils of intemperance, we can obtain what we wish from our Savages. . . . I think you have heard that nine or ten Cabins left the Sault mission last year, because they said that they had withdrawn there solely to live in peace, far from the disorders caused by intemperance; but that they found themselves as greatly annoyed by drunkards as they were in their own country. I have also said that this prohibition respecting drunkenness was the means of making our Savages happy among the french; and it is one of the arguments that have most impressed their minds, in making them cheerfully submit to all the orders promulgated against intemperance, especially of late. "See, my children," I said to them, "how the Great Captain loves you. He wishes you to be happy; that you should want for nothing; that by means of your hunting you should provide for all your petty needs. He desires that the french should not deceive you, by giving you nothing but bad liquor instead of good blankets and good coats to cover yourselves and your children. . . ."

D. Evaluations of the Assimilation Policy

It is evident to the historian today that many of the factors involved in the assimilationist experiment—such factors as cultural clash, requisites for assimilation, environmental influences, the Indian sense of identity and worth, and contradictory and complementary economic and social forces—were not fully understood by those who sought to evaluate such efforts in the 17th century. On what did contemporaries agree? What were the main points of disagreement? Which analysis seems more accurate?

Document D–1

MONTAIGNE—ANOTHER WORLD

(Excerpt taken from Donald M. Frame [ed.], *The Complete Works of Montaigne, Essays, Travel Journal, Letters* [Stanford, Calif., 1957], Book III, p. 693.)

Montaigne in writing about "our world has just discovered another world" offered one point of view. How familiar was he with actual conditions in New Spain?

I am much afraid that we shall have very greatly hastened the decline and ruin of this new world by our contagion, and that we will have sold it our opinions and our arts very dear. It was an infant world; yet we have not whipped it and subjected it to our discipline by the advantage of our natural valor and strength, nor won it over by our justice and goodness, nor subjugated it by our magnanimity. Most of the responses of these people and most of our dealings with them show that they were not at all behind us in natural brightness of mind and pertinence.

Document D–2

LE CLERCQ—RELATION OF FAILURE

(This excerpt is from Chrestien Le Clercq, *Nouvelle Relation de la Gaspésie qui contient les Moeurs & la Religion des Sauvages* [Paris, 1691], pp. 276–79.)

Father Chrestien Le Clercq, a Recollet, worked among the Indians of Gaspesia from 1675 to 1679. On the basis of experience he argued a quite different position from that of Montaigne.

It is true that several of our Gaspesians hope at present to be instructed, ask for Baptism, and even seem externally quite good Christians after having been baptized, zealous in the ordinary morning and evening prayers, modest in Churches, and given to confessing their sins in order to approach the holy Communion worthily.

But one may say that the number of those who abide by the rule of Christianity and who do not fall back into the irregularities of a brutal and savage life is very small, either because of the natural insensibility of these people to matters of salvation or because of drunkenness, their delusions, their superstitions and other great defects to which they are addicted. From this it follows that although several Missionaries have worked much for the conversion of these Infidels, one sees nevertheless, no more than among the Savage Nations of New France, a solidly established Christianity; and that is perhaps why the Reverend Jesuit Fathers, who have laboured with so much fervour and love in the missions they formerly had at Cape Breton, Miscou & Nipisiguit where our Gaspesians live to this day, have found it wise to abandon them in order to establish others among far away Nations situated in the upper country of the St. Lawrence river, in the hope of making greater progress there, and this furthermore in spite of the fact according to the testimony of these Reverend Fathers that the Gaspesians are the most docile of all the Savages of New France & the most susceptible to the instructions of Christianity.

It is true that the slight progress I had made in four years of labour with all the application I could muster to convert these Peoples, in addition to the deep displeasure of not finding the response I hoped for on the part of our Gaspesians, the majority of whom were Christians only in appearance, the indefatigable labour of so many illustrious and zealous missionaries who preceded me notwithstanding caused me to hesitate to abandon the work but I had no cause to hope for a happier success in future. Meanwhile, not to rush matters in such a consequential affair, I asked the Holy Spirit for the light I needed in order to know the will of God and to give myself wholly to it. . . .

Document D—3

DABLON—REPORT ON A RESERVE

(This report appeared in the final installment of "Etat présent des Missions . . . 1675," published in R. G. Thwaites [ed.], The Jesuit Relations and Allied Documents [Cleveland, 1896–1901], Vol. LX, pp. 27-31.)

In 1675 Father Claude Dablon made a full report on the Indian reserve at Lorette (formerly Notre-Dame de Foy). Did he think the reserve system aided Frenchification? Did it assist evangelization? Were these synonymous aims?

This Mission, which formerly bore the name of Mission of Notre Dame de Foye, and which during two years has been called the Mission of Notre Dame de Lorette,—on account of the change of village that had to be effected last year, as described in the preceding relation,—now consists of about 300 souls, both Huron and Iroquois. This number is small, in truth, compared with that of the other Missions; but they are all chosen persons, who openly profess Christianity and the most sublime virtues that are practiced therein.

This Christian settlement has the advantage, over the other Christian communities of natives of the country, of being a *Church fully formed*; and we no longer count therein the number of the baptized, except by that of the children who come into the world. Should it nevertheless happen that some Iroquois abandon their country to take refuge in this village, as in a sure port of safety, we baptize them after carefully instructing them; and this year we have administered baptism to twenty-two adults of this class. With respect to this, I must not omit to mention the zeal manifested for their countrymen by our Iroquois, of both sexes, who have dwelt in this Mission many years; for I may say that the foundation of the instruction received by our newly-arrived neophytes is given them by the older residents, who very frequently go to seek them in their cabins, to instruct them in the mysteries of our holy Faith.

Document D—4

DENONVILLE—THE GOVERNOR'S VERDICT

(P.A.C., Series C11A, Denonville to Minister, November 13, 1685, Vol. VII, pp. 45–47.)

Government of the North American colonies was conducted by correspondence, with the flow of information from trusted officials in the New World forming the basis of instructions dispatched from the royal camp in France to the appointed officials and Sovereign Council of Quebec. Denonville's appraisal of the situation in 1685 is particularly revealing.

It seems to me that this is the place, Monseigneur, that we have to take into account the disorders which occur not only in the woods but also in our settlements. These disorders have come to the Youth of this country only through the laziness of the children, and the great liberty which the light control of fathers and mothers and Governors have exercised over youth in allowing them to go into the woods on pretext of hunting or trading. This has reached the extremity, Monseigneur, that as soon as the children can shoulder a rifle the fathers can no longer restrain them and do not dare to make them angry. You may judge what evils may ensue from such a manner of living. These disorders, Monseigneur, are greater among the families of those who are *gentilshommes*, or those who have set themselves up to be such, because of idleness or vanity, having no means of subsistence except the woods because not being accustomed to wield the axe or pick or guide the plow their only recourse is the rifle. They have to pass their lives in the woods, where there are neither priests to trouble them, nor fathers nor Governors to constrain them. There are, Monseigneur, among those men some who distinguish themselves above others in these disorders and against whom I have promised to employ the authority which the King has entrusted to me to punish them severely. I am persuaded, Monseigneur, that you will acknowledge and will approve that I do not amuse myself

with a formality of justice which would tend only to subtlety in order to hide the vice and leave the disorders unpunished. Convincing proof not always being readily established I believe, Monseigneur, that military justice in this case is more suitable than any *arrêt* of a judge.

Mr. de la Barre has suppressed a certain order of *chevaliers*, but he has not taken away its manners or disorders. A way of dressing up like savages, stark naked, not only on carnival days but on all days of feasting and debauchery, has been treated as a nice action and a joke. These manners tend only to maintain the young people in the spirit of living like savages and to communicate with them and to be eternally profligate like them, I could not express sufficiently to you Monseigneur the attraction that this savage life of doing nothing, of being constrained by nothing, of following every whim and being beyond correction, has for the young men.

It was believed for a long time that approaching the savages to our settlements was a very considerable means of accustoming these people to live like us and to be instructed in our religion. I perceive, Monseigneur, that the very opposite has occurred because instead of training them to our laws, I assure you that they communicate very much to us everything that is meanest in them, and themselves take on only what is bad and vicious in us. I have been somewhat lengthy, Monseigneur, in giving you the details of all these matters so that you may provide the remedies by the orders you give me.

I find that all the savages we have established in *bourgades* such as Sillery, Lorette, Sault de la Prairie, the Mountain of Montreal, are in truth kept in a discipline and order which are delightful to behold. There is not, to be sure, a town or village in France so well ordered than these places mentioned so long as no drunkenness comes over from our settlements. But, Monseigneur, with regards to the other savages who are wanderers and vagabonds about the private seigneuries without being gathered together in reservations like the others, you could not believe, Sir, the harm this does to the good order of the colony. For not only the young but the Seigneurs become accustomed to live in licence like them, and even abuse the savage women and girls which they entertain amongst them and take on their hunting trips in the woods, where often they suffer hunger to the point of eating their dogs. . . .

Nothing is finer nor better conceived than all the regulations for this country, but I must assure you that nothing is so badly observed as regards the fact that trade is to be carried on only in the towns of Quebec, Trois Rivières and Ville-Marie as well as everything else that regards good order.

PROBLEM 2

The Soldier in New France, 1663-1759

ANDRÉ LACHANCE
Université de Sherbrooke

From 1609 to 1760, New France was almost always under siege. The continued existence of this state can be explained partly by the geographical and demographic situation of the French colony in North America (12,000 souls in 1684): it bordered on New England (about 250,000 inhabitants in 1684) and prevented the excess British population from reaching beyond the Alleghanies. Another reason for the precarious position of New France can be found in the fur trade. During the entire French regime, this trade constituted the economic mainstay of the colony. Furs, the essential product of the economy of New France, were to be found mainly around the Great Lakes, particularly to the west and north of Lake Superior, and Hudson Bay; these regions were all neighboring on, if not included in, the hunting grounds of the Iroquois Confederation of the Five Nations, and the English possessions in North America.

In the process of preserving the furs—the almost unique commodity which New France could offer in exchange for the manufactured products of the mother country—incidents developed which in the end led to war. At the end of the 17th century, war became for the French in North America a permanent means of safeguarding their relations with the fur-trading Indians, whom the English merchants sought to subvert. There was war, or at least a state of siege, in New France from 1609 to 1713 and from 1744 to 1760; the French colony knew peace only for 30 years. Peace, however, was only relative, since during it New France twice had to fight the Fox Indians and continued to strengthen its position against the English colonies. So important was the sense of danger that the army became in importance the second, if not the first, industry of the colony.

For most of its history, New France was truly a military camp. The supreme authority in the colony, the Governor General, was ordinarily a career soldier, either a member of the land forces like Montmagny and Frontenac, or a member of the troops of the Marine like Callières and the two de Vaudreuils. He was the commander in chief of the troops in the colony. Soldiers also headed the governments of Quebec, Three Rivers, and Montreal, and the representative of the supreme authority in the parish was a soldier: the captain of militia.

Military life was thus the dominant feature of all the activities in the colony. The trading posts outside the St. Lawrence Valley were also forts, and the official censuses of the 17th and 18th centuries were always taken in terms of the militia, the totals always given as those of men able to bear arms. Under those conditions, the Canadian, whose life was spent amid military activity, could hardly avoid becoming integrated into it. He worked and lived with soldiers, whom he had to billet; he was subject to compulsory military service in the militia. The Canadian could not escape, for wherever he went in New France, he met soldiers who would remind him that the French colony in North America was an "armed camp."

And "armed camp" means soldiers. In the texts that follow, we will attempt to describe the soldier in Canada and to show how much he influenced the life of the colony.

Was the Canadian way of the life transformed by the presence of the soldier in New France? How did the soldier live? Did he influence the Canadian economy and society? How did he influence the Canadian in terms of outlook? To what point was the soldier integrated into the colony?

No comprehensive study has ever been particularly devoted to the soldier in New France. To those who would want to examine the question in more detail, we would recommend the excellent work by André Corvisier, *L'armée française de la fin du XVIIᵉ siècle au ministère de Choiseul. Le soldat* (2 vols., 1964). They will also read with profit the manuscript dissertation by Donald Fraser McOuat, "Military Policy and Organization in New France" (1947). Also worthy of attention are the studies on military organization in Canada by Gustave Lanctôt, "Les troupes de la Nouvelle-France," *Canadian Historical Association Report*, 1926, pp. 40–60; and Gérard Malchelosse, "Milice et troupes de la Marine," *Cahiers des Dix*, Vol. XIV (1949), 115–47.

The military history of the period and the part played by European and American wars in the history of New France are well covered in Jean Bruchési, "Le sort des armes," *Cahiers de l'Académie canadienne-française*, Vol. II, pp. 167–188; and in George F. G. Stanley, *Canada's Soldiers* (1960), pp. 12–97.

An historical overview of the period is available in W. J. Eccles, *Canada under Louis XIV, 1663–1701* (1964), and in Gustave Lanctôt, *Histoire du Canada*, Vol. II: *Du Régime royal au traité d'Utrecht, 1663–1713* (1963), and Vol. III: *Du traité d'Utrecht au traité de Paris, 1713–1760* (1964).

Two studies to be consulted about the Regiment of Carignan-Salières are: Régis Roy and Gérard Malchelosse, *Le régiment de Carignan. Son organisation et son expédition au Canada. Officiers et soldats qui s'établirent au Canada, 1665–1668* (1925), and the more recent one by Father Germain Lesage, O.M.I., on one of the companies of the Regiment, that of the Sieur de la Fouille, and on one of his officers, Manereuil: *Manereuil, fondateur de Louiseville, 1665–1672* (1966).

On the Canadian militia, one must mention the studies by Benjamin Sulte, "Canadian Militia under the French Regime," *Mélanges Historiques*, Vol. I, pp. 127–46; and "The Captain of Militia," *Canadian Historical Review*, Vol. I, No. 3 (September, 1920), pp. 241–45, as well as the already listed works by Lanctôt and Malchelosse.

A. The Regiment of Carignan-Salières

Since 1660 New France had been living under the threat of an Iroquois onslaught. Following representations in 1663 by Governor Davaugour, Mgr. de Laval, and Pierre Boucher, Louis XIV decided to administer the colony himself and to send troops to humble the Iroquois. The colony could now breathe more easily. These troops, the Regiment of Carignan-Salières, arrived in Canada in 1665, and from this point until the end of the French regime, the soldier would be a dominant factor in Canadian life. Canadian society could no longer remain a society of mystics, but became one in which could be found, as elsewhere, rich and poor, city and country people, scholars and illiterates, virtuous individuals and others less so. In short, it became a "man-size" society. How and how much was Canada transformed by the arrival of the Regiment of Carignan-Salières? How did these troops take root in the country?

Document A–1

FROM A SOCIETY OF MYSTICS TO A "MAN-SIZE" SOCIETY

(Soeur Morin, *Annales de l'Hôtel-Dieu de Montréal* [Montréal, 1921], pp. 114–15.)

But the Lord was blessing the deeds of this small people so much that they were reaping as much wheat from the seeding of a single *minot* as we do today from that of 28 or 30, without exaggeration. They were living like saints, all together, and with a piety and religion towards God, just as today the good religious people do. The one from among them who had not heard the Holy Mass on a work day was considered almost as if excommunicated unless he had reasons and impediments as strong as those required today to be exempted from a mortal sin on holidays and Sundays. One could see the working men attending the first mass which was said before daybreak in winter and, in the summer, at four o'clock in the morning, as modest and pious as the most devout religious could be; and all the women, at another which was said at eight o'clock, were no less pious or virtuous than their husbands. Nothing required lock and key, neither the house, nor chests, nor cellars; everything was kept open and nothing was ever lost. Whoever had a surplus would help him who had less, without ever awaiting a request; on the contrary, being pleased to anticipate and to give this token of affection and esteem; when fits of impatience had led to harsh words to one's neighbor or other person, one would not retire without having asked forgiveness on one's knees. One never heard of the vice of lust, which was held in horror, even by those men who were the least devout. Altogether, it was an image of the primitive Church that one could find in this dear Montréal in its beginnings, that is, during 32 years, or thereabouts; but this happy time has gone forever, the continuous war by the Iroquois having forced the King to send into Canada on several occasions five or six thousand men, soldiers and officers, who have ruined the Lord's vineyard and brought with them vice and sin, which is now almost as common as in old France. Even the worst crimes are committed, bewailed by the good people, particularly the missionaries, who forever preach and exhort without seeing much result, tearfully regretting those happy years when Virtue was flourishing.

Document A—2

THE SOLDIER TAKES ROOT IN NEW FRANCE

("Lettre du Ministre Colbert à Talon [20 février 1668]," *Rapport de l'Archiviste de la Province de Québec pour 1930–31* [Québec, 1931], pp. 91–92.)

Paris, February 20, 1668

Upon his arrival, your secretary handed me your memorandum of the 27th of the month of October last and, at the same time, a judgment of the 25th, 26th and 27th of the same month together with another memorandum concerning all those things which you consider necessary to be solved for Canada in accordance with the present constitution of affairs in that country.

Before dealing with them, I consider it well that I inform you of the resolutions which His Majesty has taken regarding the troops and the officers who command them as well as the Colony, which have obliged Him to make some reflections.

Firstly, He sends his orders to have the Carignan Salières Infantry Regiment return, with 20 companies and the four companies detached from the Pordou group under Chambellé and Ligniers, except for four of the said companies which he leaves in the country to man the most exposed and the most important forts, to protect the inhabitants and guarantee them from attack by the Savages and any other enemy nation, in case they came to break the peace which has been granted them; the said four companies will be selected from those whose captains have married in the country or are about to marry.

I inform you further that the King would be pleased that the soldiers of these troops remain in Canada, and that His Majesty will be more pleased with those Captains who, having their companies in the country in good shape, will bring them back to France very weak, than with the others who will do everything to have them return in large numbers. And, as proof of this wish, His Majesty has earmarked a large sum, as you will see hereunder, to be distributed among the soldiers who will marry and remain and among those composing the four remaining companies who will receive their pay as heretofore. . . .

His Majesty has bestowed a gratification of 1500 livres upon Sieur de La Motte, first captain of the Carignan Salières Regiment, for services rendered in Canada in the construction of forts and in the expeditions which have been made against the Iroquois, for the marriage which he made in the country and for his decision to remain there; He has further ordered a sum of six thousand livres to be distributed to the officers of the same troops who have already married or will be married there hereafter, to give them the means to establish themselves and to further their resolution not to return again to France.

He also earmarked a fund of twelve thousand livres to be distributed to the soldiers who will remain in the said country or who will marry there, other than those of the four companies which He leaves there, the latter being kept through the payment of their salary. He leaves it to you to use this sum well, which undoubtedly you find large; the proper use will not fail to produce great results to the advantage of the colony.

B. The Soldier and the Army

After the Carignan-Salières Regiment departed in 1668, Canada remained almost entirely without regular troops until 1684, when the King, under Governor La Barre's pressing representations, decided to send three companies of the troops of the Marine. Thereafter, Canada would not again be deprived of regular troops.[1]

How were the troops of the Marine structured? What was the value of those troops which were sent to Canada? How good was their discipline? How did they live in the colony and what were their pay, rations, clothing, quartering, and duties? The following documents, typical of the Ancient Regime where everything had been carefully forecast by the paternalistic state, will provide some answers.

---

[1] From 1684 to 1755, the soldiers who came to New France were all members of the troops of the Marine; in 1755 the first *troupes de terre* (land troops) were sent. Unlike the former, which were under the control of the Ministry of the Marine, the latter came under the direct control of the Ministry of War and of its Minister. The eight battalions sent to Canada were part of the French regular army.

Document B–1

STRUCTURE OF THE TROOPS OF THE MARINE

("Ordonnances du Roy portant augmentation dans les troupes du Canada, 10 avril 1750"; Gustave Lanctôt, "Les troupes de la Nouvelle-France," CHAR, 1926, p. 56.)

His Majesty wishing to increase the troops of the detachment of the Marine which He maintains in Canada, He would have given his orders for the raising of the necessary recruits for the said increase and wishing to explain his intentions on the matter, He has ordered and orders as follows.

ART. I

There will be maintained in the Colony of Canada 30 Companies of 50 men each, not including the officers, that is two sergeants, three corporals, one cadet, one soldier cadet, two drummers and 41 soldiers, each of the said companies will be commanded by one captain, one lieutenant, one ensign and one supplementary ensign; and each of the soldier cadets will be provided with an order signed by the Governor Lieutenant General of the Colony recorded with the control of the Marine in Quebec.

2.

The said 30 Companies of 50 men each will be formed from the 28 Companies of 28 men each which are the present garrison of the Colony, and of new recruits raised in the execution of His Majesty's orders. The Sergeants, Corporals, Cadets and Soldiers of the said old companies will be divided equally in accordance with the specific orders which His Majesty will send to the Governor and his Lieutenant General in the said colony; and there shall be further in the said Companies a drummer major with fifer, the former to be paid 18 livres per month, the latter as a drummer.

3.

The Captains, Lieutenants and Ensigns who command the 28 old Companies will keep their rank and their seniority from the date of their commission and service Certificates; and the officers of the new companies will take theirs similarly from the date of their commissions and service Certificates.

4.

The allowances for the Captains, Lieutenants and Ensigns who will command the two new Companies, and the salaries of the Sergeants, Corporals, Cadets, Drummers and Soldiers will be paid on the same level as those of the old Companies, according to the Rolls which will be sent annually for the expenses of the said Colony.

Document B—2

QUALITY OF THE TROOPS

("Lettre de M. Chaussegros de Lery au Conseil de Marine, 29 octobre 1719," in P. G. Roy, *Inventaire des Papiers de Lery conservés aux Archives de la Province de Québec* [Québec, 1940], Vol. I, pp. 51—52.)

I have the honor to point out to the Council that the greatest resource which I have to erect the fortifications are the troops, most of whom are young men or children quite unsuited for such labors and even less for war and who will not soon become fit; I beg the Council that the recruits who will be sent to this country be not like those of the past years: they who have requested from the Council young men or children, saying that they adapt to the country better than grown men, have their reasons to speak thus, just like the officers who recruit them in France.

A man fit for service costs more to recruit than a child, and a grown man or an old soldier in the colony complains when he is wronged.

I beg the Council to consider that in the past in Canada the troops were strong and good throughout the country, which kept the inhabitants and the Indians quiet: they are quite different now, and insubordinate; heretofore the men sent from France were well drilled and capable of serving upon their arrival, but now young men and children are sent, most of them undrilled. It is impossible to form a solid body of troops with such recruits, experience has often proven it; after having waited for a few years, it happens that some of these young men have matured as small disabled men, weak and unfit for soldiering, all men not being capable of service; that is the reason why the troops are in a bad state.

In the past the Carignan Regiment had been sent to the colony; upon its arrival, it marched to war. Thereafter, troops of the Marine were sent which served the colony well, all these men adapted to the country more easily than children would; the oldest inhabitants served in these troops and the young ones are their children.

The climate being quite cold, it is sure that a strong and vigorous man will resist better than a young boy; he will also be able to serve upon his arrival, and we will be assured to have good men in the troops, fit for war and for the labors which soldiers are used to doing in France.

Document B—3

THE PROBLEM OF REPLACEMENT

("Lettre de M. Chaussegros de Lery au Conseil de Marine, 22 octobre 1720," in P. G. Roy, *Inventaire des Papiers de Lery* . . . [Quebec, 1940] Vol. I, pp. 62—63.)

Quebec, October 22, 1720

The recruits which the Council sent this year are good for this country, being good men, and almost all tradesmen and workmen; if such men are sent every year, assuredly the troops will improve. There is here a tradition which is detrimental: when the troops are incorporated into the companies, at the same time a few soldiers are discharged, some to return to France, others to marry in this country. Ordinarily the best ones are thus discharged, and there remain in the companies only those who have not been able to be discharged. When troops must be improved, the bad soldiers must be discharged, and those capable of serving must be kept; to replace the discharged bad soldiers with good ones is the only means to improve the troops in a short time.

The tradition has been to discharge the good soldiers and they have been replaced by those who have arrived as recruits in the previous years, the majority of whom were not capable of serving. If troops are to be improved, it is necessary every year when the recruits arrive from France to discharge the bad soldiers to remain in the country and to replace them with better ones.

I have the honor to point out to the Council that it would be necessary that there be here someone who took care of fulfilling the function, as the inspectors do in France, of discharging only the soldiers who cannot serve, sending to the Council every year a roll of the troops, indicating the age, the height and the strength of every soldier, and the names of those who will have to be discharged the following year so that the Council send good men to replace them.

C. Discipline of the Troops

At the outset, when the troops of the Marine began to live in the colony, discipline was relatively severe. (See "Reglement du Roy, Pour la Conduite, Police et Discipline des Compagnies que Sa Majesté entretient dans le Canada, Du 30 May 1695," in G. Lanctôt, *CHAR*, pp. 51 ff.) Gradually, however, they became an integral part of the colony and the officers, more concerned with their civilian responsibilities than with their military duty, neglected the discipline of their troops. Left to themselves most of the time, the soldiers often took to the worst excesses.

Desertions, like epidemics, were the bane of the armies of the Old Regime. Troops in New France were affected as much as those in France. But when one reads the regulations for the infantry companies in France (see G. Lanctôt, *CHAR*, pp. 49 ff.) and compares the regulations which the king had enacted for the troops in Canada, nothing about deserters is found quite similar to the metropolitan regulations. Was it that there were already many deserters from the companies maintained in New France and the king had felt it necessary to draw up severe regulations? Was the reason for so many desertions not that the country was so vast and the deserters knew that the military authorities could never apprehend them?

Document C–1

BEHAVIOUR OF THE TROOPS

("Dissertation sur le gouvernement, in Les Papiers La Pause," *RAPQ*, 1933–34, p. 208.)

This body of troops behaved much better in the past and is degenerating daily: the example of the comfort of the troops from Europe, the number of French officers who have been commissioned, the scarcity of rewards and appointments, and the absence of opportunity, have led those officers to neglect their preparations for party warfare with the Indians and their capacity for hardships; today there are no more than a few Ensigns and two or three lieutenants in this whole body who are fit for this type of warfare; some are in business, others are soliciting positions or the opportunity to exploit a post on someone else's behalf, but very few worry over war and military spirit. Soldiers are almost always scattered and away from their officers' control; the majority of the latter no longer care for the detailed administration of their companies, the paymaster paying the soldiers often individually. The officers barely know the soldiers who are in their company, or where they are, and the latter seldom know their officers; in spite of all that they are given for their upkeep, which is quite considerable, they are very badly maintained and badly disciplined.

Document C—2

THE KING'S SEVERITY TOWARDS DESERTERS

("Reglement du Roy, Pour la Conduite, Police & Discipline des Compagnies que Sa Majesté entretient dans le Canada. Du 30 May 1695," G. Lanctôt, CHAR, p. 53.)

The Sergeants shall twice daily visit all the soldiers of their squad to be continuously informed of their disposition and their behavior, in order to inform their Captain and to warn him of any desertion.

A fine of two *écus* will be deducted from the pay of those Sergeants who shall not have informed their Captain within twelve hours of the desertion of one of their soldiers.

If a Sergeant commits the same offense a second time, he shall lose his rank.

Two *écus* shall be given, by order of the Intendant, to any soldier who informs on the desertion of another, on condition that the information be provided within two hours of the desertion.

The Captain commanding the area from which a soldier has deserted, the Major of the Troops and the Captain of the soldier having deserted, shall write individually to the Governor General and to the Intendant, giving the name and description of the soldier, and shall at the same time give an account of the efforts made to arrest him, and which officers have been thus employed.

The deserters of the Companies shall pass in judgment in the area where the officers are numerous enough, according to the prescription of the Ordinance of the Marine of April 15, 1689; and if there are not seven Captains present in the area to make up the required number of judges, the Commandant shall call upon the Lieutenants and the Ensigns of the Companies who shall be twenty-two years old, to whom His Majesty grants permission to be members of the Courts martial, when Captains are not in sufficient numbers.

Document C—3

THE SOLDIERS' LICENTIOUS MORALS

("Lettre du Père Etienne de Carheil, de la Compagnie de Jésus, à l'Intendant de Champigny, 30 août 1702," Francis Parkman, The Old Regime in Canada [Toronto, 1899], Vol. II, pp. 243–46.)

If His Majesty desire to save our missions and to support the establishment of Religion, as we have no doubt he does, we beg him most humbly to believe what is most true, namely; that there is no other means of doing so than to abolish the two infamous sorts of commerce which have brought the missions to the brink of destruction, and which will not long delay in destroying these if they are not abolished as soon as possible by his orders, and be prevented from ever being restored. The first is the commerce in brandy; the second is the commerce of the savage women with the French, which are both carried on in an equally public manner, without our being able to remedy the evil because we are not supported by the Commandants who, far from attempting, when we undertake to remonstrate with them, to check these trades, themselves carry them on with greater freedom than do their subordinates and so sanction them by their example, so much so that blank permission is taken and a guarantee of impunity assured which make those vices common to all the French who come here to trade, so that all the villages of our savages are now only taverns for drunkenness and Sodoms for immorality, from which we must withdraw, abandoning them to the just anger and vengeance of God.

You see by this that, in whatever manner the French trade is established among the Savages, if it be desired to retain us among them, to maintain us and to sustain us as missionaries in the exercise of our functions with the hope of our efforts bearing fruit, we must be delivered from the Commandants and their garrisons, who, far from being necessary, are on the contrary so pernicious that we can truly say that they are the greatest scourge of our missions, being detrimental to the ordinary trade of the travelers and to the advancement of Faith. Since they have come up here, we have seen only universal corruption which they have spread by their scandalous conduct to the minds of all those nations which are now contaminated. All the pretended service which is sought to make people believe that they render to the King is reduced to four chief occupations of which we beg you to inform the King.

The first consists in keeping a public tavern for the sale of brandy, wherein they trade it continuously to the Savages, who do not cease to become intoxicated, notwithstanding our efforts to prevent it. Vainly we talk to them to stop it; we gain only to be accused of opposing the King's service and of wishing to prevent a trade which is permitted to them.

The second occupation of the soldiers consists in being sent from one post to another by the Commandants in order to carry their goods and their brandy, after having made arrangements together, none of them having any other object than to help one another in their traffic; and in order for that to be executed the more easily on both sides as they wish, it is necessary that the Commandants shut their eyes not to see any of the disorders occasioned by their soldiers, no matter how visible, public and scandalous they be, and it must be that the soldiers, besides trading their own goods, be traders as well for those of their Commandants who often force them to buy from them before they allow them to go where they wish.

Their third occupation consists in making of their fort a place that I am ashamed to call by its proper name, where the women have found out that their bodies might serve in lieu of goods and would be still better received than beaver, so that it is now the most usual and most continual commerce, and that which is most in fashion. Whatever efforts all the missionaries may make to denounce and abolish it, this traffic increases, rather than diminishing, and grows daily more and more; all the soldiers hold open house for all the women of their acquaintance; from morning till night, the women spend full days, the ones after the others, sitting by their fires and often on their bed in talk and action fitted to their trade which ends ordinarily but at night, the crowd being too dense during the day for them to complete the transaction, although often they arrange to leave a house empty not to defer the completion till night.

The fourth occupation of the soldiers is gambling, which occurs when the traders assemble; it sometimes proceeds to such excess that they are not satisfied with passing the whole day, but they also spend the whole night in this pursuit; and it happens too often that, in the ardor of their application they forget, or if they remember, they fail to mount the guard of the posts. But what makes their misconduct even worse is that so persistent an attachment to the game hardly ever goes without a general intoxication of all the players, and that drunkenness is almost always followed by quarrels which arise among them and which, taking place publicly in front of the Indians, cause among the latter three great scandals: the first, of seeing them drunk; the second, of seeing them fighting among themselves so furiously as to take their rifles to kill one another; and the third, of witnessing the missionaries' inability to stop this.

Such, My Lord, are the four sole occupations of the garrisons which have been maintained here for so many years. If occupations of this kind can be called the King's service, I admit that they have always rendered him one of those four services; but I have observed none other than those four; and consequently, if such services are not considered necessary to the King, there has never hitherto been any necessity for keeping them here, and after their recall, there will be no necessity of sending them back.

D. Standard of Living

Document D–1

RATIONS

("Lettre de Doreil au Ministre, 16 juillet 1755," RAPQ, 1944–45, p. 21.)

The soldier on garrison duty receives rations of one and one half pounds of good bread, four ounces of lard or, on some occasions, one-half pound of fresh beef in lieu of lard; he is also given daily four ounces of dry peas. When he serves in an outpost or on the march, he is given two pounds of bread and, with it, two gulps of brandy.

The troops of the colony are not usually provided with salt and tobacco; I am, however, pressing M. Bigot in this matter.

I have already obtained that our troops, according to my rolls indicating their number, be given one pound of tobacco per man per month. I dare not hope for the same success in the case of salt, but I will not desist.

I have also obtained from M. Bigot that our sick and wounded in the hospitals be provided with wine when the doctors and surgeons will allow them to drink it. It has never been the custom to give any to the soldiers of the colony.

Document D–2

SOLDIERS' CLOTHING IN NEW FRANCE

(G. Lanctôt, CHAR, p. 55.)

Clothes to be sent in the year 1729 for the troops of the Colonies [Maurepas, 26 October, 1728] to Quebec, on board the storeship Elephant for 28 Companies consisting of 812 men:

56 coats for Sergeants of blue Lodève broadcloth
756 coats for soldiers of blue lined Mazamet

812 breeches for sergeants and soldiers made of the same Mazamet
56 Sergeants' Hats with gold braid
756 Soldiers' Hats with yellow braid
56 pairs of blue stockings from Nimes for Sergeants
756 pairs of blue stockings from St. Maixant for soldiers
1624 red linen shirts
1624 white cravats of St. Jean de Lyon linen
1624 pairs of double-soled shoes

Document D–3

MEDICAL CARE

(W. Marchand [Ed.], Peter Kalm, *Voyage en Amérique* [Montréal, 1880], p. 102.)

The hospital (Hôtel-Dieu de Québec), as I have before mentioned, forms a part of the convent. It consists of two large halls, and some rooms near the apothecary's shop. In the halls are two rows of beds, one on each side. The beds next to the wall are furnished with curtains, the outward ones are without them. In each bed are fine bed clothes with clean double sheets. As soon as a sick person has left his bed, it is made again to keep the hospital clean and orderly. The beds are two or three yards apart, and near each is a small table. There are good iron stoves, and fine windows in this hall. The nuns attend the sick people, and bring them their meals and care for their needs.

Besides them there are some male nurses and a surgeon. The royal physician is obliged to come to the hospital once or twice a day; he goes from bed to bed and orders his prescriptions. Sick soldiers are normally received into this hospital; they are very numerous in July and August, when the King's ships arrive, and in time of war. But at other times, when there are not many sick soldiers, other patients take their place, as beds are free. The hospital is amply provided with everything which is required for the care of the sick: provisions, medicines, fuel, etc. Those who are very ill are put into separate rooms, that they be not troubled by the noises.

E. Payment of the Military

Document E–1

FOR THE EXPENSES OF CANADA DURING THE YEAR 1743

(A.P.C., "Canada, dépenses générales, 1741–1746," CII^A, Vol. 115–1, p. 111ff., fol. 50–51, 58.)

9 June 1743

Pay of the Companies

For Twenty eight companies of soldiers composed of 29 men each with one Captain, one Lieutenant and two Ensigns the Sum of one hundred and fifty four thousand eight hundred and twelve livres. That is:

	livres
For the Captain of a Company per month	90
For the Lieutenant	60
For the appointed Ensign	30
For the supplementary Ensign	25
For two Sergeants at 20.5 each per month	40.10
For three Corporals at 12.15 idem	38.5
For three Lance-Corporals at 9.15 idem	29.5
For one cadet	15
For Twenty Soldiers at 9. each per month	180
Total for one Company per month	580

And for the Twenty eight Companies on strength the sum of one Hundred and Seventy thousand six hundred and eighty eight livres 170,688

From which must be subtracted 18^d per day from the pay of each Cadet and Soldier to a sum of 45^s each per month and per Company 47.5 for clothing provided, the yearly sum being 15,876

Therefore remains to be paid 154,812

Salaries and Subsistence of Employees in the Stores and Offices

In Quebec

For six Scribes attached to the Office of the Intendance and to that of the Control for the munitions store, five of whom at VIe and the other at IIIIe IIII^xx per year, the sum of 3,480

For one Boat and Canoe Keeper at XXV per month 300

For one Clerk for the issuing of rations at XX 240

For three bakers at C IIII^xx each per year 540

For one Interpreter of the Iroquois Language attached to the General, the sum of 400

For another of the Abenakis Language	300
For another of the Ottawa Language ..	200

In Three Rivers

For one store keeper, the Sum of	150
For one Surgeon	200
For one Baker	72
For one Interpreter of the Abenakis Language	100

In Montreal

For two Scribes attached to the Office of the Commissary and to the munitions store, at VIᶜ each	1,200
For another Scribe taking care of the journeymen, boats and canoes, idem	600
For one Control Clerk at XL per month	480
For one Clerk in the munitions Store idem	480
For one Clerk for the issuing of Rations at XX	240
For one Clerk in charge of the fur trade done at Fort Frontenac on behalf of the King at LXXV	900
	9,882

On the other side	9,882
For one Clerk for the Fur Trade of Lake Ontario, the sum of	350
For one Clerk for the Trade at Niagara at 50	600
For one store keeper at Fort Chambly at XXX	360
For one boat Builder at L	600
For one Surgeon at X	120
For two Armourers, one at IIIIᶜL and the other at 375 per year	825
For one Interpreter in the Iroquois Language at 16.13.4	200
For one in the Algonkin Language at XII.X	150
For another in the English Language idem	150
For another in the Iroquois Language who works at his trade of blacksmith at XXXIII.VI.VIII	400
For two men who help in the trade of Ontario and Niagara at 300 each	600
For three bakers at CIIIIˣˣ each	540
For another Baker at Fort Chambly at 10	120
For two other Bakers for the garrison of Fort St. Louis where the Iroquois Indians have settled	144
For one woman who handles the housework and the cleaning of the chapel linen	120
Sum XVᵐCLXI	15,161

"Marine 1743
From the funds of the Domaine d'Occident
9 June 1743"
Justice and Police Officers
In Quebec

For the first counselor of the Superior Council of Canada for his allowances the Sum of five hundred livres	500
For ten other Counselors of the council at 300 each the Sum of	3,000
For the Attorney general idem the Sum of Fifteen hundred livres	1,500
For the Clerk idem, the Sum of Seven hundred livres	700
For the Bailiff the sum of One Hundred livres	100
For the Lieutenant general of the Prevosté the Sum of Seven hundred livres	700
For the special lieutenant idem, The Sum of Six hundred livres	600
For the King's Attorney the Sum of Three hundred livres	300
For the Clerk, The Sum of one hundred livres	100

In Montreal

For the Lieutenant general, for his allowances the Sum of Four hundred and fifty livres	450
For the King's Attorney, The Sum of Two hundred and fifty livres	250

In Three Rivers

For the civil Lieutenant for his allowances the Sum of four hundred and fifty livres	450
For the King's Attorney, the Sum of Two hundred and fifty livres	250

Other Justice and Police Officers Attached to Quebec

For S. Lanoullier Desboiscler, Road Supervisor, for his allowances, the Sum of Six hundred livres	600
For the Prevost Marshal, the Sum of Five hundred livres	500
For the Watch Officer, the Sum of Three hundred livres	300
For Four Archers at 175 each per year, the Sum of	700
	11,000

On the other side	11,000
For the Executioner, the Sum of three hundred livres	300
For him for his board, Thirty livres	30
Sum XIᵐIIIᶜXXX	11,330

Document E–2

COULD THE TROOPS LIVE FROM THEIR SALARY ALONE?

(Mémoire sur les postes du Canada adressé à M. de Surlaville, en 1754, par le chevalier de Raymond," *RAPQ*, 1927–28, p. 334–35.)

I have told you that it was not rank or seniority which had been, since I Came to Canada, and which has been until now the criterion in the selection of officers to commands in those posts, that it was favoritism and almost always to the same persons and the same families to whom the rich posts were granted. . . . Many other families and French officers are deprived, although they have given on several occasions satisfactory proof of their knowledge, of their application, of their zeal and unselfishness; they are officers who know only how to care for their affairs and to whom, however, these commands have been denied, which would have enabled them to support their career; they remain in poverty and cannot support their families. The French and Canadian officers who are not married receive a captain's allowances of 1062 livres; can this be sufficient to pay 1200 livres for room and board without a servant or 1600 livres with a servant? Yet it is common knowledge that this is their situation. Where can they find the difference? Where can they get the required money when they have no other resources in a country where even living is beyond price? What must they do to keep body and soul? It is the least one can do for the lowliest of humans. However, persons of rank, old and trusted officers, do not have the means to do it. In order to achieve it, must they steal? No. How then can they act in the face of harsh necessity? They borrow from merchants, almost all of whom lose what they have loaned when the officers die bankrupt. This would never happen if, instead of granting favors and clutching at all possibilities in complicity with one's favorites, the officers were to be named to these posts one after the other. All the officers who cannot obtain one of these commands are despised by those who are favored thus, even by their soldiers and the people. The result is unbelievable insubordination. The young officer who is rich because of such favors hardly acknowledges an old captain who has become grey under the weight of arms. He will not even give him the deserved respectful treatment. What else is the result of such policy? A disgust with service, loss of care for application and zeal, loss of interest for the service of the King. Such are the fruits of discontent among officers who are neglected, rebuffed, left in poverty in spite of their pressing requests that they be used in the service.

Document E–3

CONDITIONS OF TROOPS SERVING IN FORT ST. FREDERIC

(Kalm, *Voyage en Amérique*, pp. 13–16.)

The soldiery enjoy such advantages here as they are not allowed in any part of the world. Those who formed the garrison of this place had a very plentiful allowance from their government. They get every day a pound and a half of wheat bread, which is almost more than they can eat. They likewise get plenty of peas, bacon, and salted or dried meat. Sometimes they kill oxen and other cattle, the flesh of which is distributed among the soldiers. All the officers kept cows, at the expense of the king, and the milk they gave was more than sufficient to supply them. The soldiers had each a small garden outside the fort, which they were allowed to attend and to plant in it whatever they liked. Some of them had built summerhouses in them and planted all kinds of vegetables. The governor told me that it was a general custom to allow the soldiers a plot of ground for kitchen gardens, at such of the French forts hereabouts as were not situated near great towns, from whence they could be supplied. In time of peace the soldiers had very little guard duty when at the fort; and as the lake close by was full of fish, and the woods abounded with birds and animals, those amongst them who chose to be diligent could live extremely well and like a lord in regard to food. Each soldier got a new coat every two years; but annually, a waistcoat, cap, hat, breeches, cravat, two pairs of stockings, two pairs of shoes, and as much wood as he had occasion for in winter. They likewise got five *sols* apiece every day, which is augmented to thirty *sols* when they have any particular labor for the king. When this is considered it is not surprising to find the men are very healthy, well fed, strong and lively here. When a soldier falls sick, he is brought to the hospital, where the king provides him with a bed, food, medicine, and people to take care of and serve him. When some of them asked leave to be absent for a day or two to go away it was generally granted them if circumstances would permit, and they enjoyed as usual their share of provisions and money, but were obliged to get some of their comrades to mount guard for them as often as it came to their turns, for which they gave them an equivalent. The governor and officers were duly honored by the soldiers; however, the soldiers and officers often spoke together as comrades, without any ceremonies, and with a very becoming freedom. The soldiers who are sent hither from France commonly serve till they are forty or fifty years old, after which they are honorably discharged and allowed to settle upon and cultivate a piece of ground. But if they have agreed on their arrival to serve no longer than a certain number of years, they are dismissed at the expiration of their term. Those who are born here commonly agree to serve the crown during six, eight, or ten years, after which they are discharged and settle down as farmers in the country. The king presents each discharged soldier with a piece of land, being commonly 40 arpents long and but three broad, if the soil be of equal goodness throughout; but they get somewhat more, if it be poorer. As soon as a soldier settles to cultivate such a piece of land, he is at first assisted by the king, who supplies him, his wife and children with provisions during the first three or four years. The king likewise gives him a cow and the most necessary instruments for agriculture. Some soldiers are sent to assist him in building a house, for which the king pays them. These are of great help to a poor man who begins to keep house, and it seems that in a country where the troops are so highly distinguished by royal favor, the king cannot be at a loss for soldiers. For the better cultivation and population of Canada, a plan was proposed some years ago for sending three hundred men over from France every year, by which means the old soldiers might always be retired, marry, and settle in the country.

Document E–4

TROUPES DE TERRE'S MATERIAL STANDARD OF LIVING

(Mémoire des choses qui seront fournies aux troupes de terre en Canada, Papiers La Pause, 22 mars 1754," RAPQ, 1933–34, p. 225.)

1o The officers and soldiers of those troops shall be fed during the crossing.

2o Upon arrival in the colony each soldier will receive one jacket, one coat, one pair of breeches and one hat, all new; the old ones to be stored for cleaning and mending as much as possible, to keep them for the return trip or to be used in case of emergency.

3o Each soldier shall also receive two pairs of shoes, two pairs of stockings, two pairs of soles, one pair of gaiters, or linen to make them, a black cravat, one pack, and three shirts. These items, and the breeches, shall be replaced as necessary.

4o Upon arrival in Quebec, each soldier shall receive one knife, one spoon and one fork, and each Company a certain number of canteens, mess-tins, razors, scissors, ironing stones, needles and thread.

5o Food will be provided for sergeants, corporals, (*anspessades*) and soldiers in the garrisons of Quebec, Montreal and Three Rivers, on the scale of rations provided for the troops of the colony; and the officers on garrison duty shall live from their allowances.

6o Officers and soldiers in outposts will be fed during the campaign on the same scale as the officers of the colonies.

7o Officers and soldiers, sick and wounded, shall be received and treated until recovery in the hospitals of the country, together with the sick and wounded of the troops of the colony, and the surgeons who go across with the battalions shall be paid allowances similar to those of the surgeons in the colony.

8o Powder, shot and flints will be provided not only for the campaigns, but also for garrison duty, and they shall be given weapons to replace those damaged or lost.

9o Each soldier shall receive one *pistole*, who continues to serve beyond his term when he ought to have been discharged had he remained in France; in accordance with the ordinance which will be issued on the matter.

10o When the troops are in the field, the officers and soldiers will receive the same equipment, clothing and weapons, etc. which are provided for the officers and soldiers of the troops of the colony.

11o All these provisions shall be provided without any withholding on the officers' allowances or the soldiers' pay.

Document E–5

THE CONDITIONS OF A SOLDIER ON GARRISON DUTY IN THE 1750'S

(J.C.B., *Voyage au Canada dans le Nord de l'Amérique septentrionale fait depuis l'an 1751 à 1761* [Québec, 1887], pp. 37–41, 45.)

After having spent five days visiting all that was worth seeing, I then found myself in need and idleness, and I therefore determined to join the army, a course which, although appearing rigorous, would at least solve my embarrassment.

This decision was dictated only by the circumstances, because I believed that I had talent for more rewarding positions; I made up my mind and, of my own free will, I left the merchant where I was boarding and went to the artillery commandant to join this corps because, according to my information, this type of service would be more to my liking; the salary was sixteen and eighteen *francs* per month. Having informed this officer of my voluntary decision, he found that I was weak and too short for artillery service; happily for me, however, he had with him three ladies who, perhaps because of my meek attitude, became interested in my fate. After I had answered the officer's several questions to the best of my ability and with my usual frankness, he decided, at the request of the ladies, to make me a gunner. They thanked him and, to indicate their happiness, they decided immediately on a stage-name for me, and called me Jolicoeur; with the name came one *louis*, in paper money current in the country, which one of them gave me and which I accepted the more willingly that I was without a *sou*. At the same time, the commandant ordered me to be at the Place d'Armes where the Governor General was to preside, on the following day, November 12, over the bringing of the recruits on the strength of the various companies of troops which were the town garrison and were not yet incorporated: they are called the companies *franches* of the Marine. I did not fail to appear for the review: all the troops were under arms in three ranks, eighteen companies in all; the recruits were facing them, without arms and in two ranks. The governor, with his staff, arrived about noon; I took my place, on my own, at the end of the two companies of gunners who in this country act as grenadiers, and the inspection began with them; the commandant having spoken to the governor, he examined me and was informed of all about me; he then went to the other companies and finally to the recruits, from whom each captain, according to his seniority, beginning with the gunners' captain, took the number of men who were assigned to him; the gunners' commandant selected ten men, not counting me, and the other captains followed. After the division, each company withdrew with its recruits; I was assigned the fifth rank in the second company, which was located on St. John's Gate. The next day, we were clothed and armed.

Several persons of the most distinguished society in the town, drawn by curiosity, watched the review; I saw my three patronesses, who curtsied to me and gave me eighteen *francs* in hard money: this generosity augured well. When I returned to the company, I paid out the eighteen *francs* to arrange my welcome according to the established custom: this

guaranteed me friends like the soldiers have. I paid no attention to that except insofar as it could serve my interests and this, without taking to the visiting of taverns.

I was given as bedmate, for we slept in pairs, a Parisian who, although he had a pretty face made to draw attention, liked to drink and gamble; he was also cruel, quarrelsome, and too often put his hand to his sword without provocation or reason; however, with time, I gained upon him so much influence that I could put an end to his anger by my very presence. When he was sober, he was kind and gracious, especially to women, whom he took great pains to cheat. He was very fond of dancing,—he excelled at it—and I acquired a taste for it as well, since he took me with him to balls and taught me the steps; so much so that, within three months, I was almost as proficient as he was in the art, which did not fail to divert him from his vices, at least for a time; but, when I neglected him for a while, he returned to his old habits. My kindness had allowed him to use my clothes, but he was wearing all I had and I could not go out: he was taking the best of what I had and my money. This behavior cooled my friendship and led me to break off our relations.

I was offered, sometime in December, a position with a merchant to keep his books and learn his trade; I took it without hesitation, having made a ruling for myself, because of the unknown future, to learn all I could use later, knowing that he who has a single purpose may find himself embarrassed when the purpose fails. I went therefore to work for the merchant; since I appeared full of zeal for his interests, we developed a friendship. I pleased him enough that he decided to try and obtain my release. This benevolent act of kindness was rewarded with my gratitude, which I showed with all my heart. He went through all that he believed necessary, but he was unsuccessful. This honest man, I have learned since indirectly, had planned to obtain my release, to have me made his partner, to make me heir to his business and to marry me to his only daughter, a young person well-learned and pretty. Thus, fortune rendered me a disservice on this occasion and I much regretted my military engagement.

I had not lost sight of my three patronesses; I had visited them on several occasions during the winter, and I was always well received with true kindness. One day, without my knowledge, three officers of their families, who had met me there on several occasions, reproached them their relationships, although they were perfectly free to receive me in their home. These three relatives, after their failure to convince them not to receive me any more, resorted to other means which proved more successful: they went and saw the commandant of the gunners and had him intervene with his authority and forbid me to continue my visits to those Ladies. I was informed to meet him and, when I arrived, I was forbidden to see them again under penalty of imprisonment. Since I could not disobey an order from a superior without being guilty, I had to resign myself. I immediately wrote the Ladies that I was very sorry but that

I had to cease visiting them, that an order from a superior ran against my good will and that I could do nothing but obey. I received no answer but, a few days later, I heard that the Ladies had quarrelled with their relatives and I was even sorrier to be the innocent cause of this quarrel.

YEAR 1752. In March of that year died, in Quebec, Governor General de la Joncquière, who had succeeded Comte de la Galissonnière.

Soon thereafter, a holiday was proclaimed to celebrate the birth of the Duke of Bourgogne, the Dauphin's son. Preparations were made for fireworks, the gunners were charged with the task under the commandant, and I was among the workers; this forced me to leave the merchant where I had been working and where I had been treated like an adopted son. We were busy for three months in the preparation of the fireworks. . . .

During the remainder of the year 1752, I returned to my employment with the same merchant whom I had left because of the fireworks. I used to spend the evenings in the pleasure of social balls, where I was welcome.

F. Canadian Society: Military Society?

What position did the Canadians give the army in their society? What links existed between the army and the society? These are the questions which must now be asked. Did the soldier live in isolation from society? To what extent was the Canadian "civil" society a military one, and to what extent was the army "civilian"?

Document F–1

NATURE OF AUTHORITY IN NEW FRANCE

("Dissertation sur le gouvernement. Papiers La Pause," *RAPQ*, 1933–34, p. 207.)

Canada has a military government; it has been based on sound principles for the mainstay of the country, but the abuse of the most useful things for its preservation and increase have made it turn away from this military spirit so useful to the maintenance of a new colony;

it is even to be feared that if the Court does not initiate measures to correct those abuses and laxities, this country will survive only with complete help from France. A military colony must have military laws, and there are none; it must have order and discipline, but they are known in name only; the inhabitants must be governed by and submit to military regulations, but all is arbitrary; it must avoid luxury and indolence, but one is approved and the other tolerated; it must reward merit, but all is confused; it must increase the population and the agriculture, yet nothing is done for the former, the other is degraded, and commerce alone is considered as worthwhile, and it is conducted through favors or protection. It will be very easy to prove, when dealing with finances, how much this commerce is to the prejudice of this colony.

The government of Canada is composed of four orders which are: the Church, the military, the traders or merchants, and the militia which includes artisans and *habitants*; there is a Governor General who until now has been of no higher rank than that of post captain, who represents the person of the King; he is however limited in some matters by the intendant. He has under him two local governors, those of Montreal and Three Rivers, and he is expected to fill the position of governor of Quebec himself and he receives all its revenues. Each of the three towns has a King's lieutenant, a mayor and an assistant mayor. The town-mayors are often drawn from among the senior army captains, but favoritism has often led to their exclusion; the King's lieutenants are drawn from the senior town-mayors and the local governors from the senior of the King's lieutenants; when the Governor General is absent, the senior of the local governors commands.

Document F–2

CARD MONEY TO PAY THE TROOPS

("Ordonnance de M. de Frontenac et Bochart de Champigny, 19 novembre 1689," P. G. Roy, *Ordonnances, commissions, etc., des gouverneurs et intendants de la Nouvelle-France, 1639–1706* [Beauceville, 1924], pp. 188–89.)

Having to provide for the payment of the troops to enable them to subsist next year 1690, until the funds provided by His Majesty for the said year have arrived, since there are no funds at the present time, we have considered necessary to have card money made for four *livres* and two *livres* of money of this country, as it shall be indicated on each of the said cards by the hand of Sr de Verneuil, clerk of Mr de Lubert, the treasurer of the Marine, and by him and Sr Duplessy, another of Sr de Lubert's clerks, signed and sealed; it shall be legal for the amounts inscribed as ordinary money, which no one shall be entitled to refuse under penalty of a fine of one hundred livres; we forbid expressly any person to forge the said card money under penalty of death as counterfeiters; the said card money shall be withdrawn from those who shall have received it, and we shall have them paid equal value on the said funds which will be sent by His Majesty for the expenditures of the said year 1690.

Document F–3

CENSUSES OF THE NUMBER OF MEN ABLE TO BEAR ARMS

("Lettre de Colbert à Talon, 20 février 1668," RAPQ, 1930–31, p. 94.)

I was surprised to find in the list of the inhabitants of Canada, which your Secretary handed me, only four thousand three hundred and twelve persons, including merely fifteen hundred and sixty-eight able to bear arms, and to find also only eleven thousand one hundred and seventy-four arpents of cultivated land; your Secretary informed me that there were many errors and omissions in that list because you had been unable to supervise its preparation yourself on account of your sicknesses, that he knew whole families who had not been counted and that the recruits of the last year, either men or girls and also the soldiers who have established themselves, have not been counted. And since the King wishes to be informed exactly of the number and the quality of his subjects in that country, His Majesty wishes that you prepare your other list before your departure, without any error.

Document F–4

THE ARMY AS AN INDUSTRY OF IMPORTANCE IN THE COLONY

(Canada Fiscal year 1743, A.P.C. "Canada, dépenses générales, 1741–1746" C11A, Vol. 115–1, p. 140ff., folio 60–61, 64.)

At the end of the seventeenth century, the French monarchy, which had to maintain troops in New France, became one of the most important customers of the Canadian merchants. And of all the monies which France earmarked for Canada, the army received always the highest percentage, as the following document indicates.

Mémoir on the Finances of Canada for the Year 1743

The funds provided to be drawn on the King's budget of 9 June 1743 add up to the amounts hereafter listed for the said fiscal year.

That is
Colony

	livres	s	d
For the construction and maintenance of boats and canoes	9,300		
For voyages to the interior of the colony	4,000		
For freight of foodstuff and other supplies from Quebec to various locations and for implements used for this service	6,600		
Labour costs and other works	7,300		
For purchase of merchandise, war supplies and food	12,800		
For presents to be given the Indians	22,000		
For wood for prison guards and prisons	4,000		
	66,000		
On the other side	66,000		
For subsistence, remedies, and medicines provided to the sick in the hospitals	4,200		

	livres	s	d
For the unforeseen expenses of the colony	3,000		
For the salaries of the General Officers and other salaried	52,838		
For the allowance of retired officers	7,300		
For the pay of the companies of soldiers numbering 28 men, the sum of 154812, the sum of 15876 l. already subtracted at 18 deniers per day from the pay of cadets and soldiers for their clothing	154,812		
For wages and maintenances of the employees of stores and offices in the colony	15,161		
For the rentals of stores and offices in the Colony	4,425		
For ordinary allowances	4,470		
For extraordinary allowances	5,433.	6.	8
For other divers expenses	22,195.17		

Fortifications

	livres	s	d
For expenses made for fortifications and repairs	82,457		
Total of the funds provided by the King's budget of 9 June 1743, for the expenses of the said year	422,292.	3.	8

Other funds provided by the King's budget of 26th April 1744 on the said fiscal year to pay for itemized expenses hereafter listed of the fiscal year 1743.

That is

	livres	s	d
a) Amount of the expenses made during the year 1743 for the maintenance of fortifications and of civil buildings	12,000		
Total of the funds drawn by the said King's budget for the expenses of the fiscal year 1743	12,000		

Other funds provided by the King's budget of 15 June 1745 on the said fiscal year to pay for the following articles of the fiscal year 1743.

	livres s d
For the complete payment of expenses incurred during the year 1743 for the maintenance of Fort St. Frederic	49,051.13. 5
Total of the funds provided by the said King's budget for the payment of the expenses of the fiscal year 1743	49,051.13. 5

The extraordinary revenues drawn on the fiscal year 1743 in accordance with the examination made of the accounts of the said year amount to 262,833. 5.10

Summary

Funds provided by the King's	livres s d
budget of 9 June 1743	422,292. 3. 8
On the other side	422,292. 3. 8
Funds provided by the King's budget of 26 April 1744	12,000
By that of 15 June 1745	49,051.13. 5
Amount of Extraordinary revenues	262,833. 5.10
Total of Revenues	746,177. 2.11

Done in Quebec, the 15th October 1748.

Bigot

Document F–5

THE SOLDIERS IN WINTER QUARTERS WITH THE HABITANT

("Ordonnance de M. de Denonville au sujet des soldats à Montréal (5 octobre 1685)," P. G. Roy, *Ordonnances*, Vol. II, pp. 126–28.)

The service of the King requiring that we leave five companies of infantry in the Island of Montreal for the winter, and since there is not a sufficient number of habitants for the soldiers not to become a burden, unless we prepare some regulations, the intention of the King not being that the said habitants be in any way trodden down by his troops, we have considered necessary to let it be known to the said troops that the intention of his Majesty is that the officers see to it that the troops maintain such discipline thanks to their salary which will be paid regularly for room and board, and do such that the hosts will not be any way burdened with their presence, since they will be providing only shelter, bedding, cooking utensils, and a fireplace, which fire will be kept by the habitant together with the soldier, who will have to go with the habitant to fell the wood and help him to transport it. And for the remainder of his needs we want them to live in such harmony with their hosts, that the habitant cannot have any matter of complaint. To that end, we order all the officers to visit their companies as often as they possibly can, to keep themselves informed of each soldier's behavior and attitude toward his host; and to understand that they will answer of everything unpleasant, unless they bring their own remedy by exemplary penalties to those who will not behave as we expect them to. And since there may be a need to mount guard, the intention of His Majesty is that the Captains and Commandants of Companies be required to lead their soldiers to the forest closest to the said watch post to cut the required quantity of wood to keep the fire of the said watch post. It is also required that each Captain ensure that there are ten axes per Company, to be used by the soldiers, the value of which will be withheld from their salary at the rate of two *liards* per day at most until paid. And since we are informed of several complaints that have been made that there has been failure to account for each soldier, we order that every two months a muster be conducted very accurately of all those from whom something has been withheld, without under any pretext whatever any Captain or Commandant be entitled to take for himself what is due to them of their daily salary. Further we order that all the soldiers work with their hosts, and we promise to ensure that they will not suffer from any withholding of salary.

Document F–6

THE HABITANT AND THE SOLDIER

(Mr le Baron de Lahontan, *Mémoires de l'Amérique septentrionale* . . . [Lahaye, 1703], Vol. II, pp. 77–78.)

The troops are normally quartered with the habitants of the *cotes* or seigneuries of Canada, from the month of October to that of May. The habitant who provides only the tools to his soldier employs him ordinarily for felling trees, uprooting stumps, clearing land, or wheat-threshing in the barn during that period, at a salary of ten *sols* daily plus food. The Captain also profits from this arrangement: to ensure that the soldiers give him half their pay, he forces them to report three times weekly for drill. Since the houses are four or five arpents one from the other and a *cote* is two or three leagues in front, the soldiers prefer reaching an agreement with him than having to travel such distances in snow and mire. So, *volenti non fit injuria*, is the Captain's reasoning. As to those soldiers who are good tradesmen, he is assured of their whole pay when he gives them permission to work in the cities or elsewhere.

Document F–7

THE TROOPS AS MANPOWER

("Ordonnance de M. de Meulles [28 avril 1685]," P. G. Roy, *Ordonnances*, Vol. II, pp. 96–97.)

The Governor General having been informed by us that the funds earmarked for the upkeep of the troops which His Majesty had sent two years to this country of New France are almost exhausted; and wishing to help the people of this Colony who have voluntarily taken up arms in the war which he had believed necessary to undertake last year against the Iroquois; which had forced the said habitants to make a trip which had cost them some money and much labor, most of whom having returned sick and several having died; has been pleased to give the soldiers of the said Companies the freedom to work and to live with the said habitants to earn thus their board and lodging, whilst waiting that His Majesty send us the werewithals to pay their salary as usual. This obliges us to inform all the habitants of this Colony that they may hire such soldiers as they wish to work with them according to what they consider reasonable, prohibiting them to pay each of the soldiers more than 10 or 12 *livres* per month; under penalty of a fine of 10 *livres* to be paid to the hospital of this town; for their services they shall also have to feed them on holidays and Sundays as well as other days, prohibiting the soldiers under the same penalties of asking more per month from the habitants; of using the clothes provided by the King and ordering the habitants not to tolerate such, under penalty as above. Guaranteeing to the said soldiers that they shall be paid by the treasurer as soon as the money shall have been received which his Majesty is sending for their salary.

Document F—8

THE TROOPS PROVIDE TRADESMEN

("Ordonnance de M. de Meulles [15 mai 1685]," P. C. Roy, *Ordonnances*, Vol. II, pp. 104–5.)

Because of our last ordinance rendered on 28 April last, giving permission to the habitants of this Colony to use soldiers of the troops and to hire them for work which they will consider reasonable with the defense of paying salaries of more than ten or twelve *livres* monthly; the said ordinance having been read, published and posted at the door of the parish church of this town at the end of the High Mass on the twelfth of this month and year.

Having learned since particularly that several of the said soldiers were tradesmen who wished to be hired by the day, several persons having even mentioned that since they would require these soldiers only for a few weeks, they would rather pay them by the day according to our intentions and regulations on the matter; and tending always to favor the population and to find means to maintain and feed the troops; we hereby permit all the said soldiers who are tradesmen and wish to work at their trade to work by the day for the habitants of this country prohibiting them from asking more than fifteen *sols* per day plus their food, and the habitants from paying more under penalty of a fine of ten *livres* to be paid to the poor of the hospitals of this colony, without, however, departing from our said ordinance of April 28 last, which shall remain in effect for all the soldiers who have no trade or who work by the month.

Document F—9

THE TROOPS AS SETTLERS

("Ordonnance du 21 may 1698," *BRH*, Vol. XI [1934] p. 63.)

His Majesty having been informed that among the soldiers composing the companies which He maintains in Canada, there are several who would be pleased to become habitants and who have all the qualities required to contribute to the well-being and strength of the colony, He has ordered and orders, wishes and expects that those who find it possible to establish themselves through marriage to women or widows born or settled in the said colony be discharged from the said companies at their first request, and that they keep the clothing which they have without the officers using any pretext to withhold it. And, in order to give them the means to settle and to survive while awaiting that the lands they will be given be cleared and produce wheat and the other necessities for their subsistence, His Majesty has granted them one year's salary which will be paid to them on the orders of Sr de Champigny, Intendant of the said Country.

G. Were Canadians Military Minded?

Like other men of the Old Regime, Canadians liked to own a firearm, particularly since most of the time they had to guarantee personally their own and their family's security. Travelers who visited Canada reported that possessing a firearm made Canadians feel more independent. Did this make them military minded?

Document G–1

HABITANTS AND WEAPONS

("Ordonnance de M. de Frontenac [8 janvier 1676]," P. G. Roy, Ordonnances, Vol. I, p. 179.)

Because of what has been reported to us that several persons who are not qualified either by rank or by profession to carry a sword dare carry one by day as well as by night, with other firearms, in contravention of the ordinary custom which must be the same here as in the cities of France; in order to prevent the excesses and the evil consequences which may result, we hereby strictly prohibit and forbid all bourgeois and habitants of this town who are not qualified either by rank or by profession, in particular merchants, craftsmen, sea-going people(?), hired men, servants and valets, to carry a sword or firearms by day as well as by night in this town and suburb under penalty of a fine of fifty *livres* or of imprisonment in the case of relapse.

Document G–2

HABITANTS AND MILITIA SERVICE: THE 17TH CENTURY

("Lettre de Frontenac au Ministre [2 novembre 1672]," RAPQ, 1926–27, p. 16.)

I will give my utmost care to have the habitants drilled, to regulate and to assign them into companies in those areas where this has not yet been done; although there are some of them who have not forgotten soldiering simply because they have become settlers, you know better than I do the difference which exists between disciplined troops and people who can hardly leave wife and children, who think more of their household than of orders given and who, being almost all of them without weapons because they have traded them or because they are poor or careless, are not really fit for any expedition; further, only by cutting into the periods of sowing or harvesting, could we use them for any undertaking, and this would create another problem for the colony at the very time when we are attempting to do it some good.

Document G–3

THE HABITANTS AND MILITIA SERVICE: THE 18TH CENTURY

("La mission de M. de Bougainville en France en 1758–1759: Milices du Canada," RAPQ, 1923–24, p. 29.)

The Canadian militia is very fit for party warfare, for the navigation of streams and lakes, for either summer or winter marches. But, since 1756, when war began to be conducted in America as it is in Europe, little use has been made of the militia for the following reasons:

1o Until that time, militiamen, who were enlisted for short forays only or for long trips, activities which required continuous movement, were unaware of what it was like to remain for six months together as an army corps and often in observation camps, and consequently in permanent positions.

It ensues that, in our armies, they become disgusted; they wish to return home, to sow and to harvest; soon they declare themselves sick. Either they must be sent home or they become deserters.

2o When they go into the field, the King gives them a full equipment, that is, shirts, overcoat, tight coat, gloves, etc.

They leave this equipment at home, convinced as they are that their absence will be a short one, and during the warm season at that. Furthermore, they take with them their worst rifle, hoping that, once they are with the army, the King will have to have it repaired or will have to give them another one.

There ensue great expenses for the King, a double expenditure of weapons, which are so precious; further, those Canadians who have with them only one shirt and one coat fall sick during the cold weather or even during the cool summer nights.

They are thus more of a liability than they are of use.

3o They are without tents and have no other shelter but huts made of tree bark, a very good type of shelter for forays or war parties lasting at most a month, but quite insufficient for six-month campaigns; this is a second cause of sickness.

4o Since no one is there to ensure that they use a cooking pot, when the conduct of warfare makes it possible, they feed on nearly-raw pork; this may have been possible with the old type of warfare in this country, but today it has become a third reason for the sickness and the uselessness of those militiamen.

5o Finally, it is not quite established that they respect their militia officers. The Indian example, the vastness of the lands, all conspires and inspires independence. There is among the militia men no order and no submission.

PROBLEM 3

The Great Lakes-
Mississippi-Ohio Triangle

CLAUDE THIBAULT
Bishop's University

Historians of the colonial period in North America have traditionally defined the territory of the Northwest as beginning west of the Island of Montreal and extending as far west as man reached. In New France, *Pays d'en Haut* designated that expanse of land and water, translating roughly as "Upper Country." It is too easily forgotten that under the French regime the territory from Montreal to the shores of Lake Huron—400 miles along the Ottawa route and a similar distance along the St. Lawrence–Lake Ontario waterway—was almost completely uninhabited. The location of the Iroquois Confederation of tribes to the south of Lake Ontario and their incursions ranging to the north of the Ottawa River gave little hope of white men ever successfully occupying a rich but dangerous land. Indians themselves, indeed, shunned the area and, as the Iroquois power and preponderance expanded westward, the western tribes took to detouring through other northern waterways to bring their furs down to Three Rivers via the St. Maurice and to Tadoussac via the Saguenay.

For the French in North America, the western region early became the mainstay of the fur trade. Because of its narrow economic structure based almost exclusively on furs and on begrudged grants from the French royal government, the continued control of that area and of the Indian tribes inhabiting the beaver territory became essential to the maintenance and survival of New France. The exhaustion of territories to the east of the St. Lawrence settlements and the depletion of the lands occupied by the Iroquois and Huron tribes posed a problem of fur supply. Coupled with the challenge of meeting new tribes that had never had any contact with white men, the dangling prospect of great profits in spite of the dangers and sufferings led to the penetration ever further westward by hardy explorers. Once contact was established, a continuous presence was required to maintain the Indians in allegiance and to prevent furs from being detoured to other colonizing groups or to trading agents to the north (Hudson's Bay Company), to the southeast (Carolina and Virginia traders) or to the east (Dutch Orange or English Albany). For these reasons, the triangle limited to the north by the Great Lakes, to the west by the Mississippi, and to the southeast by the Ohio River acquired great commercial and strategic importance.

This territory became the subject of many conflicting claims. At various times, the Iroquois declared that they were the possessors of much of it by right of conquest over other Indians. The English colonies, particularly those of Pennsylvania and New York, sought to assert their protectorate over the Ohio Valley and the lands to the south of the Great Lakes (Erie and Michigan) by claims of royal grants and of a suzerainty over the Iroquois acknowledged by the Confederation itself. The French colony of Louisiana attempted to make a large part of the area—the Illinois country—a food-producing territory for its own purposes. New France, founding its right to exclusive possession on prior discovery and occupancy, sought to resist all claims which could have deprived it of the mainstay of its economy and could have threatened its very existence.

In order to ensure its possession of the region, New France developed a number of routes to reach into the territory. Early contacts were made through the Ottawa River to Georgian Bay, then across Lake Huron to Michillimackinac, down the western shore of Lake Michigan to Green Bay, with portages to the Wisconsin River and canoe trips to the Mississippi. From Michillimackinac another route followed Lake Michigan to its southern end and, via the Chicagou [sic] portage, to the Illinois River and the Mississippi. A third channel of penetration followed the St. Lawrence, Lakes Ontario and Erie, the Miami River, and the Wabash to the Ohio and westward. At the end of the French regime, this route was diverted eastward through Rivière-aux-Boeufs and the Alleghany River to the Ohio.

The Great Lakes region has been variously described, usually in glowing terms which emphasized its economic and strategic value. These characteristics became apparent early and were acknowledged as prime components of the struggle between French and English colonists by the end of the 17th century. The possession of the area not only guaranteed economic wealth and territorial security but also controlled the allegiance and support of many powerful Indian tribes. From 1700 to 1760, the greatest task facing both France and England in North America was to acquire and ensure imperial rights to this territory. To the French, possession meant more-or-less continuous linear establishment from the Atlantic to the Gulf of Mexico, thus erecting a further physical barrier to English penetration from the Atlantic seaboard, already impeded as it was by the natural frontier of the Appalachians. To the English, the capture of the region—or at least its denial to the French—would bring increased economic value of their existing colonies, the breaking of the French noose, and the very real and desired possibility of westward expansion. The lines of conflict were thus clearly drawn between the two colonizing powers.

How much thoughtful consideration had ever been given by one or the other of the competitors to the long-term consequences of their ambitions cannot be readily ascertained. To the French, the beaver pelt was the attraction. Some claim that it was a mirage leading France to get mired in the quicksand of the west and to lose eventually all continental possession; too many settlers were required to people the area, and France was not prepared to encourage emigration. The movement of the English frontier westward to the Appalachian barrier was more elaborate and careful. There were early movements beyond the mountains; but their major objectives being the establishment of trade relations with Indians, they only succeeded in convincing the French of the true existence of a threat and of the necessity of guaranteeing the triangle to themselves. As

British pressures increased, so the French measures of security became ever more alarmingly apparent: the erection of fortified posts, the concentration of military forces, and the tightening of relations with the Indians. In the end the pressures exerted by both French and English against one another led to a war—there could be no other outcome—known in Europe as the Seven Years' War and in North America as the French-Indian War. The immediate prize was the triangle, but the ultimate result was the complete elimination of France as a continental power in North America.

In part the problem of possession had its origin in the differing concepts of acquisition of colonial territory. The English colonies relied on their original charters granted by the Crown of England. Any advance within the regions thus delimited (if the unknown limits of the grants of James I and Charles I can be called limiting) was considered as mere occupation of territory already legally owned. For the French, on the contrary, because of the lack of precise information about limits in their charters, possession in New France or in Louisiana came through formal acts in the presence, at times merely symbolic, of the Indian tribes occupying the territory being claimed. Any change in the territorial distribution of tribes or in the actual occupation of territory did not alter the French claims to possession.

While charges of imperialism were exchanged between French and English in North America and in the diplomatic negotiations conducted in Europe, the student would do well to consider what the characteristics of aggressive imperialism were and if the expansion of colonial claims could have been stopped by law, by treaty, or by reason. Was there an irreversible progression westward overcoming all obstacles, natural or man-made? Did New France make a calculated decision or a spontaneous move which led to decisions merely confirming an existing situation? Were the English colonies' claims logical and was the Indian trade so vital? Could the two powers have existed side by side without a struggle? Once engaged in expansionist policies, was it possible for either to retreat?

All French documents used in the preparation of this problem have been translated anew by the editor. The existing translations, while containing the gist of the documents, were rather adaptations. An effort has been made to stay as close to the original text as possible.

Material concerning the territory and the period has been printed in Pierre Margry (ed.), *Découvertes et établissements des Français dans l'Ouest et dans le Sud de l'Amérique Septentrionale* (6 vols., 1879–88); E. B. O'Callaghan (ed.), *Documents Relating to the Colonial History of the State of New York* (10 vols., 1855–58), particularly Vol. IX; and R. G. Thwaites (ed.), *The Jesuit Relations and Allied Documents* (73 vols., 1896–1901). Many State Historical Societies, particularly those of Illinois, Michigan, Minnesota, Pennsylvania, and Wisconsin, have published most useful *Proceedings* or *Collections*.

The historical background for New France is provided in G. Lanctôt, *A History of Canada* (3 vols., 1963–66); and P. G. Cornell, J. Hamelin, F. Ouellet, and M. Trudel, *Canada: Unity in Diversity* (1967). See also the various works by Francis Parkman and W. J. Eccles, *Canada under Louis XIV, 1663–1701* (1964). Explorations can best be reviewed in J. B. Brebner, *The Explorers of North America, 1492–1806* (1964). Indian conflicts are detailed in G. T. Hunt, *The Wars of the Iroquois. A Study in Intertribal Trade Relations* (1940 and 1960). A most recent viewpoint on the French in North America has been expressed by L. H. Gipson, *The British Empire Before the American Revolution* (13 vols., 1958–67), particularly Vols. IV and V.

The history of the Great Lakes–Mississippi–Ohio region has been written by C. W. Alvord, *The Illinois Country, 1673–1818* (1920), and L. P. Kellogg, *The French Regime in Wisconsin and the Northwest* (1925). Trading activities can best be studied in H. A. Innis, *The Fur Trade in Canada: An Introduction to Economic History* (1956); and in P. C. Phillips and J. W. Smurr, *The Fur Trade* (2 vols., 1961). Among the biographies, a most valuable work is G. L. Nute, *Caesars of the Wilderness: Médard Chouart, Sieur des Groseilliers, and Pierre Esprit Radisson, 1618–1710* (1943). Consult also W. J. Eccles, *Frontenac: The Courtier Governor* (1959).

Particular aspects of French policy have been detailed by Y. F. Zoltvany, "The Problems of Western Policy under Philippe de Rigaud de Vaudreuil, 1703–1725," *Canadian Historical Association Report*, 1964, pp. 9–24; and "The Frontier Policy of Philippe de Rigaud de Vaudreuil, 1713–1725," *Canadian Historical Review*, Vol. XLVIII, No. 3 (September, 1967), pp. 227–50.

CARTOGRAPHY

Carte de l'Amérique du Nord pour servir à l'histoire de la guerre de 1755 à 1760 par Mr le Cte de Malartic.

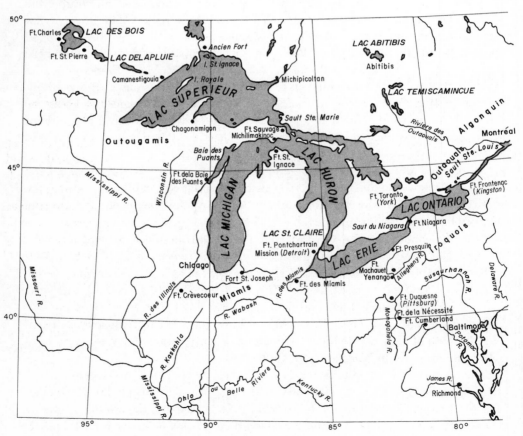

A. The Dream and the Reality of the West

For the French the idea of the West early became more than a dream. From the scanty and erroneous indications which Jacques Cartier received gratefully from the Indians of Hochelaga in 1535 to Champlain's earnest pleas for men and means to carry out explorations throughout the newly discovered continent—but most particularly westward—less than a century had passed. In threescore years, owing to the official voyages of missionaries, traders, and other accredited persons (such as Jean Nicolet, Louis Jolliet, Jean Péré), as well as the surreptitious undertakings of Radisson and des Groseilliers and many other nameless *coureurs de bois*, the routes to and the territory of the Great Lakes became rapidly well known to French colonists. The necessity of reaching a decision as to the role which this vast territory could and would play in French colonial plans in North America was soon impressed upon the French officials in Paris and Versailles by numerous written requests and reports of deeds. By the time Father Jacques Marquette had accompanied Louis Jolliet to within 700 miles of the mouth of the Mississippi, the trend had been established. Was it irreversible?

Document A—1

CARTIER'S REPORT OF THE WEST

(*Brief Recit et Succincte narration de la navigation faite par le capitaine Jacques Cartier aux Iles de Canada, Hochelaga, Saguenay et autres* [Paris, 1863], pp. 27–27v.)

And further they showed us that along the said mountains to the north, there is a large river which comes from the west, like the said river [St. Lawrence]. We believe that it is the river which goes through the kingdom and province of Saguenay; and without us making any request or sign, they took the chain of the captain's whistle, which is silver, and the handle of a dagger, which was of yellow brass like gold, hanging on the hip of one of our fellow mariners, and showed that it came from up the said river, and that there were *agojuda*, that is bad people, who were armed to the finger tips, showing us the fashion of their armor, which is of thongs and wood, laced and tied together; giving us to understand that the said *agojuda* were continually at war amongst themselves; but because of a lack of words, we could not learn how far it was to the said country. The said captain [Cartier] showed them red copper, which they called *caignetdazé*, showing them the direction of the said place and asking by signs, if it came from there. And they began to shake their heads, saying no, and showing that it came from the Saguenay.

Document A—2

CHAMPLAIN'S HOPES

(C. H. Laverdière [ed.], Oeuvres de Champlain, Vol. IV [Québec, 1870], pp. 71–72.)

As to those parts which are further west, we cannot know fully their course, all the more since the peoples have no knowledge whatever, except of two or three hundred leagues, or more, toward the west, whence the said great river comes, and passes, among other places, through a lake, in length nearly thirty days of their canoes, that is, the lake which we have named the *Mer Douce*, because of its great area, being nearly four hundred leagues long; furthermore, the Savages with whom we are acquainted are at war with other nations west of the said great lake, which is the reason that we cannot have further knowledge, except that they have told us several times that a few prisoners of a hundred leagues' distance have related to them that there are people like us in whiteness, and other details, having through them seen the hair of these people, which is quite blond, and that they have much esteem for them, since they say they are like us. I do not know what to think of the matter, except that they might be people more civilized than they who say they look like us. It would be well to know the truth by sight, but assistance is required; there is only the time and the courage of a few persons of means, who can, or want, to undertake to help in these designs, in order that one day we can discover amply and perfectly these locations, in order to have a sure knowledge.

Document A—3

TALON'S PROJECTS AND SUCCESSES

(Rapport de l'Archiviste de la Province de Québec pour 1930–1931 [Québec, 1931], pp. 50, 136–37, 157–58.)

(i) *Talon to Colbert (November 3, 1666)*

Since Canada borders upon Florida and through it upon Mexico, upon Virginia, New Sweden, and New Netherlands, there is in its vicinity a good number of the powers of Europe, which the King can attack through this place, if His Majesty were to work at the establishment of a large colony and had the lakes and river sources occupied which communicate with the countries occupied by the Europeans; what I am suggesting entails many difficulties but, since they are not invincible, I do not hesitate in putting the plans forward. To great souls like the King's, there is a need solely for great undertakings, and to spirits like yours nothing is satisfying which is lowly. That is why, My Lord, I do not mention at all the small advantages which that great and vast expanse of country can give the State through its variety of products.

(ii) *Addition to the Report of Talon on Canada to Minister Colbert (November 10, 1670)*

This country is so designed that by the river one can go up everywhere thanks to the lakes which carry its source towards the west and to the rivers which flow into it on all sides, opening the way northward and southward; it is through this same river that we may hope some day to find the passage to Mexico and it is to the first of these discoveries that My Lord de Courcelles and myself have despatched Sr. de La Salle who has much enthusiasm for such undertakings, while, through another route, I have sent Sr.

de St. Lusson to push westward as far as his food will hold out, with orders carefully to seek if there is, through some lakes or rivers, a means of communication with the South Sea which separates this continent from China, but only after he shall have given first consideration to the discovery of copper mines, which is his prime mission, and after he shall have corroborated the reports handed him concerning the said mines.

Having failed to discover for what reasons or as a result of what intrigues I had not found upon my return the explanations which I had expected from Sr. Péré sent last year with an allowance of more than one hundred *pistolles* [sic]; this Péré has not returned, but he has stayed with the [Jesuit] Fathers at the Ottawa mission; he writes only obscurely, which gives reasons to believe that he has been delayed in recognizing the mine, and prevented from communicating his information in its entirety.

I wish to mention new discoveries, and I have to say that already Mssrs. Dolier and Galinée, Sulpicians, missionaries in Montreal, have explored Lake Ontario and met hitherto unknown nations. The map herewith enclosed as Appendix C will indicate their route and the point which they have reached; the report as Appendix D, which they have written somewhat hastily and without giving it its proper format, will indicate that they have taken possession of the entire area. I will correct this crude act and I will have planted, everywhere the King's subjects shall go, the arms of His Majesty with the emblems of his religion, foreseeing that if these precautions are not useful now they may become so in another season. We are told that the Iroquois usually tear down the arms and written notices from the trees to which they are attached in the areas of which we are taking possession, and carry them to the English; thus this nation is aware that we intend to remain the masters of those lands. It is up to His Majesty to decide whether this practice of display is to be continued or to be ceased, until he is thoroughly assured all the important posts of this country.

(iii) Memorandum of Talon to the King about Canada (November 2, 1671)

Sr. de La Salle has not yet returned from his voyage to the south of this country, but Sr. de St. Lusson has returned after having reached almost five hundred leagues from here, erected a cross and raised the arms of the King in the presence of seventeen nations of savages assembled from all sides for that purpose, all of which have voluntarily submitted to the domination of His Majesty whom they consider alone as their sovereign and protector; this has happened, according to the Jesuit Fathers who have witnessed the ceremony, with all the magnificence and dash which the country would allow. I will carry with me the acts of possession which have been written by Sieur de St. Lusson to guarantee this country to His Majesty.

It is believed that from the point reached by Sr. de St. Lusson there is no more than three hundred leagues to the end of the lands which touch on the Vermilion or South Sea; the lands which touch on the Western Sea do not appear to be at any greater distance from those lands discovered by the French, according to calculations made from information gathered from the Savages. And, according to the maps, it appears that there is a navigation of no more than fifteen hundred leagues to reach Tartary, China, and Japan; these types of discoveries must be the work of either time or the King. It can be said that the Spanish have gone no further into southern American lands than the French into northern American lands.

The voyage which Sr. de St. Lusson has made for the discovery of the South Sea as well as of the copper mine will cost the King nothing. I will not enter anything into my accounts, because, having made to the Savages a grant of the lands of which he had taken possession, he received from them a present of beaver which will reimburse his expenses.

Document A—4

POSSESSION IN LAW

(Pierre Margry [ed.], *Découvertes et établissements des Français dans l'Ouest et dans le Sud de l'Amérique Septentrionale*, Vol. I, [Paris, 1879], pp. 96–99.)

Proceedings of the taking possession of the countries situated towards Lakes Huron and Superior.

June 14, 1671

Simon François Daumont, Esquire, Sieur de Saint-Lusson, Commissioner sub-delegate of my Lord the Intendant of New France for the search of the copper mine in the country of the Ottawa, Nez-Perces, Illinois, and other Savage nations discovered or to be discovered in Northern America, in the area of Lake Superior or Mer Douce.

Having received orders from My Lord the Intendant of New France, on September 3 last, signed and paraphed: Talon, and thereunder: by My Lord, Varnier, with paraph, to go to the country of the Savages, Ottawa, Nez-Perces, Illinois, and other nations discovered or to be discovered in Northern America, in the area of Lake Superior or Mer Douce, to seek and discover all types of mines, particularly copper; further, to take possession in the name of the King of all the lands, inhabited or uninhabited, through which we would pass, erecting at the first village the cross, to bring about the fruits of Christianity, and the Escutcheon of France, to guarantee the authority of His Majesty and French domination; by virtue of our commission, having first landed at the village of Sainte Marie du Sault, where the reverend Jesuit Fathers have their mission and the savage nations called Achipoes, Malamechs, and Noquets, and others, their residence, we called in assembly the largest possible number of neighboring nations, fourteen in number, that is: Achipoes, Malamechs and Noquets inhabiting the said village of Sainte Marie du Sault, and the Banabeouiks and Mako-miteks, Poulteattemis, Oumalominis, Sassassaouacottons, inhabiting the Bay known as Green Bay, who took upon themselves to inform their neighboring tribes who are the Illinois, Mascouttins, Outtagamis and other nations; the Christinos, Assinipoals, Aumoussonnites, Ottawa, Bouscouttons, Niscaks and Masquikoukieks, all inhabiting northern lands near the sea, who took upon themselves to inform their neighbors, who are held to be in large numbers inhabiting next to the sea; to whom, in the presence of the Reverend Fathers of the Company of Jesus and of all the Frenchmen hereafter named, we had our commission read and interpreted into their tongues by Sieur Nicolas Perrot, His Majesty's interpreter in these parts, so that no one could claim ignorance; we then had a cross elevated to bring forth the fruits of Christianity, and near the latter a cedar post to which we raised the arms of France, saying three times in a loud voice and with public outcry that, in the name of the Most High, Most Mighty, and Most Redoubtable Monarch Louis the Fourteenth of the Name, Most Christian King of France and Navarre, we take possession of this place, Sainte Marie du Sault, as also of Lakes Huron and Superior, the Island of Caientoton, and all countries, rivers, lakes, and tributaries contiguous and adjacent thereto, discovered and to be discovered, which are bounded on the one side by the seas of the North and of the West, and on the other side by the South Sea, including all their length and breadth, raising on each of the said three occasions a sod of earth and crying: Long Live the King, and having it cried by the whole assembly, French and Savage alike; declaring to the nations thereof that from this time forth they are vassals of His Majesty, bound to obey his laws and follow his customs; promising them on his part all succor and protection against the incursions and invasions of their enemies: declaring to all other potentates, princes, sovereigns, states and republics alike, to them and to their subjects, that they cannot and are not to seize or settle upon any parts of the aforesaid countries, save only under the good pleasure of His Most Christian Majesty, and of him who will govern in his behalf; and this on pain of incurring his resentment and the efforts of his arms. And in order that no one plead ignorance, we have attached behind the escutcheon of France an extract of this proceeding of possession, signed by us and by the persons hereafter named, who were all present.

[Done at Sainte Marie, the 14th of June, in the year of grace 1671, in the presence of the Reverend Fathers: the Reverend Father Claude D'Ablon, superior of the missions of that country; the Reverend Father Gabriel Dreuillettes, the Reverend Father Claude Allouez, the Reverend Father André, all of the Company of Jesus, and of Sieur Nicolas Perrot, His Majesty's interpreter for these parts; Sieur Jolliet, Jacques Mogras, inhabitants of Three Rivers; Pierre Moreau, Sieur de la Taupine, a soldier of the garrison in the castle of Quebec; Denis Masse, François de Chavigny, Sieur de la Chevrotière; Jacques Lagillier; Jean Mayseré; Nicolas Dupuis; François Bibaud; Jacques Joviel; Pierre Porteret; Robert Duprat; Vital Driol; Guillaume Bonhomme and other witnesses.

Thus signed:

Daumont de Saint Lusson,
with paraph

Document A–5

TO THE MISSISSIPPI

("Lettre de Jolliet au Gouverneur de Frontenac, à son retour de la découverte du Mississippi," *Rapport de l'Archiviste de la Province de Québec pour 1924–1925* [Québec, 1925], pp. 230–31.)

It is with much joy that I present to you this map which will inform you of the location of the rivers and lakes which are used to go across Canada or Northern America, more than 1200 leagues from East to West.

This great river beyond Lakes Huron and Illinois, which bears your name, that is Buade River because it was discovered in these last years, 1673 and 1674, on the first orders which you gave me upon entering your government of New France, flows between Florida and Mexico, and, before emptying into the sea, cuts through the most beautiful country to be seen. I have seen nothing so beautiful in France as the vastness of grasslands which I have admired here, or so agreeable as the diversity of groves and forests where plums, pomegranates, lemons, mulberries, and several types of small fruits which do not exist in Europe can be picked. In the fields quails can be flushed, in the woods parrots can be seen; in the rivers fish can be caught which are unknown to us for either taste or size.

Iron mines and red-tinged stones, which are found only with red copper, are not scarce; neither are slate, saltpeter, coal, marble and mixtures of copper. The biggest pieces I have seen were as big as a fist, and very pure; it was discovered near the red-tinged stones which are of better quality than those of France and in greater quantities.

Through one of these large tributaries which flows from the west and empties into the Buade River, one will find a passage to enter the Vermilion Sea. I have seen a village which was only five days' journey from a nation which trades with those of California. If I had arrived two days earlier, I would have spoken with those who had come and had brought four axes as a present.

B. French Imperial Policy

In 1663 New France became a royal colony. This momentous change in the administrative concept of territory led to the elaboration of a royal colonial policy, founded on the principle that a compact or restricted area could be readily occupied and defended by the population available. Since it did not enter into the French plans to depopulate France in favor of Canada, Colbert's policy was to impose bans on adventurous explorations and extracolonial trade. However, the Canadian inhabitants already had their eyes turned to the west, the Indians were beckoning the white man to come and trade with them, and the appeal was well-nigh impossible to resist. When governor and intendant united their efforts, the conjunction of forces made difficult any plans for limiting the expansion of New France.

After several attempts at restricting the number of Frenchmen in the Great Lakes area, ranging from forbidding trade by *coureurs de bois* to ordering the abandonment of all western posts, the French ministers decided, early in the 18th century, to occupy the West with all the means at their disposal. Why did the French government become committed to holding the West?

Document B–1

COLBERT'S STATEMENT OF POLICY

(Lettre du Ministre Colbert au Gouverneur de Frontenac, 17 mai 1674, *Rapport de l'Archiviste de la Province de Québec, 1926–1927* [Québec, 1927] p. 58.)

His Majesty's intention is not that you undertake great voyages by ascending the river Saint Lawrence, nor even that in the future the inhabitants spread themselves as much as they have done in the past; on the contrary, he desires that you labor incessantly and during the whole time that you will spend in that country to draw them together, to collect and form them into towns and villages, to place them in a much more easy position of defending themselves well, so that even if the state of European affairs should be altered by a good and advantageous peace to His Majesty's glory and satisfaction, he deems it much more satisfactory to the good of his service that you apply yourself to the clearing and settling of the tracts most fertile, nearest the sea coasts and the communication with France, rather than pushing further discoveries inland into countries so distant that they cannot ever be settled or possessed by Frenchmen.

This general rule may have its exceptions in two cases: the first, if the countries of which you would take possession are necessary to the traffic and trade of the French and if they could be discovered and possessed by some other nation which could disturb the traffic and trade of the French; but since there is none of this type, His Majesty is always of the opinion that you may and ought to leave the Savages at liberty to bring you their peltries, without giving yourself the trouble of going so far to seek them.

The other case is that the countries which you would discover could bring you closer to France by communicating with some sea which would be more southerly than the mouth of the Saint Lawrence River, such as Acadia; the reason is that you know perfectly that what is the worst in Canada is the mouth of that river which, being very northerly, does not allow vessels to enter except for four, five, or six months of the year.

Document B–2

FRONTENAC'S ACCOMPLISHMENTS AND WISHES

("Lettre du Gouverneur de Frontenac au Roi, 2 novembre 1681," *Rapport de l'Archiviste de la Province de Québec, 1926–1927* [Québec, 1927], pp. 127–28.)

The Mohawks have done nothing contrary to the protestations of the ambassadors whom they sent last fall, but the Onondagas and the Senecas have not appeared by their conduct to be in the same spirit and the same dispositions. The guile of certain people, to which the English perhaps have also added theirs, has led them to continue their war against the Illinois, in spite of all that I had said to them; they have burned a village and taken six or seven hundred prisoners, but almost all children or old women. What is most annoying is that they wounded Sieur de Tonty who attempted at first to arrange some compromise with them, and whom Sieur de La Salle had left in this village with a few Frenchmen to man the post which he had built.

. . . In the last ten years I have maintained all those Savages in a spirit of obedience, rest and peace only through skill and tact; it is difficult, when one is without anything, to do more and to prevent things which would be so easy to remedy if there was some help available. Now that the Savages are arming themselves again, what can I tell them to retain them to their duty? All those trips which they see me undertake almost every year to Fort Frontenac no longer astonish them as they used to in the beginning.

. . . Five or six hundred regular troops . . . would . . . offer the means of occupying posts on Lakes Frontenac and Erie and, with boats there, of preventing the Iroquois from openly carrying their beaver to New Netherlands; and the increase which would accrue to the farm of your Majesty would go beyond the expenses which the troops would incur, besides the assurance which they would give the nations which are under Your Majesty's protection, and the other advantages which could be drawn for communication by land routes and land clearing.

Document B–3

CLOSING THE WESTERN POSTS

(*Rapport de l'Archiviste de la Province de Québec, 1928–1929* [Québec, 1929], pp. 302–5, 311–12, 331.)

(*i*) *Mémoire du Roi pour le Gouverneur de Frontenac et l'Intendant Bochart de Champigny, 26 mai 1696*

His Majesty, having considered what the Sieurs de Frontenac and de Champigny have written about the bad dispositions of the allied Savages and of the difficulties of an unbearable expense for maintaining communications with them for war purposes, has had his Council examine anew their letters and reports, hear the persons who might have some knowledge of the state of affairs in the colony, and has resolved to have abandoned Missimakinac and all the other posts occupied in the interior of the country except for Fort Saint Louis of the Illinois, . . . wishing to reunite all the French scattered outside the colony that they may be employed to make war on the enemy, to defend the colony or for whatever other tasks will be suitable to them and to the country, that the ranging and the trade in the interior of the country be abolished forever, and that the Savages may bring their peltries to Montreal as they used to do, and the inhabitants and merchants share in the trade and sale of their goods and wares, which the *coureurs de bois* had usurped, excluding thereby the whole of the colony. This is why His Majesty wishes that the said Sieurs de Frontenac and de Champigny take the necessary measures and that the said Sieurs de Frontenac and de Champigny give orders to have all the French return with their goods in obedience of what is his intention, without any French, under any pretext, being permitted to carry goods into the interior of the country for trade, but only what will be necessary for the sustenance of those who will be sent to bring back the goods acquired in the exchange of merchandise transported before the publication of the declaration which He is sending to revoke all types of congés and permissions, in order that there be neither contravention to the said declaration nor abuses in the means of execution.

(ii) Lettre du Gouverneur de Frontenac au Ministre, 25 octobre 1696

I will not fail to put into execution the last orders which you have sent me to recall all the French who are in the woods and to send no permission or congé in the future.

. . . I would fail, nevertheless, in what I owe the King's service, if I did not make representations on the murmurings which the publication of the King's declaration has caused and the untoward and inevitable consequences which it will bring onto the colony.

Firstly, because if all the French are withdrawn generally and that there remain no commandants in the posts, and particularly at Missilimakina [sic], the Huron, Ottawa, and other Savages' nations who have for a long time wished to trade with the English, not knowing to what they must attribute this change after the great advantages which we have just gained, will believe themselves abandoned, and, seeing themselves in such entire liberty to reach their goal, will make peace with the Iroquois through whom they will soon trade.

. . . Secondly, if the Ottawa and the Hurons conclude a peace with the Iroquois without our participation and if they allow the English to enter their territory to trade, the colony will be completely ruined, since it is the only way this colony can survive; and it cannot be assured that, once the Savages have tasted once of the trade with the English, they will not break forever from the French, because these can give their goods only at a much higher price.

It is also quite easy to establish that, if this peace is ever worked out and concluded and the English trade established at Missilimakina [sic] and among the other nations who are our allies, they will strike so close a friendship based on their common interests that it will be impossible for the French, having once abandoned it, to renew it; and it will inevitably happen that, when we wish to attract them again, we shall have as enemies not only the Iroquois but also the Flemings and the English who will be there trading, and the Huron, Ottawa and the other nations of the Upper Country.

(iii) Mémoire du Roi pour le Gouverneur de Frontenac et l'Intendant Bochart de Champigny, 27 avril 1697

What they have replied to the reasons which have forced His Majesty to issue the declaration which they have received, forbidding congés and permissions to carry goods to the Ottawa and elsewhere in the interior of the country and having all the French return with their goods, containing nothing which he had not exhaustively considered, He desires that they have the declaration executed in accordance with its form and content and without exception, if upon receipt of this despatch, they had not already done so; He wishes to consider, nevertheless, the reasons which they have brought forth, regarding the posts of Missilimakinat and St. Joseph des Miamis, and he finds desirable that, if the said Sieur de Frontenac had not had them already abandoned and had not withdrawn the detachments of soldiers who were there, he leave them there until further orders; but since it must be for the sole purpose of containing the Savages and preventing their taking decisions to the prejudice of the well-being of the colony, He does not intend that under any pretext whatever the officers and soldiers who will remain there engage in trade in any way, either directly or indirectly, His intention being that they be punished severely if they contravene this order.

. . . The same reasons impel His Majesty to have Fort Frontenac continue to exist; but His Majesty is well pleased to explain that he expects the same conduct to be adhered to, that is, that there be no trade, directly or indirectly, under threat of the same penalties.

. . . He repeats once again that he has agreed to have the establishment of the Sieurs de Laforest and Tonty continue to exist only on the condition that there be no trade in beaver, and that none be sent anywhere in the colony or elsewhere.

Document B–4

VALUE OF THE WESTERN POSTS

(M. d'Aigremont ou Ministre sur l'état des différents forts et postes du Canada, 14 novembre 1708, Archives des Colonies, C 11A, 29: 25–102.)

Pursuant to the orders with which you honored me on June 30 and July 13, 1707, I left Montreal on June 5 last to go to the advanced posts of Canada, and returned on September 12 following.

. . . .

For Frontenac. It is advantageous to keep this post for, because of it, the Iroquois cannot make a move without us being warned and, since we are near them, it will always be easy to upset their projects as soon as we will become aware of them; it is a constant maxim among the Savages to abandon their undertakings as soon as they are disclosed.

Further, it is possible through these Savages to know what is happening among the English, and thus to oppose with more facility the undertakings which they might be preparing against us; it is a fact that they seek all opportunities to cause misunderstandings between the said Savages and us.

. . . .

[Niagara]. The advantages which we could draw from it, by having it fortified and by having a garrison established there, would be that there would settle there several Iroquois who would leave the villages, through whom we would always know what happens in the said villages and among the English; by this means, it would be easy to prevent any undertaking which might be prepared against us.

The Detroit is a very onerous post for the Colony of Canada, which may be lost entirely, if we continue to underwrite the post. People will say that perhaps it is true, but that, if we abandon it, the English will grab it. I do not know, but I am sure that it is more advantageous to them that we hold it than they, because it does not cost them anything while they do all the trading there. Were it true, even, that the English want to seize that post if we were to abandon it, I do not believe that the Iroquois would suffer the English there because, once the masters, they would do all the trading independently of them; this would not be very satisfactory, assuredly. They want the English to do the trading, but they want to share the advantages with them.

. . . .

Missimakinac is the most advantageous post in Canada and to show its advantages over the Detroit, I will say that, even if all the Savages of Canada were established near the latter, we could not gain the tenth part of the beaver that we can gain in Missimakinac: it would all go to the English through the Iroquois and Hurons, and even several other Savages who have learned of that route.

Document B–5

INDIAN ALLIANCES

("Mémoire du Roi à MM. de Vaudreuil et Bégon, 15 juin 1716," *Rapport de l'Archiviste de la Province de Québec, 1947–1948* [Québec, s.d.], pp. 298–300.)

His Majesty has every reason to believe that the reestablishment of the congés and of the posts among the (Western) Nations will win them over entirely to France; He recommends that the Sieur Marquis de Vaudreuil devote his full attention to this and act to disrupt the arrangements which the English may have concluded with those Savages. It is the only way of keeping the peace on the continent and to preserve the trade of the Colony in the interior of the country.

. . . .

It has been suggested from Canada to erect a small establishment to the north of Niagara on Lake Ontario about 100 leagues from Fort Frontenac. . . . His Majesty has refrained from deciding anything on this subject and is convinced that it is not convenient to establish this post without a request from the Iroquois. . . .

The said Sieur de Vaudreuil knows how necessary it is to spare those Indians. His Majesty will therefore prescribe nothing on this subject. He will recommend only that everything be done to keep them in our alliance and to prevent their undertaking of a war against the Nations our allies.

Document B–6

DIVISIONS OF THE TERRITORY

("Lettre de M. de la Galissonnière, 1 septembre 1748," *Archives des Colonies*, C 11A 91: 101–9.)

New France was not the only French colony with interests in the Triangle; Louisiana had acquired some early. The latter were concentrated in the area of the mouth of the Ohio River, and the problem of responsibility for the territory —the Illinois Country—arose in relation to defense, particularly. The settlements were a long distance away from the main area of Louisiana; but they were exposed to incursions from the English colonies, if ever a decision was taken to attack toward the Ohio. The weakness of these establishments, made obvious during the conflict of 1745–48, prompted the governor of New France, at the request of the minister, to offer suggestions on the fate of the Illinois.

Our establishments in the Illinois . . . have in common with all that relates to the Mississippi that, after having been valued more than their just worth, they are hardly considered today as useful at all. I believe that we must avoid either extreme.

. . . I believe that it is extremely necessary that Louisiana be settled so as to draw from parts nearer than the Illinois flour and other necessities. . . . But I am far from concluding that this small colony must be abandoned; I think, on the contrary, that the King must sacrifice something to sustain it.

. . . We must not delude ourselves that our colonies on the continent, that is this one (Canada) and Louisiana, will ever be as wealthy as the neighboring English colonies, or that they will ever have a very lucrative trade. . . . Of all the countries which we occupy it (the Illinois) is the one where they (the English) can come most easily with few forces and, if they were to succeed once in wedging themselves between our two colonies, the loss of the Mississippi and the ruin of the interior trade of Canada would follow; even the Spanish colonies, and Mexico, would be in very great danger.

. . . It follows that, if the Illinois were reunited to Canada, we would save little on troop expenses; it seems to me that we must increase rather than decrease their number. They are, indeed, absolutely necessary to contain the Savages, and sometimes the settlers, and to increase in time the number of the latter.

. . . It is quite indifferent, having regard to the role that the Illinois settlement may play in the defense or even the provisioning of Louisiana, that it be an officer from Canada or one from Louisiana that would be put in command there. . . . To increase wealth in this post and to promote its settlement, I see no objection that the Governor of Mississippi, as well as the Governor of Canada, grant congés to come there and trade.

C. English Penetration

The English colonies, particularly Virginia and New York, developed important interests in the west. The territory of Virginia extended to the "South Sea," and, after 1650, commercial concerns began to search for a route through the Appalachian range. By 1674 Virginians were aware of the existence of the Ohio and of its connection to the Mississippi.

Farther north, New York merchants, mainly Dutch and English traders of Albany, wanted to wrest the control of the Great Lakes fur trade from the French. They had an excellent instrument in the Iroquois Confederation, which was strategically located, powerful, and at the height of its preponderance in the western lands. The Five Nations would also be an obstacle, since they would not allow direct contact between the western Indians and the Albany traders; their intention was to keep to themselves the all-important middleman role. In the course of the last quarter of the 17th century and the first half of the 18th century, the English exerted themselves to break through the Iroquois and then to wrest from the French the allegiance of the western tribes and, in the process, their furs.

About 1730 another group, the Pennsylvania traders, appeared on the scene along the Ohio. Men like Conrad Weiser and George Croghan soon penetrated to the north of the river, and unlike the Albany merchants, they established regular trading posts. Why was trade so important to the Indians that they would forsake the French alliance for British goods?

Traders, however, were always followed in the English pattern of colonization by settlers. The penetration of the former led to plans for the creation of settlements and for the distribution of Indian lands to white men. The possibility of English settlement in that area made the French very uneasy.

Document C—1

ENGLISH TRADERS IN THE WEST

(Cadwallader Colden, *The History of the Five Indian Nations Depending on the Province of New York in America* [1866], pp. 57—59.)

The Five Nations have few or no Bevers in their own Country, and are for that reason obliged to hunt at a great distance, which often occasion'd Disputes with their Neighbours about the Property of the Bever, in some parts of the Country. The Bevers are the most valuable part of the Indian Trade. And as the Twihtwies carried their Bever to the French, the English favour'd the Five Nations in these Expeditions, and particularly in the beginning of the year 1687, made the Five Nations a Present of a Barrel of Powder, when their whole Force was preparing to go against the Twihtwies. The English were the better pleas'd with this War, because they thought it would divert their Thoughts from the Indians that were friends to Virginia:

In the mean while, a Cannoe arriv'd, which was sent by Mr. De Nonville with his Orders to the Officers. This Cannoe in her Passage discover'd some English commanded by Major McGregory, in their way to Teiodendaraghie. The English thought (after they had an account of the new Alliance their King had enter'd into with the French) that the French would not disturb them in prosecuting a Trade with the Indians every where, and that the Trade would be equally free and open to both Nations. With these hopes a considerable Number of Adventurers, went out under the Conduct of Major M'Gregory to Trade with the Indians living on the Banks of the Lakes; and that they might be the more wellcome, perswaded the Five Nations to set all the Dionondadie Prisoners at Liberty, who went along with the English and conducted them towards Missilimakinak or Teiodondoraghie. But the English found themselves mistaken, for the French Commandant at Teiodondoraghie, as soon as he had Notice of this, sent 300 French to intercept the English.

Document C—2

ENGLISH INTENTIONS IN THE 1700'S

("Lettre du marquis de Vaudreuil au ministre, 1er octobre 1701," Pierre Margry [ed.], *Découvertes et établissements des Français dans l'Ouest et dans le Sud de l'Amérique Septentrionale*, Vol. V [Paris, 1879—88], pp. 353—55.)

The general peace which M. de Callières has made with the Iroquois nations, except the Mohawks, does not fail to render the English jealous, and I have learned from a Savage of our parts, who was with the Mohawks last year and who went to Orange to a general council, which the Governor General of those parts held, that he had been deeply angered by that general peace which they have reached with us. "What!" he told them, "Don't you see that the French are lying to you? They seize your land [speaking of the Detroit]. Stay here, it is your country. I forbid you to go to Canada, unless to bring back your relatives. If you love praying, I will give you ministers." And, to offset the words of M. de Callières, who wants to be their mediator if there happens to be some quarrel: "Go ahead; if someone attacks you, defend yourselves and I will protect you from your enemies." He supported his words with considerable gifts and insisted much on the union which he wants to conclude with them.

I have also had notice, My Lord, that the news which I had received last year and which I had the pleasure of mentioning to you, that they wanted to establish themselves on Lake Ontario, was true. You made no error: the Iroquois did oppose it; there is no doubt that, if we have a war against the English, they will do all in their power to draw the Iroquois to their side.

Document C–3

THE ESTABLISHMENT OF OSWEGO

(Bégon au Ministre, Québec, 10 juin 1725," C IIA 47: 151–61.)

Since it is apparent to M. de Vaudreuil, to M. de Longueuil, and to me that it was important to take all necessary measures practicable to oppose this establishment, and that the English might drive us away from Niagara and establish themselves there, we have determined to have two barks constructed at Fort Frontenac to be used in case of need against the English to chase them from the establishment, and also to be used for the transport of materials to build a stone fort at Niagara, which we believe necessary to put that post in a good condition of defense against the English, and even to maintain it against the Iroquois, in case of need, so that the latter cannot dictate to us when they want to, by uniting with the English, since we possess only this means of preventing the English from getting themselves in spite of us into the upper country, and of safeguarding it for this colony.

("Mémoire sur les colonies de la France, dans l'Amérique septentrionale. Par M. le Marquis de la Galissonière, 1751," France, Affaires Etrangères, Mémoires et Documents, Amérique, Vol. XXIV, pp. 110–36v.)

(It) must be observed that this post [Oswego], which has always been regarded as an object of small importance, is capable of causing the complete ruin of Canada and has already dealt the colony some rude blows. It is there that the French often carry on an illicit trade which transfers to England clear profits that Canada should afford to France. It is there that the English lavish brandy on the Indians, the use of which had been forbidden them by the ordinances of our kings, because it makes them madmen. Finally it is thither that the English draw all the Indian tribes, and try by means of presents, not only to win them over, but even to induce them to assassinate the French traders scattered throughout the vast extent of the forests of New France.

So long as the English retain Oswego, we can only be in perpetual distrust of those Indians who till now have been the most faithful to the French; in the most profound peace we shall have to maintain twice the troops the state of the colony requires or permits, to build and guard forts in numberless places, and to send nearly every year numerous and expensive detachments to control the various Indian tribes.

The navigation of the lakes will always be in danger of being disturbed; the cultivation of the soil will progress only by halves and can be carried on only in the center of the colony. Finally we shall always be in a situation that has all the inconveniences and none of the advantages of a state of war. Nothing therefore must be omitted for the destruction of this dangerous post, on the first occasion for reprisals that the English afford us from the hostilities they are only too used to committing in time of peace; always supposing that it is not possible to get them to give it up of good will for some equivalent.

Document C–4

TRADE IN THE OHIO VALLEY

("Copy of Mr. George Croghan's Account of Indian Affairs from 1748–49 to General Braddock's Defeat," *Pennsylvania MSS., Indian Affairs, Vol. I, 1687–1753, Historical Society of Pennsylvania.*)

"During the late war, all the Indian Tribes living on the Ohio and the Branches thereof on this Side of lake Erie were in strict friendship with ye English in the several Provinces, or took the greatest care to preserve the Friendship then subsisting between themselves.

"At that time we carried on a considerable Branch of Trade with those Indians for Skins and furrs, no less advantageous for them than to us, we sold them goods on much better terms than the French which drew many Indians over the Lakes to trade with us; the exports of Skins and fur from this Province at that time will show the Increase of our trade in these Articles."

Document C–5

PLANS FOR SETTLEMENT

("A Plan for Settling Two Western Colonies," *Political, Miscellaneous, and Philosophical Pieces, written by Benjamin Franklin, LL.D. and F.R.S.* [London, 1779], pp. 133–43.)

The great country back of the Apalachian mountains, on both sides the Ohio, and between that river and the lakes; is now well known both to the English and French, to be one of the finest in North America, for the extreme richness and fertility of the land; the healthy temperature of the air, and mildness of the climate; the plenty of hunting, fishing, and fowling; the facility of trade with the Indians; and the vast convenience of inland navigation or water-carriage by the lakes and great rivers, many hundred of leagues around.

From these natural advantages it must undoubtedly (perhaps in less than another century) become a populous and powerful dominion; and a great accession of power, either to England or France.

. . . If two strong colonies of English were settled between the Ohio and lake Erie, in the places hereafter to be mentioned, these *advantages* might be expected:

1. They would be a great security to the frontiers of our other colonies; by preventing the incursions of the French and French Indians of Canada, on the back parts of Pensylvania, Maryland, Virginia, and the Carolinas; and the frontiers of such new colonies would be much more easily defended, than those of the colonies last mentioned now can be, as will appear hereafter.

2. The dreaded junction of the French settlements in Canada, with those of Louisiana would be prevented.

3. In case of a war, it would be easy, from those new colonies, to annoy Louisiana by going down the Ohio and Mississippi; and the southern part of Canada by sailing over the lakes; and thereby confine the French within narrower limits.

4. We should secure the friendship and trade of the Miamis or Twigtwees, (a numerous people, consisting of many tribes, inhabiting the country between the west end of lake Erie, and the south end of lake Hurons, and the Ohio) who are at present dissatisfied with the French, and fond of the English, and would gladly encourage and protect an infant English settlement in or near their country, as some of their chiefs have declared to the writer of this memoir. Further, by means of the lakes, the Ohio, and the Mississippi, our trade might be extended through a

vast country, among many numerous and distant nations, greatly to the benefit of Britain.

. . . Such settlements may better be made now, than fifty years hence, because it is easier to settle ourselves, and thereby prevent the French settling there, as they seem now to intend, than to remove them when strongly settled.

If these settlements are postponed, then more forts and stronger and more numerous and expensive garrisons must be established, to secure the country, prevent their settling, and secure our present frontiers; the charge of which, may probably exceed the charge of the proposed settlements, and the advantage nothing near so great.

D. Prologue to War

The commercial competition of French and English increased in violence, as each side sought to subvert the Indians and draw them into its allegiance. Since the ambiguity of the Treaty of Utrecht (1713) made it possible for the Indians to ally with either of the trading rivals, every means was considered to draw them. Gifts, of a type suitable to the red man, were not spared on either side. While the French displayed an eagerness for expanding their knowledge of the continent beyond the Mississippi, they did not forego their advantageous position in the Great Lakes area. From Niagara to Kaskaskia, they erected a series of fortified trading posts around which *coureurs de bois* and Indians were invited to settle. To control waterways, portages, and strategic locations, the Forts of Niagara, Detroit, Michillimackinac, St. Joseph des Miamis, La Baye, de Chartres, Miami, Ouiatenon, and Vincennes were built between 1715 and 1733. When the English pressures became too difficult to resist, the French decided on a show of force in the Ohio Valley itself. The French expeditions had no other result but to convince the English colonials that a concerted war effort alone could lead to a satisfactory final solution. How important a factor was the West in the tensions between England and France in North America?

Document D–1

PEACE WITH THE IROQUOIS

("Instructions de M. de Callières au père Bruyas envoyé avec MM. Le Moyne de Maricourt, de Joncaire et autres chez les Onnontagués, . . . [15 juin 1701]," P. G. Roy, *Ordonnances, Commissions, etc., etc., des gouverneurs et intendants de la Nouvelle-France, 1639–1706,* [Beauceville, 1924], Vol. II, pp. 290–93.)

We have received from France great news that assures us that the great Onnontio has become master of the whole Kingdom of Spain, by the death of its King, who has declared as his heir My Lord the Duke of Anjou, the great Onontio's grandson; and as this event might lead to a resumption of war between him and the King of England, if the latter wanted to prevent you from

coming, you can see the consequences of not listening to him and of not pledging to return to his side, because you would draw upon yourselves a greater war than the previous one with Onontio and all his allies; under the circumstances, be satisfied to let them settle their disputes, while you smoke peacefully on your mats; you will thus preserve free passage to go to Orange and to come to Montreal to obtain your necessities and the right to hunt without being disturbed by the Savages allies of Onnontio.

. . . If the English still wanted to use the establishment that your father Onontio will cause to be built at the Detroit, to cause you tó mistrust him, do not listen to them because I can guarantee, on his behalf, as he has already done at Teganissorens, that he has no other purpose in this matter but to keep the peace among all the Upper Nations and you; if, indeed, some quarrel occurred when you are out, the ones and the others, hunting in those parts, the Commandant whom he is appointing there will work out a compromise among you, as the Commandant at Fort Frontenac did last winter for the Nations that were hunting in his neighborhood, by sending someone to tell them from Onontio not to trouble you; indeed, when you want to go to that post, you will be received there as well as at Katarakouis, and you will find goods at a reasonable price.

. . . Your father Onontio will arrange everything; this is why you must not fail to come at the beginning of August with all your prisoners that he may cause all acts of hostility to cease. Done in Montreal, June 15, 1701.

Document D–2
TREATY OF UTRECHT (1713)
(*Mémoire des commissaires du Roi et de ceux de sa Majesté Britannique* [Paris, 1756–57], Vol. III, pp. 172–207.)

The inhabitants of Canada & other subjects of France shall not hereafter molest the Five Nations or Cantons of Indians subject to Great Britain, nor the other nations of America friends of that Crown: in like manner the subjects of Great Britain shall behave themselves peaceably towards the American subjects or friends of France, and the ones and the others shall enjoy full freedom to associate for the good of trade; & with the same freedom the inhabitants of those regions shall be allowed to visit the French & British colonies for promoting trade on one side and the other, without any molestation or hindrance: further the Commissioners will determine exactly and distinctly who are those who shall be or shall be deemed subjects & friends of France or of Great Britain.

Document D–3
CELORON DE BLAINVILLE'S EXPEDITION (1749)
(Pierre Margry [ed.], *Découvertes et établissements* . . . [Paris, 1879–88], Vol. VI, pp. 666–726.)

COPY OF THE MINUTE CONCERNING THE LAYING OF A LEAD PLATE AND OF THE ARMS OF THE KING AT THE SOURCE OF THE BEAUTIFUL RIVER, TOGETHER WITH THE INSCRIPTION

In the year one thousand seven hundred and forty nine, we, Céloron, Knight of the Royal and Military Order of Saint Louis, captain, commanding a detachment sent by order of M. the Marquis de La Galissonière, commandant general of Canada, to the Beautiful River, otherwise named the Ohio, accompanied by the main officers of our detachment, have buried at the foot of a red oak, on the southern shore of the said Oyo and of Chanaouagon, and by 42° 5′ 23″, a lead plate with the engraved inscription.

Inscription

In the year 1749, . . . of the reign of Louis XV, King of France, we Céloron, commandant of the detachment sent by M. the marquis de La Galissonière, commandant general of New France, to restore tranquillity to a few villages of these cantons, have buried this plate at the confluence of the Ohio and Kanaouagon, on the 29 July, as a memorial of the renewal of possession that we have taken of the said Ohio River and of all those who flow into it and of all the lands on both sides up to the sources of the said rivers, as have enjoyed or ought to have enjoyed the previous Kings of France, and have maintained themselves by arms and by treaties, and especially by those of Riswick, of Utrecht and of Aix-la-Chapelle; we have, further, displayed at the same place on a tree the arms of the King.

In attestation thereof, we have prepared and signed the present report, done at the entrance of the Beautiful River, the 29 July 1749.

COPY OF THE DEMAND MADE TO THE ENGLISH OF THE BEAUTIFUL RIVER

We Céloron, captain, Knight of the Royal and Military Order of Saint Louis, commanding a detachment sent by M. the marquis de La Galissonière, commandant general of New France, have demanded that the English traders, who were trading in a Savage village located on the Beautiful River, withdraw from that country with their goods and baggages under threat of being treated as interlopers in case of a refusal. To which demand the English have answered that they would withdraw into their country with their belongings.

Done in our camp of the Beautiful River.

Document D–4
DESTRUCTION OF PICKAWILLANY (1752)
("Letter to Governor Dinwiddie, 22 June 1752," C.O. 5: 1327, pp. 561–62.)

"They had two Hundred & forty Fighting-men, appeared suddenly & took us in Surprise, when they had sent us Wampum, & a fine French Coat, in token of Peace & good-will, just to deceive, & draw our People out a Hunting, & then fall on us as a more weak & defenceless Part, being only Twenty men able to bear arms, & nine of them were our Brothers the English who helped us much. But their Stores & Houses being on the out side of our Fort, our enemies plunder'd them, & took six of our Brothers the English's Goods, & to our great loss their Powder and Lead. . . ."

Document D–5
FORT DUQUESNE
("Duquesne à Contrecoeur, Montréal, le 27e janvier 1754," Archives du Séminaire de Québec, V–V 2, p. 146.)

I

It is proper to inform you that my intention is that you leave only eighteen men in the Fort of Presquisle and twelve in that of Rivière-aux-Boeufs, officers included; I may hope, then, that you will enter into the Beautiful River with 600 men, fully equipped, whose appearance will be more striking to the Savages than if this detachment were made up of twice as many, but of the type of those who were ordered last year.

Although I have no reason to suspect that the English or the Savages have any idea of opposing with open force the taking possession of a land which belongs to us, it is prudent and cautious that, from the moment you have reached the source of the Rivière-aux-Boeufs with the last convoy of goods, you hurry to go and build Fort Duquesne at Chinengué or in the neighborhood and on a site which will appear to you most advantageous.

If it is true that there is a river six

leagues above Chinengué, which is said to be the ordinary route of the English coming from Philadelphia, you will locate the fort at that site to block their passage and to obstruct their trade; I have been assured that there would be another advantage to placing the fort near this river: Chinengué lacks wood, which is plentiful there; this has decided me to a change which appears altogether advantageous. It would have been desirable that we could investigate the behavior of the Savages of this village, but I hope that they will settle closer to the fort when they see us established there.

(Pennsylvania Gazette, 9 May 1754.)

II

Philadelphia, May 9 [1754]

Friday last an Express arrived here from Major Washington, with Advice, that Mr. Ward, Ensign of Capt. Trent's Company, was compelled to surrender his small Fort in the Forks of Monongahela to the French, on the 17th past; who fell down from Venango with a Fleet of 360 Battoes and Canoes, upwards of 1000 Men, and 18 Pieces of Artillery, which they planted against the Fort; and Mr. Ward having but 44 Men, and no Cannon to make a proper Defence, was obliged to surrender on Summons, capitulating to march out with their Arms, &c. and they had accordingly joined Major Washington, who was advanced with three Companies of the Virginia Forces, as far as the New Store near the Allegheny Mountains, where the Men were employed in clearing a Road for the Cannon, which were every Day expected with Col. Fry, and the Remainder of the Regiment—We hear farther, that some few of the English Traders on the Ohio escaped, but 'tis supposed the greatest Part are taken, with all their Goods, and Skins, to the Amount of near £20,000. The Indian Chiefs, however, have dispatch'd Messages to Pennsylvania, and Virginia, desiring that the English would not be discouraged, but send out their Warriors to join them, and drive the French out of the Country before they fortify; otherwise the Trade will be lost, and, to their great Grief, an eternal Separation made between the Indians and their Brethren the English. 'Tis farther said, that besides the French that came down from Venango, another Body of near 400, is coming up the Ohio; and that 600 French Indians, of the Chippaways and Ottaways, are coming down Siota River, from the Lake, to join them; and many more French are expected from Canada; the Design being to establish themselves, settle their Indians, and build Forts just on the Back of our Settlements in all our Colonies; from which Forts, as they did from Crown-Point, they may send out their Parties to kill and scalp the Inhabitants, and ruin the Frontier Counties.

Document D—6

OPENING OF HOSTILITIES

(Mémoires et réflexions politiques et militaires sur la guerre du Canada depuis 1746 jusqu'a 1760, par Chevalier de la Pause," Rapport de l'Archiviste de la Province de Québec, 1933–1934 [Québec, 1934], pp. 147–49.) [Editorial Note: The left-hand column is the text of the Mémoires, while the right-hand column refers to notes on the text. The disposition is that of the original.]

In 1753, My Lord Duquesne sent Sieur Marin, captain, with 2,000 men to the Oyo to establish a communication from that river to Lake Erie to base the planned establishment on the said river the more

5. For this expedition nothing had been provided, nothing was known of what we were getting into. Our colony was unable to support so distant an establishment and to sustain it against the forces of the

solidly and the farther down possible.[5]

After this line of communication was established preparations were made to go down the Oyo. The English, learning of these moves, took up arms and in greater numbers went to trade. They sent someone to ask the French commander what the motives were of our movements in these parts and sent detachments forward. An officer was then despatched with a small detachment to order them not to enter under arms onto the lands of the King of France. This officer was ambushed and killed[6] with part of his detachment; the remainder was captured and taken away. We then took steps to build a fort; it was erected at the mouth of the Monongahela, in the Oyo, and it was named after the Governor general. The English also built one on the Monongahela, which they named Necessity.

In 1754, Sieur Villiers, captain, Sieur Gernonville's brother, requested that the governor put him in charge of a detachment to avenge his brother's death. He was given 600 men, with whom he attacked Fort Necessity and forced the place to capitulate. It is thus that the war began without having been authorized by the Court.

At that time, and even before having learned of the expedition mentioned, it had been resolved in old England to seize Canada. General Bradok [sic] was to leave with a body of troops ready for war before the end of the year, and the following spring was with 3,000 men to cross the Appalachians to reach the Oyo and capture Fort Duquesne; ascend that river and reach Lake Erie at Niagara, and then to Lake Ontario where he would join forces with Sieur Chirlay (Shirley) who, with 3,000 men, was to wait for him at Chouagen; from there they were to descend the rapids to Montreal, towards which another body of militiamen was to make its way via Lakes St. Sacrement and Champlain and the St. John River; in the meantime, another army was to seize Acadia. It did not seem possible that so well concerted an invasion could not succeed. Canada was without any resources to defend itself in so many places.[7]

English colonies. Our navy in Europe could not back up such enterprises.

The governors sent to this colony have never seen or known anything but through the Canadians, persons little suited to situations requiring consideration and planning. Their interest has shown them everything as easy to achieve; they have been deluded and have deluded the ministers. If we had considered how near our Oyo establishment was to the provinces of Carolina, Maryland and Virginia and how interested old England is in her colonies, it would have been obvious that the English knew of our alliances with the Savages of those parts and of the North; they could not calmly accept this establishment which lead them to fear an uprising among these barbarians and even that, in the future, Canada and Louisiana being settled and having established communications, we could seize, with the help of the Savages, their colonies, without taking into account the large losses which they suffer on our account in the fur trade.

If we had designs in this matter, it was necessary that our colonies be settled and cultivated, and that our land and sea forces be able to support them. We made them aware of all they had to fear, and this, together with their great plans for their colonies, has been the cause of our loss of Canada.

6. This officer's name was Gernonville (Jumonville). This action on the part of the English and their behavior towards the prisoners proves that it had been premeditated and can be considered as murder.

7. If the English, rather than proceeding to Beautiful River had captured the forts on Lake Ontario, the posts on the Oyo would have fallen by themselves. They would have found no other obstacle on their way to Montreal but the rapids; a little speed in the advance of the army from Lake Champlain would have been sufficient to guarantee the success of their expedition.

PROBLEM 4

Yankees at Louisbourg, 1745

GEORGE RAWLYK

Queen's University

In the early spring of 1745, thousands of New Englanders threw away their fish nets and their farming implements to volunteer to capture Louisbourg, the so-called French "Gibraltar of North America." The Louisbourg Expedition of 1745 had all the ingredients of a comic opera. One contemporary believed that it resembled a wild Harvard Commencement celebration. Another wrote:

Those who were on the spot, have frequently in my hearing, laughed at the recital of their own irregularities, and expressed their admiration when they reflected on the almost miraculous preservation of the army from destruction. They indeed presented a formidable front to the enemy, but the rear was a scene of confusion and frolic. While some were on duty . . . others were racing, wrestling, pitching quoits, firing at marks or at birds, or running after shot from the enemy's guns, for which they received a bounty.[1]

Of course, the expedition had many comic features, but it was also a crucial incident in North American colonial history. The expedition has been accurately referred to as "the most important military achievement of the American Colonists prior to the War of the Revolution."[2] It showed, among other things, that the New Englanders may have had a far more sophisticated and long-sighted grasp of military realities than the British. The "Yankees" realized that Louisbourg was a base from which the British Navy could effectively control the North Atlantic and thus strangle the struggling French colony of New France. The Louisbourg episode, especially the rather foolish return of the fortress to the French in 1748, helped to drive the sensitive New Englanders away from the Mother Country. In addition, the expedition appeared to strengthen what some scholars have referred to as New England's special sense of mission. Convinced that they were the Almighty's special instruments in the New World, the "Yankees" became increasingly confident in their superior abilities and in their

---

[1] J. Belknap, *History of New Hampshire* (Boston, 1813), Vol. II, p. 170.
[2] L. E. DeForest, *Louisbourg Journals* (New York, 1932), XV, 715.
[3] Benjamin Colman to William Pepperell, July 3, 1745, Massachusetts Historical Society *Collections*, 6th Series, Vol. X (1899), p. 307.

superior way of life. "Ye God of Heaven" was regarded as "Ye God of New England."[3] In the Louisbourg Expedition, one may begin to see a few faint traces of those forces which were destined to converge to precipitate the American Revolution.

The Louisbourg Expedition of 1745 should not be looked at in historical isolation. The expedition was one of many New England thrusts into the Nova Scotia–Cape Breton region. Throughout the 17th century and the first half of the 18th century, many New Englanders regarded Nova Scotia–Cape Breton as their northeastern frontier and as a vitally important stepping-stone to the valuable North Atlantic fisheries and to the St. Lawrence region. The expeditions of 1654, 1690, and 1710 against Nova Scotia were excellent examples of New England's economic and territorial expansionism as well as the area's natural defensive response to the threat of French encirclement. These expeditions had much in common with the Louisbourg Expedition of 1745. New England's penetration into Nova Scotia was neither purely offensive in nature nor defensive; it was both. Of course, there were other factors involved, notably the prevailing English antipathy, especially at times of crisis, toward Roman Catholics and toward Frenchmen. There was also the widely held view that the Indian threat in the northern and eastern frontiers of New England could be removed only if the French forces were driven from Nova Scotia. After the signing of the Treaty of Utrecht in 1713, which gave Nova Scotia but not Cape Breton to the British, some New Englanders eagerly awaited the outbreak of new hostilities between France and Britain so that the French could be forced to leave Cape Breton Island. These men would not be satisfied until the Island as well as the peninsula became "New England's Outpost."

Who was responsible for the Expedition of 1745? Three men, each of whom believed he was alone responsible for bringing about the expedition, played crucial roles—Governor William Shirley of Massachusetts; William Pepperell, the pious Kittery businessman and politician; and William Vaughan, the enigmatic Maine entrepreneur. Shirley espoused the cause of the expedition for two main reasons. First, he believed that unless Louisbourg was attacked early in 1745, the French would probably mount an offensive thrust against the vulnerable Annapolis Royal and perhaps even Maine. Second, Shirley saw in the expedition an excellent opportunity to gain control of new sources of patronage to consolidate his political position in the colony. Pepperell, who was extraordinarily popular, consented to be "commander in chief," because he hoped that he might receive as a reward for his services, a lucrative colonial position from Whitehall. Vaughan, too, was interested in obtaining such an office. When the Massachusetts General Court was first asked to organize the expedition, it stubbornly refused. But on February 5, 1745,[4] when the proposal was once again passionately debated, it was accepted by the narrowest margin of one vote. It was understood, apparently, not only that the British Navy would assist and that the British Government would reinburse the colony for all of its expenditures but also that the other northern colonies would join Massachusetts.

The recruiters were well received. They took full advantage of the prevailing antipathy towards Roman Catholics and Frenchmen and also the widely held

---

[4] "New Style" dates are used throughout this brief introduction even though it was not until 1752 that the British finally adopted our present calendar.

view that the Indian threat on the northern and eastern borders of New England could only be eradicated if the French forces were driven from Cape Breton. But the recruiters emphasized most of all that the Louisbourg merchants and officers possessed vast sums of money and other valuables all readily available to make each volunteer a rich man. To become wealthy was a mere matter of sailing, since the French were expected to surrender without a battle. Hundreds of men from Massachusetts, New Hampshire, and Connecticut, who craved adventure and coveted wealth, were prepared and eager to believe almost anything; and the shrewd recruiters were fully aware of the fact.

The first contingent of Massachusetts troops sailed from Boston on April 4, 1745. The voyage to the barren and inhospitable island of Canso—the place of rendezvous—was one that the volunteers would not soon forget. After the arrival of further detachments of volunteers and also Commodore Peter Warren's four British warships, Pepperell naïvely expected that Louisbourg would quickly surrender. On May 11th, a daring amphibious landing was made at Kennington Cove, some 3 miles southwest of the fortress. Raw, untrained, and undisciplined New England militia were to carry out a maneuver that would have taxed the ingenuity of the best-trained British regulars. In fact, under the circumstances, such an amphibious landing was probably beyond the capacity of most British regulars accustomed only to the barrack square and the battlefields of Europe.

For the New Englanders, the regular siege of the fort was the most disconcerting feature of the entire Louisbourg episode. Building siege batteries within shouting distance of the fortress walls was no easy job. In addition, manning the batteries was regarded as a fool's errand. Not only were the men subject to heavy French fire, but many were also forced to use artillery for the first time. These amateur gunners all too frequently doubled charged their cannon in the hope that the shot would do twice as much damage. The bursting cannon did a great deal of damage but to the wrong side!

Louisbourg was finally surrendered on June 28, 1745. Its many strategic weaknesses, the British naval blockade, and New England persistence all contributed to Louisbourg's capture. With the landing of Warren's Marines, bickering began in earnest between the New Englanders and British regarding who was in fact responsible for the fall of the fortress. Each group wished to possess all of the glory of victory and the dispute was a bitter one. New England volunteers and British sailors should have realized that neither could have succeeded alone and that, furthermore, as Lord Selkirk commented concerning another military episode: "There would appear in this celebrated campaign fully as much guid luck as guid guiding."[5]

A long and complex chain of events had led to the fall of Louisbourg. There was Massachusett's key role in originating and organizing the expedition. There was also Peter Warren's gamble in deciding to sail to Cape Breton and the enthusiasm of the British Admiralty for the expedition. Finally, there were the strategic weaknesses of the fortress and the blunders committed by Cape Breton's governor, Du Chambon, before and during the siege. But too much criticism should not be heaped upon Du Chambon. With British naval supremacy assured in the North Atlantic because of the weakness of the French Navy, Du Chambon's task was virtually an impossible one. For Louisbourg, without a powerful naval

---

[5] From C. P. Stacey, *Quebec, 1759, the Siege and the Battle* (Toronto, 1959), iii.

force to defend it, was an easy prey for any invader supported by naval strength. Furthermore, Du Chambon was not responsible for the military weaknesses of the fortress itself. Some of the walls were crumbling even before the New England bombardment began; the two isolated outlying batteries, the Grand and Island Batteries, were dominated by neighboring heights of land; and the landward defences of the fortress were grossly inadequate. What is remarkable is that under these adverse circumstances the French were still able to conduct a reasonably vigorous defence.

It is noteworthy that the siege proper took so few lives. Only 53 French troops and 101 New Englanders were killed. The capture of Louisbourg in 1745, which one New Englander thought "can scarce be parallel'd in History." showed what could be accomplished by a combined British and American force and by a combined sea and land force. But it also demonstrated that there was a widening chasm developing between Britain and her New England colonies. During the months and years immediately following the capture of Louisbourg and its return to the French in 1748, this chasm widened dangerously.

The interested student should consider the following questions: How does the Louisbourg expedition of 1745 fit into the general context of New England–Nova Scotia relations from 1630 to 1784? Was the expedition an aberration or was it what should have been expected under the circumstances? Who was, in fact, responsible for organizing the expedition and why did Louisbourg fall? Finally, what impact did the Louisbourg episode have on the New England mind in the pre-Revolutionary period?

For those interested in pursuing the topic in greater detail, the best one-volume study of the history of Louisbourg is still J. S. MacLennan, *Louisbourg from its Foundation to its Fall* (1918). For the New England background, Byron Fairchild, *Messrs. William Pepperell: Merchants at Piscataqua* (1954), and J. A. Schutz, *William Shirley: King's Governor of Massachusetts* (1961) should be consulted. For the French side see Guy Frégault, *Français Bigot, Administrateur français*, Vol. I (1948) and for the British side see Gerald Graham, *Empire of the North Atlantic* (1950). The most detailed recent study of the fall of Louisbourg in 1745 is G. A. Rawlyk, *Yankees at Louisbourg* (1967).

Of the printed sources the Massachusetts Historical Society *Collections*, 1st. Series, Vol. I and 6th Series, Vol. X, "Pepperell Papers," are indispensable as is G. M. Wrong (ed.), *Louisbourg in 1745: The Anonymous Lettre D'Un Habitant de Louisbourg* (1897). L. E. De Forest, *Louisbourg Journals, 1745* (1932), is a fine collection of 10 pertinent journals and other important documents. There are numerous available printed journals written by some of those involved in the Louisbourg Expedition. Some of the most relevant of these are E. M. Bidwell (ed.), "Journal of the Rev. Adonijah Bidwell," *New England Historical and Genealogical Register*, Vol. XXVII (1873), pp. 153–60; "Benjamin Cleaves's Journal," *ibid.*, Vol. LXVI (1912), 113–124; L. E. DeForest (ed.), *The Journals and Papers of Seth Pomeroy* (Conn., 1926); S. A. Green (ed.), *Three Military Diaries Kept by Graton Soldiers in Different Wars* (1901); C. H. Lincoln (ed.), *The Journal of Sir William Pepperell* (1910); "Journal of Roger Wolcott at the Siege of Louisbourg," Connecticut Historical Society *Collections*, Vol. I (1860), pp. 131–62.

A. The Men Responsible for the Expedition

Three men, William Shirley, William Vaughan and William Pepperell, all played key roles in bringing about the Louisbourg expedition. The following selections should reveal why Shirley was so enthusiastic about the capture of Louisbourg and how Vaughan and Pepperell viewed their respective contributions.

Document A—1

SHIRLEY'S "VISION"

(C. H. Lincoln [ed.] *Correspondence of William Shirley* [New York, 1912], Vol. I, pp. 161–65.)

WILLIAM SHIRLEY TO THE DUKE OF NEWCASTLE

Boston, N. Engld. Jany 14, 1744

My Lord Duke,

It having been represented to me by persons well acquainted with the Island of Cape Breton and the Harbour and present Circumstances of Louisbourg as practicable to surprize and take it with two thousand men, if attempted before the Arrival of their expected Supplies and Recruits from Old France, and finding the Fishermen in particular and the People of this Province in general so well spirited for such an Enterprize that it seem'd no difficult matter at this Juncture to raise that number of Men upon the Occasion in a very short time, I recommended it to the Assembly in my inclos'd Message to 'em to make a suitable provision for the Expence of such an Expedition, to which, after a close Consultation upon my Proposal for two days, and apprehending the Attempt too hazardous, they return'd me the inclos'd Answer, praying in the latter part of it that I would lay before his Majesty the Danger, which this Province and the Neighbouring Governments are expos'd to from the Situation of the French at Louisbourg, and in the name of his Majesty's most Loyal and Dutiful Subjects of this province to intreat his Majesty's Compassion-

ate Regards to these his Governments in reducing Cape Breton, and represent to his Majesty the ready Disposition of this province to exert themselves to the utmost of their Abilities in conjunction with the other Neighbouring Governments upon such an Occasion.

In Compliance with this Request I humbly beg leave to lay before your Grace, and that your Grace would be pleas'd so far as you shall think proper, to represent to his Majesty that Cape Breton, which was originally deem'd part of Nova Scotia and possess'd as such by his Majesty's Subjects, till it was conceded to the French King by the Treaty of Utrecht, is situated so as to be a most commodious Harbour, from whence the Enemy's Ships may intercept (in different Degrees) the British Trade and Navigation to and from this province, the Colonies of Connecticut and Rhode Island, and the provinces of New Hampshire, New York, the New Jerseys and Pensilvania, also supply their own Colonies with provisions from the Vessells of his Majesty's Northern Colonies, to the great Distress of all his Sugar Colonies in particular, and very much interrupt the Coasting Trade and Navigation of the Northern Colonies as far as Pensilvania, but especially of this province; And that in particular the New England Fishery, which since the French have been in possession of Louisbourg has been half ruin'd by their carrying on the Cape Breton Fishery and Encroachments upon the English Fishery in time of peace, will be now in danger of being quite destroy'd and lost to the Enemy, who have already made a Beginning by their Surprize of Canso.

I would further beg leave to represent to your Grace that the Harbour of Louisbourg is most commodiously situated for a place of Retreat for the Enemy's Ships of War navigating these Seas to refit in, and also for a Rendezvous for 'em to form Expeditions from against his Majesty's Northern Colonies, especially Nova Scotia, and as we have had a late Instance of it's being made use of as a place of Shelter and Refreshment for their East India Fleet in their Return home, and to meet Convoy for the Remainder of their passage, it seems to be a proof of what further Service it may be to 'em in time of War. But what seems a much more considerable Advantage arising to the Enemy from their possession of Cape Breton is that it is the principal Settlement of their growing Fishery, from which alone during the Fishing Season they employ seven thousand men, and from whence they may effectually protect their own Fishery and annoy the British: It would require too particular Calculations for me to pretend to ascertain what the Revenue of the whole Fishery in those Seas, clear of the French Incroachments upon it, would be to Great Britain, where the profits arising from the New England Fishery likewise chiefly center in the End; also what the number of men employ'd in the French Fishery is; But the Revenue would certainly be very large, and the Nursery of able Seamen rais'd thereby for the Royal Navy be very considerably increas'd; And it would render the Roman Catholick States in the neighbouring Seas in some measure dependent upon his Majesty's Subjects for part of their provisions.

I would further beg leave to observe to your Grace that the Reduction of Cape Breton seems almost necessary for securing to his Majesty the possession of Annapolis Royal and province of Nova Scotia, and for the Recovery of the Canso Fishery; At least the Expence of maintaining 'em whilst the French hold Cape Breton will probably equal that of his Majesty's reducing and holding that Island; And the further Consequence of reducing it would be in a great measure cutting off in present the French Navigation to and from Canada, and would probably in a little time be attended with an easy Reduction of that Country also by the joint Forces of his Majesty's Northern Colonies assisted with a few of his Ships of War and some few Troops, which Event would give his Majesty's subjects the whole Furr Trade, now chiefly in the possession of the French of Canada, and render 'em Masters of an entire Territory of about eighteen hundred miles extent upon the Sea Coast, (reckoning from Georgia to Newfoundland inclusive) which from it's production of Naval Stores and it's Fisheries, it's Demands for Woollen and other British Manufactures (that must increase in proportion to the increase of it's Inhabitants, who from the general Healthfulness of the greatest part of it's Climate make a very quick progress in the Growth of their Numbers, to which it would be difficult to set Limits in so large and healthful a Country) and from the Support it yields by Supplies of provisions and Lumber to his Majesty's Sugar Colonies, (without which they could not subsist) if the Value of a Territory to the Mother Country may be computed by the Increase of her Natural Wealth and power, which it occasions, may be reckon'd a more valuable Territory to Great Britain than what any Kingdom or State in Europe has belonging to it. And on the other hand the Loss of Annapolis Royal and whole province of Nova Scotia to the French, besides being attended with the Loss of the New England Fishery, the Destruction of it's Trade, and the breaking up of all its Eastern Settlements, and very probably of the province of New Hampshire itself by the Addition of five or six thousand fighting men (which the Enemy would gain by that Conquest) in Conjunction with the Indians of all Tribes, would, as it is a Country fruitful of provisions and nearly contiguous to Canada in which the French have increas'd their Numbers exceedingly within these few years, not only strengthen 'em so greatly in Cape Breton as to bid fair to give 'em the whole Fishery and chief Navigation of those Seas, but afford 'em such a Footing upon the Northern Continent of America as might possibly in time make 'em think of disputing the Mastery of it with the Crown of Great Britain. Such may be the Difference between His Majesty's reducing Cape Breton and holding Nova Scotia, and the French King's holding Cape Breton and gaining that province, which two last Events seem to be too closely connected together, as the Inhabitants of Nova Scotia are all Frenchmen and Roman Catholicks, and who ought to be look'd upon (be their pretensions what they will) as ready in their Hearts to join with the Enemy, whenever a French Force sufficient in their Imagination to subdue it shall appear in their Country: and so much seems to depend upon reducing Cape Breton to the Obedience of his Majesty, that the Reduction of it, if estimated from it's beforemention'd Consequences to the particular Interests of the British Crown and Dominions, might seem almost of itself to be near an Equivalent for the Expence of a French War.

As the Motives which induc'd me to propose at this time to the Assembly an Expedition from hence for surprizing Cape Breton may be thought of some force still, I shall just mention the chief of 'em to your Grace. There seem'd to be now an advantageous Opportunity to attempt the Reduction of it on account of it's present scarceness of provisions and probably of Military Stores; The Garrison, which has not yet receiv'd any Recruits since the Commencement of the War, does not exceed seven hundred men, one hundred and forty of which being Swiss and their best Troops are greatly discontented, and did not scruple to talk in a very mutinous manner when some of our people were prisoners there; And, as I am inform'd, there is an Hill on the back of the Town, and at about a quarter of a mile's Distance from it, from whence it may be extremely annoy'd with Safety to the Besiegers, and which the French level'd about twelve feet of last Summer, and will doubtless go on to level as fast as they can, but have not so lower'd yet as to take away the Danger arising from it.

I would further beg of your Grace that your Grace would be pleas'd to represent to his Majesty that his most Loyal and Dutiful Subjects within this province are not only most readily dispos'd but desirous, in case his Majesty shall be graciously pleas'd to attempt the Reduction of Cape Breton to it's former Obedience and Subjection to his Crown, to exert themselves to the utmost of their abilities upon this Occasion in conjunction with his Majesty's other Neighbouring Governments, which I have herein before mention'd to your Grace, or such of 'em as his Majesty shall be pleas'd to lay his Commands on to assist in such an Expedition; And whatever proportion of Men his Majesty shall be pleas'd to allot this province to raise and transport to Cape Breton or of the other Expences of it to bear I hope I may venture to assure your Grace of their most Dutiful and cheerful Compliance with it; And I most humbly beg of your Grace to assure his Majesty that at all Events his Majesty may depend upon my utmost Zeal and Attention in the performance of my Duty and promoting his Service upon this Occasion.

I am with the most Dutiful Regards

My Lord Duke

Your Grace's most Obedient

and Most Devoted Servant

W. SHIRLEY.

Document A—2

VAUGHAN'S CONTRIBUTION

(New Hampshire Historical Society, Vaughan Papers, Vaughan's Memorial to the King, 1745.)

That your Memorialist has for these twenty Years last past made it his constant Business to enquire after the Number, Strength, & Situation of the French and Indian Settlements between New England and Newfoundland, their Communication with each other and with Canada, in order to reduce them to the Obedience of the Crown of Great Britain; which has been attended with great Expence, as well as infinite Hazard of his Person and Settlements.

That the Declaration of a War with France (affording a favourable Opportunity to put in Practice what your Memorialist had so long meditated) he quitted without Hesitation his said Eastern Settlements, at a Time when his Presence was more than ordinarily requisite to encourage the defence of what he had done at so great an Expence: And it is currently reported that the said two powerful Tribes have since made Incursions to within eight Miles of his dwelling House, have killed many Men and Cattle, and destroyed many Houses & Mills; wherefor he has all the Reason in the World to apprehend that his Settlements are likewise fallen into their Hands.

That your Memorialist's Design in thus quitting his Settlement was to travel through the Provinces of Massachusetts Bay and New Hampshire to enquire into the Strength and Circumstances of Louisburgh, & the other French Settlements on, or adjoining to the Island of Cape Breton: & this he performed with infinite Fatigue & Hazard during the last Winter.

That your Memorialist met with several intelligent Men who had been Prisoners there the Summer before & were good Pilots; from whom he learnt the Strength (or rather Weakness) of the Enemy & such other Particulars as might encourage an Undertaking against them.

That your Memorialist likewise calculated the Force that might be raised to attack them, & having digested the whole into a regular Scheme, about the first of December last he waited on their Excellencies William Shirley & Benning Wentworth Esqrs. two Governors of New England & laid the same before them.

That about the 7th Janry. last your Memorialist's Scheme was by His Excellency William Shirley Esqr. Govr. of the province of the Massachusetts, laid before both Houses of the General Assembly then sitting, & a Committee was chosen of both Houses to consider the Affair & make a Report thereon. The Difficulties of the Undertaking & the Improbability of Success appear'd so great to the Committee, that the Scheme was for that Time laid aside, & judged impracticable.

That your Memorialist (still possessed with the Probability of carrying his Designs into Execution) thereupon doubled his Diligence, & at his own proper Costs & Charges sent Expresses through the Provinces of the Massachusetts & New Hampshire to procure authentic Evidences of the weak State of Louisbourg, & the ready Dispositions of the People to undertake the Reduction of it; which Evidences were subsisted at the sole Expence of your Memorialist. He next procured Petitions to be signed by some Hundreds of the principal Men in New England, & preferred to the General Assembly; praying that due Encouragement might be given to such as should voluntarily engage in said Expedition. Whereupon the Attempt upon Louisbourg was revived & carried in the Affirmative, in both Houses of the General Assembly of the Massachusetts. It was now necessary to promote so good a Design in the Province of New Hampshire. To which Purpose your Memorialist went thro' all Sorts of Difficulties to carry Advices from Governor Shirley to his Excellency Benning Wentworth Esqr. of the Proceedings of the General Assembly of the Massachusetts. These were immediately laid before the General Assembly of the Province of New Hampshire, then sitting, & it was thereon instantly agreed to raise two hundred and fifty men: Hereupon your Memorialist represented that the Charge would fall too heavily on the Province of the Massachusetts, unless more Men were raised by that of New Hampshire; & offer'd to mortgage his Estate in New Hampshire worth four thousand Pounds Sterling for the Subsistence of two hundred and fifty Men more for four Months, to make up a Regiment of five hundred Men: Whereupon said General Assembly passed a Vote for the raising of one hundred Men more. Your Memorialist then obtained general Orders from Governor Wentworth to all military Officers in his Province to muster their Companies at his your

Memorialist's Call, with which Orders he rode twice thro' all the principal Towns of New Hampshire, & many of those of Massachusetts furthering & encouraging the enlisting of Volunteers for the Expedition with great and surprizing success; never desisting till the whole Number was complete.

Things being brought to this forwardness by the indefatigable Pains & Industry of your Memorialist, he offer'd himself to Governor Shirley either to embark for Great Britain with any Dispatches which his Excellency should think fit to send thither, or to go with the Army to Cape Breton. The latter Duty was assigned him, & he immediately embarked in the Province Sloop of War, and landed soon after at Gabarose Bay on the Island of Cape Breton.

Document A—3

PEPPERELL'S ROLE

(Massachusetts Historical Society, Pepperell Papers, Pepperell to Silas Hooper, November 9, 1745.)

M[r] Silas Hooper, Sir,—I have wrote you several letters since I have been on this island & this place has been reduced to his Majesty, but have not been favour[d] with any from y[o]. I am apt to think my friends will be surpris[d] to think how I came to leave my pleasant seat & agreable family where I liv[d] as well as any man in New England, & my estate when I left it would allow me so to do, and when it was first mention[d] to me I was very loth to come, M[rs] Pepperrell being in an ill state of health & my business unsettel[d], but when y[e] Gov[r], Council & Speaker of y[e] Lower House told me there would be no expedition without I would head y[e]

forces, and when I consider[d] that y[e] French from this place had destroy[d] Canso & attackt Annapolis Royal, w[ch] if they had taken y[e] neutril French there would have joyn[d] them, & then I had reason to think that in time they would have destroy[d] y[e] eastern part of New England, & Newfoundland would have stood but a poor chance, so that y[e] greatest part of y[e] codd fishery in a short time would have been in y[e] French hands, and great part of our trade to New England, Verginia, &c., intercept[d] by y[m], upon these considerations I undertook this difficult hazardous enterprise, & thrô divine assistance have succed[d]. . . .

B. The Debate Concerning the Expedition

Not everybody in New England wanted a military expedition against Louisbourg. When the Massachusetts General Court finally agreed to proceed with the assault, Shirley's proposal was agreed to by the narrowest margin of one vote! Thomas Hutchinson, the Massachusetts politician-historian, who was a keen and perceptive observer of the 1740's, described the debate in the following manner.

Document B–1

THE DEBATE

(T. Hutchinson, *The History of the Province of Massachusetts Bay* [Boston, 1767], Vol. II, pp. 407–10.)

The plan of the expedition was, a land force of 4000 men in small transports to proceed to Canso, and the first favorable opportunity to land at Chapeaurouge bay, with cannon, mortars, ammunition and warlike stores, and all other necessaries for carrying on a siege and, to present a supply of provision and stores to the enemy, several vessels were to cruize off the harbour of Louisbourg, soon as the season of the year would permit. An estimate was made of all the naval force which could be procured in this and the neighbouring colonies, the largest vessel not exceeding 20 guns. With this land and sea force, it was said there was a good chance for success, and if the men of war should arrive, which there was good reason to hope for, there was all imaginable grounds to depend upon the reduction of the place. The general court being sitting the beginning of January, the governor sent a message to the two houses to let them know he had something to communicate to them of very great importance, but of such a nature that the publishing it, before they should come to any resolution upon it, might wholly defeat the design, he therefore desired they would lay themselves under an oath of secrecy for such time as each house should think proper. This they did, altho' it was the first instance in the house of representatives, without any scruple, and then he communicated to them his proposed plan of the expedition. Many of the members who had heard little or nothing of the conversation upon the subject, were struck with amazement at the proposal. The undertaking they thought to be vastly too great, if there was a rational prospect of success. However, in deference to the recommendation of the governor, a committee of the two houses were appointed to consider the proposal. Here, the proposal was for several days deliberated and weighed. Louisburgh, if left in the hands of the French, would infallibly prove the Dunkirk of New-England; their trade had always been inconsiderable, their fishery was upon the decline, and for several years past they had bought fish of the English at Canso cheaper than they could catch and cure it themselves, both trade and fishery they might well lay aside, and by privateering enrich themselves with the spoils of New England; and to all these dangers was added that of losing Nova Scotia, which would cause an increase of six or eight thousand enemies in an instant. The garrison of Louisburg was disaffected, provisions were scant, the works mouldering and decayed, the governor an old man unskilled in the art of war; this therefore was the only time for success, another year the place would be impregnable. We had nothing to fear from the forces at Louisburgh, before additional strength could arrive from France they would be forced to surrender. We had, it must be owned, no ships of strength sufficient to match the French men of war, unless, perhaps, a single ship should fall in by herself, and in that case five or six of ours might be a match for her; but there was no probability of men of war so early and it was very probable English men of war from Europe or the West-Indies would arrive before them. There was always uncertainty in war, a risque must be run, if we failed we should be able to grapple with the disappointment, although we should bear the whole expence, but if we succeeded, not only the coasts of New-England would be free from molestation, but so glorious an acquisition would be of the greatest importance to Great-Britain and might give peace to Europe, and we might depend upon a reimbursement of the whole charge we had been at.

On the other hand it was replied, that we had better suffer in our trade than by so expensive a measure deprive ourselves of all means of carrying on any future trade, that we were capable of annoying them in their fishery, as much as they could annoy us in ours and, in a short time, both sides would be willing to leave the fishery unmolested, that the accounts given of the works and the garrison at Louisburgh could not be depended upon, and it was not credible that any part of the walls should be unguarded and exposed to surprize, that instances of disaffection rising to mutiny were rare and but few instances were to be met with in history where such expectation has not failed. The garrison at Louisburgh consisted of regular experienced troops who, though unequal in number, would be more than a match in open field for all

the raw unexperienced militia which could be sent from New-England, that twenty cruizers at that season of the year would not prevent supplies going into the harbour, it being impossible to keep any station for any length of time, and the weather being frequently so thick, that a vessel was not to be discovered at a quarter of a mile's distance, that there was no room to expect any men of war for the cover of our troops, that if only one 60 gun ship should arrive from France, or the French islands, she would be more than a match for all the armed vessels we could provide, our transports at Chapeaurouge bay would be every one destroyed, and the army upon Cape-Breton obliged to submit to the mercy of the French, that we should be condemned in England for engaging in such an affair without their direction or approbation, and we should be no where pitied, our misfortunes proceeding from our own rash and wild measures. To these arguments were added the uncertainty of raising a sufficient number of men, or of being able to procure provisions, warlike stores and transports, discouragement from the season of the year when, frequently, for many days together no business could be done out of doors. Money indeed could be furnished, or bills of credit in lieu of it, but the infallible consequence would be the sinking the value of the whole currency, to what degree no man could determine but, probably, in proportion to the sum issued, and finally, if we should succeed, a general national benefit would be the consequence, in which we should be but small sharers and far short of the vast expence of treasure and perhaps of lives in obtaining it, and if we failed, such a shock would be given to the province that half a century would not recover us to our present state.

C. The Siege

In many respects the siege was a comic-opera affair. But it also had a few rather bloody episodes. The following two descriptions, one made by a Frenchman in Louisbourg under siege and the other by a New Englander, present views of the siege from two different vantage points.

Document C–1

THE FRENCH VIEW

(G. M. Wrong [ed.], *Louisbourg in 1745: The Anonymous Lettre d'un Habitant de Louisbourg* [New York, 1897], pp. 24, 37–41, 46, 48, 49–51, 56–57, 64–65, and 67–68.

We had (in 1744–5) the whole winter before us—more time than was necessary to put ourselves in a state of defense. We were, however, overcome with fear. Councils were held, but the outcome was only absurd and childish. Meanwhile the time slipped away; we were losing precious moments in useless discussions and in forming resolutions abandoned as soon as made. Some things begun required completion; it was necessary to strengthen here, to enlarge there, to provide for some posts, to visit all those on the island, to see where a descent could be made most easily, to find out the number of persons in a condition to bear arms, to assign to each his place; in a word, to show all the care and activity usual in such a situation. Nothing of all this was done, and the result is that we were taken by surprise, as if the enemy had pounced upon us unawares. Even after the first ships of the enemy which blockaded us had come we should have had time enough to protect ourselves better than we did, for, as I shall show, they appeared slowly, one after the other. Negligence and fatuity conspired to make us lose our unhappy island. . . . The enterprise was less that of the nation or of the King than of the inhabitants of New England alone. These singular people have a system of laws and of protection peculiar to themselves, and their Governor carries himself like a monarch. So much is this the case that although war was already declared between the two crowns, he himself declared it against us of his own right and in his own name, as if it was necessary that he should give his warrant to his master. His declaration set forth that for himself and all his friends and allies he declared war against us; apparently he meant to speak for the savages subject to them, who are called Indians, and whom it is necessary to distinguish from those obedient to France. It will be seen that Admiral Warren had no authority over the troops sent by the Governor of Boston and that he was merely a spectator, although it was to him that we finally surrendered, at his own request. So striking was the mutual independence of the land army and the fleet that they were always represented to us as of different nations. What other monarchy was ever governed in such a way?

The greater part of the transports having arrived by the beginning of May, on the eleventh we saw them, to the number of ninety-six, coming in order of battle from the direction of Canso and steering for the Flat Point of the Bay of Gabarus. We did not doubt that they would land there. Then it was that we saw the need of the precautions that we ought to have taken. A detachment of one hundred men from the garrison and militia was sent thither quickly in command of M. Morpain, port captain. But what could such a feeble force do against the multitude which the enemy was disembarking? The only result was that a part of our force was killed. M. Morpain found about two thousand men already disembarked. He killed some of them and retired.

The enemy took possession of the surrounding country and a detachment pushed forward close to the Royal Battery. Now terror seized us all. From this moment the talk was of abandoning the splendid battery, which would have been our chief defence had we known how to make use of it. Several tumultuous councils were held to consider the situation. Unless it was from a panic fear which never left us again during the whole siege, it would be difficult to give any reason for such an extraordinary action. Not a single musket had yet been fired against this battery, which the enemy could not take except by making approaches in the same manner as to the town and besieging it, so to speak, in the regular way. A reason for our action was whispered, but I am not myself in a position to speak decidedly. I have, however, heard its truth vouched for by one who was in the battery, but, my post being in the town, it was a long time since I had been to the Royal Battery. The alleged reason for such a criminal withdrawal is that there were two breaches which had never been repaired. If this is true the crime is all the greater, for we had had even more time than was necessary to put everything in order.

However this may be, the resolution was taken to abandon this powerful bulwark, in spite of the protestations of some wiser heads, who lamented to see such a stupid mistake made. They could get no hearers. In vain did they urge that we should thus proclaim our weakness to the enemy, who would not fail to profit by such huge recklessness, and would turn this very battery against us; that, to show a bold face and not reinforce the courage of the enemy by giving him from the first day such good hope of success, it was necessary to do all that we could to hold this important post; that it was quite clear that we could hold it for more than fifteen days, and that this delay could be utilized by removing all the cannon to the town. The answer was, that the council had

resolved otherwise; and so on the 13th, by order of the council, a battery of thirty pieces of cannon, which had cost the King immense sums, was abandoned without undergoing the slightest fire. The retreat was so precipitate that we did not take time to spike the guns in the usual manner, so that on the very next day the enemy used them. Meanwhile, some deluded themselves with a contrary hope; I was on the point of getting a wager accepted that they would make almost no delay in attacking us. So flurried were we that, before the withdrawal from the battery, a barrel of gunpowder exploded, nearly blew up several persons, and burnt the robe of a Récollet friar. It was not from this moment, however, that imprudence marked our actions; for a long time we had yielded to it.

What I had foreseen happened. From the fourteenth the enemy greeted us with our own cannon, and kept up a tremendous fire against us. We answered them from the walls, but we could not do them the harm which they did to us in knocking down houses and shattering everything within range.

While they kept up a hot fire upon us from the Royal Battery they established a mortar platform upon the Rabasse height near the Barachois on the west side and these mortars began to fire on the sixteenth day after the siege began. They had mortars in all the batteries which they established. The bombs annoyed us greatly. . . .

The *Vigilant* came in sight on the 28th or 29th of May about a league and a half distant from Santarye [Scatari]. At the time there was a north-east wind which was a good one for entering. She left the English fleet two and a half leagues to leeward. Nothing could have prevented her from entering, and yet she became the prey of the English by a most deplorable fatality. We witnessed her manœuvres and there was not one of us who did not utter maledictions upon what was so badly planned and so imprudent.

This vessel, commanded by M. de la Maisonfort, instead of holding on her way, or of sending a boat to land for intelligence, as prudence demanded, amused herself by chasing a privateer rigged as a Snow (*Senault*), which unfortunately she encountered near the shore. This privateer, which was commanded by one Brousse, manœuvred differently from the French vessel, and retreated, firing continuously, with all sail set, and leading her enemy on towards the English squadron; her plan succeeded, for the *Vigilant* found herself so entangled that when she saw the danger it was impossible to save herself. At first two frigates attacked her. M. de la Maisonfort answered with a vigorous fire which soon placed one of them *hors de combat*. Her mainmast was carried away, she was stripped of all her rigging, and was compelled to retire. Five other frigates, however, came and poured in a hot fire from all sides; the fight, which we watched in the open air, lasted from five o'clock to ten in the evening. At length it was necessary for her to yield to superior force and to surrender. The enemy's loss in the fight was heavy and the French commander had eighty men killed or wounded; his ship was very little damaged.

It is right to say to the credit of M. de la Maisonfort that he showed great courage in the struggle, but the interests of the King demanded that he should have proceeded to his destination. The Minister did not send him to give chase to any vessel; his ship was loaded with ammunition and provisions, and his one business was to re-victual our wretched town, which would never have been taken could we have received so great a help; but we were victims devoted to the wrath of Heaven, which willed to use even our own forces against us. We have learned from the English, since the surrender, that they were beginning to be short of ammunition, and were in greater need of powder than we were. They had even held councils with a view to raising the siege. The powder found in the *Vigilant* soon dispelled this idea, and we perceived that after the capture their firing increased greatly. . . .

The enemy was busy all the remainder of the month in cannonading and bombarding us without making any appreciable progress which could arouse their hopes. Since they did not attack in form, and, since they had no entrenchments to cover themselves, they did not venture to approach too near. All our shots carried while the greater part of theirs was wasted. Hence we fired only when we thought well. The enemy would fire daily from five to six hundred cannon shots to our twenty; in truth our scarcity of powder caused us to be careful. The musketry was of little use.

I have forgotten to mention that in the early days of the siege the enemy had summoned us to surrender, but we answered as our duty demanded; the officer who was sent to make the proposition, seeing that we were rejecting his offers, proposed that the ladies should be sent out with the guarantee that they should not be insulted, and that they should be protected in the few houses that were still standing, for the enemy when they disembarked had burned or destroyed nearly everything in the surrounding country. We declined the officer's proposal, for our women and children were quite safe in the shelter we had made for them. Some long pieces of wood had been put upon the casemates in a slanting position and this so deadened the force of the bombs and turned them aside that their momentum had no effect. It was underneath this that we had, as it were, buried them.

At the beginning of June the besiegers appeared to acquire renewed vigour. Dissatisfied with their slight success hitherto, they began new undertakings, and planned to attack us from the sea. In order to succeed they tried to surprise the battery at the entrance. A detachment of about 500 men, transported thither on the night of the sixth, was cut in pieces by M. d'Aillebout, captain of a company, who commanded there and fired upon them with grape shot; more than three hundred were left dead, and none were saved except those who asked for quarter; the wounded were taken to our hospitals. On this occasion we made one hundred and nineteen prisoners, and on our side had only three killed or wounded, but we lost a gunner who was much regretted. . . .

To make things worse, on the 15th a squadron of six warships from London reached the English. These, together with the frigates, cruised about in view of the town without firing a single shot. We have, however, since learned that if we had delayed capitulating, all the vessels would have brought their broadsides to bear upon us and we should have had to undergo a most vigorous fire. Their arrangements were not unknown, I will report the order that they were to keep.

The enemy had not yet used red hot bullets, but on the 18th and 19th they did so, with a success which would have been greater had there not been prompt action on our part. Three or four houses took fire, but it was quickly extinguished. Promptitude in such emergencies was our single resource.

It was without doubt the arrival of the squadron which caused this new greeting on the part of the land army, the General, who wished himself to have the honour of conquering us, being very desirous of forcing us to surrender before the fleet should put itself in a position to compel us. . . .

In consequence of this capitulation, signed "P. Warren" and "William Pepperell," the war vessels, merchant ships, and transports entered the harbour of Louisbourg on the 29th. We have nothing but praise for the polished and engaging manners of the Admiral, who had his men well under control, and showed us all the attentions that one could expect from an enemy, generous and compassionate. Mr. Warren is a young man, about thirty-five years old, very handsome, and full of the noblest sentiments. That he sought to gratify us in everything we had proof at our departure; we had need of a surgeon on the *Linceston*, the ship which carried us to Rochefort, and he obligingly gave us the surgeon of the *Vigilant*.

We have, however, much to complain of respecting the commander of the land forces, who had not the same consideration for us, and allowed us to be pillaged by his troops, in violation of the good faith due to our capitulation, and of the public security. What could we expect from a man who, it is said, is the son of a shoemaker of Boston? The Governor, whose favourite he was, had given him this command to the prejudice of better men, who had murmured loudly about it. The officers of the men-of-war had only open contempt for him; those who served under his orders did not respect him more. To punish us for not surrendering to him, he did not cease to persecute us; we can only impute to him all the harm which was done us. Constantly, ineffective complaints were carried to him against his men, who, after they were free to enter the town threw themselves into our houses and took what pleased them. Our lot was little different from that of a town given up to pillage. . . .

Such is the description of the siege of Louisbourg, which, notwithstanding our fortifications, would not have lasted so long had we been attacked by an enemy better versed in the art of war. No complaint can be made of the settlers, who served with the same precision as did the troops themselves, and had to bear the greatest fatigues. The regular soldiers were distrusted so that it was necessary to charge the inhabitants with the most dangerous duties. Children, ten and twelve years old, carried arms, and were to be seen on the ramparts, exposing themselves with a courage beyond their years. Our loss scarcely reached one hundred and thirty men, and it is certain that that of the English was more than two thousand. Yet their force was so great that for them this loss was inconsiderable. They had, at disembarking, as many as from eight to nine thousand men. We should have done them more injury if we had been able to make sorties. I have told the causes which prevented our doing this. The bombs and bullets of the enemy caused frightful desolation in our poor town; most of our houses were demolished, and we were obliged to remove the flour from the general magazine to expose it to the weather in the King's garden; we feared that it might be burned by the enemy, as most of the bombs fell upon this magazine. More than three thousand five hundred must have been fired against us. I do not know exactly how much flour remained to us still, but I know that there was a large quantity, and there were other provisions in proportion. These, however, could not take the place of the munitions of war, which were absolutely exhausted. We had no more bombs, and if we had had any they would have been perfectly useless, for our mortars had cracked, after some shots had been fired. All misfortunes were ours at once. . . .

Document C–2

THE NEW ENGLAND VIEW

(Massachusetts Historical Society, Anonymous Louisbourg Journal.)

March 24, 1744/5 [Old Style]

The forces raised within the Province of the Massachusetts Bay being about three thousand two hundred and fifty men,—exclusive of Commission officers, embarked March 24th, 1744/5 in seven Weeks from the time of the Issuing Governor Shirley's Proclamation for raising them, under convoy of the Shirley Galley, then in the employ of that Government and now his Majesty's Frigate Shirley Captain [John] Rous Commander, and arrived the fourth of April at Canso, appointed by the Governor to be the place of Rendezvous for the Transports and Cruizers, and for a communication of Intelligence between himself at Boston Generall Pepperells Camp before the Town of Louisbourg and Mr. Warren from the Ships before Harbour, and for lodging all Stores not in immediate use in the Camp and Fleet; where they found the New Hampshire Forces, being three Hundred and four inclusive of Commission officers, arrived four days before them; and were joined the 25th of the same Month by the Connecticut Forces being Five Hundred and sixteen Men including Commission officers—Chappearouge Bay, which was the place appointed for landing the Troops, being so filled with Ice as to make their landing impracticable before, they were detained there till the latter end of the month, in which Time the General drew up and reviewed the Forces on Canso Hill and formed the several detachments ordered to be employed in the several attacks proposed to be made immediately after their landing at flat point Cove, within three Miles of the Town of Louisbourgh to the W:S:W: and four Miles distance from the Grand Battery to the S:W: according to the plan of Operation concerted at Boston, and there given him in charge by the Governors written orders. During the Stay of the Troops there, a Block House was erected on Canso Hill and called Cumberland, the Flag being hoisted on his Royal Highness's Birth Day picquetted without, and defended by Eight Cannon of 9 nine Pound, and to be garrisoned by two Companies of Soldiers of Forty men each besides officers. From thence two armed Sloops were sent to Bay Vert to take or destroy some Vessels that according to information were to carry Provisions from thence to Louisbourgh. And the 18th of April the Renomee [Renommée], a French Ship of War of 30 Guns nine Pounders with three hundred Seamen and Fifty Marines being charged with publick Dispatches, fell in with the armed vessels in the Service of the Massachusetts Government before Louisbourgh Harbour; where she maintained a running Fight with them, but got clear by outsailing them: This Ship afterwards fell in with the Connecticut Troops under the Convoy of their own

Colony Sloop and the Rhode Island Colony Sloop the latter of which she attacked and damaged considerably, but finally the Sloop got off, as did the Troops with their other Convoy during the engagement and after having made two more attempts to push into the Harbour and been again hindered and chased by the Massachusetts Cruizers. returned to France without having delivered her Packetts. from whence she sailed again the beginning of July with six Ships more. being the Brest Squadron for Louisbourgh. The 22th of April Capt. [Philip] Durell in his Majesty's Ship Eltham of 40 Guns arrived at Canso Harbour from New England, having received orders from Mr. [Peter] Warren for that purpose, and on the 23rd Mr. Warren in his Majesty's Ship Superbe of 60 Guns with the Launceston of 40 Guns Capt. Kalmady [J. Calmady] and the Mermaid of 40 Guns, Capt [James] Douglas under his Command. And after staying there some Hours and conferred with the General by Letter, Mr. Warren with the rest of the King's Ships sailed to cruize off Louisbourgh.

On the 29th of April the Troops embarked in four divisions of Transports and sailed for Chappearouge Bay, under Convoy of one armed Snow, and two armed Sloops in the Service of the Massachusetts Government, under the Fire of whose Cannon they were to land. And at the same time a detachment of two hundred and Seventy men under the command of a Colonel [Jeremiah Moulton], and convoy of an armed Sloop in the pay of the New Hampshire Government, were sent to St. Peters, a small French settlement on Cape Breton with orders pursuant to the beforementioned plan of Operations to take the Place burn the Houses and demolish the Fort which was accordingly effected. On the 30th of April between nine and ten in the Morning, the Fleet having the main body of the Troops on board came to an Anchor in Chappearouge Bay, at the distance of about two Miles from flat point Cove: upon the discovery of which the Enemy immediately fired some Cannon, and rang their

Bells in the Town, to alarm and call in their people living in the Suburbs, and sent out of the Town a detachment of about 150 Men headed by Capt. Morepang [Morpain] and Mr. Boulerdrie [de la Boularderie] late an officer in the Duke of ——— [Richelieu's] Regiment in France to oppose the landing of our Troops upon the sight of which the General made a feint of landing a party of our men in Boats in Flat point Cove, in order to draw the French thither (which had its effect) and upon a signal from the Vessels the Boats returned and joined another party of Boats under his Stern, from whence under the Fire of our Cannon was landed, two Miles higher up the Bay, about 100 of our men before the Enemy could get up with them; and upon briskly attacking them, tho under the advantage of being covered with their Woods, after exchanging some shot killed six of them upon the Spot took as many prisoners (among whom was Mr. Boulerdrie) and wounded several other, forced the remainder to make a precipitate flight towards the Town, with the loss of some others, who were the next day taken prisoners before they recovered it; which was done with the damage on our part of only two Men's being slightly wounded. On the same day about two thousand of the Troops were landed without any farther opposition. And on the next day being the first of May the remainder landed, and began to get Provisions and Stores ashoar. The landing of Provisions Ammunition and heavy Artillery was attended with extreme difficulty and fatigue, there being no Harbour there, the Surf almost continually running very high so that frequently for some days there was no landing any thing at all, and when they did the Men were obliged to wade high into the Water, to save everything that would have been damaged by being wet, they had no Cloaths to shift themselves with, but poor defence from the Weather, at the same time the nights were very cold and generally attended with thick heavy fogs. By means whereof, it was near a fortnight before they could get all their Stores on shoar, and not withstanding all possible care to prevent it many Boats and some Stores were lost.—On May 2d a Detachment of four hundred men was sent round behind the Hills to the N: East Harbour, where they got about Midnight, and burnt the Enemy's Houses and stores about a Miles distance from the Grand Battery, and on the 3d of May we took possession of the Battery, which the Enemy had deserted, owing as it is supposed to the surprize they were in from the firing of the Houses in the Neighbour Towns They had abandoned this Battery in so much hurry and confusion that they had only spiked up their Guns, without breaking off any of the Trunions, or much damaging any of the Carriages. There were found here twenty eight 42 lb Cannon and two of Eighteen Pounds, three hundred and fifty Shells of 13 Inches and thirty Shells of ten Inches, and a large Quantity of Shot. The same day a party of the Enemy in Boats attempted to regain the possession of it, but were beat off by about fifteen or sixteen of our men who had before taken possession of the Battery, and stood on the Beach, exposed to the Enemy's Musquetry from the Boats and Cannon from the Town which played continually upon them. The Distance from the Grand Battery to the Island Battery is 4800 Feet. This Battery commands the whole Harbour from the entrance between the Light House Point and the Island Battery. Two Flanks of two Guns each point from hence against the Town, and a Line of Ten Guns against the Island Battery, the remainder to the N:East part of the Harbour. By the fire from hence during the Siege, the Citadel and Houses in the Town suffered very much as also the Barracks at the Island Battery: The Towers of this Battery were something damaged one man killed, and a few wounded by the Enemy's Cannon, which fired very briskly upon it, as did also their Mortars, from the Town and Island Battery, especially at the beginning. In a few days the Camp was formed about half a mile from the place where they made a feint of landing but without

throwing up lines, depending only upon their Scouts and Guards; but afterwards they encamped regularly and threw up lines nearer the place of landing their Stores. And Scouts during the whole Siege were constantly sent out, who seldom returned without bringing some prisoners, and very much confined the Enemy within their Walls, and prevented their making frequent Salies. May 4th We began to fire from the Grand Battery from three Cannon which had been cleared: as likewise to bombard the Town from Green Hill, being the place where the first Battery was planted (of one thirteen Inch Mortar one of eleven Inches and one of nine Inches, two Cannon nine Pounders and two Falconets) being two Miles distance from the Camp and fifteen hundred and fifty yards from the Citadel: Five Hundred Men were ordered to sustain this Battery; but finding the nine and eleven Inch Mortars would not reach the City they were removed the 7th of May, and planted with ten Coehorns at the distance of nine hundred Yards from the Citadel, where a Battery was erected the 10th of May of four 22 Pounders The thirteenth two of them burst, owing to their not being sound The fifteenth of May four 22 Pounders more were brought to this Battery as also the two nine Pounders and thirteen Inch Mortar from Green Hill: From this Battery the City was bombarded, and as the Shot from this Battery ranged through the Center of the City, it damaged not only the West Flank of the King's Bastion which it flanked; but also the Citadel and the greatest part of the houses in the Town and even Port Maurepas in the easternmost part of the City. This Battery was sustained by the same Forces that sustained the Battery at Green Hill. The damage received at this Battery was breaking the Trunion of one of the Coehorns and bursting another; six men wounded of whom one died, by the bursting of two 22: lb Cannon, one man killed and two wounded by the Enemy the same day. The 25th of May the thirteen Inch Mortar was burst and a Bombardier wounded, occasioned by some flaw in the Shell which broke in the Mortar. Another 13 Inch Mortar from Boston was mounted in the same place, and played the eighth day after the other was burst. The transporting the Cannon was with almost incredible labour and fatigue. For all the roads over which they were drawn, saving here and there small patches of rocky Hills, was a deep Morass, in which whilst the Cannon were upon Wheels, they several times sunk, so as to bury not only the Carriages, but the whole Body of the Cannon likewise. Horses and oxen could not be employed in this Service, but the whole was to be done by the Men. themselves up to the knees in Mud at the same time; the nights in which the Work was done cold and for the most part foggy; their Tents bad, there being no proper materials for Tents to be had in New England, at the time the Forces were raised. But notwithstanding all these difficulties, and the people's being taken down with Fluxes, so that at one time there was no less than 1500 Men incapable of duty, occasioned by their fatigue, they went on cheerfully without being discouraged or murmuring, and by the help of Sledges of about sixteen feet in length, and five feet in Width, and twelve Inches thick they transported the Cannon over these ways, which the French had always thought impassable for such heavy Bodies; and was indeed impracticable by any people of less resolution and perseverance, or less experience in removing heavy Weights; and besides this they had all the Provisions, Powder Shot and Shells, that they daily made use of, to transport over the same Ways, upon their Backs. During this time the French erected two Cavaliers of two Guns each, upon the Rampart of one of the Faces of the Kings Bastion; planted a great number of Swivel Guns upon the Wall facing the Harbour; and to secure the low Wall at the South East part of the Town, added to the top of it a Plank Work picketted, to raise it to the same height with the rest of the Wall, and a range of Pallisadoes at a little distance within the Wall, and raised a little

Battery of three small Guns upon the Parapet of the lower South Bastion fronting Cape Noir, a small Hill which very much commands the Town. May 7th a Flag of truce was sent into the Town with a Summons to deliver it up to his Brittanick Majesty to which an Answer was returned by Mr. [Louis] Du Chambon, Commander in chief, that the King his Master having intrusted him with the defence of the Island, he could not hearken to any such proposal, till after the most vigorous Attack, and that he had no Answer to make but by the Mouth of their Cannon. May 8th. The Enemy made a Sally, but were soon repulsed—The 13th. Notwithstanding all the Care and Vigilance of the Men of War and the Colony Cruizers, a Snow from Bourdeaux got in, which they attempted to fire by a Fireship from the Grand Battery, but in vain. May 16 The Coehorns and nine and eleven Inch Mortars were removed to a hill within 440 Yards of the West Gate, from whence they annoyed the Enemy very much and received no damage at all.—A Party of a hundred men came out of the Town in the night, and landed near the Light House Point, and the next day attempted to surprize a party, that was posted at the Light House, who first discovered the Enemy from an Eminence, where they were on Guard; forty only of our men advanced towards them; the Partys met in a Wood, and the Enemy was routed, five of them killed, and a Sixth the Lieutenant wounded and taken Prisoner; The rest that escaped joined some others and 80 Indians about Mera [Miré], and were attacked two days after by another Party of our Forces that were out on a Scout, this dispute lasted a considerable time, and several of our men made thirty discharges each on the enemy, who were again routed. In this Action there was but one Prisoner taken. Upon the return of this Party another Scout was sent out the next day, who returned in two days and brought ten Prisoners, who reported that many of their People were killed and wounded in the last skirmish. Our Scouts and Cruizers at different times took and burnt most of their small settlements near and took about 300 Prisoners.— The 17th of May the Advanced Battery was raised bearing W: b: N: ½ N 230 Yards distance from the West Gate, and one Eighteen Pounder mounted and the next night another Eighteen Pounder and two 42 Pounders were mounted; these were all brought from the Grand Battery upwards of two Miles as the Road goes, over a very rough rocky hilly way from hence not only the West Gate was beat down, but a breach made in the Wall adjoining, and the North East Battery was damaged and rendered almost useless, their Guns lying entirely open to the Fire from this Battery. This Battery being so near the Town, there was no safety in loading the Cannon but under the Fire of the Musquetry, which was very smart on both sides. The Enemy generally opened the Action in the Morning, with the Fire of their small Arms which we returned with Advantage, We were likewise warmly entertained by the Enemy from a Flank of their North East Battery, from the West Gate Battery and the West Flank of the King's Bastion, which had flanked this Battery and therefore on the 20th [May] a trench being dug on the South End, one Eighteen Pounder and two nine Pounders were brought from the Eight Gun Battery and mounted upon the South Line against this Flank, which with the remainder of the Guns at the Eight Gun Battery, dismounted some of the Enemy's Cannon, and annoyed them so much, that they were silent the rest of that day which was often the Case afterwards, particularly May 22d. The Fire was very hot on both sides till 12 a Clock at noon when the French were beat from their Guns, The 23d of May the Enemy mounted two new Guns at the West Flank of the King's Bastion but in four hours were forced to leave them. The 6th of June They had two Guns run out of new Embrazures cut thro the Parapet near the West Gate, which soon began to play with great fury, and we were obliged to turn three Guns against them, and in three hours we dismounted one and silenced

the other for that day. The nine and eleven Inch Mortars with constant use straining their Beds, occasioned their being removed to this Battery, which was nearer the Enemy, as were also the Coehorns. The Bombs in great number fell all round, but did very little damage. There were ten Men killed and fifteen or sixteen wounded several of them with Musquet Balls. In the meantime the Enemy worked constantly in the night to barricade the Gate way where a Breach was made; they also made a retrenchment across the Circular Battery, and raised another work to cover their Magazine, and laid a Boom before the Town to hinder Boats from landing under the Walls. At the same time our Men of War and Cruizers were very diligent, and took several Prizes and on the 19th of May there was an Engagement off the Harbour in sight of the Camp between some of our Ships and a French Man of War. The 21st a letter came to the General from Commodore Warren, acquainting him that he had taken the Vigilant a French Ship of 64 Guns, Besides the Superbe the Mermaid, Eltham, Massachusetts Frigate and Shirley Galley were all in the Engagement and at the taking of her Three days after the taking of the Vigilant Captain Edwards in the Princess Mary of 60 Guns joined the Commodore, and the next day Capt. [Frederick] Cornwall in the Hector of 40 Guns. The 20th of May the N: West Battery commonly called Titcombs Battery was erected, bearing N: W: b: W: about Eight Hundred Yards distant from the West Gate, and two 42 Pounders mounted, which were brought from the Grand Battery, and about a fortnight after were brought three 42 Pounders more. This Battery did great Execution against the Circular Battery. By means of this Battery and the Advanced Battery, not only the West Gate was demolished, but a large breach was made in the Wall to within ten feet of the Bottom of the Ditch, the Circular Battery was almost entirely demolished but three Guns out of Sixteen being left standing, and these so exposed to the N: West Battery that nobody could keep the Platform. The West Flank of the King's Bastion was almost entirely ruined, but in some Measure repaired with Timber This Battery the advanced Battery and the Eight Gun Battery were sustained by thirteen hundred and fifty Men. After many fruitless preparations for an Attack on the Island Battery, it was attempted on the 26th of May at night by a party of 400 Men, but from the Strength of the Place, and the advantage the Enemy had of being under cover and our men exposed in open Boats, which a Musquett Ball would sink, the Surf running very high, and their not being thoroughly acquainted with the best place of landing, they were repulsed, with the loss of about Sixty killed and drowned and a hundred and Sixteen taken prisoners. The 10th of June the Chester arrived from England, and joined the Comodore, and on the 12th the Canterbury and Sunderland, as did likewise the Lark with a Store Ship under her Convoy bound to Annapolis Royal. It being of the utmost consequence to be Masters of the Island Battery (The Island Battery is a strong Fort at the entrance into the Harbour, mounted with thirty twenty eight Pounders, and seven Swivels, having two Brass ten Inch Mortars, and garrisoned with 180 Men) and after the last Attempt thought impracticable to reduce it by Boats, it was determined to erect a Battery near the Light House opposite to it which would be 3400 feet distant and in such a manner, as to be opposed to the Fire of but Four of the Enemy's Guns, and at the same time to Flank a line of above twenty of their Guns, which, notwithstanding the almost insuperable difficulties that attended it, was happily effected, and two Eighteen Pounders mounted the 11th of June and by the 14th four more sustained by three hundred and twenty Men. (The difficulties were the transporting of the Cannon in Boats from Chappeaurouge Bay to the Eastward of the Light House, the getting them up the Bank of the Shoar, which was a Steep craggy Rock, the haling them a Mile and a quarter over an incredible bad way of Hills and Rocks and Mor-

asses.) Powder growing short, the Fire had for some days been very much slackened, and the French began to creep a little out of the Cazmates of Cover, where they had hid themselves during the greatest fierceness of it. But this being the Anniversary of His Majesty's happy Accession to the throne it was determined to celebrate it as became loyal Subjects and brave Soldiers, and Orders were given for a discharge of all the Cannon from every Battery at twelve a Clock, which was accordingly done and followed by an incessant fire all the rest of the day, which much disheartened the Enemy, especially as they were sensible, what must necessarily be the consequence of this New Battery. It was now determined as soon as possible after the Arrival of the Canterbury and Sunderland, to make a general Attack by Sea and Land, accordingly, they arriving the next day all the transports were ordered off to take out the Spare Masts Yards and other Lumber of the Men of War: the Soldiers were employed in gathering Moss to barricade their Nettings, and Six Hundred Men were sent on board the King's Ships at the Commodore's request, the Large Mortar was ordered to the Light House Battery; and a new supply of Powder arriving the fire was more fierce from this time to the fifteenth than ever; when the Mortar began to play from the Light House Battery upon the Island Battery, out of nineteen Shells seventeen fell within the Fort and one of them upon the Magazine, which together with the Fire from the Cannon, to which the Enemy was very much exposed, they having but little to shelter them from the Shot that ranged quite thro' their Barracks, so terrified them that many of them left the post and run into the water for refuge.

The Grand Battery being in our possession, the Island Battery being so much annoyed by the Light House Battery, the North East Battery so open to our Advanced Battery, that it was not possible for the Enemy to stand to their Guns, all the Guns in the circular Battery, except three, being dismounted, and the Wall almost wholly broke down, the West Gate demolished, and a large Breach in the Wall adjoining, the West Flank of the King's Bastion almost ruined, all the Houses and other Buildings almost tore to pieces, but one house in the Town being left unhurt, and the Enemy's Stock of Ammunition growing short, they sent out a Flag of Truce to the Camp, desiring time to consider upon Articles of Capitulation, this was granted till the next morning, when they brought out Articles, which were refused; and others sent in by the General and Commodore, and agreed to by the Enemy: Hostages were exchanged and on the seventeenth of June the City and Fortresses were surrendered and the Garrison and all the Inhabitants, to the number of two thousand capable of bearing Arms, made Prisoners, to be transported to France with all their personal Effects. During the whole Siege we had not more than a hundred and one Men killed by the Enemy and all other Accidents, and about thirty died of Sickness. And according to the best Accounts there were killed of the Enemy within the Walls about three Hundred, besides numbers that died by being confined within the Cazmates.

D. The New England Reaction to the Capture of Louisbourg

New Englanders welcomed the news of the fall of Louisbourg with an outburst of prolonged and unprecedented celebration. Numerous thanksgiving sermons were preached by gleeful clerics and many would-be-poets cranked out special broadsides to commemorate Louisbourg's capture. New England's special sense of mission was strengthened and an increasing number of inhabitants began to think that they were innately superior to any other nation. For did not one of the leading French officers captured at Louisbourg declare "that he thought the New England men were Cowards—but now he thought that if they had a pick ax and spade—they would dig their way to hell and storm it?"

The two following documents are examples of the broadsides and sermons published in New England in 1745.

Document D–1

NEW ENGLAND BRAVERY: BROADSIDE

(————, *New England Bravery* [Boston, 1745].)

Come all New England's gallant Lads,
and lend to me an Ear,
And of your Brethren's Acts
I will in short declare.
Brave Pep'rell with Three Thousand Men,
(perhaps some hundreds more)
Did land the very first of *May*,
upon *Cape Breton* Shore:
And tho' opposed by Morepang
with full two hundred Men,

A handful of our gallant Lads
did drive them back again.
Some few were taken Prisoners,
and many kill'd out-right
Which taught the *French* at *Louisbourg*
New England Men can fight.
The *Monsieurs* all astonished
to see our Armament,
Were griev'd to see that they must be
within Stone Walls all pent.

In haste they call in to their Aid
the Men upon the Isle
Forgetting their own Poverty,
(such things would make one smile)
But what is vastly more absurd
Then anything like this,
They quitted the *Grand Battery*,
The Glory of the Place.
Of which our *English* Lads did take
Possession quietly,
And with the Guns did ever since
the Enemy annoy.
They also did with mighty Toil
their Batteries erect,
Against the Town and Citadel
which play'd with good Effect.
They sent such Showers of Bombs and Balls
as made the *Frenchmen* quake,
And sputter out such words as these,
Those Dogs the Place will take.
Our Men did also batter down
The West Gate and the Wall,

And made therein so large a Breach
That to the French they'd call,
Come out; Jack Frenchmen, come to us,
and drink a Bowl of Punch.
Jack Frenchman *cries, you English Dogs,
come, here's a pretty Wench.*
But by and by they change their Tones,
and after Terms of Peace,
Which if consented to they would
surrender up the Place.
(For they were so severely maul'd
by Cannon Shot and Shells,
That they no Place of Safety found
on Platforms or in Cells. . . .)
Our Gen'ral upon this Success
did send *Monsieurs* Words,
If they would not give up the Place,
He'd put them to the Sword.
And now not daring to withstand
The Force of all our Bands,
They gave up all their Fortresses
into our *English* Hands.

Document D–2

THE GENERAL THANKSGIVING SERMON

(T. Prince, *Extraordinary Events the Doings of God, and marvellous in pious Eyes* [Boston, 1747], pp. 33–35.)

And now who can in common Reason deny a *particular Providence* in this great Affair? Who can in Reason imagine that such a *Multitude* of *various* and *contrary* running *Wheels*, both of *material Causes* and *spontaneous* Agents, shou'd all be made to work together, and in the midst of Thousands of Difficulties and Contingencies, in the happiest Seasons coincide, to accomplish *this* great Event; without a supream *Contriver, Mover* and *Director?* We may a thousand Times more consistently apprehend the *most curious Engine* in the World to be made without Design, and to work without a moving Power.

Yea, Those who own not *These* to be the *Operations* of God, as a wife, sovereign, free and actual Ruler among Men and Elements; must not only deny the *Scriptures*, but even the very *Foundations* of all Religion, or Adoration of this supream Governour. For they must deny there is any Need, or Duty, or Wisdom, of fearing Him, or praying to Him, or

hoping on Him in any Emergencies; or of acknowledging, admiring, praising, loving, or thanking Him, for the *greatest* and *most marvellous Salvations.*

But as for *Us*—In the *Name* of God, *our* God in Christ, yea in the *Name* of the Son of God, as supream Lord and Ruler of Heaven and Earth, of Men, Angels and Elements, we lifted up our Banners: To *Him* we looked and prayed: In *Him* we put our Trust and fought: And now, *He* has heard and prosper'd, to *Him* we will ascribe *the Praise.*

Whatever *Instruments* or *Means* He us'd, we will bless Him for them; we see them form'd, endow'd, excited by Him; we see them in his mighty and all-active Hands, deriving Strength and Guidance from Him, and employ'd continually to fulfill his Pleasure. We will own, the Work is his in the highest Sense: It was all comprehended in his sovereign View, Design and Providence; begun, carried on, accomplish'd by his all-governing Wisdom,

Power and Efficacy; and the Whole together is marvellous in every serious Eye.

When the Tydings came on our *Commencement*-Morning *July* 3, of surrendring the City, 'we were like them that dream: 'Our Mouth was fill'd with Laughter, and 'our Tongue with Singing: Even the 'Heathen said, *The* Lord *hath done great* 'Things for them; and We—*The* Lord 'hath done great Things for us, whereof 'we are glad. Not unto us, O Lord, not 'unto us, but unto thy Name give Glory: 'Our God hath done whatsoever he 'pleased: The Lord hath been mindful of 'us: And we will bless the Lord, from this 'Time forth and for ever. Thine O Lord is 'the Greatness, and the Power, and the 'Glory, and the Victory, and the Majesty: 'For all that is in the Heaven and in the 'Earth is thine; thine is the Kingdom O 'Lord, and thou art exalted as Head above 'all: Both Riches and Honour come of 'Thee, and thou reignest over all, and in 'thine Hand is Power and Might; and in 'thine Hand it is to make Great, and to 'give Strength to all: Now therefore our 'God, we thank Thee and praise thy 'glorious Name. Give Thanks to the Lord, 'call on his Name, make known his Deeds 'among the People: Sing unto Him, sing 'Psalms unto Him, talk ye of all his 'wondrous Works: Declare his Glory 'among the Heathen, his marvellous Works 'among all Nations.'

O that when we have *sang his Praise*, we may not ungratefully *forget his Works*, or return to *Sin*; which is to rob Him of his deserved Glory and fly in the Face of our great Preserver and Benefactor: It is the vilest Degree of Ingratitude and provoking Baseness: It is to fight against Him, who has been marvellously fighting for *us*, and given us a wondrous Series of great Salvations. Yea, this will be the dangerous Way to move Him to turn *our Enemy*; to change the Course of his slighted Dispensations, and give *the Place* into our Adversaries Hands again, with a more dreadful and mischievous Increase of Power than ever, to punish us. And the

Sins of *Drunkenness, Profanation* of the *Name* and *Day* of God, *Uncleanness, Injustice, Oppression, Contempt* of Christ, and *Opposition* to the *Purity, Power* and *Practice* of *his holy Religion*; are some of the highest and most dangerous Provocations and Preparatives to ruinous Judgment.

Yea, *distinguishing Appearances* of God to save and prosper us, are *distinguishing Obligations*, not only to *distinguishing Degrees* of *Joy* and *Praise*, but also to *distinguishing Degrees* of *Piety*: i.e. of active Gratitude and Love to God, of perpetual Contrivances and Labours to promote his Glory and holy Kingdom in Ourselves and Others, and a constant Life of Service to His Cause and People. And as the *Failure* of this, will not be a rendring to Him according to his signal Benefits, but a most *ungrateful* Treatment of Him; *His Eyes* are always on us, to observe us *now*, and to judge and Recompence us *Here* or *Hereafter*.

But let us rejoice, not only in *our own Salvation*, the Salvation of *all our Colonies*, and some of the most important Branches of the *British Trade*;—But let our Joy rise higher, that hereby a *great Support* of *Antichristian* Power is taken away, and the *visible Kingdom* of Christ enlarged. Methinks, when the southern *Gates of Louisbourg* were opened, and our Army with their Banners marching in; *the Gates were lifted up—the Gates were lifted up—and the* King *of* Glory went in with them. Even the Son of God, the Lord of Hosts, the Lord strong and mighty in Battle—having gain'd the Conquest, he rode in in Triumph and took Possession. He set up his Standard, proclaim'd his Gospel of Peace, the Glad Tydings of Salvation, open'd the Prisons, redeem'd his Captives, and began to receive his grateful Incense of pure Adorations. O that There, in Purity of Worship, Doctrine and Conversation, in the Power of his Grace and in the Glory of his Holiness, He may reign and shine to all the Islands round about, as long as the Sun and Moon endure.

PROBLEM 5

The Quebec Schools Question, 1784-90

L. F. S. UPTON
University of British Columbia

Canadian history has been punctuated with controversies over education from primary school to university. This issue was one of the most divisive in the Union of the Canadas that preceded Confederation; New Brunswick in the 1870's, Manitoba in the 1890's, and Ontario in the second decade of this century all found themselves in bitter struggles that carried across provincial boundaries to affect the whole relationship between French and English Canadians. The issue is now thought of in terms of language, but it was originally a religious conflict between Roman Catholic and Protestant. The 19th-century Canadian could get more excited over religion than over any other question, and when religious enthusiasm ebbed, it was replaced by racial pride. The contest centred on the schools because they were the transmitters of culture; control of them meant control of the future.

The contest began in the 18th century with the cession of New France to Britain and the introduction of a culture that measured itself in Protestant, English-speaking, and mercantile terms. Education had been entirely in the hands of the Roman Catholic Church orders, and the conquerors viewed such men with disfavour. Higher education languished, and since the church's ties with France were cut, there was a decline in both the quality and the quantity of the parish clergy who were responsible for primary schooling. As the literacy rate declined, the majority of the inhabitants did indeed become ignorant peasants, and the English assumed that it was all part of a popish plot to keep the faithful in darkness. But the English cast them further into the darkness when they converted the Quebec seminary into a barracks, an act that summed up their contempt for Roman Catholic education. Since the natives were so ignorant, the highest positions in business and government went to the newcomers, who had received their education elsewhere.

A whole generation passed before the government attempted to raise the general level of education. French Canadian voices were heard, in a mildly secular tone, demanding that improvements be made; English merchants who had come to stay and were raising families demanded better standards; Loyalist

97

refugees from the old colonies saw education as a basic social right. And although all were concerned with education from the primary level, all concentrated their attention on the future university that was to crown the system. The university would train the governing class of the future and all those who would fashion Quebec after their own image. And what was that image to be? The ensuing controversy brought to light the whole range of ambitions and suspicions and animosities that were to become so familiar in the years ahead.

Personalities played a large part in the development of the controversy, but each individual stood for a train of thought that was to have a long life. The Roman Catholic Bishop, Hubert, fearful of a covert attack on religion, argued that a university was unnecessary in a land of pioneer farmers. This defensive reaction was typical of his church's mentality until the ultramontane revival of the 1840's turned the negative aspects of this same agricultural society into positive virtues. The Coadjutor Bishop, Bailly, had thrown his lot in with the English, and had been advanced to his high position in the Roman Catholic Church as the governor's man. Obviously anxious to ingratiate himself further, he took an essentially secular attitude toward education that was, despite his motivation, a true forecast of *rouge* arguments in later years. The spirits of Hubert and Bailly have wrestled for the control of Quebec's education to this day.

The only Anglican bishop in British America was Charles Inglis, Bishop of Nova Scotia. He was a Loyalist, convinced of the necessity of a strong state church to support the government and instruct subjects in their duties to the king. Failure to create such a church, as he knew to his cost, had helped lead to revolution. He had to ensure that his church gained the same special relationship to the state in Quebec that it held in England. Successive Anglican bishops in Canada and the Maritime provinces fought to attain that position down to the eve of Confederation, and one of their principal weapons was the control of university education. They were tenaciously opposed by other Protestants, dissenters from the Anglican Church, who argued that religion had no place in what should be a public institution. Such a man was the Presbyterian Chief Justice William Smith, a Loyalist as was Inglis, but of very different beliefs. He had led a campaign in New York in the 1750's to prevent the Anglicans from controlling that colony's first university. He had failed then and did not intend to fail again. As chairman of the Quebec council's committee on education he was in a good position to advance the cause of a state-controlled university that ignored denominational religion. The spirits of Inglis and Smith wrestled for the control of English Canada's education for 80 years before Smith won.

The rivalries of Hubert and Bailly, of Inglis and Smith, should not obscure what was immediately at stake. Education had developed in New France as a branch of the missionary effort among the Indians, and it was inevitable that it should be considered as having a fixed purpose beyond the mere dissemination of knowledge. That object was the inculcation of virtue as defined by the Roman Catholic Church. But if education came into the hands of the state, would it not continue to inculcate virtue? And who would then interpret virtue? Presumably the Protestant, English-speaking mercantile minority that ruled Quebec on behalf of Britain. The imperial government agreed that education was basically a form of state propaganda. The attempt to renovate a defective school system failed because education could not be separated from the clash of cultures.

For those interested in further study, the best treatments of education in Quebec are Louis Philippe Audet, *Le Système Scolaire de la Province de Québec*, Vol. II (1951), and Abbé Lionel Groulx, *L'enseignement français au Canada*, Vol. I (1931); see also Armand Martineau, "Programme des études au Canada durant la periode 1760–1790," in *Révue de l'Université d'Ottawa*, Vol. XXXVII, No. 2 (1967), pp. 206–30. The background for this period can be studied in A. L. Burt, *The Old Province of Quebec* (1933), and Hilda M. Neatby, *Quebec, the Revolutionary Age* (1967).

A. The School System

No survey of the school system in Quebec was attempted until 1789 when the council committee on education circulated a questionnaire. The reply of Bishop Hubert gave a survey of education carried out under the auspices of the Roman Catholic Church. English language education was offered by a number of individual schoolmasters, and the reply of one of them, Daniel Keith, describes a typical private school of the day.

How adequate was this system for a colony with a population of about 150,000? What differences in emphasis were there between French and English language schools?

Document A—1
ROMAN CATHOLIC EDUCATION IN QUEBEC

(Bishop Jean François Hubert, November 18, 1789, in *Report of a Committee of the Council on the Subject of Promoting the Means of Education* [Quebec, 1790], pp. 11–15, 17–18.)

Question: What schools are there, and what kind of instruction? What their support?

Answer: The reverend fathers the Jesuits of Quebec, before the year 1776, always kept or caused to be kept a well regulated school, where young persons were taught reading, writing and arithmetic. This school was free to every one. But government having thought fit to lodge the records of the province in the only apartment of the house where scholars could be admitted, the reverend fathers could not continue the good work.

There are some Canadian masters in town, who for payment, teach reading and writing. Their schools are regular and daily, and pretty well frequented. The parents of the children sent there are tolerably well satisfied with the progress they make.

At Montreal, the seminary ever since the time of its institution, has supported a free school, where children of all ranks are taught reading and writing. Books are given them gratis. This school, remarkable for its extreme regularity, has had 300 children at a time.

The nuns or congregated sisters at Montreal have a numerous boarding school for the instruction of young gentlewomen. The Ursuline nuns at Quebec and Three Rivers have each another boarding school. Also the nuns of the general hospital of Quebec. The young ladies in these schools are taught reading, writing, needle and other work suitable to the sex, such as embroidery, etc. But above all things, they are taught virtue. Public schools are also kept for young women in the three towns of the province: one at Montreal by the congregated sisters, one at Three Rivers by the Ursulines, one at Quebec by the Ursulines and one by the sisters in the Lower Town. The schools kept in the country parishes by missions from the congregated sisters, must not be forgotten. They spread a great deal of instruction. These communities at their own charge support their respective schools; and they are also supported and encouraged by the attention and vigilance of the superiors of the church, who are careful to see that the intent of the establishments be fulfilled. Above all things, the minds of the children in those schools are inspired with morality, and a love and veneration for religion, the principles of which they are taught to understand.

There are some English masters who teach schools at Quebec, Montreal and Three Rivers, but I do not know their different branches of instruction, nor their support.

Question: Can it be true that there are not more than half a dozen in a parish that are able to write or read?

Answer: Such a report, it is true, is publicly spoken of, and if I mistake not, maliciously spread abroad, to disgrace the Canadians. . . . I am convinced that upon an average, from twenty-four to thirty persons may easily be found in every parish who can read and write. 'Tis true the number of women so instructed exceeds that of the men.

Question: The cause of the imperfect state of instruction. What kinds of public and general tuition are established? What the funds? What the income? To what the uses and ends?

Answer: Classical learning and rhetoric are publicly taught in the College of Montreal since the year 1773, and geography and arithmetic are beginning to be taught. I have reason to expect this establishment will in time produce a good effect. The proprietors of the college solicited me in September last to let them have a professor of philosophy and mathematics, and I shall do all in my power to procure them one. The college belongs to the administrators of the parish church revenues of Montreal, it has no other fund than the board paid by the students, and the liberality of the ecclesiastics of the seminary. . . . Boys, who cannot afford to live in the college as boarders, are received as day scholars, for the moderate sum of one guinea per annum.

The seminary at Quebec was founded and endowed by Mr. Francis De Laval Montmorency, first bishop of Canada. Its own revenues support it. . . . This seminary, by its constitution, is only held to instruct young clergymen for the service of the diocese; but since the conquest of the province by his Britannic majesty's arms, public instruction has been voluntarily and gratuitously given. Theology, the classics, rhetoric, moral and natural philosophy, geography, arithmetic, and all the different branches of the mathematics are taught. It has produced, and produces daily, learned men in all the sciences they have studied, capable of doing honor to their education, and to their country. . . .

When English young gentlemen have desired to come into the seminary, they have been admitted there upon the same footing with Canadians, without any distinction or partiality. They were exempted, however, from attending religious duties, differing from the principles of their belief. . . .

Question: Whence proceed the discouragements and faults?

Answer: It may be answered, that of all the young gentlemen, naturally studious and virtuous, who have begun their studies at a fit age, not one has been discouraged at the seminary; . . . some of stubborn dispositions, little adapted for the sciences . . . have gone away ignorant, and unfortunately, judging by their incapacity, an unfavourable opinion is entertained of the learning to be acquired in the seminary. Hence proceeds the idea, pretty generally propagated, that none are admitted into the classes there, but such as are disposed to take up an ecclesiastical life; that their instruction is directed only to that study, and otherwise very contracted; an idea, that could not be repressed even by the publication in the Quebec Gazette . . . which announced to the English and French youth the opening of the ordinary mathematical class at the seminary, wherein would be taught, according to usage for twenty years back, arithmetic, algebra, geometry, trigonometry, together with the conic sections and tactics, in both languages, and without expence to the scholars.

The preference given to old subjects [English], and even to strangers, over the Canadians, in appointments to public offices and places of trust may, perhaps, be an additional cause of discouragement: but this is not within my sphere, nor is it with me to enquire whether such complaints are well or ill founded. . . .

Question: By what means can a taste or desire for instruction be excited in the parishes?

Answer: This, in my opinion, should be committed to the zeal and vigilance of the curates, supported by the country magistrates.

A calumnious writer hath maliciously reported to the public, that the clergy of this province do all in their power to keep the people in ignorance, in order to domineer over them. I do not know upon what ground he has been able to found so rash a proposition, contradicted by the care always taken by the clergy to procure to the people such instruction as they are susceptible of. The severity of the climate of this country; the distances between the houses of its country inhabitants; the difficulty of assembling the children of a parish into one place, especially in the winter as often as it would be necessary for their education; the inconvenience to a teacher of going daily to a great number of private houses: such are the obstacles that have rendered useless the desires of many of the curates, whose efforts to instruct the children of their parishes are within my knowledge. But in towns or villages, such as l'Assomption, Boucherville, La Prairie de la Madeleine, Terrebonne, La Riviere de Chesne, etc., we have the pleasure of finding the people, in general, pretty well informed; most of these villages are supplied with schoolmasters.

Document A–2

ENGLISH LANGUAGE EDUCATION IN QUEBEC

(Letter of Daniel Keith, October, 1790, in State Records of the Executive Council of Quebec, R.G. 1, E 1, Vol. CXV, pp. 416–19, *Public Archives of Canada*.)

In consequence of your application I send you the following particulars.

1st. The number of my scholars, at present, does not exceed thirty two. They are of various ages from eight to seventeen.

2d. They are instructed in the following branches, *vizt*: Reading and spelling English, writing, cyphering, bookkeeping, geometry, mensuration, plain and oblique trigonometry, the elements of algebra, the use of the globes, the Latin and Greek languages and the grammatical part of the French language.

3d. Mr. Selby Burn, my brother-in-law, a very worthy young man, and who writes an elegant hand, has been two years my assistant. He understands and figures perfectly. His age is twenty one, my own is thirty one.

4th. Six guineas yearly, including pens, paper, ink and fire, have been my ostensible fees for four years past. From this sum I have been obliged in some cases to deviate, in order to suit the circumstances of my employers. In no case, however, have I received less than four guineas, except for a few poor ones, whom I have taught gratis. My boarders, if under twelve years of age, pay twenty five pounds currency. Washing, lodging and education are included. If above twelve years of age, they pay thirty pounds yearly. These prices have never been increased, but frequently diminished according to circumstances.

My present number of scholars is not so great as it has been. Many of my young pupils have left me last summer, being thought qualified to enter business. Their places might have been supplied from the lower schools in town, if I had thought it proper to admit them upon their terms.

For three years I employed a French teacher recommended by Mons. St. Hu-bert the Cure of Quebec and gave him a decent allowance for his trouble. Since June last, I have endeavoured myself to supply his place, having a tolerable knowledge of the grammatical part of the French language.

It is now five years since I began my labours in Quebec and can honestly say, that meat and drink have not been more agreeable to me than my daily work. In the course of it I have met with many difficulties from untoward children, indulgent parents and precarious payments; yet upon the whole I have the happiness to think, that many have profited under my tuition and that my school merits some degree of fame.

B. Criticism

The English who had come to live in Quebec were appalled at the low quality of education and were very free with their condemnation. Hugh Finlay, a member of the colonial council, argued that the widespread ignorance made political reform impossible. This deplorable situation had come about largely due to the English conquest itself, according to a petition signed by 195 persons, both French and English. A council committee reviewed the situation early in 1787 and suggested changes.

Who had the responsibility for education in the province? How disastrous had been the results of the conquest? Where would financial support for education be found?

Document B–1

AN ENGLISH COMMENT

(Hugh Finlay to Evan Nepean, October 22, 1784, in Adam Shortt and Arthur G. Doughty [eds.], *Documents Relating to the Constitutional History of Canada, 1759–1791* [Ottawa, 1918], pp. 739–42.)

The advocates for a house of assembly in this province take it for granted that the people in general wish to be represented; but that is only a guess, for I will venture to affirm that not a Canadian landholder in fifty ever once thought on the subject and were it to be proposed to him, he would readily declare his incapacity to judge of the matter. Although the Canadian peasants are far from being a stupid race, they are at present an ignorant people, from want of instruction —not a man in five hundred among them can read; perhaps it has been the policy of the clergy to keep them in the dark, as it is a favourite tenet with the Roman Catholic priests, ignorance is the mother of devotion. The females in this country have great advantage over the males in point of education. The sisters of the congregation, or grey sisters as they are called, are settled in the country parishes here and there to teach girls to read, write, sew, and knit stockings: there's only a few of that sisterhood—they are the most useful of any of the religious orders in Canada.

Before we think of a house of assembly for this country, let us lay a foundation for useful knowledge to fit the people to judge of their situation, and deliberate for the future well-being of the province. The first step towards this desirable end, is to have a free school in every parish— Let the schoolmasters be English if we would make Englishmen of the Canadians; let the masters be Roman Catholics if it is necessary, for perhaps the people, at the instigation of the priests, would not put their children under the tuition of a protestant. . . .

Document B–2

A CITIZENS' PETITION

(November 19, 1787, Colonial Office Records, Q Series, M.G. 11, Vol. XXXV, pp. 64–117, Public Archives of Canada.)

A public and free education is essentially necessary and advantageous in every good government, which cannot subsist without citizens, nor the citizens without virtue. To make them men, and virtuous, they should receive instruction early in life. If, from their infancy, they are trained up to observe good precepts, to nourish humanity in their bosoms, to have a proper knowledge of their existence, of the social duties and of the true interest of their country, which is that of their sovereign, and to consider themselves, only in the relation they bear, individually, with the great body of the nation, they perceive themselves becoming members of the state, they support it, contribute to its prosperity, and love it with those exquisite sentiments which, for want of education, the unimproved and ignorant man, has for himself only. Children, brought up in common upon the footing of equality, instructed in the laws of God and man, respecting and fulfilling them; surrounded with examples and objects of liberality, who converse with them about the mother country that protects them, about the affection which she has for them, and the acknowledgements they owe in return; these learn first by education, and afterwards by sentiment, to substitute manly actions for that dangerous slothfulness and poverty in which a state of ignorance, and of indifference for great things, absorbs them. In a word, virtue, acquired and cherished by the hand of education, makes them good and enlightened subjects, transforms their idleness into activity, their cowardice into magnanimity, and their poverty into riches or industry, so as to harbour no fear of any attack or invasion from a neighbouring enemy, and to become, gradually, the defenders, resembling the fathers, of that country where of they shall have been the children.

If, in every country, the education of youth is found to be so necessary and profitable to mankind, and even to the government, how much more indispensibly so is it in Canada, from its unhappy situation, where both the soil and climate impose the necessity of procuring, by activity and industry, that which wild nature lavishes to more fortunate climates? Greatly distant from the mother country, the inhabitants of this province should be sufficiently instructed, sufficiently vigorous, interested and active, to resist the unforeseen or sudden attacks of their neighbours, who have not been negligent of their colleges for education, their estates, their power or their ambition.

The first settlement of Canada could

not seriously be undertaken without a college for a public and free education. Its first sovereign should have been the founder; but in order to render that respect to literature which no doubt they had received, virtuous citizens anticipated the royal grace, by giving estates and monies to build and perpetually support the college of Quebec, for the instruction of its natives and inhabitants. The then sovereign, or the antient government, was only the powerful and constant protector.

The Canadians of the present generation owe it to themselves, as well as the succeeding generations, to prevent the reproaches which could be imputed to them, on account of that state of ignorance in which the far greater part of the youth of the present day are lost, for want of a public education since the conquest, altho' endued naturally with propitious dispositions, and endowed with a college for their free instruction. Various troubles, the instability of the municipal laws, the people without a sufficient representation expecting everything from the goodness and justice of government; the fear of the teachers to continue teaching without the direct approbation of government, possession of the college taken for the use of the troops for ten years past; the hope that at the last peace things would have been put upon a better footing; these, and many other causes may be considered as a sufficient excuse for the time past: but now, when the public tranquility allows the mother country to put her colonies in the most flourishing state, the province would be wanting to itself and to government, whose interests are inseparably united, if it neglected humbly and confidently to represent . . . the principal causes that have deprived the Canadians of their education in the College of Quebec since the conquest. . . .

The managers and professors of the college, altho' they remained in possession [after the conquest], did not obtain the approbation of government to continue the education of youth, from whom heretofore civil officers, good militia officers, commercial persons, navigators, and intelligent tradesmen were formed. All, for want of a public education, remained in ignorance of the laws divine and human, of reading, writing, and even of the English language, which they should learn in their college, and which it was the interest of the new government to encourage by the education and advantage of a foundation so antient and profitable to the state.

The citizens were divided; there were no municipal officers for affairs of this nature; and no representatives for the Canadians. Fathers of families who were unable to pay, or could find no schoolmaster to teach grammar, or even the first principles of learning in which the College was bound to instruct their children, wept for their fate. . . . The youth remained in ignorance; the greater part of them deprived of their patrimony, ruined by the war and the discredit of their paper money, grew old in misery. 'Tis true, the managers of the college not being permitted to teach, employed their revenues in charities, which want quickly consumed without procuring the advantages perpetuated by education.

In 1770 the best families were become poor and indolent, their property diminished at least two thirds in their value, and various reasons had occasioned a remarkable emigration since the conquest; consequently commerce languished, and the mother country suffered by it. At that time the governor had the best intentions for the province, but it was necessary that some constitution should be fixed for it, and it was found difficult to do so in England. A number of the most considerable Canadian subjects sent home to administrations their most humble supplications for their college of Quebec; but probably the multiplicity of business prevented attention to that object, they remained unanswered. . . .

In 1776 his majesty's troops were lodged in the college which is situated in the center of the Upper Town of Quebec; many reasons justified it, it was thought to be only for a short time; but it still continues, though those reasons may have ceased, and the neighbourhood, composing the most elegant quarter and the most frequented, receives a foetid air and is continually mixed with the troops. . . .

The college is for education that which the parochial church is to Christians; the one makes them children of God, the other children of the state, by instructing them and rendering them capable to know their country, to love it, serve, support and contribute to its prosperity by their abilities and virtue. Parish and college often go together in the settlement of a colony, which was the case in Canada. . . .

The causes that have deprived the Canadians of their education in the college of Quebec since the conquest having ceased, nothing seems to be required from the bounty and justice of government than to dislodge the troops, and to allow a lawful and competent assembly of his majesty's faithful Canadian subjects whether natives or residents in the province, possessing lands and indiscriminately being heads of families, having an essential interest therein for themselves and their posterity, for the purpose of electing a proper number to represent them as directors or managers of the said college and its estates; to preserve them, collect the revenues, sue or defend by the titles and the laws of this country which establish their functions, cause exactly to be fulfilled the wishes of this laudable foundation, by soliciting the approbation of government to restore the antient professors of the college or to name others, and regulate the recompence due to their talents and attentions.

Document B–3

A COMMITTEE REPORT

(January 5, 1787, in Shortt and Doughty, *Documents*, pp. 907–8.)

The Report of the Committee of Council on Commerce and Police. . . . Article 22d:

The establishing of schools and seminaries for the education of youth, from those funds now unemployed as well in England as in this province, and particularly a respectable college in this city, with able professors, and erecting free schools at convenient distances throughout this extensive province, for the purpose of opening and enlarging the human mind, conciliating the affections of all his majesty's subjects, and having a tendency to render this a happy and flourishing province.

Observation: The education of youth in this province except in the cities where indeed the schools cannot be boasted of, is confined altogether to the female sex, there are some five or six small indifferent schools dispersed thro' the country kept by nuns called sisters of the congregation, for instructing girls, but not a single one that deserves the name for educating boys, hence all the inhabitants are unhappily ignorant of the use of letters, and incapable of reading or writing, a situation truly lamentable!

We are informed that the fund in England piously and generously contributed for the propagation of Christian knowledge in foreign parts, is in a great measure now unemployed, from the circumstances of the United States of America having separated themselves from Great Britain.

We are also informed that the society of Jesuits is shortly to be suppressed and dissolved and their property and estates vested in the crown.

We understand that the estates granted to the Jesuits were for the purpose of building a college and endowing it and the revenues arising therefrom to be applied to the education of youth, and that before the conquest of Canada a very considerable number of students were constantly educated in that college. Such being the deplorable state of this country with respect to useful learning, and such the ample provision made as a remedy to so great a misfortune as a state of ignorance confessedly is.—We have humbly to recommend that application be made thro' the proper channel for a participation of the first mentioned fund, and we humbly trust that his majesty out of his paternal goodness will be graciously pleased to direct that the Jesuits estates and the revenues thereof, may be applied to the endowment of a college or university in this city with able professors for the education of the youth of all British America and for building and maintaining free schools with proper masters for teaching the English language and other branches of education throughout this extensive province on an approved liberal plan. Posterity requires at our hands our endeavour to procure them so great a blessing which we supplicate both on their behalf and our own. . . .

C. The Conflict of Ideas

Charles Inglis, Bishop of Nova Scotia, the only Anglican prelate in British America, was consulted on the means of improving Quebec's education. He advised the creation of a university that would impress the virtues of Anglicanism on the future rulers of the province. The Roman Catholic Bishop, François Hubert, was afraid of this very thing, and saw educational reform as a vehicle of Protestantism and anglicization. His coadjutor, and next in line as bishop, Charles-François Bailly, poured scorn on Hubert's objections, a breach of ecclesiastical discipline for which he was to beg forgiveness on his deathbed. Chief Justice William Smith, the chairman of a council committee on education, hoped to avoid religious strife by excluding theological instruction of any sort and by keeping the university and school system under the control of the state.

What were Inglis' arguments for favoring the Anglican Church? How did Hubert make his objections known, and what did he suggest? Were Bailly's counterarguments factious or well founded? Did Smith's plan represent a practical compromise?

Document C–1

THE ANGLICAN VIEW

(Bishop Charles Inglis to Governor Lord Dorchester, December 27, 1787, Correspondence of Bishop Charles Inglis, M.G. 23, C 6, Vol. I, pp. 26–30, *Public Archives of Canada.*)

It gives me much pleasure to find that the establishing of a university in the province of Quebec "is greatly desired by many of the respectable inhabitants." Such an institution, if properly conducted, cannot fail of being attended with the most salutary consequences. . . .

I shall take the liberty to suggest two or three general observations. . . . It is universally allowed that youth is the properest time for having the principles of religion and virtue, as well as those of science, impressed on the mind; and hence, the general principles of the former are universally inculcated in some shape or other, with the principles of the latter, in all seminaries. It will be expected and it seems indispensably necessary, that, where a number of youths are collected for the purpose of education, they should be called together twice a day to prayers; on Sundays, especially, they should attend divine worship: how can all this be done . . . without a clergyman in the college? Or without some distinction in the mode of divine worship?

In a province, like Canada, where Roman Catholics are so numerous, every reasonable concession should certainly be made that would tend to gain them, or conciliate their affections, or even soften their prejudices. But then, there is a line which prudence forbids us to pass in making concessions; because, if we go beyond that limit, the concessions will sink in the estimation of those to whom they are made, and consequently miss the end that was aimed at. Roman Catholics are strongly attached to their peculiar principles, and think that attachment meritorious. They will not unnaturally judge of others by themselves. If we go too far in our concessions, will they not be apt to have an unfavourable opinion of us? And to think that we place little or no value on those things which we easily give up? This extreme, I apprehend, should be avoided, as well as the opposite one, of rigidly adhering to every little punctilio, without giving up anything. In short, if the happy medium of showing a liberal spirit, or the desire to meet them where it is proper, and yet avoiding whatever might diminish a due respect to government and the national church, could be hit on, it evidently appears to be the most eligible.

Document C–2

THE ROMAN CATHOLIC VIEW

(Bishop Jean François Hubert, November 18, 1789, in *Report of a Committee. . . .*, pp. 6–10, 15–17.)

Nothing is more worthy of the wisdom of the government under which we live, than the encouragement of science by every possible means; and with respect to myself, let me assure you, nothing can be more agreeable to my views and wishes. At the name of an university in the province of Quebec, my *native* country, I bless the Almighty for having inspired the design, and my prayers are offered for the execution of it. However, as you give me to understand, that my opinion will be received with pleasure, I ought to suggest to the honorable council and to the committee, in whose name, I conceive, you have written to me, the following observations:

1. It is very doubtful whether the province can, at present, furnish a sufficient number of students to occupy the masters and professors that would necessarily be required to form an university. While there remains in Canada so much land to clear, it is not to be expected that the country inhabitants will concern themselves about the liberal arts. A farmer in easy circumstances, who wishes to leave his children a comfortable inheritance, will rather bring them up to agriculture, and employ his money in the purchase of lands, than procure them learning of which he knows nothing himself, and of the value of which it is scarcely possible he should have any idea. Every nation upon the globe has successively given proof of my assertion, the sciences having flourished only, when there have been more inhabitants than necessary for the cultivation of the land. This is not yet the case in Canada; an immense space of country, where the lands, little improved, offer on all hands the wherewithal to exercise the industry, and stimulate the interest of the settlers. The towns therefore stand alone for furnishing students to the university.

There are but four towns in the province: William Henry, still uninhabited; Three Rivers, scarcely meriting the name of a town: the inhabitants of Quebec and Montreal, it is known, are not very numerous. Besides, is it probable, considering the present scarcity of money and the poverty of the citizens, that Montreal can send many youths to the university? In the course of every two years, ten or twelve scholars are sent from thence to Quebec to study philosophy; if more should come from thence, the whole town would murmur. Many, for want of funds, are compelled to finish their studies when only in the class of rhetoric. Yet the Seminary of Quebec teaches philosophy gratis, as well as the other branches of science, and the greatest sum required from a student, never exceeds twelve pounds sterling per annum. Hence I conclude, that the period is not arrived for founding an university at Quebec.

2. I understand by *university*, a company, community or corporation composed of several colleges, in which professors are placed to teach several sciences. The foundation of an university presupposes an establishment of colleges dependent thereon, and furnishing students for it. According to the most esteemed chronologists, the University of Paris, the most ancient in the world, was only founded in the twelfth century, tho' the kingdom of France had subsisted from the fifth. Nothing therefore seems to urge such an establishment in a province newly risen into existence, where there are but two small colleges, and which might, perhaps, be obliged to apply to foreign countries for professors to sit in the chairs, and for scholars to receive their lectures.

It will be objected that the Anglo-Americans, our neighbours, tho' the settlement of their country is not of long date, have nevertheless furnished themselves with one or more universities. But it must be observed, that their proximity to the sea, which is not the case with us, having rapidly extended their commerce, multiplied their towns, and increased their population, and it is not to be wondered that they should be more advanced than we are, and that the progress of two countries, so differently situated, should not be exactly alike.

3. Supposing the two foregoing reflections refuted by others more judicious and wise, I wish to know by what plan it is proposed to govern the administration of this community, before I take any step respecting the clergy of my diocese or the Canadians collectively. . . . Is it intended that it should be governed by one rector, or by a society of directors? If by a rector, is the appointment to be for life, or is he to be removable at the end of a given number of years? Who are to be the persons to nominate either him, or the directors. . . . Would it be the king, the governor, the citizens of Quebec, or the province at large? What rank or character would be given to the bishop, and what to his coadjutor in the establishment? Would it not be proper that both, or one at least of them should hold a distinguished station?

This is not all. *An union protecting the Catholic and Protestant subjects* has been previously announced. These terms are very vague. What are the measures to be taken to procure so necessary a junction? Will it be answered by proposing for the university, *persons unprejudiced in their opinions?* . . . in the style of modern writers, *a person unprejudiced in his opinions*, is one who opposes every principle of religion, who, pretending to conduct himself by the law of nature alone, soon becomes immoral and not subordinate to the laws, so necessary to be inculcated upon youth, if it be intended that they should conduct themselves uprightly. Men of this character (and this age abounds with them, to the misfortune and revolution of nations) would by no means suit the establishment proposed.

. . . In order to put the province in a state of enjoying, in the process of time, so precious an advantage as that of an university, it is necessary to use all possible means of supporting and encouraging the education already taught in the College of Montreal and Seminary of Quebec. . . . Another object, not less essential, for the present, would be to procure a third place of public instruction for youth. . . . There is in the center of Quebec a handsome and spacious college, the greatest part of which is occupied by the troops in the garrison. May not that college be drawn nearer to its primitive institution by substituting instead of those troops, if it should be his excellency's pleasure, some useful classes, such as the civil law, and navigation, to which may be added, if approved of, the mathematical class now taught at the seminary? Might not that college itself, in the course of time, be constituted an university, and support itself, in part, with the revenues of the estates now belonging to the Jesuits? This mode of proceeding gradually to the establishment of an university appears to me much more prudent and sure. . . . But to whom ought the government of the Jesuit's college belong if it were again set on foot? First, to Father Glapion [the Superior of the Jesuits] for his life, and afterwards to those who should be appointed by the bishop. Does any one wonder at such a plan? I will state the principles upon which I ground it. 1st. The funds of the college will only consist of the estates of the Jesuits. 2nd. The province has no right to appropriate them to itself but for their original destination. 3rd. The propagation of the Catholic faith is the principal motive assigned in all the title deeds. 4th. The circumstances of the donations, and the quality of the donors would alone prove that to be their intention. The Canadians, considered as Catholics, have therefore a right to those estates, which appears incontestible. . . .

Document C–3

A ROMAN CATHOLIC DISSENT

(Bishop-Coadjutor Charles François Bailly to the Council Committee on Education, April 5, 1790, in H. Tétu and C. O. Gagnon [eds.], *Mandements, Lettres Pastorales et Circulaires des Évêques de Québec* [Québec, 1888], Vol. II, pp. 398–409.)

In the report of a committee on the subject of education which has lately been sent me, I have seen a letter signed Jean François Hubert, Bishop of Quebec. Having read it with the utmost attention . . . I have come to the unalterable conclusion that it is a fraud made in the name of our dear bishop. . . . Even supposing that this letter really was from him, it contains only one point of view, and not that of the whole province, as requested.

Allow me, gentlemen, to communicate my observations. . . . The rhapsodist, under the name of the Bishop of Quebec, begins by declaring the joy which the establishment of a university would give him: "these are my wishes." He thanks God "for having inspired the design, and my prayers are offered for the execution of it." But straightway this joy, this trust in God, disappears. . . . Why? Because he does not believe that the province provides enough students.

If it is necessary to wait until we have cleared lands up to the arctic circle, and our youth, without masters or professors prepares itself for a university on its own, from all appearances we will find ourselves one fine day transported to the valley of Jehoshaphat.[1] . . .

A farmer who is well off, he adds, who desires to leave an inheritance to his children, would do better to put them to work at farming "and use his money to buy them lands, than procure them learning of which he knows nothing himself." He supposes that our first settlers are

---

[1] "Then he said, I did see all Israel scattered upon the mountains, as sheep that have no shepherd; and the Lord said, these have no masters. . . ." (II Chronicles 18, 16.)

directly descended from those men Saint John described in the third chapter of his gospel as preferring the dark to the light. However it is put, this is exactly the evil, and the very great evil, which the worthy representative of his majesty in this province wishes to remedy: it is for this reason that he has established a committee of distinguished and enlightened men who have undertaken the most exhaustive research to find a way to stop the father from passing on his ignorance from one generation to the next as part of the inheritance. And what better remedy than the establishment of a university? . . . A glance at the colonies [i.e., U.S.A.] will convince us that the sciences can and do flourish where the vast amount of land yet uncleared far exceeds the numbers of farmers. And France, with twenty two universities, Italy and Spain both crowded with them, are nevertheless short of farmers. . . .

Quebec, the residence of the commander in chief of North America, could become the centre for great numbers of students from all his majesty's different provinces. There are towns in Nova Scotia, New Brunswick, and the western areas as well as in the different parts of Quebec, which, if they are neither London nor Paris, can hardly be called deserted. Quebec, Montreal, Three Rivers, William Henry have more people than the rhapsodist credits them with. Is it through malice or ignorance that he speaks neither of the new Johnstown, nor of Lunenburg and several other sizeable towns and boroughs either in the west or on the Bay of Chaleurs, which will provide large numbers of students? Should it not be said that a large part of those who attend what we in Canada call college, come from the countryside? The clergy lets them in, and they are certainly not the least respectable part; and there is no doubt that their numbers would grow considerably according to the rewards which came to them from a liberal education under capable masters. To reject the means of education suggested is thus to prefer the greatest evil in the province

to its general good, and the incalculable advantage of seeing it flourish a little.

The following objection is also very badly grounded: France existed from the fifth to the twelfth century. Doubtless she would have existed to the present day under kings as despotic as they were ignorant. Would he persuade us that we, who can count not quite two hundred years, must remain in ignorance for another thousand? . . .

As to the different questions he proposes with regard to the direction of the university. . . . I will say that a university has never been, and never will be, anything but a body of professors and students established by public authority to teach the higher sciences and arts. Who should control it? I ask him, who must establish it? The king! well then the control belongs to the king. . . . What place would the bishop and his coadjutator have there? the place which knowledge and merit deserve in any university. There is no university in Europe where the mitre does not take second place to the cap and gown of Aristotle. Bishops will not be more exalted than the body of the university.

He says he wants a union that will protect Catholics and Protestants; but this, he says, is "a very vague term." . . . He is afraid; as far as I am concerned, I would be happy to see Catholic and Protestant equally protected by a wise and prudent administration. In our professorial chairs there would be none but learned professors, on the benches none but studious scholars, in the streets and public places none but citizens who support and love each other according to the Gospel. I am not going to hide myself in a corner of the bedroom to see if the mother of the family, after having worked all day in the house, and the father who has toiled outdoors, make the sign of the cross with holy water before going to bed. . . .

Unprejudiced men also appear to his mind as a hidden snare; he is afraid to be caught. If there is a trap, it is hidden by few leaves and little foliage, and no one but he believes there is one. Men without prejudice, by definition, cannot be anything but men of good morals: no loose-liver or miser or debauchee will be found among the ranks of unprejudiced men, however free he may be in his way of thought. . . . The man uniquely qualified to fill a chair in our university will be he whose lessons are free of all irrelevant and useless considerations.

Who would not die laughing . . . if he heard his professor of philosophy or astronomy begin with a treatise on the right of bishops to explain the laws of the motion and orbit of planets; or a professor of anatomy demonstrating the circulation of the blood in our veins through the canonical authority of the Epistle of St. Paul to the Hebrews. . . .

What means can be adopted for the establishment of preparatory schools? What is the point of having preparatory schools if the time has not yet come for a university? . . . How to create a taste for learning in the various parishes? Why inspire them with a taste for learning if you refuse them the means of perfecting it? A writer is accused of libelling the clergy by publishing that it was their policy to keep the people in a state of ignorance. Is the reply to this aspersion satisfactory? He opposes the gracious methods offered us by the government and the council. The time has not yet come to let the light of learning shine on the poor Canadians; their eyes are too weak. . . .

You have asked my opinion on the plan proposed and on the means of putting it into effect. . . . Yes, it is high time to establish a university in Canada; to confine yourself to unveiling the project in public and then to stop would be to create a universal discouragement, and a distrust from which it would be difficult to revive enthusiasm. Dare we hope to see scholars coming from all parts, if it is not put into practice? Sadly, our best citizens will be torn between sending their children away on the one hand, and ignorance and idleness on the other. Has there been any establishment in the world that has not been started on a small scale? . . . Not all the professors will be found in this province, but a mutual freedom will procure them for us very soon. Irreproachable manners, intelligence embellished by study and a taste for knowledge will qualify them and allow us to choose them. Christian theology being left to the care of each communion, it can matter little who teaches Aristotle or Euclid. Further, all jealousy will disappear between Catholics and Protestants who are the object of a just and constant protection, and our wise and sympathetic government will give a fine example in this union which has been so long desired.

Document C–4

THE SECULAR VIEW

(Observations by Chief Justice Smith to the Council Committee on Education, November 26, 1789, in *Report of a Committee. . .*, pp. 19–25.)

To what extent or degree it was expedient to introduce the means of education in this province?

That certainly there could be no division of sentiment, repecting that elementary instruction, necessary to the lower classes in all countries; the want of which left a people in a state of *base barbarism*. By these he meant,

1. *Parish* free-schools, or a school in every village, for reading, writing and the four common rules of arithmetic.

2. A *County* free-school, one at least for further progress in arithmetic, the languages, grammar, book-keeping, gauging, navigation, surveying and the practical branches of the mathematics.

The next step in civilised countries, was an university or a collegiate society, for instruction in the liberal arts and sciences; and how far the province was prepared for such an institution, was the point which the right reverend bishop had with much reason made the subject of his deliberation.

The chairman concurred with the venerable bishop, that the erection of an university, measuring it by the European scale, would be extravagent, as neither adapted to the abilities, nor the wants of a country, not yet consisting of one hundred and fifty thousand inhabitants, who had a wilderness before them, to be brought into cultivation for obtaining the necessaries of life.

It was nevertheless to be wished that the youth of the province might not be estranged from it, by an education in foreign parts, but find *at home* sufficient means to qualify them for the trusts, offices and honors of their native *community*.

Tho' the idea therefore of establishing such a fountain of light *here*, as is found in the universities of the old continent, for the diffusion of knowledge among the nations, and thro' the immense regions of his majesty's inland dominions, which is only to be indulged as an object of distant prospect, the great and important questions still remained.

How far the necessities of the colony demand, and its abilities will permit, of a college or academy for that improvement of the mind, presupposed in every advancement to real usefulness in any of the learned professions, and indispensibly necessary to every great social collection; and without which, it must be indebted to emigrants from other countries.

A college under one rector and four tutors, dividing the labour between them, would, in his opinion, be sufficient for instructing the students to be expected from all the provinces on this continent now remaining to Great Britain, in grammar, logic, rhetoric, mathematics, natural philosophy, metaphysics and ethics; and these sciences made the path, which all were obliged to walk in, to obtain any degree of eminence in the learned professions, to give a man distinction among his fellow citizens, and to enable him to come forward to the magistracy and other important services of his country.

The chairman added, that tho' an institution of this extent could not be very extensive, it would nevertheless require an union of hearts and hands, to give it the desired prosperity; and this it certainly could not want, by due guards against the illiberality of a contracted and sectarian spirit. To which end, it was his idea, the state of the province considered,

That Christian theology be no branch of instruction in this college; but left to be provided for by the two communions that divide the province, in such a way as they elect, and by such means as they respectively possess or may acquire.

That a corporation be created by letters patent, capable of donations, and perpetual succession, and with authority to make by-laws.

That the visitation be vested in the crown.

That the king's judges and the bishops of the province for the time being, both Catholic and Protestant, be members of the corporation; and the rest to sixteen or twenty, of the principal gentlemen of the country, and equal number of both communions; and that vacancies be filled, by the majority of the voices of the whole body.

That proper clauses be inserted in the charter to repel every appropriation and by-law, touching the funds or government of the college, to any other than the promotion of science *at large*, as aforementioned; in exclusion of all biasses, ceremonies, creeds and discriminations, either of the Protestant or Catholic communion. . . .

Advanced to the institution of a college, the committee must perceive, that like a reservoir for watering the surrounding fields, this, as a fountain, would find candidates *in the province*, for the care of all the inferior schools, in our expanded population, to the extremity of the British dominions in the west; and that therefore, tho' this was mentioned last in the chain of deliberation, it ought to have the chief influence, even with those, who might before have been only advocates for those lower exertions, immediately necessary to the village and county schools.

D. The Remedies

At a time when unanimity was very rarely achieved at its meetings, the council voted unanimously in favour of a state-run school system. A public petition supported their decision. Bishop Inglis urged that the only way to overcome Hubert's opposition was to retire him and divide his diocese. Lord Dorchester wrote to the British government seconding the council's decision and emphasising the use that could be made of a state directed educational system.

Were Bishop Hubert's fears of an assault on French and Roman Catholic culture justified in the light of these suggestions?

Document D–1

THE COUNCIL ADVISES

(Meeting of November 26, 1789, in *Report of a Committee . . .*, pp. 25–26.)

After deliberating upon the subject at large,

Agreed, that the general question of concurrence be put upon all the resolves; and it being put accordingly, the Committee concurred in them, and ordered that it be reported to his lordship as their *unanimous opinion.*

First, That it is expedient without delay, to erect parish or village free-schools, in every district of the province, at the determination of the magistrates of the district, in their quarter sessions of the peace.

Second, That it is also expedient, that each district have a free school, in the central or county town of the district.

Third, That the tuition of the village schools, be limited to reading, writing, and cyphering.

Fourth, That the instruction in the district or county schools, extend to all the rules of arithmetic, the languages, grammar, book-keeping, gauging, navigation, surveying, and the practical branches of the mathematics.

Fifth, That it is expedient to erect a collegiate institution, for cultivating the liberal arts and sciences usually taught in the European universities; the theology of Christians excepted, on account of the mixture of two communions, whose joint aid is desirable, as far as they agree, and who ought to be left to find a separate provision for the candidates in the ministry of their respective churches.

Sixth, That it is essential to the *origin* and *success* of such an institution, that a society be incorporated for the purpose; and that the charter wisely provide against the perversion of the institution, to any sectarian peculiarities; leaving free scope, for cultivating the *general circle* of the sciences.

Document D–2

CITIZENS FOR EDUCATION

(Records of the Provincial and Civil Secretaries' Offices, Series, R.G. 4, A 1, Vol. XLVIII, pp. 15908–15911, *Public Archives of Canada*.)

Your petitioners have with regret long seen and lamented the low and depressed state of science in this province,

That they have been without the means, owing to the want of an university or college of giving their youth a liberal education,

That the heavy expence of sending their youth to Europe for an education on the one hand, and the danger that they might be estranged from the province by an education in the American states on the other, have deprived many of them of those advantages which are enjoyed in most parts of his majesty's dominions,

That altho' your petitioners, from the infant state of the province, and their want of abilities, see great difficulties and embarrassments opposed to the erection and accomplishment of an institution so necessary and useful, yet when they contemplated the benevolence and patronage of his majesty, the assurance of your lordship's auspices, the generosity of the nation to which they belong, and the encouragement and assurance it has ever afforded to similar institutions . . . they look forward with confidence and a pleasing hope to the establishment and completion of an university.

Your petitioners therefore humbly pray your lordship that an university may be erected in this province wherein youth may be instructed in the learned languages and sciences (excepting theology) that it may be established on the most liberal principles and terms, be free and open to all denominations without any regard being had to their different tenets in religion; and that your lordship will be pleased to grant his majesty's charter of incorporation to erect and establish an university in the province of Quebec by the name and style of the University of the Province of Quebec to be erected in such a place, and under such regulations as to his majesty may seem expedient.

Document D—3

INGLIS TO THE ATTACK

(Bishop Charles Inglis to Governor Lord Dorchester, April 15, 1790, Inglis Papers, M.G. 23, C 6, Vol. I, pp. 198–200, *Public Archives of Canada.*)

I am favoured with your lordship's letter of Feb. 13, together with six printed copies of the legislative council's report on the subject of education; for which I return you many thanks.

The report is curious and interesting, and throws much light on the state of the province. Whilst it manifests the laudable attention which your lordship has paid to the instruction of the Canadians; and to the means of diffusing literature and liberality of sentiment among them; it also evinces that there are many difficulties to obstruct those measures. Poor Bishop Hubert seems to be frightened at the idea of having a college erected at Quebec; and indeed whoever wishes to prolong the reign of bigotry and ignorance will naturally be of his mind and join him. . . .

I know it is your lordship's wish to unite the Canadians with the Protestants in this design; and certainly this wish is dictated by benevolence and good policy —the question is—can it be effected? I very much doubt it, in the present state of things. It appears to me impracticable, any otherwise than by adopting a proposal which has been lately suggested from Quebec, and wish I shall communicate to your lordship in confidence. . . . The proposal does not come from a Protestant but from a very zealous Roman Catholic; it does not come from a layman, but from a churchman of respectable character, and anxious to preserve the just rights of the clergy. . . .

The proposal came to me in a letter from Quebec. The letter, with much good sense laments the ignorance and bigotry which prevail and are daily gaining ground among the Roman Catholics, and the separation which is kept up between them and the Protestants, and which the author wishes to be removed; it states that those Roman Catholics who possess liberal sentiments are discouraged, and injured, that this is particularly the case of Mr. Baillie, the coadjutor, who notwithstanding his own great merit and your lordship's countenance and support, is so often insulted, and has no suitable increase of salary or authority allowed; of several St. Sulpicians and other clergy, men of chief merit, who are injuriously treated. The principal causes assigned for this are the weakness and narrow principles of Bishop Hubert, who is entirely influenced by his secretary and grand vicaire at Quebec, two hot headed men, and is himself frequently *non compos*. This letter sets forth that these and the other leaders of the clergy will resist any measures that would promote literature and enlighten the Roman Catholics, or unite them more closely to the Protestants. . . .

The remedy proposed for removing these inconveniences is briefly this—to divide the Popish bishopric of Quebec into two sees; to place Mr. Baillie immediately in one of them; and a native of his majesty's European dominions, a Roman Catholic, in the other; Bishop Hubert to retire like his predecessor, on a provision out of some part of the church funds. It is presumed that the European bishop, born in the king's dominions, will be attached to the constitution; and being free of those narrow prejudices that are commonly imbibed by the natives of Canada, and having an enlarged and liberal turn of mind, will assist in rooting out those prejudices, in cultivating knowledge, and in promoting a more friendly and intimate intercourse between his majesty's old and new subjects.

I scarcely dare hazard an opinion concerning this plan. Were it practicable, and could those ends be thereby attained, it would well deserve attention; but there may be obstacles in the way, of which I know nothing. I am assured that a large majority of the Romish clergy are disgusted with the indiscreet violent measures that are pursued by their leaders. . . . The plan would be of the utmost service to order, literature and the best interests of the province.

Document D–4

THE GOVERNOR REPORTS

(Lord Dorchester to Secretary of State William Grenville, November 10, 1790, in Colonial Office Records, Q Series, M.G. 11, Vol. XLIX, pp. 26–30, *Public Archives of Canada*.)

The inclosed schedule will serve as an index to the council meetings relating to the state of the church and schools in this country, and the means proposed for the advancement of education.

The encouragement of academies for elementary knowledge ought not to be omitted in any of the provinces, but the establishment of a university in Lower Canada[1] appears to be most proper to give energy, uniformity, and extent, to the cultivation of the higher branches of science throughout the British dominions on this continent.

The place recommended by the committee appears to be well adapted to the present condition of the country, and open to such extension as an increase of wealth and population may require.

It will be very material so to organize and endow this institution, that the inferior schools, pointed out by the committee throughout the country of Upper as well as Lower Canada, may be subordinate to the government, and in some measure dependent upon it for support, so that the whole system may be animated by one common principle, under the eye and control of the crown.

For this purpose there should be an adequate fund created to defray the expense of the whole establishment.

A royal charter incorporating the immediate trustees or governors of the

---

[1] The Constitutional Act, 1791, was to divide Quebec into Upper and Lower Canada, with the old French settlements along the St. Lawrence to the Ottawa River being Lower Canada.

university will secure the property they may acquire, and enable them to apply the revenue to the intent, and in the manner therein to be expressed, under the visitatorial authority of the crown.

For extending the influence of the institution to the regulation and inspection of all inferior schools and academies dependent upon it, in the two provinces, as well respecting the nature of the tuition, as the conduct of the teachers, and the government of the schools, the legislative interposition may be necessary, and if so, a parliamentary regulation to that effect would perhaps be preferable to any provision to be concerted within the province by their several legislatures.

.   .   .   .

In the new districts a glebe of two hundred acres has been set apart in every township for the support of a free school, but until the value of these lands is enhanced by an increased population, the erection of school houses, and other improvements through the joint exertions of the inhabitants, little or no advantage can be expected from them. Some other temporary aid will therefore be indispensable. At this time the introduction of masters for these free schools from Britain is much to be wished, particularly in Lower Canada.

Hereafter the university and its subordinate branches of education may supply competent instruments for this necessary service.

The exclusion of theology recommended by the committee and prayed for by the petitioners, is judged necessary for obtaining the greatest degree of advantage from this institution to all classes of inhabitants.

And the benevolent design of his majesty to secure to his colonies a succession of respectable ministers of religion by a provision for some of their youth at the English universities, which cannot fail to produce the most salutary effects in every point of view, at once removes the chief objection, that might otherwise have been raised against this restriction. I should think the admission of three or four young men from Canada to a participation of these benefits sufficient for the present. . . .

PROBLEM 6

The Great Awakening in Maritime Canada

J. M. BUMSTED
McMaster University

In 1775 the American Revolution began. Although Maritime Canada did not become a centre of rebellion, it was nevertheless greatly affected by the Revolution. The presence of British military bases, the coming of the Loyalists, and the subsequent reorganization of what remained of British North America all were fundamental components of Maritime development. But the Revolution and the shock waves it produced were not the only occurrences of momentous significance for the area at this time. Simultaneously with the beginning of war came the stirrings of a great religious revival in Maritime Canada, which in a variety of subtle ways itself altered society in the region. The revival—usually called the Great Awakening—is a subject relatively unfamiliar to most undergraduates studying Canadian history, for most textbooks give it little attention. Nevertheless, insight into the Awakening and the evangelical pietism which it fostered is essential not only for an understanding of the Maritimes but of Canadian development itself, since evangelical Protestantism continued to be a basic component of Canadian society and Canadian personality well into the 20th century. Evangelical pietism soon spread into all of Canada, bringing religion into backwoods areas, battling the Anglican establishment in church and state, and contributing to sabbatarian and temperance sentiment. While the source material in this problem will focus on revivalism and pietism in the Maritimes at the end of the 18th century, the phenomena continued into later periods in other regions. A careful study of the Great Awakening in Maritime Canada, therefore, serves as a useful basis for understanding Protestant evangelical movements wherever and whenever they appear in Canada. The fundamental beliefs and techniques of pietism remain as unchanging as do the criticisms and attacks directed against it.

The religious currents which produced the Great Awakening in the Maritimes were international and almost a century old in 1775. Evangelical pietism had begun in Lutheran circles in Germany at the close of the 17th century, had made its way to England to influence the Wesleys and George Whitefield, and had come to colonial America to contribute to the outbreak of an extraordinary religious revival there between 1720 and 1745. In the New World, the area most strongly affected by revivalism was New England, the source of most early settlement in Nova Scotia. Despite this background, it would be a mistake to see the Awakening in the Maritimes as nothing more than a late manifestation of a long-standing phenomenon. The revival which began in 1775 with the conversion and decision to preach of Henry Alline (1748–84) owed a good deal to the international evangelical spirit, but it was also an indigenous response to peculiarly local problems. Nova Scotia's scattered settlements teetering on the brink of economic disaster lacked the ability to produce—much less support—the cultured, well-educated, and settled clergy which traditional Protestantism demanded. Moreover, the coming of the American Revolution combined with socioeconomic discontent to produce a crisis of identity for many Maritime settlers who were sympathetic to the rebels but could not afford to join them. Revivalism offered an alternative to revolution, since it insisted that what mattered was not the individual's earthly status or actions but his ultimate salvation.

Henry Alline was soon joined in his evangelical activities by others. Some were converts of Alline's preaching, but others like William Black (1760–1834) and his Methodist colleagues apparently arrived at a similar point independently of Alline's New-Light movement. Following Alline's death in 1784, his followers split, most ultimately becoming Baptists. By the 1790's, the main competition among the evangelicals was between the Baptists and the Methodists, although the Loyalist migration of the 1780's had provided a number of Anglican clergymen who offered the major Protestant alternative to pietism until the arrival of large numbers of Presbyterians at the beginning of the 19th century. Whatever else the revival had or had not done, it certainly contributed to a religious pluralism in the Maritimes which made it impossible for any single denomination to gain a dominant position.

Evangelical pietism was a reaction against traditional religious assumptions and it rejected many of them. It insisted that everyone could be saved and that all who were truly converted were equal in the sight of God. In this sense it was antiauthoritarian, democratic, and socially leveling, but whether it was as politically subversive as many opponents (especially Anglicans) charged is a matter for the student to decide on the basis of the evidence. Besides subversion and disloyalty, critics of the evangelical movement also charged it with fanaticism, narrow-mindedness, and religious division. Some of these accusations strike a very modern chord, but whether or not they should be accepted without qualification is another matter entirely. Before concurring in the condemnations, the thoughtful student must ask whether pietism served any useful function at the time, or whether at the beginning of the revival the critics offered the population any realistic alternatives. The student must also ask whether the pietists would not themselves concur in some of the criticisms of extremism leveled against the movement, and—given the assumptions about religion and salvation which the evangelists held—whether their actions were inconsistent, unreasonable, or undefensible. In short, what sorts of conclusions about evangelical pietism and religious revivalism should the dispassionate observer make based upon an objective study of the historical record?

For those interested in further study, the best treatments of the American context of early revivalism are E. S. Gaustad, *The Great Awakening in New England* (1957), and W. W. Sweet, *Revivalism in America* (1944). For Canada, see S. D. Clark, *Church and Sect in Canada* (1948), and W. H. Elgee, *The Social Teachings of the Canadian Churches* (1964). Historical background for the Maritimes is provided by W. S. MacNutt, *The Atlantic Provinces* (1965), and *New Brunswick: A History, 1784–1867* (1963); J. B. Brebner, *The Neutral Yankees of Nova Scotia* (1937); B. Murdoch, *A History of Nova Scotia* (3 vols., 1865); and A. B. Warburton, *A History of Prince Edward Island, 1534–1831* (1923). The classic work on the Maritime revivals is M. W. Armstrong, *The Great Awakening in Nova Scotia* (1948). Professor Armstrong has also produced important statements in "Backgrounds of Religious Liberty in Nova Scotia," *Nova Scotia Historical Society Collections,* Vol. XXVII (1947), pp. 17–32, and "Neutrality and Religion in Revolutionary Nova Scotia," *New England Quarterly*, Vol. XIX (1946), pp. 50–62. For the Baptists, consult G. E. Levy, *The Baptists of the Maritime Provinces, 1753–1946* (1946), and for the Methodists, G. S. French, *Parsons and Politics* (1962). Among the works on individual evangelists, the most useful are Matthew Richey, *A Memoir of the Late Rev. William Black* (1839); Nathan Bangs, *The Life of the Rev. Freeborn Garrettson* (1829); and John Davis, *Life and Times of the Rev. Harris Harding* (1866). The editor of this problem has in preparation the first full-length biography of Henry Alline, to be published by the University of Toronto Press.

A. Leadership

Most traditional Protestant churches insisted upon an educated and settled clergy. The minister was expected to be learned—in ancient languages, in theology, in moral philosophy—and was ordained or installed over a particular church or congregation. The Maritimes lacked any educational institutions before the Revolution to provide a learned ministry, and the scattered settlements found it difficult to support one. A few educated clergymen were imported from outside the region, chiefly from colonial America and Britain, but a native ministry was impossible under existing assumptions and circumstances. The frontier conditions of the Maritimes could be overcome only gradually over a very long period of time, but the assumptions hampering religious development could be overturned very rapidly. The following selections indicate the ways in which tradition was rejected and altered by various evangelical leaders—Henry Alline of the New Lights, William Black of the Methodists, and Joseph Crandall (1772–1858) of the Baptists. What did the evangelicals consider to be the essential qualifications for the ministry? What was the minister's primary task? Were such pietists anti-intellectual?

Document A–1

THE CONVERSION OF HENRY ALLINE

(Henry Alline, *The Life and Journal of the Rev. Mr. Henry Alline* [Boston, 1806] pp. 35–48.)

[1775]

O the astonishing wonders of his grace, and the boundless ocean of redeeming love! millions and millions of praises belongs to his name. O how shall I make the least return! O what a wretch have I been to stand it out against such love. I have long and often wondered, that God did not have mercy on me and convert me; but now I saw it was my own fault, and wondered why he waited so long upon such miserable rejectors of his grace. O how black appeared all my righteousness, which I saw I had hugged so long. And O the unspeakable wisdom and beauty of the glorious plan of life and salvation. I have often wanted some things in the world, and some plans to be altered, and wished this thing and that thing was not so, because it seemed hard, and not agreeable to my carnal mind and human reasonings; but I would not now have any alteration for ten thousand worlds. Every thing that God did was right and nothing wanting: I did not want then that God should alter any thing for me, but I was willing, yea chose (for it was the food and joy of my soul) to bow to him, to be ruled by him, to submit to him and to depend wholly upon him both for time and eternity; and it was the joy of my soul that he would be God alone forever. . . . O I would rather be a door-keeper in the house of my God than to dwell in the tents of wickedness, crowned with all the dignities of this lower world, surrounded with all the enjoyments of time, and the most exalted pleasures of sense.

In the midst of all my joys, in less than half an hour after my soul was set at liberty, the Lord discovered to me my labour in the ministry and call to preach the gospel. I cried out amen, Lord I'll go, I'll go, send me, send me. And although many (to support the ministry of antichrist) will pretend, there is no such thing, as a man's knowing in these days he is called to preach any other way, than his going to the seats of learning to be prepared for the ministry, and then authorized by men: yet blessed be God, there is a knowledge of these things, which an unconverted man knows nothing of. For my own part it was so clear to me, that I had not the least doubt, but I should preach the gospel; although to all appearance in the sight of man, there was none appeared more unlikely: for my capacity in the world was low, being obliged to labour daily with my hands to get a living; my father's estate was not very large, and my parents being almost past labour, I had the whole care of these temporal concerns. As for learning, it was true I had read and studied more than was common for one in my station, but my education was but small: what I had of human literature, I had acquired of myself without schooling, excepting what I obtained before I was eleven years of age, for I never went to school, after I came to Nova-Scotia; so that if learning only would make ministers of Christ, as the world vainly imagine, I had it not: but, blessed be God, I trust I had that to go with me which was better than all the wisdom and learning; neither had I the least doubt, when I was near to God, of being not qualified, though after that, when I got in the dark, I had: but said with all my soul, I'll go, I'll go; send me, send me with the glad tidings of salvation and messages of peace to my fellow-men: yea, my whole soul thirsted to go; and at that time found nothing of the fear of man or the storms and trials of a frowning world in the way: although before I had any liberty for my soul from the 40th Psalm, those words, as before observed, were spoken to me: "Many shall see it, and fear, and shall trust in the Lord." O that ever God should make me instrumental in bringing one soul to the knowledge of a Saviour! O Lord, send me with meekness and humility. . . .

One day, being under great trials of mind, one of my brothers in law spoke to me, and asked me if I was fully satisfied, that I was called to preach the gospel? I told him yes. He asked me then, what I was waiting for? If God had called me, I ought immediately to go, and not wait for any more learning; God was able to give me all the assistance that I needed. I answered, that although I was convinced that God had called me, yet I could not think that it was his will for me to proceed, until that he had given me more human wisdom. Why, said he, has not Christ learning enough? Is he not able to teach you in half an hour in his school, more than you'll be able to obtain in the seats of human learning all your life. This I told him, was very true; yet I thought I needed more of man's wisdom and learning than what I had. He told me that my success in the gospel did not consist in knowing so much myself, as in the spirit of God's going with me, which certainly would go with me, if God had called me. I told him if the Lord designed that I should preach with no more learning than I had, he would certainly have made it manifest some way or other. He answered, he thought it was already evidently manifest, when a small number of people did meet in the town every sabbath day, and I with them, and no minister, nor any one to give a word of exhortation; and I believe it would be very acceptable to the christians of that society, if you was to improve. This bore much on my mind, and led me to examine more closely whether the Lord had really called me; and what he would call me for, if he did not intend that I should preach: but still I thought he was confined to human learning, and that he would not send me without it; but would find out some way to give it to me. O the prejudices of education! I had heard so much of ministers coming through the orders of men, that it seemed to be an infallible rule. But, blessed be the Lord, he still followed me with divine impressions on my mind to that degree, that I could hardly engage in any worldly employment; for it seemed as if it was not my work, and that I was out of my duty all this time. . . .

About the 13th or 14th day of April, 1776, I began to see that I had all this time been led astray by labouring so much after human learning and wisdom, and had held back from the call of God. One day in my meditation I had such a discovery of Christ's having every thing I needed, and that it was all mine, that I saw I needed nothing to qualify me but Christ; and that if I had all the wisdom that could ever be obtained by mortals, without having the spirit of Christ with me, I should never have any success in preaching; and if Christ went with me I should have all in all. And O what a willingness I felt in my soul to go in his name and strength, depending on him alone. I found I had nothing more to inquire into, but whether God had called me: for he knew what learning I had, and could have in the course of his providence brought me through all the seats of learning, that ever man went through, together with all the orders of men; but he had not; therefore I had nothing else to observe, but the call of God: and when I got near to him and enjoyed a sense of divine things, I was fully convinced (though in the dark I would often doubt) and was now determined to come forward the first opportunity I could get. . . .

It being reported at this time that Henry Alline was turned New-Light preacher, many would come from other towns, even whole boat-loads. Some came to hear what the babler had to say; some came with gladness of heart that God had raised up one to speak in his name; and some come to make a scoff, but it did not seem to trouble me much; for I trust God was with me and supported and enabled me to face a frowning world. The greatest trials I met with were from my parents, who were so much against my improving, as sometimes to leave the house as I was speaking. O how it would cut me sometimes: but, blessed be God, he not only carried me through these trials; but likewise so opened their eyes, that they were as much engaged for me to preach the Gospel, as I was, and would have plucked out even their eyes for my encouragement. Thus God was kind to me in every respect, and ever worked for my good. He blessed my soul, supported my body, blessed my labours in some degree, increased my desires and my resolutions, lifted me above the fears and trials of the world, weaned me in a great degree from the flattering charms of this world of sense, and increased my faith.

Document A—2

THE CONVERSION OF WILLIAM BLACK

(Matthew Richey, *A Memoir of the Late Rev. William Black, Wesleyan Minister* [Halifax, 1837], pp. 18–20.)

In the year 1779, I saw, if I would go to heaven, I must lead a new life. But I did not know I wanted an inward change, or see the deplorable state I was in by nature, till I was at a prayer meeting held at Mr. Oxley's. While they were praying, my heart began to throb within me, my eyes gushed out with tears, and I cried aloud for mercy; as did most that were in the room, about fourteen in number. One, indeed, could not hold from laughing, when we began to cry out; but it was not long before he cried as loud as any. In a few moments it pleased God to fill Mrs. Oxley with joy unspeakable. After this, we went almost every night to Mr. Oxley's to sing and pray. Going thence one night, and seeing the Northern Lights, I thought, 'What, if the Day of Judgment be coming?' I threw myself down on the ground, and cried to the Lord for mercy. On Sunday, Mr. Wells, an old Methodist, came to Amherst, and gave us an exhortation, in which he said, 'Sin and repent, sin and repent, till you repent in the bottomless pit.' The words went like a dagger to my heart; and I continued mourning after God for five weeks and four days, till our monthly meeting. I was then strongly tempted to put an end to my life; but God enabled me to resist the temptation. Two days after, an old Methodist, after praying with me, said, 'I think you will get the blessing before morning.' About two hours after, while we were singing a hymn, it pleased God to reveal his Son in my heart. Since that time I have had many blessed days, and many happy nights.

One Sunday night, after my brother Richard and I were gone to bed, I asked him, 'Can you believe?' He answered, 'No.' I exhorted him to wrestle hard with God, and got up to pray with him. But he was unbelieving still: so I went to sleep again. Yet, not being satisfied, after talking largely to him, I got up again, and began praying for him; being fully persuaded that God would set his soul at liberty. And so he did: he pardoned all his sins, and bade him 'go in peace.'

It being now between twelve and one, I waked my brothers John and Thomas, and told them the glad tidings. They got up. We went to prayer; and when we rose from our knees, Thomas declared, 'God has blotted out all my sins.' I then went to my father and mother, (who were both seeking salvation,) and told them the joyful news. My father said, 'Willy, pray for *us*.' I did; and earnestly exhorted him to wrestle with God for himself. So he did; and it was not long before God set his soul also at liberty. The next morning it pleased Him to show my sister Sarah his pardoning love. Blessed be his name for all his benefits!

Not long after, Mr. Oxley's son came to our house; and lay with me, and complained of his hardness of heart. After I had talked with him a little while, the Lord laid his hand on him in a wonderful manner; so that he rolled up and down, and roared as in the agonies of death. But between one and two in the morning, he likewise could rejoice in God his Saviour. These are a few of the wonderful works of God among us; but he is also working upon the hearts of the inhabitants in general.

Document A—3

THE CONVERSION OF JOSEPH CRANDALL

("The Autobiography of Joseph Crandall," ms. in Maritime Baptist Historical Collection, Acadia University, Wolfville, Nova Scotia, pp. 1–10.)

I was born in a place called Tivertown in Rhode Island. My parents Webber Crandall and Mercy Vaughan, emigrated from that country to Nova Scotia about one year before the revolution. The country was extremely poor, and but thinly settled. The inhabitants were poor and there were no schools there at that time. When I was ten or twelve years of age I was sent from home. The woman with whom I lived taught me to spell a little. Afterwards I attended an evening school for about three months. . . . I recollect one day a couple of strangers came to the house where I was living. They talked of a strange man that was preaching in Windsor and adjoining places; he preached in the night and people were becoming crazy and talked about their souls. My father had heard this man preach and as he happened to be there at the time he explained to the strangers that this preacher Henry Alline was a "New Light" and that the "New Light" were the people of God for they were Christians and that none could go to Heaven unless they were converted. Some time after this Mr. John Sargent came to Chester. He was called a "New Light" preacher; then came Handly Chipman and Harris Harding. Their arrival was followed by a great excitement among the people. Quite a number professed to be converted, among the number being the Vaughans, the Floyds, and many other families followed the new preacher. Some young people about my own age professed to be converted, and although I attended all the meetings and fully believed it was the Lord's work, yet my heart was hard and unmoved and I thought at the time that the Lord had left me to perish in my sins, and justly too, for I was one of the greatest sinners on earth. From that time I became more hardened in sin and was often in despair,

sometimes I wished I had never been born. . . .

I left Chester and went to Liverpool, N.S., where I remained two years—was employed at this place in Cod fishing. My life in Liverpool was exceedingly sinful. From Liverpool I returned to Chester. From there I went to Falmouth and then to Newport, was employed for a time in freighting lumber from Shubenacadie to Windsor. About this time there was to be a meeting of the Christians from different parts of the country. David Vaughan had promised that the Schooner in which I sailed should carry the pilgrims to Onslow. After some hesitation I consented that they should be carried with us, but my cousin John Vaughan refused to go. We left Newport on Friday and reached Onslow on Sabbath morning. The next week I collected a number of young men and we went down the bay to have a regular pleasure sail. We returned on Saturday and Sabbath morning I went to the meeting which was held at the house of Mr. Philip Higgins. I cannot say that I had any great anxiety about the meetings, except my desire to see Harris Harding, who was high in my esteem since the time of the reformation at Chester. When I entered the house, the meeting had commenced. I have no knowledge of anything that was said by any person in the meeting. The moment I entered the house, the glorious majesty of the Divine Being appeared to open before the eyes of my understanding (I beheld no object with my bodily eyes) and I saw myself justly condemned to endless misery. I saw no way of escape until suddenly a glorious light shone from the excellent majesty and I saw the way of salvation was Gods work and not mine. I felt as I had never felt before, although amongst strangers, I could not hold my peace. My hard heart was at last broken, and I had such a view of a perishing world lying in ruin as I never could express. To the great surprise of all present I began to speak and try to tell what I felt and saw. My mind was completely absorbed in the solemn and marvellous scene. I appeared to me that the whole human race lay in open ruin and were altogether at the disposal of that Holy Being whose bright glory had so overwhelmed my soul. I saw mercy so connected with the justice of God that they were both one, that what God had done in the person of Christ was alone sufficient to save all that came to God for mercy through Jesus Christ. I felt that the whole world ought to know what I felt and saw, for indeed it appeared of more importance to me than the whole world. I continued speaking (as the people told me afterwards) for more than an hour for I could not hold my peace, for it was a stream of living water flowing into my soul and then bursting forth like a stream from an overflowing fountain. The work of sinners lay before me, like a broad field to which I could see no end. When the scene had passed over and I looked around me, the two ministers, Joseph Dimock and Harris Harding were weeping and many more were weeping with them. The next day we embarked for Newport where we arrived in safety; this was in July 1795. I spent that summer in Newport, but O how changed the scene, the *world* had no charms for me now. . . .

In the autumn of that year I returned to Chester and remained for some time there. . . . Some of the Christians said I was called of God to preach. Others said, "That poor, illiterate boy, preach indeed! It is a shame to think of such a thing." And I must confess that I thought at the time that the ones who opposed it were about right in the matter. But I had no

rest. I dare not go back to my former pleasures. They seemed like thorns to my soul. . . . In November of that year Elder Harding came to Chester on his way to Liverpool and invited me to go with him. I went, thinking I might be of some use to help him convey his luggage. When we arrived at Liverpool, there was no small stir among the people when they heard of the professed conversion of that wayward boy Joseph Crandall and that he had come to exhort the young people to turn from their evil ways. As it was early in the week when we arrived, we held a number of meetings before the Lords day, but nothing special transpired. On the Sabbath we met in the Meeting house. Elder Payzant preached in the morning and Harris Harding prayed and exhorted. In the afternoon Elder Harding preached, and when done called on me to pray. I had not expected to be called upon and felt much cast down in my mind, but I thought it would seem very unkind in me to refuse when invited to pray. Besides, I felt a great want in my own soul. It seemed as though a dark gloom of spiritual death surrounded me. But when I commenced to pray the scene changed, the light of heaven shone into my soul. How long I prayed, I know not, but when I opened my eyes and looked around all was changed. The two ministers were weeping in the pulpit and the whole congregation seemed to be melted down under an awful sense of eternity. From this time the work of the Lord commenced. The two ministers said I had a special call to preach and on the next Lords day they insisted on my ascending the pulpit. But oh! how I trembled, my great fear that I was not called by God to the work of the ministry. But when I began, my fears all left me for a time. . . .

B. Techniques

The presence of a few enthusiasts does not by itself produce a popular movement. But men like Alline, Black, and Crandall were eminently successful in bringing their message to the people of the Maritimes and in making converts.

In the selections which follow, the evangelists record (and at times analyze) their techniques and the reasons for their gains. Why were the evangelicals so successful? What was characteristic of all their methods? What other approaches could have competed with theirs?

Document B–1

THE PREACHING OF HENRY ALLINE

(Alline, *Life and Journal*, pp. 82–83.)

[1780]

March 10th. I set out from Annapolis on snow shoes; as there was no riding on account of the depth of the snow. A young man went with me to carry my saddle-bags. We had to walk forty miles before we could ride. I travelled the forty miles in five days. The next day I preached and found the work of God reviving. Some who were opposers, the last time I was there, were now falling in with the work and inquiring what they must do to be saved. One man took me by the hand, saying I am rejoiced at your return this way, although the time has been when I have seen you passing my house, if it had not been for the law, I would have murdered you. O the power and goodness of God among the sons of men! . . .

I remained riding about from place to place, and preached often, until the 21st of April, when I went on board of a vessel to sail to St. John's, and arrived there the next day. I preached on the Sabbath, remained there until the next Sabbath day, and spent my time in a chamber by myself, chiefly at my pen, which may be a blessing to some, after I am in my grave. I then went on board a vessel to go up the river, but by reason of a head wind, was four days going up; but I still employed my pen, and could not but admire the wisdom of God in this particular; for when I was on land, I preached so often, that I could not get much time to write. . . .

I remained preaching and visiting from place to place, passed through many trials, and enjoyed many happy hours until the 5th of June, and then began to go down the river. I preached at several places, as I went down; but the work of God was not so powerful as it had been, although many of the christians were very happy, and some souls were born to God. O may Jesus continue a good work in the land, and bless them with the outpouring of his spirit. Much company went with me from place to place, sometimes six or seven boats loaded with people. When I came to the river's mouth I was obliged to tarry a fortnight waiting for a passage, but I hope it was not in vain; for I preached and visited the people.

Document B–2

THE PREACHING OF WILLIAM BLACK

(Richey, *Memoir of William Black*, pp. 102–5.)

Thursday, 22d of May, I set sail from Halifax for LaHave, and arrived the following day in time to get the people together for meeting. I preached from, 'If the trumpet give an uncertain sound, who shall prepare himself for the battle?' After having preached ten times to them, many of them accompanied me to the shore, where we had an affecting parting. . . .

I sailed for Liverpool, where we arrived about four o'clock in the afternoon, and a little after seven we had about three hundred to hear. . . .

Sunday, June 1st.—The Rev. Mr. Frazer preached in the meeting house twice, and I once. At noon a multitude of persons followed me to Mr. Smith's; the house was pretty well filled, and the Lord was in the midst of us. Many were deeply convinced of sin, and many were exceedingly happy, praising the Lord.—On Monday I preached on the east side of the river; and oh! what a meeting. . . .

I think there were about fourteen crying out in great anguish of soul; while others were shouting for joy. Such affecting heart-piercing cries as were uttered by one, my ears never heard. 'Oh!' she vehemently cried, 'oh! what shall I do to be saved? O my Jesus! My Jesus! What shall I do—what shall I do to be saved?' and she continued thus for the space of two hours.—In the evening I preached at the meeting house; this also was a solemn time. After the meeting, some wanted me to go this way, and some that; their entreaties were so importunate, and yet so opposite, that I was involved in much perplexity. I concluded to go over the river to brother Dean's. We kneeled on the shore, prayed and parted with those who could not accompany us. Those who conveniently could, went over the river with us, to whom I proposed that we should spend part of the night in prayer. The power of God descended upon the people; cries, groans, or rejoicing were on every hand. Thus it continued till about one o'clock in the morning, soon after which we retired.

Document B–3

A BAPTIST REVIVAL

(The Reverend James Manning to Mrs. Manning, Chester, June 14, 1806, ms. in Maritime Baptist Historical Collection, Acadia University.)

Dear Janey:

With delight I Emprove these few moments to let you know I am well. I have been getting better Sence I left home. The Lord has conducted my Steps to this place for good. I have no dubt but in my mind but our Coming to Chesster Will be had in eternal remembrances. There was a Church meetting on Satterday and the Lord was very preasant with many. It was a time of Refreshment from the Glorioys Lord. Likewise on Lords day I think it was one of the best Sabbaths I Ever Saw in my life. Mr. Chipman Spoke Very Well. The People ware much affected and in the intermishon the Saints of God at least some of them felt their Souls deliver'd. You could Scarce See a dry eye in all the house and so in the afternoon and in Sacrament time the Lord appear'd at his own table and people stay'd all most till night at the meeting house. It was hard to get any Sleep a tall. Monday a very grate audance attended and the people ware very Sollom but no grate appearance of any thing very Extraordinary. But after business was over the fire broke oute on every side. Saints Rejoiced indeed and poor sinners all in tears and Some backsliders with sorry and joye enterwoven in all there Countennaces. I think it was one off the best days I ever saw. Nor I was so much Engadged but to see and hear the fathers & mothers in Israel praying and adoring God for the many blessing they ware bless'd with and Young men and women they kept it up till night.

Document B–4

A METHODIST EVALUATION OF SUCCESS

(Joshua Marsden, The Narrative of a Mission, to Nova Scotia, New Brunswick and the Somers Islands [2d ed., London, 1827], pp. 23–24.)

Other ministers both of the Church of England, and the Scotch Church, are chiefly stationary; they are pastors of separate flocks, and seldom go far from their centre. Your missionaries, sir, are the *pioneers* of the army of Jesus; they break up new ground, they explore new scenes of labour they rove far and wide: one night they preach in the hut of a fisherman, the next in a log cottage in the forest, and the night following in the house of a farmer, or the parlour of a merchant. In summer he travels on horseback; and in winter, sometimes on horseback, and sometimes in a sleigh or sled; or when the snow is too deep, on foot, or on snow shoes. By this you will perceive, sir, that the Methodist missionary in this country, should have little of the fastidiousness of the fine gentleman about him; his motto should be, "in labours more abundant." To such an one, when entering upon his mission, the following questions might be innocently asked: will you "endure hardness as a good soldier of Jesus Christ?" Will you trample upon the "counsel of flesh and blood?" Will you, when your appointment requires it, trudge through the drifting snow, and carry your saddle-bags upon your shoulders? Will you ride upon the ice of the rivers and bays? Are you afraid to cross rapid rivers in log canoes? Are you averse to long and solitary rides in the wilderness? Can you sit in a smoky hut and are you satisfied with buck-wheat cakes for your food? Will your constitution bear cold fourteen degrees below the freezing point? Can you brave in the summer, myriads of musquitoes; and thankfully take up your lodgings in a cottage in the wilderness?

C. Doctrine

Whatever their particular religious preference, most Maritimers of Protestant persuasion were Calvinists and had therefore been brought up to believe in both limited atonement and unconditional election. Christ had died, not to save all mankind, but only those whom God in His infinite (and inscrutable) wisdom chose to save. Most Maritimers also believed in the baptism of infants in order to admit them into a religious environment which would hopefully prepare them for salvation. Limited atonement, unconditional election, and infant baptism all came under attack by various wings among the pietists. Most saw Calvinism as a hindrance to revival, a point which greatly distinguished the Maritime Awakening from those which had earlier occurred in North America. Many came to see the rejection of infant baptism as the logical extension of their revival beliefs. How do these doctrinal points assist in understanding the pietists?

Document C–1

HENRY ALLINE ON ELECTION

(Henry Alline, *Two Mites Cast into the Offering of God for the Benefit of Mankind* . . . [Dover, N.H., 1804], pp. 15–18.)

But to proceed; as I promised, you are now to receive the impression of some undeniable truths upon your mind, and carry them till your dying day; consider first the electing love of God which is as unbounded as himself, has this instant broke forth in the creation of a world of immortal vessels, capable of drinking in this electing love to all eternity, the very same instant Man has rebelled, and so ruined himself; but electing love still being as unbounded as before, pursues the guilty race, and therefore has laid help on one mighty to save even to the very uttermost all that will or can possibly be redeemed:[1] the very same instant this great restorer of mankind rides triumphant over death and hell, opens this electing love to all the fallen race,[2] and declares that the great work of Man's redemption is finished,[3] that very same instant he knocks at the sinner's door, declaring that his electing love is so great and unbounded, that it determines the salvation of every soul, that will only consent to be made a partaker of it;[4] and he that consents shall certainly be saved, but he that rejects this electing love, reprobates himself, and therefore must be damned.[5] And thus my dear Reader, you see the redeeming and electing love is so unbounded, that it fain would make every creature a partaker of it; yea you may see that it is impossible to be otherways if God himself is unlimited. And now, if you should ask (as perhaps some may) if they were not elected before? I answer no; because there never was such a period before. Well, but this is wholly a new doctrine, says one; for I have been taught, that God first determined the happiness of the one, and the misery of the other without any reference to their consenting or rejecting; and after that, by way of succession, makes use of means to bring to that place and station, which he had before intended; and that he could, if he pleased, have brought them all to a state of happiness, true dear Reader, you have been so taught, which is the way that election is generally held forth by some Men; though I presume to say, that God never sent them on that errand, for to shut up, and limit that unbounded ocean of electing and redeeming love which he has opened at no less expence than the gift of his own Son: And you see, that such a principle cannot stand any longer than it is supported by almost blasphemous reflections upon the Deity; and even, against his own word, charge him with partiality:[6] neither can I see, how such Men dare presume to declare free Grace, and unbounded Grace; when at the same time they have got the Plan contracted, and scaned in their own head so scant, as to believe, that there is not one drop of mercy for the greatest part of their Hearers; and that God never intended any for them; but only makes them a sham offer, which must of course, too shocking to be mentioned, charge God with that mockery and flattery. which, I dare say, they would not be willing should be charged against themselves. Instead of this, my Reader, I think, I have sufficiently proved, that the very nature and Decrees of God are such, as to withhold no good thing from any of his creatures, and that his electing love is so unbounded, as to fill every vessel that can possibly receive it: and therefore every creature that is lost, either angels or men, are the authors of their own misery; and that against the very nature and decrees of God.

[1] Heb. 7. 25.
[2] Heb. 2. 9. 1 John 2.2.
[3] John 19. 30.
[4] Mark 16. 16.
[5] Revel. 3, 80. 2 Pet. 3. 9.
[6] Ephe. 6. 9. Rom. 2. 11.

Document C–2

WILLIAM BLACK EXPOUNDS METHODIST DOCTRINE

(William Black to Freeborn Garrettson, Halifax, February 14, 1787, reprinted in Richey, Memoir of William Black, pp. 166–72.)

According to your desire and my promise, I now send you my thoughts on the propositions you mention. You justly observe, as they are so zealously propagated through the province, they must certainly do much harm.

1. It is affirmed, that 'man has nothing at all to do; that if he lift a hand towards his own salvation, he will be damned? But is not this contrary to the words of St. Paul,—'Work out your own salvation, with fear and trembling.' If indeed by

'towards salvation,' they meant, towards *purchasing* it, they would affirm nothing but the truth; but if they refer to our obtaining salvation, the assertion is utterly false. For though Christ has died for us, he has neither repented nor believed for us; still, therefore, if we repent not, we shall perish—if we believe not, we shall be damned. The Scriptures urge us to *turn, seek, knock, strive, wrestle, run,* &c. And is this, I would ask, doing nothing? absolutely *nothing?* Is it not for *salvation* that we are to seek, ask, wrestle and run? Does the sinner repent that he may perish, or believe that he may be damned? or rather does he not do both in order to salvation? Is not believing itself called a work?— 'This is the work of God that ye believe;' and St. Paul says, 'We have believed that we might be justified,' that is plainly, in order to justification, and of course, to salvation. Shall we then be damned for attempting to stretch forth the withered hand, and touch the hem of his garment? Does not the Gospel call upon us to renounce our self-righteousness, to fly to Christ, and to lay hold on the hope set before us? And can any soul be saved without doing this? Does not Christ command us, if we would be his disciples to deny ourselves? Is the man in his proper senses who would affirm that all this is nothing?

2. It is vehemently contended that 'neither repentance nor prayer precedes the new birth.' This also is contrary to the Scriptures.—With regard to *repentance,* John the Baptist thus opens his mission, 'Repent ye, for the kingdom of heaven is at hand;' and our Lord began to preach in the same words. Matt. iv: 17. The Apostles proclaim the same doctrine —'Repent and be converted that your sins may be blotted out.'—Now here repentance is put before forgiveness. Simon Magus was exhorted to repent. Acts viii: 20. 'God commandeth all men every where to repent.' Acts xvii: 30. Paul showed to both Jews and Gentiles that they should repent, and do works meet for repentance. Acts xxi: 20. But enough of this.————In relation to *prayer,* it may

be observed,—Some well-meaning people, apprehensive lest sinners should put prayer in the place of the Saviour, have gone very unscriptural lengths; and sometimes from the pulpit have said more against praying than against swearing. 'No unconverted man,' say they, 'ought to pray; it keeps him from Christ, and he will never be converted till he leaves off praying.' I am really of opinion that many of those who speak thus, wish well to the cause of religion; and seeing many rest in the bare form of prayer, and building on their self-righteousness, were, in order to avoid this rock, before they were aware, led into serious error; and instead of opposing the *abuse,* have inveighed against the *use* of a precious ordinance of God. . . .

3. An extremely dangerous notion has of late been received by many, respecting sin in believers. Those born of God are said to be *dead unto sin* and *alive unto God.* They are no longer slaves unto sin that they should obey it in the lusts thereof, but *new creatures* in Christ Jesus. But we are told that true faith may not only exist *without good* works, but that it may consist *with the most diabolical* works of *darkness*—that a man may be a drunkard, an adulterer, and even a murderer, without forfeiting his title to the favour of God. One told me, the other day, that if he were to live in the forementioned vices, from that day till the day of his death, his title to heaven would remain secure, nor would he be a whit the less a child of God, than when walking in the obedience of love. 'It is true,' said he, 'I do not wish to do so. If I were, it would becloud my evidence.' Yes, replied I, and forfeit your title too; for 'faith without works is dead,' and 'when the righteous man turneth away from his righteousness, and committeth iniquity, and dieth in them; for his iniquity that he hath done shall he die. . . .'

One of their teachers on a certain occasion illustrated his sentiment by this (beautiful?) simile—'A believer,' said he, 'is like a nut; it may fall into the mud, but the kernel will not be in the least defiled.' What a dreadful insinuation is here; for mark the explication:—'Though we sin with the body, the soul remains pure and undefiled.'

I also heard another of their teachers affirm that, 'a man might live in adultery and murder ten months together, and yet be a child of God—a man after God's own heart—that his soul might never sin all that time.' To prove this, he produced the case of David. That noble testimony concerning David, they forget, was not given when he was covered with the guilt of uncleanness and blood. Nor can they ever prove that David was 'a man after God's own heart' when he perpetrated those evil deeds, unless they can make it appear that the holy God delights in murder and adultery; that he forbad David to do the thing he willed he should do; that he reproved him for fulfilling his will; and that he punished him severely, inwardly and outwardly, in his person and in his family, for accomplishing his will and pleasure.

After all, I cannot but form a favourable judgment of many who hold these unscriptural tenets. I believe many of them would shudder at the thought of reducing them to practice. Many of them, I doubt not, are real lovers of Jesus. I desire always to distinguish between a man and his opinions. You may make of this letter what use you think proper.

Document C–3

HENRY ALLINE ON BAPTISM

(Alline, *Life and Journal*, p. 84)

[1780]

July. I came to Cornwallis, and remained there about four days, and found too much of the disputes about water-baptism existing among some of the christians. O how much advantage does the enemy get in the minds of christians by those zealous disputes about non-essentials; making that the chief subject of their discourses when the essentials or work of God is neglected. I have often observed in the short compass of my ministry, that when the christians get much of the life of religion with the love of God in their souls, those small matters were scarcely talked of, but whenever they met their discourse was about the work of God in the heart, and what God had done for their souls; inviting sinners to come to Christ, and setting forth in their conversation the important truths of the gospel; but as soon as religion grows cold, then they sit hours and hours discoursing about those things which would never be of service to body or soul, and proving the validity of their own method or form of some external matters, and condemn others, who do not think as they do. Ah, how many hours have I seen spent even among christians to prove the different methods of water-baptism either to infants or adults, either by sprinkling or immersion; when it would not at all help the poor soul in the least out of its fallen state back to God without the true baptism of the spirit of Christ, which alone can. O that all the distinction might be made only this, to wit, christians and the world: converted or unconverted. And that the christians or children of God might go hand in hand, as if there was no difference among them, since they are all agreed in the essentials: yea methinks every thing else is too small to be mentioned among them.

Document C—4

JOSEPH CRANDALL ON BAPTISM

("Autobiography of Joseph Crandall," pp. 20–21.)

At the commencement of our revivals in Salisbury, there was a pious man in the neighbourhood—William Linton Esq.—who would not come to hear me preach on account of the ordinance of immersion. But the Lord converted all his children, and when he observed the change in them he ventured on Lords Day to come to meeting and at the close invited me home with him and showed me great kindness. Said he was glad to see such a decided change in his children but hoped I would not persuade them to go into the water, for said he, "You are killing yourself." I told him it was not my custom to persuade people to go into the water, but I persuade them to read the Lords word. "Oh," said he, "that is right; I will not forbid them but give them advice." The Lords work prospered and they were all immersed. . . . The aged Esquire often combatted me about the "infant exclusion" as he termed it, till one day I said to him, we will dispute no more on that subject until you can show me some portion of Scripture where one person was baptised on the faith of another, for according to the word of the Lord, "Without faith it is impossible to please God" and we know that a child has no faith, and I know of no command for infant baptism on the faith of the parent or Minister. This ended all our controversy. He was indeed a convicted disciple! . . . One year later the old Esquire, while standing on the bank of the river, said in the presence of a great multitude, "for more than twelve months I have been convinced that there was not one single word in all the bible for sprinkling or pouring on infants and yet tradition was so strong that my stubborn heart would not yield. But now I come at the eleventh hour to obey my Lord and master." Thus we led the old English seceder into that ordinance practised and commanded by the holy son of God.

D. Attitudes Towards Authority

One of the major difficulties faced by the evangelicals was that Anglicanism was the established and favoured religion in every Maritime province. By and large, the pietists attempted to avoid conflict with the authorities of church and state both from conviction and out of practical considerations. In the selections which follow, the fundamental attitude of the evangelicals toward government and public authority is revealed. Why did pietism tend to avoid political involvement? What limits did the pietists place on their acceptance of Anglican establishment?

Document D—1

HENRY ALLINE ON POLITICAL OFFICE HOLDING

(Alline, *Life and Journal*, p. 44.)

[1776]

About this time I was solicited by some of the officers to put in for a commission in the militia; I utterly refused to take one step in pursuit of it; yet after this, when I got a little in the dark, I began to wish that I had taken it; for that grandeur and the esteem of the world, which the devil and my own corrupt nature suggested, I might obtain by success in a few years, began to look pleasant to me, like Eve's apples, pleasant to the eyes, and a fruit to be desired: but while I was meditating on this, the Lord broke into my soul with the revivals of his grace, the sweetness of his love; and shewed me the vanity of all things here below, and the worth of souls, which gave me such a longing desire to go forth with the gospel, and proclaim the Redeemer's name, that my soul cried out, Send me, send me, O Lord God, in thy blessed name, and take away all honour, but the glory of the cross, and all commissions but a commission from heaven to go forth, and enlist my fellow-mortals to fight under the banners of King Jesus: and my soul rejoices to take it for my whole portion, while on this mortal stage. Sometimes I feared that I was only imposed upon by the devil and my proud heart, and tried myself, whether I did not covet to have a great name in the world, and to become popular.

Document D-2

PIETISM AND THE AMERICAN REVOLUTION

(Henry Alline, A Sermon on a Day of Thanksgiving . . . on the 21st of November, 1782 [Halifax, 1783], pp. 22-23.)

Think O my hearers, how infinitely we are indulged, invironed with the arms of omnipotence, wrapped in the mantle of love, and cultivated with the word and spirit, under the balmy wing of everlasting kindness. O how largely have we been made to partake of the goodness of God, and share in the favours of his hand! and O how little returns! yea and if I come a step nearer still omiting our being excluded from heathenish darkness and from the cruelty of oppression and tyranny, how are we screened from the trials of our (once happy) Nation in the convulsions of the present day? how have we sat in peace while this inhuman war hath spread devastation thro' our Neighbouring Towns, and Colonies like a flood! not my dear hearers because of the cleaness of our hands, or past righteousness: for surely we have not only had our hands equally engaged in the sins that have incurred the lamentable disorder; but have likewise perpetrated the same crimes, and remained unfruitful and incorrigible under such distinguishing advantages.

Yea and when we have daily expected the impending cloud, and to share in the bitter cup, heaven's indulgent hand has interposed and averted the blow.

Yea, and more to be admired still we have not only been excluded from the destructive scene, but while they were involved in the dreadful calamity, we have been blest with that unparellel blessing the moving work of the Spirit of God; a work of grace, and the advancing of the Redeemer's kingdom in almost every corner of the Province; which, blessed be God, (although many may and do despise it) I have been an eye witness to, and a happy partaker of; yea, and many hundreds will likewise forever adore God for the blessed Work.

Document D-3

METHODIST RESPONSE TO ANGLICAN CRITICISM

(Marsden, Narrative, pp. 185-88.)

Ah sir! how truly pitiable is the case of the rich and great; frequently placed out of the range of those powerful means, that might arouse the guilty conscience from its delusive slumbers, or bring home the truth of God to the heart. . . .

Life passes in a circle of amusement, compliment, and frivolity: fashion and pleasure, are the order of the day. Truth, in its pure form, they are taught to call fanaticism; religious conversation, cant; strictness in religion, methodism; and the vital experience of godliness, enthusiasm. For their amusement, the buffoon and the mimic, dress true piety in the fool's coat of caricature, and the theatre, not the bible, gives the *cue* to religion. The poor in spirit are deemed hypocrites, the evangelical christian is nicknamed a saint, and places where the gospel is preached in its purity, conventicles. How truly thankful should we be, that our lot is cast in the middle walks of life, far from that magic circle, where the gay throw fortune, conscience, health and time away. While colonel B. was wicked in the worst sense of that term; an unbeliever, a man of pleasure, a carousing, profane, and dashing officer, no fault was found with him; but alas, he had become moral, serious, and godly, and withal was united to a body of christians odious in the sight of many of the rich and gay: hence, a certain c———n, offended that God had made the methodists the humble instruments of conveying his truth to the colonel's mind, was pleased to observe, that his religion was only the half-way house to atheism; and he was no longer deemed fit company, either for the clergy, or the venerable bishop. But God forbid, that a line of mine should ever underrate the character of those who are set apart to serve the sanctuary, for whether he be in or out of the established church. . . .

. . . But when a bishop or a clergyman is an enemy to all religion, save and except what flows through the channel of canonical or high church episcopacy, when all others, whatever good the blessed God may do by them, however amiable in their lives, respectable in their acquirements, or various in their learning, are deemed *unauthorized* teachers, and out of the *true* pale. I am ready to say in the language of a pious formula "from envy, hatred, and all uncharitableness, good Lord deliver us." For where in such a case, is the liberal and catholic spirit of the blessed Redeemer? where is the love that hopeth all things? where is the "meekness instructing those that oppose themselves;" if God peradventure will give them repentance to the acknowledging of the truth; that they may recover themselves out of the snare of the devil." Some of the colonel's relations, in writing to him, after the garbled accounts they had heard, begged of him for God's sake to think upon his military honours, and not tarnish his respectable family and name, with such a low drivelling thing as fanaticism, alias, enthusiasm; alias, methodism; alias, experimental and vital religion. The witty said he kept three chaplains to pray for the good of his soul, and the wicked and incorrigible hated him, because, as a magistrate, he put the law in force against swearing and sabbath-breaking. Thus, when a man of dignified station becomes truly godly, his former gay companions stigmatize and vilify him, and consign him over as a person of a little mind to oblivion; so it often fares, O blessed Jesus! with thy pure religion and gospel.

E. Criticism

Revivalism had many enemies, particularly within the more traditional religious denominations. The Anglicans, the older New England–oriented Puritan ministers, and many Presbyterians attacked evangelical principles and activities on a variety of grounds. How legitimate are the criticisms made in the following selections? How would a pietist answer them?

Document E–1

A LAYMAN'S VIEW: PIETISM AS FANATICISM

(Patrick Campbell, *Travels in the Interior Inhabited Parts of North America. In the Years 1791 and 1792* [Edinburgh, 1793], pp. 310–11.)

I set out from Frederick Town on foot; and walking through Maugerville along the river side, I fell in with a gentleman travelling the same way. As we were conversing along, I heard a great noise in a house at some distance, on which I stopped to listen, and told the gentleman that there were some people fighting in that house; at which he smiled and answered, "That he knew the place well; that it was a house of worship, where a number of religious fanatics preached, every one prayed for himself, and the louder they roared, the more sincere and devout they were supposed to be; so that the one vied with the other who should bawl out loudest." When we had come nearer I was struck with amazement at the hideous noise they made, and which could be heard at a considerable distance; I asked him if he supposed they would permit me to go in to see them; he said I might, provided I behaved properly, and did not laugh, or offer to ridicule them in any shape; that they would not prevent me, or give me the least trouble; thus encouraged, I went in, and found they consisted of about three score persons, of both sexes, all on their knees, and in tears, every one praying for himself, as already said, and bawling out, O Lord! O Lord! which were the only expressions I understood of what they said. After standing for a few minutes in the house, my hair almost standing on end at the horror of the scene these miserable people exhibited, I returned, and just as I was passing the window of their apartment, some one called out, that the devil was among them; upon which they all gave a yell, louder and more horrible than any Indian war hoop I had ever heard; and if the devil himself was to show his physiognomy in all the frightful grimaces ascribed to him in the middle of them, every door bolted, so that none could escape his clutches, their screaming could not have been louder or more horrible. I returned to the road with deep impressions of the deplorable effects of fanaticism on the human mind. . . .

Document E–2

THE PURITAN VIEW: PIETISM AS DIVISION AND SCHISM

(Jonathan Scott, *A Brief View of the Religious Tenets and Sentiments, Lately Published and Spread in the Province of Nova Scotia* [Halifax, 1784], pp. 218–20.)

This is one of the strong Refuges that those betake themselves to, who by their bold, ignorant and absurd Assertions, and imprudent, irregular, and disorderly Practices, bring all to Confusion in the Church of God. They have it at their Tongue's End, Christ came to send Division, and was opposed and contradicted and his Life sought to be taken away; and all the Apostles were persecuted and vilified and counted as the Offscouring of all Things, and therefore it is not strange that we should be blamed and charged with Error and Disorder. Whereas the Case may be widely different, and certainly is so in many Cases: Christ was opposed and persecuted for the Truth only, and for good Works, and not evil Actions; and the holy Apostles and other Ministers of Christ were persecuted for their pure and holy Doctrines, Reproofs and Instructions, and for their holy Walk and Behaviour. But these suffer for their *Faults*, their Errors and disorderly Walk and Practices, whereby they bring Difficulty on themselves and others and Confusion into the Church; and then fly to, and alledge the *Example of Christ* and his *Apostles*, that they were greatly opposed and persecuted; and here they quiet and harden themselves in Wickedness, and are remote from all Repentance; while the Cause of Christ bleeds through their Means, and others with Tears and Grief are left to undo what they have done. Until Ministers and Churches are made wise to bring out *Seducers* and *disorderly Persons* from this secret Refuge, and strong Hold, where they constantly shelter, there is but finall Prospect of Safety from this Quarter. . . .

Not only is our Land overspread with Tenets and Principles, which by their plain Construction and Meaning, and their most natural and direct Tendancy, overthrow and destroy the Truths and Doctrines of divine Revelation; but also this Province is overspread with religious Contentions, Divisions and Separations; so that there is scarce a Church or religious Community that I can hear of in this Province, but what our Author [Henry Alline] has broke in upon, and drawn off a Party from it by some Means or other.

Document E–3

THE OFFICIAL ANGLICAN VIEW: PIETISM AS SEDITION

(John Wentworth to Secretary of State, Halifax, July 27, 1801, ms. in Nova Scotia State Papers, Vol. A133.)

He [Anglican bishop Charles Inglis] fully concurs with me, in opinion that every exertion should be made to provide for constant performance of public worship according to the Church of England, both in Halifax, and in other parts of this Province, where it is certain Missionarys are most seriously wanted to preserve the poor dispersed settlers from the dangerous fanatical assiduity of mendicant, migratory new light teachers, who are generally as badly disposed to the dutys of loyalty as they are to our religious establishment. Nor have I doubt that among them are artful people, acting under the wicked influence of democratic, foreign Anarchists. Their mischief can only be counteracted, and His Majesty's subjects best preserved from civil and religious distractions, by the establishment of additional Missionarys in several parts of the Province—Five or Six might be employed immediately with the highest usefulness— Their salarys not less than one hundred pounds sterling per Annum would be infinitely compensated by the advantage— From Halifax to the remotest bounds of the Province on the Gulf of St. Lawrence, there is but one Missionary of the Church of England—It was happily observed that in his Parish the people were peaceable, orderly, sober and without itinerant Teachers—I found the contrary without exception on all the rest of my progress, and could trace it to the mischievous pursuits of Itinerants, unchecked by any regular Church establishment—Their arts are so exerted, and toward such a dispersed various people, that the Laws do not reach the evil, nor is it at all times prudent to afford opportunity to such persons to misrepresent the proceedings of law, as the influence of persecution and intolerance.

Document E–4

THE PRESBYTERIAN VIEW: THE PIETIST AS BIGOT

(Thomas McCulloch, *The Letters of Mephibosheth Stepsure* [Halifax, 1862] pp. 91–94.)

Mrs. Sham and Miss Clippit were exceedingly religious in their own way, and zealous, too, in proportion. Accordingly, they spent most of their time running about the town to tell everybody their experiences and how they felt. How many believed them I cannot exactly say; but, as people by practice improve in religion as well as in other things, these ladies at last became to acute, that, by looking in a person's face, they could ascertain his state precisely; and when they found it bad, they could even do a great deal for his conversion.

When my neighbour Scantocreesh came to our town, because he wrought pretty hard, Mrs. Sham declared him to be in a natural state. But Saunders was not easily alarmed: he said that slothfulness in business is no mark of fervency of spirit. At last the two ladies sent him word that they designed to hold a meeting in his house, in order to pray for him and convert him; and, as Mrs. Sham could recount something very like miracles, as seals of her ministry, she was pretty confident of success. Saunders did not know very well what to make of it. He said that, in Scotland, neither the Stuarton sickness nor the Cambuslang work (both businesses of the same sort) had done much good; and he doubted that his conversion would come on slowly in their hands. He let them know, however, that as they seemed to think his house nearer heaven than their own, it was the best place for praying with a prospect of being heard; and, therefore, they were welcome to come and try their hand at the business. At the same time, he gave notice to a few of us that he was going to be converted, and asked us to step over and witness the process.

When the time arrived, we were all there, to see what would become of Saunders; and, really, everything looked as if some strange event was about to happen. My neighbour is a hard-faced Scotchman; but, as if he had set his face against conversion, it seemed harder than usual. The two ladies, also, when they arrived, along with the others, to assist them in holding the meeting, appeared exceedingly solemn. Instead of being cheerful and chatty, as Widow Scant usually was, they looked as grim as if they had been going to hang Saunders. Before they had well sat down, Mrs. Sham began to tell him what miserable sinners she and Sister Clippit had been,

to which my neighbour nodded a cordial assent; but, when she recounted the joys which succeeded their conversion, he seemed to examine their grim countenances with a great deal of care. She then ran over with much volubility, what she called marks of grace, and the experiences of gracious souls; and was just beginning to tell him about the day of judgment and its consequences to himself, when Saunders interrupted her by saying that he did not expect his conversion to be an easy job, and that we had better first take something to eat. To such a reasonable proposal nobody objected. My neighbour, who is a very hospitable man, gave us his very best cheer and I could easily see, that, though the two ladies had perceived nothing to be commended in Saunders, they found something very good about his house. After our repast my neighbour observed that, about a business of this sort, he understood there was always a good deal of tumbling and roaring. He therefore proposed, that, as the evening was very fine and his house small, we had better all go to the smooth green before his door, where we would have plenty of room. Accordingly, we turned out, one after another, as fast as possible.

When we were all upon the green, Saunders said to the two ladies, that he had now got them out of his house, and would tell them a little of his mind before they began; and first of all, that if he needed to be converted, he was resolved that it should be done by the word of God and his own minister, who had some sense and religion; and not by silly women like them, ladened with sins, and as ignorant of true godliness as his young stots. He told Mrs. Sham that, before running about the country, pretending to convert sober, industrious folks, she had better show a little Christianity at home, by lessening that misery in which her idleness, ill-management and ill nature had involved her family. As for Sister Clippit, he advised her to find a husband for herself, and get children, as the Bible bid her. This, he assured her, would be more to her credit than tattling through the town about her experience and marks of grace, when everybody could see nothing about her but marks of corruption; and, therefore, concluded her to be one of Solomon's foolish women, who are clamorous and know nothing. They, and the like of them, he said, were a disgrace to religion. Instead of minding their own affairs, and living comfortably like other decent folks, they ran about the country in idleness, living upon their neighbours the one half of the time, and starving the other; and if it fared ill with themselves, it fared worse with their religion. Every fool among them was a preacher and a converter; and when a decent minister who could put a little sense in them happened to come among them, they soon starved him away. They would give him plenty of prayers, and long stories which they had heard from one another, about their conversions, and experiences, and marks of grace. But, when necessity forced the poor gentleman to remind them that the labourer is worthy of his hire, his whole congregation would forsake him to run after the like of Shadrach Howl, whom no careful man would trust with the feeding of his swine. With their groaning and whining, and slang about religion, he said they had made decent people who have some sense of it, almost ashamed to mention many of its doctrines. At last, Saunders concluded with advising them to go home, read their Bible, and mind their own calling, and let ministers mind theirs. This, he said, would help them to redeem their character, which they would soon find to be necessary; for he hoped to see the day in this province when everybody, instead of running after them, would, according to the Bible, believe them to be silly women, who had turned aside unto Satan.

PROBLEM 7

The Goderich Memorandum

J. E. REA

St. Paul's College, University of Manitoba

In April of 1832, William Lyon Mackenzie, the stormy petrel of Upper Canadian politics, set sail for England. He found the trip relaxing; as indeed he might, since for the past few years he had been intimately caught up in the hurly-burly of Provincial politics, with little effect, from his point of view. Most recently, his strictures against the so-called "Family Compact" of Upper Canada had resulted in his being thrice expelled from the House of Assembly. And now he was returning to Britain, armed with petitions with which to persuade the Colonial Secretary that only radical changes would placate the discontented people for whom he had been deputed to speak.

With what hope of success he viewed his mission, it is difficult to say. Mackenzie was becoming embittered by the failure of Reformers to influence the development of Upper Canada. Indeed, the voters of the province had returned a Tory majority to the Assembly in the election of 1830. It was almost incomprehensible to the future rebel that the people could be so deluded. What was there in the Tory ideology that could attract them? Mackenzie could see only grasping and conniving men bent on solidifying their political power and enriching themselves from government patronage. But the Upper Canadian Tory was more than a self-seeking oligarch.

The constitutional difficulties which were disrupting the province, and had resulted in the clashes between Reformers and Tories, grew out of the Constitutional Act of 1791. In this document the British Government had created the political framework for Upper and Lower Canada. It was very much an 18th-century solution to the problem of reconciling liberty and order; in another sense, it represented the British conception of the political breakdown which had provoked the American Revolution. The essential failure, it was felt, had been an unbridled colonial assembly which had arrogated to itself the bulk of political power at the expense of the executive authority. A remedy for this weakness in the structure of Upper and Lower Canada was considered vital to their continuance within the Empire.

Yet, it was recognized that a repressive reaction would never be permanently acceptable in a North American environment involving British people. Some method must be devised whereby the popular voice could be given expression and, at the same time, controlled. The Constitutional Act of 1791, it was hoped, would accomplish this objective. It provided for an Assembly elected on a relatively broad franchise. But it also provided for a Legislative Council which would serve as a check upon the popular body. Indeed, it was intended at the time to make this Legislative Council an hereditary group—an attempt to create a colonial aristocracy. While this became a dead letter, the upper chamber did constitute an independent element in the legislative process through its ability to reject measures of the Assembly. The executive, thus, would not be placed in direct confrontation with an overpowerful Assembly.

As a further conservative influence, it was intended to give the Church of England a preferred position in the colony. This would, firstly, serve as a constant manifestation of the British character of the province. Secondly, and equally as important, the Anglican Church would through its ministry instill the precepts of loyalty and social order which would strengthen and stabilize the imperial connection. To this end, the hierarchy of the church were accorded political appointments, and a patrimony was established by extensive grants of crown land.

The scheme seemed to work well in the early years. There was little political debate, except as to the proper methods of representation in a frontier society. The sheer physical obstacles to settlement, and the sparse population, proved serious inhibitions to political sophistication. Since there were few well-educated people who could afford the time, appointments to the Legislative Council did not arouse much controversy. They were, as a rule, conservative, and kept a wary eye on the bustling democracy next door. The War of 1812 seemed to confirm their darkest suspicions. The emotional upheaval of the war, and the fact that the population of Upper Canada was heavily American in origin, inspired a reaction in the years which followed.

The sense of being threatened by a rising tide of democracy was exhibited in an attempt to stifle dissent and equate loyalty with anti-radicalism. The Conservatives, or Tories, found their greatest defense in the restrictive forms of the act of 1791. As the Reform spirit grew during the 1820's, they relied more and more on the constitutional irresponsibility of the executive, and the protective outwork of the Legislative Council's virtual veto of legislation. Yet, it is important to recognize that throughout the period they were able to win their share of electoral victories. It was this apparent paradox that so distracted Mackenzie and the more zealous Reformers.

Thus, the Family Compact had a not unacceptable vision of the future of a British province in North America. But it was a vision based on certain immutable convictions—the maintenance of the British connection and a contempt for the American republican experiment, a strong and necessary bond between church and state, a hierarchial society, and steady economic progress. To the Tories, the activities of Mackenzie and those who followed his lead were at best mischievous, at worst, seditious. They posed a threat, not only to their positions, but to their conception of a viable British society in North America. Their value system was an integrated whole and must be defended as such.

Whether Mackenzie charged the Legislative Council with obstructing the will of the Assembly, or attacked Bishop Macdonell and Archdeacon Strachan as "political priests," the Tories would close ranks. Criticism would be equated with disloyalty.

The fact that Lord Goderich, the Colonial Secretary, gave careful attention to Mackenzie during his stay in London, was bad enough. But when he apparently gave credence to his charges, the Tories were appalled. The success of their design for Upper Canada depended, they were convinced, on firm support on the part of the home government. If there were any wavering, the province would be inundated with republican ideas. Thus, the Tories and their newspapers tended to overreact when Goderich sent a long commentary on the condition of Upper Canada to Lieutenant-Governor Sir John Colborne. It seemed clear that while the Colonial Secretary discounted much of Mackenzie's more abusive rhetoric, he was prepared to recognize some substance in the criticism.

The particular issues which Goderich took up, and which produced the greatest reaction in Upper Canada, were interrelated—the composition and powers of the Legislative Council, and the presence, in that body, of high-ranking clergymen. Legislative Councillors were appointed by the Crown (in fact, on the recommendation of the Provincial Executive) and, in practice, held their positions for life. Since they were not amenable to popular pressure, they could block legislation with immunity. In theory, the Legislative Council, in a balanced constitutional system, would perform a dual function; it would protect the popular assembly from the encroachments of the executive, and at the same time, protect the executive from the popularly elected body. It would, in other words, be the balance wheel. Mackenzie charged, however, that in Upper Canada, the Legislative Council and the Executive were mutually sustaining, indeed, indistiguishable. He had arrived at the conclusion that, because of this imbalance, the constitution was really unworkable without drastic modification. The Legislative Council, for its part, would consider any weakening of its position as a concession to democracy. Any revision of its independent character would upset the whole constitutional framework.

This same attitude is evident in the Tory reaction to the Colonial Secretary's suggestion that Strachan and Macdonell might better serve their interests by resigning their Council seats. Anglicanism and Catholicism were class religions in their social implications. The insistence that man should accept his lot in life, that his reward would be otherworldly, was a buttress to a stable society. The inculcation of the concepts of loyalty and submission provided the necessary bulwark against the democratizing influence of frontier "enthusiasm." Thus it was the social utility of the Church-State connection that the Tories felt must be preserved.

This ideological immobility of Upper Canadian Toryism was both a strength and a weakness. As it was articulated and institutionalized, it appeared to become entrenched.

But were the Tories right in thus attempting to isolate Upper Canada from American influence? Was it even possible for a political framework such as that established by the Constitutional Act of 1791 to survive in the North American environment? Did Tory intransigence make Mackenzie's pathetic revolt inevitable?

For further reading, the best general treatment of the period will be found in Gerald Craig, *Upper Canada, The Formative Years* (1963). On the Family Compact specifically, there are some older studies: W. S. Wallace, *The Family Compact* (1915); A. Dunham, *Political Unrest in Upper Canada* (1922), chapt.

ii; and E. Ewart and Julia Jarvis, "The Personnel of the Family Compact," *Canadian Historical Review*, Vol. VII (1926). A good, brief description is R. E. Saunders, "Who was the Family Compact," *Ontario History*, Vol. XLIX (1957); also David Earl, *The Family Compact: Aristocracy or Oligarchy* (1967). The most perceptive examination of Tory ideology will be found in S. F. Wise, "Upper Canada and the Conservative Tradition," *Profiles of a Province* (1967).

A. The Memorandum

On November 8, 1832, Lord Goderich, the British Colonial Secretary, sent a lengthy memorandum to Sir John Colborne, Lieutenant-Governor of Upper Canada. Goderich had listened patiently to Mackenzie and forwarded his collected impressions of the state of Upper Canada and his thoughts on needed change. What does the letter reveal of the nature of the colonial relationship? Is Goderich critical of the government in power? What does the discussion of representation illustrate about the political difficulties of newly settled areas? To what extent does the Colonial Secretary seem determined to preserve the constitutional arrangements adopted in 1791? What is his view of the proper function of the Lieutenant-Governor? Does he accept the position assumed by the "Family Compact"?

Document A—1

TEXT OF THE MEMORANDUM
(Public Archives of Canada, Record Group 7, G 1, Vol. LXIX.)

Downing Street, 8th Nov. 1832

Sir:

During several months past I have been in occasional communication with Mr. William McKenzie upon the subject of the grievances said to exist in Upper Canada, and for the redress of which various petitions have been addressed to His Majesty.

As Mr. McKenzie has been the bearer of those Petitions to this Country, I have gladly availed myself of his residence here to obtain such information as he has it in his power to give respecting the opinions and wishes of that portion of the inhabitants of the Province by whom he has been deputed to act; and altho' I have adhered to the general rule of declining to explain the views of His Majesty's Government on questions of Canadian policy to any person except the Governors of the Province, I have been

anxious to afford Mr. McKenzie the most ample opportunity of doing justice to the case which he laid before me. From the voluminous mass of that Gentleman's correspondence I have selected three documents which profess to embody the entire substance of that case as it affects the present condition of Upper Canada; of these documents I have the honor to enclose copies for your information.

I propose in this dispatch to follow Mr. McKenzie thro' those parts of his statements respecting the Representation of the Inhabitants in the House of General Assembly which appear so essential to the consideration of the practical questions he has undertaken to agitate. But conforming myself to what I consider as really relevant, I shall necessarily pass over in silence some details which have been introduced with no perceptible tendency to elucidate the subjects in discussion, and much invective and sarcasm which would have been far more conveniently spared. It is with no intentional disrespect to Mr. McKenzie that I remark that he has adopted a style and method of composition singularly ill adapted to bring questions of so much intricacy and importance to a definite issue. But however discursive may be his papers, or however acrimonious their tone, I am not on that account disposed to withhold my attention from any useful suggestions they may contain for the public good.

I am more induced to devote to this discussion such leizure [sic] as I can command, because I am solicitous that the comparatively small body of persons whom Mr. McKenzie represents should have no reason to think that their complaints had been overborne by the contrary declarations of the much more numerous bodies opposed to them. Mr. McKenzie indeed would have himself understood as speaking the sentiments of the entire population of Upper Canada, excepting only a few public functionaries, whose sentiments are opposed to those of the public at large. It is not necessary, however, to have a very long experience of public controversies of this nature to be aware of the levity with which such pretensions are continually advanced upon the slightest and most inadequate grounds.

Almost all complaints, the most opposite and contradictory not excepted, which reach this office are nearly as a matter of course preferred in the name of the collective society, and it becomes necessary to distinguish carefully in such cases between mere rhetorical embellishments and statements made in the cautious and measured tone of truth. Now in the present instance I find that Mr. McKenzie's views are supported by 44 petitions, which have been signed on the whole by 12,075 persons. On the other hand, I have before me no less than thirty-three petitions from the different Counties, Districts, Towns and Townships of the Province signed by 26,854 persons, who concur in expressing their cordial satisfaction in those Laws and Institutions which the other set of petitioners have

impugned. Such a body is far too numerous and many of the individuals composing it are far too considerable in their station and character to justify the supposition that they can be in a state of dependence on the local Government, or controlled by any unworthy influence in their public conduct. I am driven to the dilemma of either supposing this great mass of the people of Upper Canada ignorant or corrupt, or of concluding that a very small minority of the whole population concur in Mr. McKenzie's views. The former supposition is as improbable as it is offensive. The latter however contradictory to Mr. McKenzie's assertions, is verified by many of the particular facts which he has advanced or admitted. But altho' I conceive this gentleman's constituents to be opposed by the general current of public opinion, I do not in the slightest degree mean to dispute their collective or individual respectability; and there is no class of the Canadian People, however small, nor individual amongst, however obscure his station, to whose petitions His Majesty does not require that the most exact and respectful attention should be given.

I shall in the first place advert to the paper to which Mr. McKenzie has given the title of "Observations on the State of the Representation of the People of Upper Canada in the Legislature of that Province."

In performing this task, however, I must decline to pursue the discussion into those redundant and misplaced details with which Mr. McKenzie has encumbered it.

The great object of Mr. McKenzie's censure is the Election Law, which was passed by Lieutenant-Governor, Council and Assembly of Upper Canada in the year 1820. I might perhaps, not without reason, raise a preliminary objection to the discussion of that subject at all. If the Election Laws of the Province require amendment, the change must originate not with the Executive Government, but with the popular branch of the local Legislature. Any interference of the Ministers of the Crown would be reprobated, probably by Mr. McKenzie himself, and certainly by his brother Journalists as an unconstitutional encroachment. If, therefore, I advert to the question at all, it is because, in the prospect that such a discussion will be provoked by the petitioners, I think it fit that you should be apprised of the views which His Majesty's Government entertain on this subject, that you may not be destitute of a rule for your guidance in the acceptance or rejection of any Bill which may be passed by the Legislative Council and Assembly for the amendment of the Election Laws.

If I have found occasion to lament the redundancies, I cannot less regret the deficiencies of Mr. McKenzie's documents. He has travelled thro' this protracted discussion without finding himself called upon to notice, still less to refute the arguments by which it has been usual to vindicate the Constitution of the Provincial House of Assembly. Yet it is impossible that he can be ignorant, nor credible that he should regard them as deficient at least in plausibility. An ignorant reader of his papers might be left with the impression that the question was altogether new, and that the existing Constitution had never been vindicated on the principles and on the example of the most free and independent Governments. How utterly remote this is from the fact, is clear to every man whose attention has been given to the affairs of Upper Canada for the last few years.

It is a fact familiar to all who are conversant with the Legislative history of North America that a problem of no light difficulty has continually arisen respecting the distribution of the elective franchise amongst the inhabitants resident in different parts of the same State or Province. The surface of the country is generally divided for political purposes into sections of nearly equal areas. But those Counties or Townships which are in the immediate vicinity of the Capitol, or which are intersected by great navigable streams or bounded by lakes, are peopled with far greater rapidity than the more remote Districts. Hence it has repeatedly hap-

pened that a single Metropolitan or trading County has contained a population exceeding in wealth and number many newly settled Counties of similar dimensions. Accordingly when capital and numbers have been made the exclusive bases of the Representation, one portion of the State or Province has acquired an influence in the Legislature which has reduced to comparative insignificance the weight of all the other divisions of the Country. The favored district has thus been able, thro' its Representatives, to throw upon the less fortunate sections a most unequal weight of taxation, and to refuse to them a fair participation in the benefits of the Judicial and other Institutions, to the support of which the Revenue was applied. Local interests have predominated over the general interest, and discontents have been engendered, threatening the stability of the Government and tending to an abrupt severance of one part of the State or Province from the rest.

It appears however to have been perceived by the Upper Canadian Assembly in the year 1820 that they might extricate the Province from one difficulty at the expense of another yet more considerable. A County might contain a very inconsiderable body of persons for some time after it was first redeemed from the wilderness and thus a choice of Members might actually be committed to a very few Electors who might themselves be subject to some unworthy influence. It was therefore required that no County should be represented in the Assembly by a District Member until the inhabitants numbered one thousand at least. But with the foresight which is perceptible in every part of this law it seems to have been perceived that there was considerable danger in leaving any body of new settlers unrepresented, and to obviate that inconvenience the inhabitants of each County whilst yet below the required number were authorized to vote in the least populous adjoining County.

I cannot suppose that a Gentleman who has taken so active a part in the affairs of the Province as has fallen to the share of Mr. McKenzie should have been really unapprised of considerations so familiar to every man acquainted with the subject as those to which I have adverted, tho' as a controversial writer he may perhaps have not consulted [them] for the momentary success of his argument, in suppressing all allusion to them.

I must entirely decline as perfectly irrelevant to any practical question the enquiry whether at a comparatively remote period prosecutions against the Editors of Newspapers were improperly instituted or not. It is needless to look beyond Mr. McKenzie's Journal to be convinced that there is no latitude which the most ardent lover of free discussion ever claimed for such writers, which is not at present enjoyed with perfect impunity in Upper Canada.

I next reach a statement that the local Government encourages dependent persons, holding offices during pleasure, and "debarred by the Laws of England from being concerned at Elections, to use the great influence attendant upon office, to secure seats in the Representative Body in order that its voice may be wholly under Executive control, altho'," adds Mr. McKenzie, "it is an undoubted truth that the interests of the local authorities and those of the Colonists are separate and distinct." As a writer habitually engaged in political controversies, Mr. McKenzie may not be fully alive to the injustice of advancing charges against the Servants of the Public unsupported by distinct evidence of their truth; but it is my duty to refuse credit to such imputations as I have quoted, unless they should be clearly substantiated by evidence. For widely as I dissent from the assertion so confidently made that the interests of the local Government are distinct from those of the inhabitants at large, I admit that the abuse of the influence attendant upon office for the purpose of exercising improper control over Elections would justly expose to the heaviest censure those to whom it could with truth be imputed. On this subject, however, in the absence of any more definite statements, I can only instruct you

that His Majesty expects and requires you neither to practice nor to allow on the part of those who are officially subordinate to you any interference with the Right of His Subjects to the free choice of their Representatives.

It is represented that to raise up and multiply the friends of arbitrary and exclusive privileges, persons in authority in and out of the Assembly resist all plans of general Education, and that places of learning are established only for the children of those who hold Government offices and a few other wealthy and influential individuals. It is not easy altogether to repress the expression of those feelings with which I cannot but receive such unworthy imputations upon the character of so many upright and enlightened men, unsupported by any proof whatever, except a general reference, which I am unable to verify, to a report said to have been made on some occasion by the present Chief Justice of the Province.

Even assuming, what is most improbable, that Mr. Robinson really obstructs to the utmost of his power the advance of general Education and knowledge from the base motives so lightly imputed by Mr. McKenzie, I utterly deny that the King's Government either in this Country or in Upper Canada, are responsible for the opinion which Mr. Robinson may some years ago have advocated in the House of Assembly. It is, however, not unimportant to advert to this subject, because Mr. McKenzie cannot assert more peremptorily that I deny the existence of any such narrow and preposterous policy as that of consigning the Children of the Yeomanry to ignorance, lest knowledge should render them independent in action or in thought. His Majesty now directs me to instruct you to forward to the very utmost of your lawful authority and influence, every scheme for the extension of Education amongst the Youth of the Province, and especially amongst the poorest and most destitute of their number.

I deeply regret that in some parts of his papers Mr. McKenzie should have left in much obscurity the simple matters of facts which it might have been really important to consider. Thus he speaks of Preachers taught to meddle in the political quarrels of Factions and parties and of their leaders being "accomodated with Seats in the political Councils of the State" and of the Governemnt "keeping in pay a Political Priesthood." It would surely have been as impressive and more useful to have stated that the Bishop and the Archdeacon are both in the list of the Legislative Council, but that it is expected of those Gentlemen that they should altogether abstain from interference in any secular matters which may be agitated at the Board. Whether, even under this restriction, their holding such Seats is really desirable is a question upon which I am fully prepared to listen with the utmost attention to any advice which I may receive from yourself, from the House of Assembly or from any other competent authority. I have no solicitude for retaining either the Bishop or the Archdeacon on the list of Councillors, but am, on the contrary, rather predisposed to the opinion that by resigning their Seats they would best consult their own personal comfort and the success of their designs for the Spiritual good of the People. But any such resignation must be voluntary, since the office is held for life and were it otherwise, no consideration could induce me to advise His Majesty to degrade the Bishop or the Archdeacon from the Stations they occupy except on the most conclusive proof of misconduct. But even Mr. McKenzie does not impute any violation of duty to them.

Mr. McKenzie has concluded this paper by predictions of bloodshed and Civil War, and a dissolution of the connexion between Upper Canada and this Kingdom. He may well suppose that such a prospect would be regarded by His Majesty's Government with a degree of concern and anxiety to which it would be difficult to give any adequate expression. But against gloomy prophecies of this nature every man conversant with public business must learn to fortify his mind. They have ever been the resource of those who endeavour to extort from the fears of the Government concessions in favor of which no adequate reasons could be urged. I will not adopt the injurious opinions which Mr. McKenzie seems to entertain of the People of Upper Canada. I reject as a libel on that loyal and enlightened race of men the supposition that they would violate their sworn fidelity to the King and desolate their native land with blood.

B. Reaction to the Memorandum

The Goderich Memorandum was met by varying responses within the Province of Upper Canada. The Legislative Council, the Assembly and the press all offered their own interpretations. What are the assumptions of the Legislative Councillors about the nature of Upper Canadian society? What do they conceive their own role to be in the constitutional structure? How would you describe their reaction to intervention by Great Britain in Upper Canadian affairs?

What does the rather peremptory response of the Assembly reveal of that chamber's relationship with the Colonial Office? What does it indicate about the temper of political life in Upper Canada?

What does the newspaper account tell us about the role of the press in Upper Canada?

Document B—1

THE LEGISLATIVE COUNCIL

(Journal of the Legislative Council of Upper Canada, 1833.)

His Honor the Speaker, reported, that His Excellency the Lieutenant Governor had been pleased to reply thereto, as follows:—

Gentlemen,

I shall lose no time in transmitting to the Secretary of State for the Colonies, this address to the King, in order that it may be laid before His Majesty.

Pursuant to the order of the day, the address to His Excellency the Lieutenant Governor, on the subject of a Despatch from His Majesty's Secretary of State for the Colonies, was read a third time, and passed, (nemine contradicente) as follows:—

To His Excellency Sir John Colborne, Knight, Commander of the Most Honorable Military Order of the Bath, Lieutenant Governor of the Province of Upper Canada, and Major General Commanding His Majesty's Forces therein, &c. &c. &c. May it Please Your Excellency.

We His Majesty's dutiful and loyal Subjects, the Legislative Council of Upper Canada, in Provincial Parliament assembled, beg leave to express our thanks to Your Excellency, for laying before us an original Despatch, written to Your Excellency by the Right Honorable the Secretary of State for the Colonies, on the 8th of November last, containing His Lordship's observations at great length, upon a variety of statements made to him by Mr. William Mackenzie, an inhabitant of this town. Having perused this Despatch we comply with Your Excellency's desire in returning it to Your Excellency, taking it for granted, that the only reason for laying it before the Legislative Council was the direction contained in the Despatch, that it should receive publicity.

The statements upon which these comments have been framed have also been laid before us by Your Excellency, but without entering into any particular consideration of their contents, with which the Council had little desire to become acquainted, enough appears in the tenor of His Lordship's observations to make it manifest, that these statements have been made with a very unusual disregard of truth, and in a spirit of wanton and intemperate hostility to the Legislative and Executive authorities in this Province. If sufficient internal evidence of this character did not present itself to His Majesty's Secretary of State, in all such parts of these documents as relate to the affairs of this Colony, we must infer from the observations of His Lordship, that it was abundantly displayed in the principles, motives and conduct, ascribed to His Majesty's Ministers in England, upon which His Lordship has necessarily the means of forming a correct opinion.

We cannot say that it may not possibly give satisfaction to some persons in this Province, to observe the condescending and respectful manner in which representations of so peculiar a description, proceeding from an individual, have been received and replied to, notwithstanding it is evident that they were outrageously insulting to all the constituted authorities of this Colony, and scarcely less so to the people at large, in imputing to them sentiments and feelings by which they never have been, and we are convinced, never will be actuated. It is not in the nature of things, however, that the Legislative Council, or that any portion of the people in this Province, of sound hearts and understandings, having the truth under their view, can regard such statements as compose Mr. Mackenzie's voluminous correspondence with His Majesty's Secretary of State, in any other manner than with the most unqualified contempt; a contempt, which upon every principle on which character is required or lost, we think it must be more conducive to the public interests and honor, and to all the ends of good Government, to avow than to disclaim.—So far, therefore, as the Despatch of His Majesty's Secretary of State is to be considered as a reply to those statements, or as a commentary upon information derived from the same source, we cannot regard it as calling for the serious attention of the Legislative Council, but it is scarcely necessary to say, that in any other point of view, this expression of the sentiments of His Majesty's Government upon several of the matters discussed by His Lordship, must be received by us with the greatest interest.—Upon some of these matters it may become the duty of the Legislative Council to address themselves respectfully to their Gracious Sovereign, because they deeply concern the permanent interests of this Province; but we think that we shall best consult the respect due to the other branches of this Legislature, as well as to ourselves, by forbearing to enter into any discussion upon them in connection with these documents.

We appeal, however, to the intimate knowledge of this Colony which Your Excellency has acquired during a residence of four years, for a confirmation of our remark, that upon several of the questions which in this Despatch are most elaborately discussed, no dissatisfaction or difficulty prevails, or ever has prevailed, that no person living here ever heard or imagined before that they were seriously talked of, or thought of as grievances, and that the minds of the people are so far from being disquieted by them, that it is probable not a word would be heard upon them in travelling from one extremity of the Province to the other, and in mingling with its industrious population throughout every portion of it. We appeal also to Your Excellency for a confirmation of the statement, that from the day on which the author of these abusive papers left this Province to the present hour, the people of Upper Canada have pursued their avocations as contentedly and happily, with as kind and liberal a confidence in the justice of their Government, and as respectful a submission to the laws, as can

have prevailed throughout the same period in any part of the dominions of the Crown, not excepting the most peaceable county that could be pointed out in either of the United Kingdoms.

It cannot but be highly gratifying to the Legislative Council to observe how rightly His Majesty's Government estimates the sincere and ardent attachment which binds the great body of this people to the Person and Government of their Sovereign, and to the Constitution under which they live. It would, indeed, be folly to expect that in so large a population there may not, at any time, be found some individuals who desire to disturb the existing order of things, from the same motives, and for the same purposes, which have prompted to similar attempts in all ages, and countries, and under all forms of Government.—And it is not strange that there should be among three hundred thousand persons, a very considerable number who from want of information, or of sufficient reflection, or from dispositions unfavorable to candid inquiry, may be too easily deceived, and brought to unite for a time, in measures which they would not, and could not approve of, if the truth could be brought clearly under their view. But in respect to our fellow Subjects in Upper Canada, speaking of them collectively as a people, we do them sincerely the justice to believe, that it is not necessary to conciliate their good will by overlooking upon any occasion the broadly marked distinctions, between truth and intentional misstatement, between honor and dishonor, patriotism and sedition.

Upon the manner in which His Majesty's Government might choose to notice the petitions of any number of the inhabitants of this Province, upon public or private grievances, expressed, as we must conclude they would be, in the ordinary language of serious remonstrance, or complaint, it would be presumptuous in us to offer any remark; but the documents before us are the productions of an individual supplied and reasoned upon as matters of information upon the general policy of this Government, and the conduct of its Officers; and they consist, in a great measure, of extracts from articles that have, from time to time, appeared in the columns of a newspaper, and which cast unmerited insults upon the Representative of His Majesty in this Province, upon both branches of the Legislature, upon Members of each House individually, and by name, and upon some of the most worthy and irreproachable inhabitants of the Country. These, strung together with little order or connection, and bearing upon the face of them the most palpable marks of a reckless mind, have been unscrupulously thrown before His Majesty's Government, in disregard of the respect due to the high authority to which they were addressed, and in violation of the official form and decorum which constitute, in general, some protection against contumely and abuse. It has been painful to the Legislative Council to see, that in a discussion founded upon these documents, the office of Lieutenant Governor of this Province, and the names of some of the most respectable of the King's Servants are, even hypothetically, connected with imputations which no one can easily tolerate to find associated with his name.

We confess that it has not been without some degree of alarm that we have observed the great stress laid by His Majesty's Secretary of State, in the course of his discussions, upon the fact that the Petitioners, who, it seems have supported by their signatures some of the statements advanced by Mr. McKenzie, are very much outnumbered by the signers of Petitions avowing opposite opinions. The Provinces of Canada are a most valuable portion of the British Empire, and their rapidly growing importance well justifies the anxious interest, and the minute attention with which the welfare and the wishes of their people are consulted by our paternal Government; but, for the sake of the very numerous population which now inhabits this portion of the King's Dominions, and for the sake of the millions who, at no very distant period, will be comprehended within its limits, we earnestly hope that the stability of those In-stitutions, upon which our social happiness depends, is so far secure, that there are some points, which from their vital importance, will be firmly and inflexibly maintained, and for reasons more satisfactory and conclusive, than an accidental preponderance in the number of Petitioners on one side or the other; and that the government of our Mother Country will feel it to be an indispensable duty to uphold them with constancy, against any unfounded prejudice or complaint, however supported.

The Legislative Council feel it right also, in candor, to declare to your Excellency that they have perceived, in various parts of His Lordship's Despatch, and not without extreme regret, that to the complaints urged against the Executive Government of this Colony, and its Officers, charging them with actual misconduct, or with culpable indifference to the interests of the Colony, and the happiness of its people, it seems to have been thought material, if not satisfactory, to reply, in substance, that if indeed such imputations could be truly made, no blame can attach to His Majesty's Government in England, either because these abuses occurred in times that are past, or because the responsibility rests wholly with the persons inculpated; and in some instances a degree of color is given to the complaint, by an express direction to Your Excellency not to practise or to suffer any such abuse in future, or to give your utmost attention to the particular subject in discussion, which it might, from thence be supposed, has thus been brought, for the first time, under the attention of His Majesty's Government.

The Legislative Council trust they may be permitted to remark, that if the many faithful Subjects of His Majesty in this country, whose knowledge of the truth, and whose sentiments led them justly to appreciate the acts and intentions of His Majesty's Government, had always contented themselves with vindicating them, in the same spirit, against aspersions unsupported by evidence, and advanced for the sole purpose of weakening the respect which should be felt for them, there might have been found somewhat less of that confidence in the Government of the Mother Country, which every good man has felt it his duty to maintain and cherish.

And they cannot but think it much to be deplored, that on some most interesting public questions, whatever the Government and the Legislature of this Colony have done, and are doing, in the zealous discharge of their duty, seems to have been unfortunately, for the time, lost sight of so much, as to leave ground for the inference that it was necessary to quicken attention, even to the obvious duty of promoting the religious and moral instruction of the people, by enforcing the suggestions of an individual who, unhappily employs the education he has received in misleading public opinion, and in sowing discontent among a happy and loyal people.

We have not failed to remark, that in the observations which His Majesty's Secretary of State has made upon the subject of the Legislative Council, it seems not to have been present at the moment, to His Lordship's recollection, although it must of course have been familiarly known to His Lordship, that that branch of the Legislature is not composed here, as in many chartered Governments, of the same body which constitutes the Executive Council of the Governor. It is therefore, as we most respectfully suggest, not accurately spoken of as "a Board,"—being in fact a deliberative Assembly, distinct from the Executive Department, constituted by a British Act of Parliament, and composed of Members from various Districts of the Province, who hold their offices for life, whose duties are exclusively Legislative, and in which all that is done is openly and publicly discussed, and proceeded in according to the same formalities as are observed in the Representative branch of the Legislature. Under this constitution, which created and preserves them an independent body, the Legislative Council has, for a long series of years, and for many successive Parliaments, proceeded in a spirit of perfect harmony with the House of Assembly, with but one interruption, occasioned by a discussion on a point of privilege, in which each branch doubtless maintained those principles which it thought essential to its just independence.

.   .   .   .

The Legislative Council feel it necessary also, at this time, after perusing the Despatch of His Majesty's Secretary of State, to declare with what disappointment and regret they perceive that in an official communication which is directed to be made public, and which has been elicited by the extraordinary representations alluded to, His Lordship has thought it necessary to make express and particular reference to individual Members of the Council, commenting upon the profession to which they belong, declaring the line of conduct which His Majesty's Government has enjoined upon them while they continue to be Members, and intimating His Lordship's preference that they should resign their seats. In respect to the part which the Members alluded to shall take in the measures and deliberations of the Legislative Council, it is well known to the Council, that nothing could have been less called for than the injunction which has been thus publicly announced; and it is much to be regretted, that the expression of this injunction upon such an occasion, and in such a manner, should now render it difficult for those Gentlemen to persevere in a line of conduct into which their own inclination and convenience had led them, but which they could not honorably have consented to adopt, either upon compulsion or upon any other suggestion than that of their own judgment.

The Council takes this occasion to remonstrate respectfully, but earnestly, against this assumed right of influencing the conduct, or controlling the attendance of individual Members. They claim to be regarded as a perfectly independent branch of the Legislature; they feel it to be their duty to the people of this Province no less than to themselves, that they should really maintain that character, and they are painfully sensibly that the honor of the Council collectively, and of each Member of it individually is concerned, in their asserting to the full the privileges which the Constitution has vested in them. They observe with pleasure the declaration of His Lordship in one part of this Despatch, that His Majesty's Government has no right to interfere in the proceedings of the Council, and they should have felt most happy if the same conviction which dictated that declaration had also suggested that no individual Member can constitutionally be instructed upon the part which he may take in those proceedings. If instead of being appointed to the Council for life, the Members of that body had held their seats at the pleasure of His Majesty, it would seem but a reasonable consequence that either that pleasure should be conclusively expressed by absolutely removing the Member, or that he should be left to be freely governed by his own discretion in respect to the frequency of his attendance in his place, as well as the extent to which he may participate in the acts and deliberations of the House.

The Legislative Council observes that His Majesty's Secretary of State adverts in the Despatch to a statement, that Mr. Hume had excited expectations of certain measures in regard to this Colony, which expectations ought not to be disappointed. Upon this point it is not unimportant in the opinion of the Council, to observe that, if reliance could be placed on the same source of authority on which most of those assertions rest, which have occupied so much of the attention of His Majesty's Government, Mr. Hume would, indeed be responsible in no small degree, for any discontent which may in time be produced in this Province, in respect to its Constitution and Government. But the Council sincerely trusts that it is not with truth represented that the measures beginning to be introduced into this prosperous Colony, for establishing political unions, which threaten alike the peace and liberty of the people, are pursued under his recommendation. The Council indeed, are bound at present to discredit it. It would

be difficult to conceive what motives could justify, or what feelings could impel any one of our fellow Subjects in England to such a proceeding. The people of Upper Canada are at this moment, among the most favored on earth. They enjoy peace, liberty, security and abundance, on a fertile soil and in a healthy climate, with an almost total exemption from burthens of any kind; and they enjoy these at a time when distress, tumults, and the prospect of war, occasion suffering and anxiety in most countries of the world. If under these circumstances, there can be any considerable number who are really not contented with their lot as inhabitants of Upper Canada, the only cause of their unhappiness must be that they have not the disposition to be thankful.

The Legislative Council, after perusal of this Despatch of His Majesty's Secretary of State, have thus frankly expressed to your Excellency those sentiments which, if they had foreborne to give them utterance, must nevertheless have remained impressed upon their minds. It is their earnest hope that they may not be thought to have departed, on this occasion of unusual delicacy, from that respect to His Majesty's Government of which they are conscious that the Legislative Council has never been unmindful. They do not entertain the thought that a Minister of the Crown can ever apply himself to the affairs of this Colony, with any other wish or intention than to do good; and they recognize in the voluminous Despatch which has been placed before them the most anxious desire to place in their true point of view some questions to which the attention of His Majesty's Government had been called, not merely, as the Council is aware, by the representation of an individual, but by the petitions of a number of His Majesty's Subjects in this Province. For the desire thus shewn, the Legislative Council cannot be otherwise than thankful, and they lament the more that in a document in which an anxiety to allay prejudice, is on the whole so manifest, occasion should have been given for the expression of deep regret at the impressions which some of its passages are calculated to produce. The Council with the greatest deference to His Majesty's Government, beg further to add that, although they are far from thinking that no importance should be attached to the respectability of the source from whence information upon the public affairs of this Colony or the conduct of its Government is sought and derived, yet with respect to various opinions expressed, it would have seemed to the Council to evince a departure from all former usage, almost equally to be regretted, to have found His Majesty's Government involved in public discussions upon the composition and proceedings of the Legislative Assemblies of this Colony, in consequence of the representations of any one of its most respectable Inhabitants.

Your Excellency having transmitted to the Legislative Council the Despatch and Documents referred to, as the only method which we feel could have been consistent with the dignity of the Government for giving to them the publicity required by His Majesty's Minister, we have thought it the more regular and respectful course to address to your Excellency our unanimous sentiments upon them, under the expectation however, that your Excellency will deem it proper to transmit a copy of this Address to His Majesty's Secretary of State for the Colonies. . . .

Document B—2

THE ASSEMBLY

(*Brockville Recorder*, Thursday, February 21, 1833.)

Address of Assembly:

We, His Majesty's dutiful and loyal subjects, the Commons of Upper Canada in Parliament assembled, return our thanks for Your Excellency's message of the 12th day of January last, transmitting a despatch of the Right Honourable the Secretary of State for the Colonies, in answer to certain letters and documents addressed to His Lordship, for the purpose of proving that the people of this happy and prosperous colony are oppressed and burthened with grievances and have become discontented, that there is danger of revolt and bloodshed unless those alleged burthens and grievances are removed and redressed.

We most readily concede that the Noble Secretary of State was actuated by the best motives in framing the Despatch in question, but we cannot refrain from expressing our great regret that it did not occur to His Lordship, that allegations thus deeply affecting the character of His Majesty's subjects in Upper Canada rested on no better testimony than that of an individual who has been twice expelled [from] this House, and who in conse-quence of his having fabricated and reiterated libels of the grossest description, had been declared unfit and unworthy [of] a seat in the Assembly during the present Parliament. If this fact had occurred to His Lordship, it is reasonable to suppose, that he would not have felt himself at liberty to recognize the author of this additional calumny on the people of this province, as the agent; or as speaking the sentiments of any portion of the loyal inhabitants of the Province of Upper Canada, and would therefore have considered it utterly unnecessary to enter into so elaborate an examination or refutation of anything advanced by him.

The House of Assembly are unwilling to occupy Your Excellency's time or attention by commenting on the details of the Despatch or on the different matters referred to in it as constituting grounds of complaint on the part of a few people of this Province; they will merely remark that the remedy for any ills alleged to exist is placed in the hands and is within the constitutional power of the Legislature of the Colony; and the noble Secretary of State does the people of this Province but justice in believing "that there are no people on earth who are less likely to yield to the unmanly weakness of despairing of the public good, and of betraying their most sacred duties in a pusillanimous spirit.

Acting upon principles and feeling diametrically opposite to those imputed to them, we are confident that they will take care to exercise their rights as freemen and British Subjects in such a manner as will assure the election of Representatives who will maintain our excellent Constitution, guard our rights, and with the concurrence of the other branches of the Legislature adopt such measures as may appear necessary for removing any just grounds of complaint.

Carried 18–10.

Document B–3

THE PRESS

(Cobourg Reformer, cited in Brockville Recorder, February 28, 1833.)

Every attentive reader of Lord Goderich's Despatch, cannot fail to perceive, that the several points brought under the notice of the Colonial Secretary, were considered by him of much more importance than the members of our Legislature are willing to admit, and on that account are mortified in no small degree that so much attention and labour has been given to them. Whether they, or His Lordship are in error—whether the Colonial Secretary has furnished an elaborate document, without cause—or whether he has consulted his own sense of duty in giving the several points laid before him his deliberate attention, the Province will determine. What he has done, has been well and wisely done; and must, in the judgment of every impartial man, place him among the friends of Canadian interests. Every line of this despatch, furnishes the strongest evidence of stern and unbiassed integrity; neither warped by misrepresentations of this government nor carried away by the strong and impassioned sentiments of Mr. Mackenzie; for to the influence of both these circumstances, was his Lordship liable. When these facts were taken into the account, we cannot too much admire the tenor of the whole Despatch. Lord Goderich had been furnished with a mass of the foulest slander—the private and public character of Mr. Mackenzie had been laid open, and every fact, with all the colouring which envy and malice could give it, was industriously collected and carefully brought to bear against him. Petty underlings were engaged in collecting together a heap of trash, and nothing was rejected that could by any possibility contribute to blacken his reputation and lessen his credit at the Colonial Office— but the whole has completely failed. Instead of turning Mackenzie out of the office, it would seem, that the scheme has recoiled on the heads of the slanderers and if we mistake not Mr. Draper—who acted in this business as *Scavenger* in chief, must have been bowed out of the office and his filth thrown out after him.

We are rather pleased than offended at his Lordship's critical acumen displayed at the expense of Mr. Mackenzie's diplomatic communication; we are not insensible of the exuberance and impetuosity of that gentleman's mode of speaking and writing; we are aware that all the points of importance might have been arranged with more precision and with less redundancy of reference and illustration. But all this only serves to set the conduct of Lord Goderich in a more favourable point of view; he has thought it necessary to wade through all the voluminous communications—industriously and carefully to select what was important and true, to distinguish *facts* from assertions,—and having made the selection, he betakes himself to the honest and honourable task of adjudication. He cooly investigates the causes of Complaint, and proceeds in recommending their removal. Herein consists the front of Lord Goderich's offering; had he lost sight of his dignity and become a party of their low and detestable attack—had he dismissed Mr. Mackenzie and refused all intercourse with him—then the Colonial Secretary would have received as much applause from our law officers as he has on the contrary shared of their abuse; but had he done so, he would have done himself dishonour, and this country great injustice. He could not have acted otherwise without betraying a sacred trust, without disobedience to the express commands of His Majesty, which is, that, *"the most exact and respectful attention should be paid to the petition* of the most obscure individual." But further, under the circumstances of the case, he could not have acted otherwise than he did, without offering a personal affront to that gentleman by whom he was introduced at the Colonial Office. Such a line of proceeding would have brought the Colonial Secretary under the severe censure of Joseph Hume, Esq., the member of Middlesex. But giving to Lord Goderich the full credit for all the justice and liberty to which he is entitled, we cannot close our eyes on one fact—the approach of the new reformed Parliament must have weighed with his Lordship and shown to him the propriety of doing something for this Colony which had so long been derided.

Having rendered that justice which the Despatch is designed to render, the ministry can with confidence defend themselves against the charge of indifference and injustice which has too long and too justly been chargeable against his predecessors in that office.

C. Church and State

One of the suggestions of the Colonial Secretary in his memorandum had been that Anglican Archdeacon John Strachan and Roman Catholic Bishop Alexander Macdonell should resign their seats in the Council. What is the Tory's view of the proper relationship between church and state? What does Macdonell's letter reveal of his feelings on a well-ordered society? Was he a "Political Priest"?

Document C–1

EDITORIAL IN *KINGSTON CHRONICLE & GAZETTE*

(*Public Archives of Canada,* C.O. 42, Vol. 414.)

February 23, 1833

Although we have stated that there seemed to be a spirit of fairness prevailing throughout the Despatch we would decidedly except that part of it which alludes to the impropriety of clergymen becoming members of the Legislative Council. The members of the clerical profession who at present hold seats in that body in this province derived them from the highest authority in the kingdom—as a testimonial of the confidence of their Sovereign. We know they were not called to their situation without a sufficient reason, and it can be but a matter of very little importance to them whether the Colonial Secretary has any "solicitude for their retaining their seats," or not, and of just as little importance whatever opinion he may entertain in regard to the propriety of their doing so. It appears, to say the least, indecorous in him to announce his private opinion in a public document, and for which we are inclined to think there is a further motive than what meets the eye.

Document C–2

EDITORIAL IN THE *STAR*
(Enclosed in Colborne to Goderich, 27 March 1833, C.O. 42, Vol. 414.)

February 20, 1833

. . . we allude to [Goderich's] reply to Mackenzie's complaint that the Bishop and Archdeacon sat in the Legislative Council. In no other terms than those of unqualified and unmixed disapprobation can we speak of the undignified tone in which he advises those gentlemen for their personal comfort and the success of their designs for the spiritual needs of the people, voluntarily to resign their seats in the Council. Never perhaps did a minister of the British Cabinet commit a more wanton, and unprovoked insult than the Colonial Secretary here inflicts on them. He honorably admits that no charges are brought against them of violations of duty: he confesses he has no power to remove them, that no consideration could induce him to degrade them from the seats they occupy, and yet he significantly advises them to withdraw. Lord Goderich must be aware in wishing such advice to be made public, it will be imagined that the presence of the Bishop and the Archdeacon is not needed in the Council, and that he entertains a belief of some misconduct on their part; and if so, he will regret his foul outrage on private feelings, for an expression of this nature, coming from a person of his high station, must necessarily poison the peace of two most amiable men. . . . If every offence to embruted ignorance [Mackenzie's attack] is to subject a Legislative Councillor to be bearded by the Colonial Secretary whoever he may be, and subject to his taunting language, we demand where is their vaunted independence as a Legislative Assembly, where their power as a conservative body to resist such rash innovations of popular phrenzy.

Document C–3

LETTER FROM BISHOP MACDONELL
(Bishop Alexander Macdonell to J. Joseph, Secretary to His Excellency, Sir Francis Bond Head. Macdonell Papers; *Archives of the Archdiocese of Kingston, Ontario.*)

Kingston, 7 March 1836

Sir,

I have the Honor to acknowledge the receipt of your communication dated the 17th Ulto. conveying to me Extracts from Dispatches of Earl Ripon and Lord Glenelg and of an address of the House of Assembly of this Province dated the 15th of the last month to His Excellency Sir Francis Bond Head.

The Lieutenant Governor will I trust have the goodness to indulge me with the liberty of making some remarks on a few passages of this Extraordinary production of the Honorable the House of Assembly.

The Asertion in the Address that the Country has long felt much grieved by observing the appointment of the Chief Justice to a Seat and the Speakership in the Legislative Council is wholly groundless and has not the least foundation in truth.

No suspicion of partial or impure Administration of Justice as regards the present Chief Justice was ever harboured in any other breast but in those of the Framers of the Address who form their judgement of the honor and integrity of others from the total absence of the virtues from their own minds; nor was the slightest suspicion of the kind ever expressed by any other but by such as had been carefully tutored and drilled to echo the Clamours of a reckless faction who finding their wicked attempts to overturn the Government frustrated have determined to persevere by every means in their power in disturbing the Peace of the Province.

In regard to the Archdeacon of Toronto [Strachan], having so seldom had myself the Honor of attending the Legislative Council all I can say is, that I never saw him engaged in any political discussion of any kind and never heard of his being engaged in political strife, but of his universal attention to his Pastoral functions and his Charity to the Poor and indigent of his own and other persuasions I can bear ample testimony, and I believe that all the Respectable characters in the Province will join me in that testimony.

As to the charges against myself, I feel very little affected by them, having the consolation to think that Fifty Years spent in the faithful Discharge of my Duty to God and to my Country have established my character upon a foundation too solid to be shaken by the Malicious Calumnies of two notorious slanderers.

I must indeed be possessed of more than common share of vanity if at the advanced age of seventy-four years, with a worn out constitution and in a very frail state of health, I could encounter the fatigues of a Winter journey of Four Hundred miles through bad roads and bad Accommodations, for the Honor of sitting for a few days in the Legislative Council, were I even sure that the State of my Health after such a journey would enable me to enjoy that honor. The very idea is absurd, and only shews the vindictive Malice of the two individuals who brought the charge against me, knowing it to be false, and merely to expose my name to public censure and obliquy, having drawn upon myself their mortal hatred by a Conscientious discharge of a paramount duty; that of the one by dismissing him from the Sacred Ministry on account of scandalous and immoral conduct, and that of the other by instilling in the minds of my Flock principles of attachment and Loyalty to their Sovereign and the Constitution of their Country and thus preventing his mischievous endeavours to alienate their minds from the one and the other by his Revolutionary and Rebellious harangues and writings. If this be a crime, it is a crime for which I can never expect forgiveness. So far indeed from repenting of it that neither Racks nor Gibbets shall ever deter me from persevering in so Sacred a duty.

The next charge against me in the Address is that I neglect my Spiritual functions and the Care of Souls to devote my time and talents to political strife and secular measures.

To refute this false and malicious charge, it may not be improper to look back to the state of the Province when I arrived in it in the year 1804. There were then but two Catholic Churches and two Catholic Clergymen in the whole of Upper Canada. One of these Clergymen soon deserted his post, and the other resided in the Township of Sandwich in the Western District, and never went beyond the limits of his missions. So that, upon entering upon my Pastoral duty, I had the whole of the Province besides in charge and without any assistance for the space of ten years.

During the period I had to travel over the Country from Lake Superior to the Province of Lower Canada in the discharge of my Pastoral functions, carrying the Sacred Vestments sometimes on Horseback, sometimes on my own back, and sometimes in Indian Birch Canoes, living with Savages without any other shelter or comfort but what their Fires and their Fares, and the Branches of their trees afforded; crossing the Great Lakes and Rivers and even descending the Rapids of the St. Lawrence in their dangerous and wretched crafts. Nor were the hardships and privations which I endured among the New Settlers and Emigrants less than what I had to encounter among the Savages themselves in their miserable shanties exposed on all sides to the Weather and destitute of every comfort. In this way I have been spending my time and my health year after year since I have been in Upper Canada and not clinging to a Seat in the Legislative Council and devoting my time to political strife as my Accusors are pleased to assert.

The Erection of Five and Thirty Catholic Churches and chappels great and small, altho many of them are yet in an unfinished state built by my exertions: and the zealous exertions of two and twenty clergy men, the major part of them have been educated at my own expense, afford a substantial proof that I have not neglected my spiritual functions or the care of the Souls under my charge: and if that be not sufficient I have satisfactory Documents to prove that I have expended since I have been in this Province no less than Thirteen Thousand pounds of my own private means, besides what I received from other quarters in Building Churches, Chappels, Presbyteries and schoolhouses, in rearing young men for the Church and promoting general Education.

With a full knowledge of those facts established beyond the possibility of a Contradiction, my accusers can have but little regard for truth when they tax me with neglecting my spiritual functions and the care of souls.

The Framers of the Address to His Excellency knew perfectly well that I never held or enjoyed a situation of place or profit or emolument, except the salary which my Sovereign was Graciously pleased to bestow upon me in reward of Forty two years faithful services to my Country. Having been instrumental in getting two Corps of my flock raised and embodied in Defence of their Country in critical times viz. The First Glengarry Fencible Reg't was raised by my influence as a Catholic Corps during the Irish Rebellion whose dangers and Fatigues I shared in that distracted Country and contributed in no small degree to repress the Rapacity of the Soldiery and bring back the deluded People to a Sense of their Duty to their Sovereign and Submission to the Laws. Ample and Honourable testimonies of their services and my conduct may be found in the Government Office of Toronto.

The Second Glengarry Fencible Reg't raised in this Province when the Government of the United States of America invaded and expected to make a conquest of the Canadas was planned by me and partly raised by my influence.

My zeal in the service of my Country and my exertion in the defence of this Province were acknowledged by his late Majesty through Earl Bathurst then Secretary of State for the Colonies.

My salary was then increased and a Seat was assigned for me in the Legislative Council as a Distinguished Mark of my Sovereign's favour. An Honour I should consider it a disgrace to resign, altho I can hardly expect ever to sit in the Council nor do I believe that Lord Glenelg who knows something of me would expect that I should shew so much imbecility in my latter days, as to relinquish a mark of Honour conferred upon [me] by my Sovereign to gratify the vindictive malice of a few unprincipled radicals who made a fraudulent trade of politics under the delusive pretex of patriotism. So far however from repining at the cruel and continued persecution of my Enemies, I pray God to give me patience to suffer for Justice sake, and to forgive them their unjust and unmerited conduct toward me.

I have the Honour to be

Sir

Your most Obed't, and very Humble

Serv't

Alexander McDonell

D. The Political Climate

In 1833, the *Brockville Recorder* reported an account of a public meeting called to consider the Goderich Memorandum. What does it tell us of political life at that time?

Document D—1

A NEWSPAPER ACCOUNT

(Brockville Recorder, March 14, 1833.)

Agreeable to notice, the Members of the County of Leeds attended at Farmersville, for the purpose of submitting to their constituents a petition to His Majesty, founded on [Goderich's memorandum]. About the hour appointed Mr. A. N. Buell called the attention of the people to this subject, and proposed Mr. Fairbairn, (a respectable Scotchman and merchant of this town) as chairman of the meeting. Mr. Gowan opposed it, and proposed Col. Fraser. Those in favour of Mr. Fraser were then desired to go to the left and those for Mr. Fairbairn to the right. An outcry was immediately set up by a gang collected immediately in front of the place of meeting, who were in favour of Fraser that they would not go to the left, as they were determined to have the right. Rather than dispute a point of so little importance, Mr. Buell reversed the proposition and requested those for Fairbairn to go to the left and those for Fraser to the right. Notwithstanding the Fraser men kept their position in front saying he had the majority, and should be the Chairman, at the same time brandishing a number of Shilalahs. Mr. Buell finding that there was no chance for a fair expression of public opinion as no division could be got, left the stand. Those in favour of Fairbairn were then requested to draw off to the left, which being done, exhibited the diminished numbers of those who supported Mr. Fraser, there being about two to one in favour of Mr. Fairbairn. He was accordingly requested to take the Chair, in front of Mr. Wing's store. Mr. Samuel Pennock was then appointed Secretary. Mr. Wm. Buell, one of the Members of the County briefly addressed the Meeting and proposed the Petition as given below. [The petition was favourable to Mackenzie.] Mr. Pennock proceeded to read it. While this was doing, a band of ruffians left the other meeting, some with clubs and some without and making their way up to the chairman pulled him off the platform on which he was at the time standing, and struck him several blows on the head with sticks. The Chairman however shortly after, again resumed his place, when another more desperate rush with an increased number of Shillalahs was made upon him, and he was again dragged from the platform. In the *rencontre* which followed, in order to rescue him, a number of persons received contusions and the Chairman was severely cut on the head. Except in self defence no offer of violence was made by any of those favourable to the objects of the meeting. Having come there to exercise quietly the privileges of freemen, they chose to respect the laws and show themselves the supporters of order and good government; and as they could not, without endangering the lives of their fellow subjects, proceed with the matters they desired, it was thought advisable at that time to defer any further measures.

Meanwhile, R. D. Fraser, Esq. took the chair of the other meeting supported by Shillalahs, and Mr. Ogle R. Gowan, the prime mover of discord in the country proceeded to address them. But what he said or did we are not informed, other than by the effects produced in the outrages committed on the peaceable portion of the community.

A few persons and we are glad that they are few from whom we should have expected better things, suffered the light of their countenance to shine on the disgraceful deeds of the day. Archibald McLean, Esq. who was on the ground, and at one time commanded the peace, was driven from his position by a band of Shillalah-men. And, we understand, that at a later period in the day, John Deming, Esq. in making an attempt to preserve the peace, was saluted with a blow of a stick over the head. This is what we suppose Mr. Gowan will term *loyalty,* and for which he will bestow the mawkish commendation of his vile pen on the *brave lads* who had sufficient recklessness to enact their part so much to his satisfaction.

The proceedings of the day, will, no doubt, be dubbed, a "Glorious Triumph"! May he enjoy the full credit of it. No honorable man will desire to share in such a Victory.

While we are led to express our unqualified abhorence of the conduct of Mr. Gowan and such of his deluded followers as *he* can control, we rejoice for the sake of the Irish character, to have it in our power to bear testimony to the merits of a large number of the more respectable portion of them; among whom we reckon some valuable friends and acquaintances. To these we would suggest the propriety of impressing upon their countrymen, the impolicy as well as the highly mischievous tendency of the measures to which they have been urged, by falsehood and the specious pretensions of a man whose real character needs but to be known to be detested.

PROBLEM 8

Electoral Battles in French Canada, 1792–1848

JACQUES MONET, S.J.

Loyola College, Université de Sherbrooke and University of Toronto

Before the election of 1792, French-Canadians had never been consulted on a political question, or even been encouraged to express an opinion on public issues. Except for those who at times had been asked to select a church warden, they had never voted. The only open meetings they had attended were assemblies in church. Yet by 1848, they had become so accustomed to elections, so familiar with politics, that they could determine the outcome of a general election, and command the choice of their leader, Louis-Hippolyte LaFontaine, as the first "Prime Minister" of Canada. They had learned this lesson well: in debates that contained as much high principle as demagoguery, in party organization worked out by shrewd trickery as well as by sound constitutional doctrine, in electoral contests filled with excitement, if not corruption and violence. They had learned in the best British tradition . . . and not without a sense of humour.

The Constitutional Act of 1791 began the electoral phase of the Old Regime, that which would close with Responsible Government in 1848. In a proclamation issued in May, 1792, Lower Canada was divided into election districts drawn up to choose 50 Members for the Assembly: 39 from the counties, 11 from the cities and boroughs. According to the custom of the day, candidates need not reside in the districts they sought to represent, and as the elections took place on different days in different ridings, many of them frequently ran in several at once, or, having lost the first, consecutively. Nor did they need to be present for a campaign. Many, in fact, were acclaimed *in absentia*. They did need however to be 21-year-old British subjects who had the franchise. No special electoral privileges were accorded to the Seigneurial class either for candidacies or in the franchise. One of the long-term effects of the Constitutional Act was thus to weaken and eventually destroy any influence the Seigneurs once enjoyed.

For French-Canadians, electoral involvement began slowly. Before 1800 many of them took a very moderate interest in elections. They let not a few seats go uncontested; and in those where contests were held, election agents in the pay of the government often "organized" the voters to give a "safe" election to their candidate. One of these agents, Pierre-Aimable De Bonne (1758–1816) continued in politics even after his appointment to the bench. (His eventual defeat in 1810 after several elections showed how much the Canadiens' understanding of British constitutional practice had deepened.) In the same manner, Returning Officers also frequently controlled the outcome of the voting. So, in some places, did incipient traditions: in the dual ridings of Quebec and Montreal, for example, a tacit agreement provided for the choice among the candidates of one Member with a French name and another with an English. But gradually, as nationalist issues arose during the first decade of the 1800's, and as Louis-Joseph Papineau (1786–1871) emerged as undisputed leader of the several Canadien factions, French-Canadians became more committed as a "party." Newspapers began to take sides and politicians submitted to more disciplined organization. After the rebellions and the proclaiming of the union in 1841, parties took on more definite and permanent structures. Their direction became professional as party managers like Alexandre-Maurice Delisle (1810–80) and Joseph Cauchon (1816–85) began a tradition of manipulating elections that was long in dying.

Pressures upon the voters were, of course, all the easier to apply because of the open vote, and because of the practice of erecting hustings about the polls, from which the candidates could harangue the crowds of voters and each other. But political corruption and violence must not be allowed to overshadow the fact that without electoral contests won by disciplined parties, neither would Responsible Government have been possible, nor Canada's peaceful evolution toward full political sovereignty.

The following documents, drawn mainly from French and English newspapers running from 1792 to 1849, are placed in the logical order in which they would have appeared in an election chronology. After the first electoral law in the Constitutional Act of 1791 and a contemporary comment, the documents follow the order: the announcement of the candidacy, the campaign, the voting day, and the election either by acclamation or by voting; violence, victory, thanks, and triumphant celebration.

Those interested in further study may consult: Jean et Marcel Hamelin, *Les Mœurs électorales dans le Québec* (1962); H. T. Manning, *The Revolt of French Canada, 1800–1835* (1962); Thomas Chapais, *Cours d'Histoire du Canada* (8 vols., 1919–34); Frenand Ouellet, *Histoire Economique et Sociale du Québec, 1760–1850* (1966); and my own *"La Crise Metcalfe and the Montreal Election, 1843–44"* in the *Canadian Historical Review* 1963, pp. 1–19; and *The Last Cannon Shot, A Study in French-Canadian Nationalism, 1837–1851*, soon to be published at the University of Toronto Press.

A. The Law Governing Elections

The demand for parliamentary government in Lower Canada originated principally with the English-speaking members of the commercial communities of Quebec and Montreal. Since as early as 1773, and for a variety of motives, these had been petitioning the Mother Country for that most characteristic of all British institutions, a representative Assembly. Frustrated by the Quebec Act in 1774, they founded *Town Meetings*: special committees whose purpose was to keep alive and boost the idea of a Parliament for Canada among politicians in Britain and the Canadiens at home. These latter in fact had petitioned the Imperial Government against an Assembly, the Seigneurs and clergy being suspicious of unknown systems. By 1784 the *Town Meeting* in Quebec was so far successful as to forward to London a petition covered with some 2,300 signatures, of which 1,500 were French. In 1788 the *Town Meetings* delegated Adam Lynburner to the House of Commons to plead on their behalf. And by 1791, such pressures and others—Loyalist petitions, the beginnings of settlement in the Upper Section of the Province, the repudiation of the *Coutumes de Paris*, to list but a few—convinced the Colonial Office to act. And so, despite renewed efforts against it by the Canadien *élite*, the new Constitution became the law of the land on December 26, 1791.

During this same December 1791, the members of the *Town Meeting* met for the last time at the Merchant's Coffee House in Quebec. Their dream had come true. They dissolved the Association . . . but not without founding a new one: the Constitutional Club. This latter aimed to "inform" the public on the meaning of the Constitution. They commissioned one of their numbers to write a commentary which they published in February and March, 1792, in a special supplement to Canada's oldest newspaper, the *Quebec Gazette*. The following two documents speak for themselves. The clauses of the Constitutional Act regulating elections give the framework within which each electoral contest would be waged for the next 50 years. The selections from the *Supplement to the Quebec Gazette* provide the contemporary Canadian reaction. How is it that the Canadians have a proportionately wider franchise than the British at the time? Could this possibly influence Britain's future policy toward the Assemblies in the colonies? And, in the context of the early 19th century, what is the "great tenderness" that is shown to the "consciences of voters"?

Document A—1

THE CONSTITUTIONAL ACT, 1791

(W. P. M. Kennedy [ed.], *Statutes, Treaties, and Documents of the Canadian Constitution, 1713–1929* [Oxford University Press, 1930].)

(An Act to repeal certain parts of an Act, passed in the fourteenth year of His Majesty's reign, intituled "An Act for making more effectual provision for the Government of the Province of Quebec, in North America," and to make further provision for the Government of the said Province.)

Whereas an Act was passed in the fourteenth year of the reign of his present Majesty, intituled "An Act for making more effectual provision for the Government of the Province of Quebec, in North America": And whereas it is expedient and necessary that further provision should

now be made for the good Government and prosperity thereof: May it therefore please your most Excellent Majesty that it may be enacted; and be it enacted by the King's Most Excellent Majesty, by and with the advice and consent of the Lords Spiritual and Temporal, and Commons in this present Parliament assembled, and by the authority of the same, that so much of the said Act as in any manner relates to the appointment of a Council for the affairs of the said Province of Quebec, or to the power given by the said Act to the said Council, or to the major part of them, to make ordinances for the peace, welfare, and good Government of the said Province, with the consent of His Majesty's Governor, Lieutenant-Governor, or Commander in Chief for the time being, shall be, and the same is hereby repealed.

. . . .

XIII. And be it further enacted by the authority aforesaid, that for the purpose of constituting such Assembly as aforesaid in each of the said Provinces respectively, it shall and may be lawful for his Majesty, his heirs or successors, by an instrument under his or their sign manual, to authorize and direct the Governor or Lieutenant-Governor, or person administering the Government in each of the said Provinces respectively, within the time hereinafter mentioned, and thereafter from time to time as occasion shall require, in his Majesty's name and by an instrument under the Great Seal of such Province, to summon and call together an Assembly in and for such Province.

XIV. And be it further enacted by the authority aforesaid, that for the purpose of electing the members of such Assemblies respectively it shall and may be lawful for his Majesty, his heirs or successors, by an instrument under his or their sign manual, to authorize the Governor or Lieutenant-Governor of each of the said Provinces respectively, or the person administering the Government therein, within the time hereinafter mentioned, to issue a proclamation dividing such Province into districts, or counties, or circles, and towns or townships, and appointing the limits thereof, and declaring and appointing the number of representatives to be chosen by each of such districts, or counties, or circles, and towns or townships respectively; and that it shall also be lawful for His Majesty, his heirs or successors, to authorize such Governor or Lieutenant-Governor, or person administering the Government, from time to time to nominate and appoint proper persons to execute the office of returning-officer in each of the said districts, or counties, or circles, and towns or townships respectively; and that such division of the said

Provinces into districts, or counties, or circles, and towns or townships, and such declaration and appointment of the number of representatives to be chosen by each of the said districts, or counties, or circles, and towns or townships, respectively, and also such nomination and appointment of returning-officers in the same, shall be valid and effectual to all the purposes of this Act, unless it shall at any time be otherwise provided by any Act of the Legislative Council and Assembly of the Province, assented to by his Majesty, his heirs, or successors.

XV. Provided nevertheless, and be it further enacted by the authority aforesaid, that the provision hereinbefore contained for empowering the Governor, Lieutenant-Governor, or person administering the Government of the said Provinces respectively, under such authority as aforesaid from his Majesty, his heirs or successors, from time to time to nominate and appoint proper persons to execute the office of returning-officer in the said districts, counties, circles, and towns or townships, shall remain and continue in force in each of the said Provinces respectively for the term of two years from and after the commencement of this Act within such Province, and no longer; but subject nevertheless to be sooner repealed or varied by any Act of the Legislative Council and Assembly of the Province, assented to by his Majesty, his heirs or successors.

XVI. Provided always, and be it further enacted by the authority aforesaid, that no person shall be obliged to execute the said office of returning-officer for any longer time than one year, or oftener than once, unless it shall at any time be otherwise provided by any Act of the Legislative Council and Assembly of the Province, assented to by his Majesty, his heirs or successors.

XVII. Provided also, and be it enacted by the authority aforesaid, that the whole number of members to be chosen in the Province of Upper Canada shall not be less than sixteen, and the whole number of members to be chosen in Lower Canada shall not be less than fifty.

XVIII. And be it further enacted by the authority aforesaid, that writs for the election of members to serve in the said Assemblies respectively shall be issued by the Governor, Lieutenant-Governor, or person administering his Majesty's Government within the said Provinces respectively, within fourteen days after the sealing of such instrument as aforesaid for summoning and calling together such Assembly, and that such writs shall be directed to the respective returning-officers of the said districts, or counties, or circles, and towns or townships, and that such writs shall be made returnable within fifty days at farthest from the day on which they shall bear date, unless it shall at any time be otherwise provided by any Act of the Legislative Council and Assembly of the Province, assented to by his Majesty, his heirs or successors; and that writs shall in like manner and form be issued for the election of members in the case of any vacancy which shall happen by the death of the person chosen, or by his being summoned to the Legislative Council of either province, and that such writs shall be made returnable within fifty days at farthest from the day on which they shall bear date, unless it shall at any time be otherwise provided by any Act of the Legislative Council and Assembly of the Province, assented to by his Majesty, his heirs or successors; and that in the case of any such vacancy which shall happen by the death of the person chosen, or by reason of his being so summoned as aforesaid, the writ for the election of a new member shall be issued within six days after the same shall be made known to the proper officer for issuing such writs of election.

XIX. And be it further enacted by the authority aforesaid, that all and every the returning-officers so appointed as aforesaid, to whom any such writs as aforesaid shall be directed, shall, and they are hereby authorized and required duly to execute such writs.

XX. And be it further enacted by the authority aforesaid, that the members for the several districts, or counties, or circles of the said Provinces respectively shall be chosen by the majority of votes of such persons as shall severally be possessed, for their own use and benefit, of lands or tenements within such district, or county, or circle, as the case shall be, such lands being by them held in freehold, or in fief, or in roture, or by certificate derived under the authority of the Governor and Council of the Province of Quebec, and being of the yearly value of forty shillings sterling or upwards, over and above all rents and charges payable out of or in respect of the same; and that the members for the several towns or townships within the said Provinces respectively shall be chosen by the majority of votes of such persons as either shall be severally possessed for their own use and benefit of a dwelling house and lot of ground in such town or township, such dwelling house and lot of ground being by them held in like manner as aforesaid, and being of the yearly value of five pounds sterling or upwards, or, as, having been resident within the said town or township for the space of twelve calendar months next before the date of the writ of summons for the election, shall bona fide have paid one year's rent for the dwelling house in which they shall have so resided, at the rate of ten pounds sterling per annum or upwards.

XXI. Provided always, and be it further enacted by the authority aforesaid, that no person shall be capable of being elected a member to serve in either of the said Assemblies, or of sitting and voting therein, who shall be a member of either of the said Legislative Councils to be established as aforesaid in the said two Provinces, or who shall be a minister of the Church of England, or a minister, priest, ecclesiastic, or teacher, either according to the rites of the Church of Rome, or under any other form or profession of religious faith or worship.

XXII. Provided also, and be it further

enacted by the authority aforesaid, that no person shall be capable of voting at any election of a member to serve in such Assembly, in either of the said Provinces, or of being elected at any such election who shall not be of the full age of twenty-one years, and a natural born subject of his Majesty, or a subject of His Majesty naturalized by Act of the British Parliament, or a subject of his Majesty having become such by the conquest and cession of the Province of Canada.

XXIII. And be it also enacted by the authority aforesaid, that no person shall be capable of voting at any election of a member to serve in such Assembly in either of the said Provinces, or of being elected at any such election, who shall have been attainted for treason or felony in any Court of law within any of his Majesty's dominions, or who shall be within any description of persons disqualified by any Act of the Legislative Council and Assembly of the Province, assented to by his Majesty, his heirs or successors.

XXIV. Provided also, and be it further enacted by the authority aforesaid, that every voter before he is admitted to give his vote at any such election shall, if required by any of the candidates, or by the returning-officer, take the following oath, which shall be administered in the English or French language, as the case may require:

I, A. B., do declare and testify, in the presence of Almighty God, that I am, to the best of my knowledge and belief, of the full age of twenty-one years, and that I have not voted before at this election.

And that every such person shall also, if so required as aforesaid, make oath previous to his being admitted to vote that he is, to the best of his knowledge and belief, duly possessed of such lands and tenements, or of such a dwelling house and lot of ground, or that he has 'bona fide' been so resident and paid such rent for his dwelling house as entitles him according to the provisions of this Act, to give his vote at such election for the county, or district, or circle, or for the town or township, for which he shall offer the same.

Document A–2

THE CANADIAN COMMENT

(From *Supplement to the Quebec Gazette.*)

TO ACCOMPANY THE NEW CONSTITUTION

February 23, 1792

The Constitutional Club having avowed that the objects they have in view are, by informing and instructing the people, to diffuse a proper knowledge of our new government and of the principles of the British Constitution; and for the attaining of that end, having invited the citizens individually to communicate their sentiments and opinions for the advantage of the whole, we judge it will not be an unacceptable service if we undertook to divest the Act which forms the new Constitution of the formal circuitous Language which all acts or ordinances are unavoidably subject to, so as to make it the more intelligible to the mass of the good people of this province. It is but just to acknowledge that the last Act which forms our present government is very explicit and clear, and easily understood; but the windings and turnings of law language, however proper and necessary in public ordinances, are apt to tire the patience and confuse the notions of plain men. . . . We consider it a duty incumbent upon the Curés, Seigneurs, Notaries, schoolmasters and traders to disperse these our productions among the people, to read and explain them, so that while knowing what a liberal constitution and free government is, they may not remain ignorant of its nature and value. . . .

SOLON

March 8, 1792

XIII, XIV, XV, XVI, XVII, XVIII, XIX, XX, XXI, XXII, XXIII clauses. Too much praise cannot be bestowed on the British Parliament for the enlarged and liberal plan upon which they have decreed the House of Assembly shall be formed, as well as with regard to the Electors as the Representatives and Officers. No citizen is compelled to serve as Returning Officer more than once, nor for more than one year after the first nomination, which shows the attention paid to the avocation of every citizen: The limitation for the number of Representatives is very liberal; the whole Kingdom of Great Britain, containing about ten millions of souls, is represented by 558 Members only; the two Provinces of Canada do not contain the sixtieth part of the number of inhabitants of Great Britain, and yet are represented by no less than 66 Members only; of which 50 are for Lower Canada; this is a distinguished mark of favor, and will prove highly beneficial to the country; it gives great scope for men well acquainted with the situation and resources of the Province to render themselves useful to it by public services. Besides its natural independence arising from the choice of the people, it has an additional one arising from so great a number.

The wisdom and justice of the British Parliament are likewise conspicuous in qualifying almost every inhabitant to vote; very few indeed are excluded, which is a very peculiar advantage; the people of Canada will be more purely and more fully represented than the inhabitants of Great Britain.

XXIV clause. In this clause great tenderness is shown to the consciences of Voters. They are required only to declare that they have attained the years of maturity, and have not given any vote before, and that they are possessed of the small qualification required by the Act.

B. The Candidate

The candidate always issued a manifesto to his constituents. Usually it was very laconic, sometimes it included something that might be construed as a pledge, always it was couched in very flowery and obsequious language. The documents in B–1 show these characteristics. Documents B–2, B–3, B–4, and B–5 point to what type of person often ran for election. Documents B–2 and B–3 concern the famous case of the election agent, Aimable De Bonne, returned for Quebec City in 1792, for Trois Rivières in 1796 and 1800, and again from 1804 to 1810, although he had been appointed to the Bench in 1794. Document B–3 is by Jean-Antoine Panet (1751–1815) who served as first Speaker of the Lower Canadian Assembly, and was defeated in his riding by the influence of De Bonne (cf. C–3, E–3). It illustrates how a candidate could change ridings and/or run in two places during a same campaign; also how he could be acclaimed *in absentia*. B–4 is a letter to the Quebec newspaper *Le Canadien*, revealing a Seigneurial reaction to certain candidates. What does it say of the leveling effect of the franchise? What does Document B–5 expose about the Canadiens' reaction to the type of man who often ran for office? About their own political morals?

Document B–1

THE MANIFESTO

(Part (a) is from *Supplement to the Quebec Gazette*; part (b) from the *Montreal Herald*.)

Thursday, May 21, 1792

(*a*) TO THE ELECTORS OF THE COUNTY OF QUEBEC

Friends and Countrymen,

With confidence I sollicit your Votes, to be elected one of your Representatives in the ensuing Assembly.

If true patriotism, liberality of sentiment, and some knowledge of the principles of free government are titles to obtain your acceptance of my services, be assured that my wishes and endeavours will ever be for the welfare of my Country and the Happiness of my fellow Citizens.

Your zealous countryman,

Pierre Ls. Panet

(*b*) TO THE ELECTORS OF THE COUNTY OF MONTREAL

Gentlemen,

Having in consequence of the distinguished support of the majority of the County, been elected your Representative in the late Provincial Parliament, I deem it my duty, respectfully, to renew the offer of my Services, and propose myself as a Candidate for the honor of your Suffrages at the approaching Election.

I have the honor to be,

Gentlemen,

Your most faithful and obedient humble

Servant

J. Stewart

Document B–2

TYPES OF CANDIDATES, I

(*Le Canadien*, 21 mai, 1808; trans. Jacques Monet, S.J.)

Reasons why members of the electorate should not vote for Judge De Bonne:

1. Because he receives more than 4000 dollars from the government annually *during good pleasure*, and his reputation is such that the ministry can easily find good reasons for removing him if he does not support all their measures in the House.

2. Because he came to the House only very rarely in the last four years, except to support and vote in favour of government measures. This is easily proved by the Journals of the House.

3. Because he is a judge, and as such should have no likes or dislikes among those who may be on trial, and because it is impossible not to have preferences when one has fought an election.

4. Because as a judge with such a bad reputation, many will want to vote for him in hopes of winning their case, and others will fear to vote against him lest he turn their case against them. This is of course the worst kind of corruption, tending to destroy political morality, to weaken confidence in the administration of Justice, to overturn the Constitution and the Government or else to set up in this country a system of slavery supported by corruption.

5. Because the electorate should support the Assembly (which decided unanimously that judges should not be elected in the districts where they hold office) against the Legislative Council which is the aristocratic branch of the Constitution, and in which there are no more than two Members who are not receiving large salaries from the government *during pleasure*. If our representatives are not upheld [by the electors] they will never have the power to correct wrongs and defend our rights.

Document B–3

TYPES OF CANDIDATES, II

(From *Le Canadien*, 11 juin 1808; trans. Jacques Monet, S.J.)

TO THE FREE AND GENEROUS ELECTORS OF THE COUNTY OF HUNTINGDON, DISTRICT OF MONTREAL

Gentlemen,

More than twenty-four years of zeal in addition to assiduous and unremunerated services in favour of obtaining and implementing our happy Constitution had led me to desire repose. I had hoped that after the expressed wishes and unanimous resolutions of the Legislative Assembly, old antagonists and younger ones who have joined them recently, would have refrained from using a Judge-Candidate to destroy free elections. Yet by means of intrigue, of imaginative lies, and of a front candidate, on the very eve of election day in the Upper Town of Quebec, they were successful in catching one third of the electorate by surprise, rendering another inoperative, and with the third, forcing the outcome of the election in a most incredible manner. You heard of it, Gentlemen, by others than myself. I remained in the background to see Liberty pit herself against Corruption, the better to ascertain her true nature. This was enough; for the candidates in your riding nobly resigned their places and you, Electors whose merit is past praising, have freely and unanimously chosen me one of your representatives. This action is an obvious proof of how well you know how to use your electoral privileges to resist illegal influences which are contrary to true constitutional Liberty. In this singular manner you have elected me to the place which one of our opponents was canvassing for himself. Please accept, Gentlemen, my most humble thanks for the immeasurable honour which you have just given me, while awaiting the next few days when I shall come up to the riding to reiterate them in person and place before you the causes and effects of our opponents actions, the better to know your wishes and the more zealously to work at fulfilling them.

I have the honour to be,
Gentlemen,
most respectfully,

Your most Humble and Obedient Servant,

J. A. Panet

Document B–4

TYPES OF CANDIDATES, III

(A letter to the Editor from *Le Canadien*, 25 juin, 1808; trans. Jacques Monet, S.J.)

Dear Mr Printer,

As one of your subscribers I would appreciate the following being included in *Le Canadien*.

A few days ago, a certain great and noble demagogue, after his dinner, seized upon the fact that someone had mentioned the word *elections*, to vent his anger on what he calls the *rabble*, the *riff-raff*, the *scum*, the *vile mob*. The *ignorant* populace, he raged, had preferred to elect common people, rather than nobles; bakers and tavern-keepers had had the impudence to become candidates. He added that it was the English who had spoiled the *Canadiens*; that it was the English who had destroyed ordinary people by bringing in these ideas of equality, and that it was a fact unheard of for everyone to want to equal the nobility. At that moment a very respectable English Gentleman came in, saying about the nobility: "Assuredly I do not know any nobleman personnally, but . . ." "I am of the nobility, I am of the nobility," our demagogue began crying as he loudly thumped himself upon the chest. The English Gentleman began to laugh, saying: "This may well be; I do not know this gentleman's ancestry. But I do know he takes his title from a certain place where he never owned an inch of land— not even enough to be buried in, although he is a small man."

One of Your Subscribers

Document B–5

TYPES OF CANDIDATES, IV

(Supplement to Le Canadien, 1807; trans. Jacques Monet, S.J.)

AN EVENING CONVERSATION BETWEEN A CANDIDATE AND HIS LADY FRIEND

—My dear, what are you thinking of this evening with such a dreamy look? Are you still reflecting on your elections and on your quarrels with the government? This cursed nonsense will do you harm. It keeps you busy all day and makes you talk in your sleep all night. . . . It is time we led a more quiet life.

—Don't worry, my dear, all will be right; the Canadiens are on my side. [Sings] "The Canadiens are jolly fellows, biribi, ah! ah! ah!"

—You mean the Canadiens you betrayed so often?

—Don't get so angry, my dear, I know the Canadiens and I'm sure of them.

—Come now! After making fools of them in the way you boast about so much, you expect they hold nothing against you. . . .

—You don't know the Canadiens my dear. I can make fools of them as often as I like, and I can bring them back any time; all they need are a few songs! They love to be told they are jolly fellows and other such drivel. Then they give me whatever I want of them. A few salutations will win them over; a few sentences against the English will work them up. I'll easily get the better of them.

—That worked once; and you have been successful before, I know; but don't you think they will remember how you betrayed them after you had won their support, and how you made fools of them since.

—The Canadiens are good people, my dear, they do not hold grudges.

—You mean to say they are stupid and without heart.

—Precisely, my dear: it is easier to win their respect by making fools of them than by serving them faithfully. They are just like you women: you scorn a sincere and worthy lover, and you run after those who betray you.

C. The Campaign

Until the 1830's, few election campaigns turned upon ideology or principle. The main division between candidates seems to have been the nationalist issue, which began more or less during the first decade of the 1800's and grew in vigour and intensity well into the 1840's. Documents C–1 and C–2, chosen out of a plethora of similar ones, illustrate the changing outlook upon each other by members of either national group. After 1834 the Ninety-Two Resolutions became the focus of political tendencies, as did the doctrine of Responsible Government after 1839. Rhum, gold, personal antagonisms, clever trickery, bold manipulation, often spoke louder or convinced more firmly than 20 orators. Document C–3 refers again to the case of Aimable De Bonne (cf. Documents B–2, B–3, and E–3) to show the role women might play in a campaign. Document C–4 underlines the advantages accruing from clever management.

Document C–1

THE NATIONALIST ISSUE, I

(From *The Montreal Herald*, July 1, 1820.)

Wednesday last being the day fixed for the Election of the Members of the West Ward of the City, George Garden and L. J. Papineau Esquires, were unanimously chosen as Members. The Returning Officer having read the writ and explained to the Electors the duty for which they were assembled Mr Papineau came forward and offered himself in a neat and appropriate speech from the Hustings. He commenced by stating that the reason they were called upon to discharge the duty of Electing Members of Parliament was the much lamented death of our late revered Sovereign. He next took a view of the great and progressive blessings the Canadas had enjoyed under his long and glorious reign, enumerating the inestimable privileges they now posessed, and their great capabilities for improvements which were daily progressing since they became part of the British Empire. To place this in its most vivid colours he contrasted it with the wretched state of Canada, while it was a Province of France, detailing how it was at that time kept as a military garrison for the purpose of making excursions on the neighbouring nations, and that all the advantages of soil, climate, and industry were totally neglected under the sway of the old French despots. He proceeded by a natural transition to mention the important duty of guarding those great privileges and blessings for the benefit of

our children; and that there was no more effectual means of doing this than by fixing on judicious and proper representatives. This led him to touch upon the duties of representatives and to a description of a rigid adherence to the law which ought to be their continual rule of action. In conclusion, he said, having had the honour of representing them in their Parliaments, and feeling that a very distinguished and flattering career as they were the Electors of the most populous, most enterprising, most rich as well as the most intelligent part of Lower Canada, he again sollicited their suffrages. Adding that it should be his study to attend to their interests, to the best of his abilities, if he again became the object of their choice.

He was followed by Mr Garden, who excused himself from addressing the Electors at great length, from the circumstance of his being unaccustomed to speak in public. He modestly declined having any intimate knowledge of legislating, but hoped that from his long residence, and intimate intercourse with many parts of the services, he would not be found unrepresentative of those things most conducive to their interests. He declared that if they elected him, he would be a rigid attendant to their wishes and endeavour to merit the confidence they would place in him.

Document C–2

THE NATIONALIST ISSUE, II

(A letter to the Editor from *La Minerve*, 27 octobre, 1834; trans. Jacques Monet, S.J.)

For a long time now I have known that the English are really partial to all that pertains to *animals*. Thus, they are mad about horses, on which they ruin themselves in bets. In London it is even very fashionable for a Lord to act as a Coachman. They like cocks, despite the horror their women have at the very mention of the fowl's name, and they attend the fights with the same nervous tensions and contortions as the Spaniards have at a bull fight. As for dogs, they go into a mad fury about them. In Paris, a wealthy nabob was known to have filled his living chambers with some two to three hundred specimens of this four-legged animal, and never to have entered a coach unaccompanied by a pack of the hairy gentlemen. Recalling all these eccentricities, it is not surprising that Englishmen have the bad taste to prefer *horses* to Canadiens, or that in the kind of bacchic fury which is common to them, they should refer to the latter as *dogs*.

But now, one of their oracles, Mr.

Neilson, writing an editorial in his insane *Quebec Gazette*, goes one better than most of his noble compatriots and has the extreme honesty to refer to the Canadien population as *pigs*. This is really not worth being angry about, especially since the poor fool of an editor who has never given any proof that he could write French, may have mistakenly taken this vulgarity for a compliment. Besides, he has just sought an excuse for himself in his issue of October 23 by saying that if *some* writers of his highly moral sheet have used such a word they are surely very ill-bred. This last confession is so naïve that it must disarm all censure. As for myself I accept Mr Neilson's apology, and I ask all Canadiens to believe that the editor of the *Quebec Gazette* really intended to pay the Canadiens a visit, for in writing the word *pig*, he was probably thinking to register his own name at their doors.

One of the Thinking Animals
of Canada

Document C–3

THE ROLE OF WOMEN (!)

(*Le Canadien*, 21 mai, 1808; trans. Jacques Monet, S.J.)

TO THE ELECTORS OF QUEBEC COUNTY

Gentlemen,

Although it is not customary for women to address you at election time, I hope you will forgive the liberty of an unfortunate soul who has no other resource than to appeal to your sense of justice. To whom else could I appeal? The ungrateful wretch I complain of is the Judge himself.

You know well enough, Gentlemen, the trouble I went to in working for him during the election campaign at Charles-

bourg four years ago; he had suffered badly in the election in the Upper Town; and out of pity, as many of you did, I worked as hard as I could to assure his triumph. Gentlemen, you witnessed this triumph of which he boasted so much. Yet, no sooner had he won than he forgot all I had done for him, and, coward that he is, abandoned me. He had the insolence to tell me that it was I who was harming his reputation among you. Gentlemen, will you let this kind of treachery go unpunished? Will your votes in his favour reward his betrayal? Will you elect him for having broken faith with me?

The ingrate even got married, and began to frequent the Church; this was to obtain your votes. He is inconstant I assure you; I know him, he will use any means to achieve his end.

He makes promises to you, but how many promises did he make to me? He will deceive you as he deceived me. He will deceive you as he deceived the Lower Town. How many promises did he not make to the voters on the day of his triumph four years ago?

This false man has never been able to win an election except in Three Rivers. . . . What honour will you gain in electing him? The Upper Town scorned him four years ago, Deschambault had driven him out, Nicolet had driven him out. Will it be that Charlesbourg will join Three Rivers in electing him!

What will be said of Charlesbourg? What will be said of Beauport, where he is so well known? People will say that it was because he was a Judge, that it was out of fear of losing their cases in court that voters elected him. Did the Upper Town succomb to such fears? Did Deschambault and Nicolet? What now! Canadiens who never feared enemy fire in battle will become cowards for fear of losing a court case!

What an honour for Canadiens to see *their judge* running for election, to see him profane the image of the King whom he represents so unworthily? Do English judges run in elections? . . . Only Canadiens so dishonour themselves. I am a Canadienne, Gentlemen, and I would die rather than consent to such dishonour.

The Unfortunate Jeannette

Document C–4

INDIRECT MANIPULATION

(Letter from Joseph Cauchon to Louis-Hippolyte LaFontaine, November 15, 1849, *Public Archives of Canada*, M.G. 24, B 14; trans. Jacques Monet, S.J.)

I had lost a great deal of personal influence in the riding because of Rhéaume who had been successful in turning against me a population which had completely trusted me until then. . . . I felt the need to discredit once and for all the man, Rhéaume, who had caused such foolish and damaging agitation, who had organized the reception for Papineau, as well as several meetings in my own riding in which I was almost murdered. I therefore published a "Confession of Jacques" (. . . for which instead of suing me for libel he challenged me to a duel.) I accepted without hesitation for I knew that if I declined I would thereby destroy the moral strength of the party in Quebec and rob my own writings of any weight. . . . Rhéaume had expected that I would refuse because I had censured duelling in my newspaper and I had said elsewhere that I would refuse a duel from a motive of religious scruple; he also thought that as I was in close touch with the clergy I

would not endanger this relationship to the point of accepting. As a second, I chose Fiset, who had himself fought twice. As soon as Rhéaume found out I had accepted, he made every effort to have himself arrested by the police, and he was almost successful. The seconds had to change the meeting place three times within an hour, for as soon as a place was agreed upon, it would immediately be made public. Rhéaume's relatives tried to embarass me by hiring my father-in-law to have me arrested, and he would have done it had I not threatened to hate him for life. Rhéaume's father-in-law went twice to see my wife to tell her we were to fight at three o'clock, and my desperate wife took to running through the streets to look for me. She never found me because I had hidden. When I saw there was a warrant against me, I hurried to the *rendez-vous* with Fiset. It was an hour and a quarter before the time agreed upon. Rhéaume was strolling through the streets. He had gone to bid farewell to his brother and tell him he was duelling at three o'clock. His father, his father-in-law, his brother, all had a warrant issued and told the police to prevent the duel at three o'clock: the time we had fixed was a quarter past four, but he did not want the police to be late. He had a *rendez-vous* first with his second, Okill Plamondon, but he did not go; and Plamondon joined us alone. Rhéaume finally arrived and began to walk up and down in the street, obviously trying to get arrested, which he very soon was; for his father-in-law arrived with the police. Plamondon drew up a report in which he declared that Rhéaume had dishonoured himself and forfeited the right to call himself a gentleman. This report was signed by both seconds. Then Plamondon, carried away by his enthusiasm, wrote out a paragraph at the bottom of his report: "M. Cauchon—M. R. conducted himself as a most conspicuous coward in regard to his debt of honour towards you, and I regret to have been taken in for so long by a man with no heart." This whole story has of course had a tremendous impact, and the annexationnist party confide that it robs them of all credit forever, for they were the ones who had urged Rhéaume on, to better their own reputation. . . . We sent a copy of Plamondon's Report to Rhéaume with a note threatening to publish it the first time he speaks in public. . . . Now we are rid of his nuisance forever, and I have regained all the influence he had made me lose. . . .

D. Election Day

Unless a candidate won by acclamation, very rarely did election day pass without violence. The following documents speak for themselves.

Document D–1

ELECTION DAY IN QUEBEC CITY (1792), I

(From *Supplement to the Quebec Gazette*, June 21, 1792.)

LOST

Yesterday morning in the Poll Room a metal watch (maker's name, Sanderson no 1749). Any person to whose cloths [*sic*] it might have become entangled in the crowd or into whose hands it may have fallen since, that will return the same to Mr Neilson, the printer hereof, shall have one Guinea reward and no Questions asked. Quebec, June 12, 1792. N.B. All persons to whom the above may be offered for sale are desired to stop it and give information to the printer.

Document D–2

ELECTION DAY IN QUEBEC CITY (1792), II

(From the *Quebec Gazette*, July 5, 1792.)

TO THOSE ELECTORS OF THE COUNTY OF QUEBEC

Who have voted, and those who were prevented from voting in my favour the 25th, 26th, 27th June last:

The more obstacles you have surmounted, you have shown the greater wisdom and firmness, in a country where liberty is but just dawning; for the general good and at the same time of esteem for myself, in thinking me worthy of being a representative; penetrated like yourselves with patriotism and gratitude for so distinguished a degree of your confidence, I entreat you to accept my sincere thanks and to be persuaded that I will neglect nothing for the accomplishment of your wishes and to obtain the justice due to us.

I cannot help observing on the silence kept by the *Quebec Gazette*, with respect to the extraordinary circumstances of the Upper and Lower town of the County of Quebec, particularly on the abstract and mysterious turn that the *Quebec Gazette* of Thursday last has given to what passed at Charlebourg during the election for the County of Quebec, doubtless the author of that paragraph is one of those who heretofore have so much fatigued themselves to write, print, and vaguely cry against the laws of this country, against the Honourable profession of Advocate, and who have employed such low means as those known to the public, but who have found no advantage in publishing the true facts arising from the Constitution; I shall not, however, undertake to establish them in this paper, the election for this County of Quebec being intended to be a subject for examination and I hope of just censure in the House of Assembly, I confine myself at present

to inform the public of the state of the poll,

Salaberry, Esq.	515
Lynd, Esq.	462
Berthelot, Advocate	436

it is evident that I find myself the lowest by 26 votes, but the public cannot be ignorant how many are to be deducted from the other two candidates of persons who are neither proprietors nor naturalized; I might depend on this point alone or contest the election altogether, by the means contained in my protest signified by two Notaries when the poll was unexpectedly closed. 62 Voters more on the spot presented themselves in my favor and formally protested even in the building where the election was held, from which they were chased by some gentlemen who demolished it by force, but they continued their protest and finished it in the neighbourhood.

I hope that the country and the truth will not fail to direct *resources*, and that no personal influence will deprive my fellow countrymen of the advantages of our Constitution, which is in itself so good that the elections have made known the good subjects in this country, as well as the intentions and cabals of some others who have preached up union and non-distinction of birth, while they would secretly favourize a certain class of men who alone are neither able to effect the welfare or the peace of this colony.

Berthelot Bartigny

Document D–3

ELECTION DAYS IN MONTREAL (APRIL 16, 17, 1844), I

(Letter from A. M. Delisle to D. Daly, April 16, 17, 1844, *Public Archives of Canada*, M.G. 24, A 15; Lord Metcalfe to Lord Stanley, April 29, 1844, with enclosure.)

My dear Sir,

Since seven o'clock this morning I am at my work, and I have at this moment two Companies at the St. Anne's Market under Command of the Mayor, and I have as many in Barracks next my Office, where I now am, ready to act in Case of need. I apprehend no violence or disturbance

to-night, however, for all is unusually quiet.

A few minutes after 9 o'clock this morning I was called to the St Mary's Ward by my Deputy, & aided by Ermatinger & Coffin rode off & succeeded in restoring something like order after making a few prisoners. The Canallers were,

I understand, (& I fully believe it, though I Could not distinguish them) all in town & took possession of all the polls, but were not armed. Their numbers however supplied this. Whilst at that Ward I was called to the Queen's Ward, then to the West; then to the Centre & subsequently to the St Lawrence Ward. In the meantime my Deputy in the St Mary was Compelled to call troops who were placed under the Superintendence of Ermatinger. From that moment all went well. I regret that notwithstanding our previous understanding some of my Deputies declined to call the Military, stating that there was no disturbance to justify that Act.

You are aware, I suppose, that my deputies are exclusively masters of their polls and that while there they alone are responsible for what takes place. I could not therefore thrust troops upon them against their will. No lives have been lost. The St Mary's, Queen's & St Lawrence Wards will have troops to-morrow, the Deputies having resolved to have them and made requisitions for that purpose.

Brush (Queen's Ward) was compelled to adjourn at one o'clock till 9 to-morrow, & Laviolette (St. Lawrence Ward) at about ½ past 2; both because Drummond-ites or rather Canallers had taken exclusive posession of the polls.

It is strange that the Canallers were not armed, their chief missiles being stones which as you know abound on our Macadamized roads. Drummond, I believe, on all the polls was 160 ahead; but this election will not give the strength of parties here. To-morrow matters will go on quietly, I hope with the Military at the most turbulent polls. One of my Deputies, Larocque (Centre Ward) was struck by the mob and was forcibly dispossessed of his sword. Such was the violence there, that instead of adjourning he *closed*, which I believe invalidates the election. He had, moreover, the folly, on being summoned by Drummond to resume, to continue after this *faux pas*—and again adjourned for violence. Yet this *I regret to say* weak gentleman will have no troops. It is sheer weakness. The law

forbids my interfereing with him; yet I may feel justified in case of excesses to strain a point & call them. I must endeavour, however, to get over all this without the effusion of blood if I can. Where the troops were called Molson polled vote for vote, and we shall see to-morrow if he can keep head at the Wards where they will be.

It is morally impossible in two days to poll one half the votes in the three large Wards, & so far the law is very deficient. I expect, of course, that people will assail me for all this, in ignorance of the law which ties my hands during the polling days. If my Deputies only make me the returns they should make I do not see how I can proclaim Mr. D. elected with any majority. I must make a special return. I myself was obeyed wherever I went; but I could only act in preserving order and no more. In that I assure you I succeeded beyond my expectations. My Deputies for the large Wards particularly I hear have acted with strict impartiality, & I believe it.

I shall write again soon. I am Completely done up.

Yours truly,

(*signed*) A. M. Delisle

P.S. The East Ward has no disturbance, & in this Drummond was 6 over Molson on adjournment. Hincks has brewed all this mischief & would do more if he could. He is a designing villain.

17 April, 9 A.M.

The most desperate preparations are making by the Irish this morning. They have compelled several large establishments where their people were at work to close, & they will be again in posession of the polls at the opening, but my Deputies have all promised to ask aid of troops. There are troops now at Queen's, St Anne's & St Lawrence Wards.

Yours in haste,

(*signed*) A.M.D.

Document D–4

ELECTION DAYS IN MONTREAL (APRIL 16, 17, 1844), II

(Extracts from a letter from Montreal, *Public Archives of Canada*, M.G. 24, A 15; Letter from Lord Metcalfe to Lord Stanley dated April 26, 1844, with enclosure.)

Montreal, April 19, 1844

The mail which carries you this will of course take you an account of Delisle's proclamation of this day—fancy Drummond duly elected according to law. When Larocque closed his poll the first day without saying when it would be opened again; had his sword taken from him and just escaped with his life—Judah the second day abandons his poll and goes off walking about the streets. Some of Molson's voters go to vote, and there is no returning officer to take their votes. The whole town under a mob and the troops called out to protect the lives of the citizens. In consequence of the illegal proceedings of Larocque, Judah, and Brush, the latter of whom neglected to take either the residences of the voters or the real estate or what not they claimed to vote on, Molson's people were advised by their lawyers that the whole proceeding was a nullity, and it would be idle in them to expose their heads or persons to record an empty vote which could lead to no result. Delisle actually favoured this belief and expressed his opinion in many quarters that Larocques proceeding would prevent any but a special return being made—and yet had the audacity, the baseness, the treachery to outrage every honest feeling in the community by publickly proclaiming an untruth in broad daylight, in the open streets; and to show you in what hands we have been, his worthy confrère in conserving the peace, Ermatinger [the Superintendant of Police], at the close of the farce goes off, arm in arm with La Fontaine to Drummonds house to assist in the glorification and speechifying out of the windows.

The canal gentry, it appears, did not find work on their return from their vile mission, and already begin to express dissatisfaction with their political employers. They behaved like devils and I really think it will be a good lesson to them if you would cause Killaly to stop the work for six months. The outrage has been felt severely, and is bitterly resented. Numbers of gentlemen have this day turned off their Irish Roman Catholic Servants and I have heard several express their determination never again to employ them. To the residents of Montreal who witnessed the election, all is well understood and Drummond is regarded only as the representative of the labourers on the Lachine Canal, but I fear it will not be understood throughout the Country, and that the effect will be damaging in the extreme. . . .

E. Post-Election Celebrations

Rarely did election day end with the laconic letter of thanks which was always published in the newspaper. (Document E–1). For the victor, serious celebration was always in order. Occasionally, he might announce a special grant (Document E–2); but more usually his campaign workers and voters joined in a triumphant parade that might turn against the defeated candidate (E–3) or against those who had been misguided enough to vote for the wrong man (E–4).

Document E–1

ANNOUNCEMENT

(Part (a) is from the Quebec Gazette; part (b) is from The Vindicator.)

June 14, 1792

(*a*) TO THE FREE ELECTORS OF THE LOWER TOWN OF QUEBEC

Gentlemen and Fellow Citizens,

Impressed with a lively sense of the distinguished honor conferred on me by being returned one of your Representatives in the ensuing House of Assembly, I take this immediate opportunity of offering my most sincere acknowledgements for the liberal support I have received from so respectable a majority of my fellow citizens, and I trust my conduct will ever be such as to prove my gratitude and merit a continuance of your friendship.

I have the honor to be, Gentlemen, and fellow citizens,

Your most obedient and humble servant,

Robert Lester

October 1, 1830

(*b*) TO THE ELECTORS OF THE WEST WARD OF MONTREAL, FELLOW CITIZENS,

I request you to accept the assurance of my entire devotedness to your interests and my most sincere thanks for the honor you have done me in again electing me your representative to Parliament, and for the approbation you have thereby given to all my preceding efforts.

The more true, independent and inviolable is the people's representative with regard to what he says and does in that capacity, the more is then weakened and annulled his legal responsibility.

In his double character of Legislator and Guardian of the people's rights, his duties are infinitely varied, important, and difficult. He whom you have elected is not the man that in the discharge of such duties shall never fall into errors; but he shall increasingly use his best efforts to fall as seldom as possible; posessed of the firm disposition never to commit them voluntarily. To do so indeed, would be unpardonable.

I remain, respectfully, Gentlemen,

Your obedient, humble, servant,

L. J. Papineau

Document E–2

REWARD

(From the Quebec Gazette, June 21, 1792.)

On the Close of the poll, yesterday, Mr Panet, much to his honor, in his address of thanks to the Electors, declared it to be his intention, to give 100 Louis d'or to the poor without distinction. It is fervently to be wished that the sums of money (if any) bestowed in elections in future, may be no worse employed.

Document E–3

WOE TO THE CONQUERED, I

(From Le Canadien, 4 juin, 1808; trans. Jacques Monet, S.J.)

The Polling began on Tuesday, May 24, the candidates being Messers Panet and Blackwood, the retiring Members, and Claude Dénéchaud. At the end of that day polling closed with 55 votes difference between Mr Panet and Mr

Dénéchaud. Most of the voters had come from Saint-Jean Ward. Few people from within the City Walls had voted; those dependent upon Government men [for their livelihood] seemed to be in ferment; and word was circulating that the Advocate-General had promised his Vote and his Influence to Mr. Dénéchaud. Most people were of the opinion that the Government had decided against Mr Panet.

On Wednesday, the voters from Saint-Jean ward and those from the City who depended on the Government continued to vote. Mr. Perrault, surrounded by his paid ruffians, attacked one of Mr Panet's people and fought; Judge De Bonne came to vote after his Court prorogued, about 11:30 a.m. As soon as he appeared in the Square, Mr Dénéchaud and his group went towards him, cheering with many an *Hurrah*! Then he voted. Mr Panet insisted that he take the oath that he was indeed qualified and a resident of the Upper Town. After he cast his vote, Mr Dénéchaud raised three cheers for him. At noon the workers from the Royal Shipyards came to vote for Mr Dénéchaud. Returns at 3 o'clock were as follows:

Blackwood	388
Dénéchaud	286
Panet	134

and polling was adjourned until Friday. While Mr Panet's people were leaving the poll, Mr Dénéchaud's group were crying out: "*Vive les bonnets rouges!*" and "*Vive les sans culottes!*" On Friday a letter was brought to the Returning Officer from Mr Panet in which he stated his intention to retire from the contest. After it was read, Messers Blackwood and Dénéchaud were declared duly elected. Mr Shaw's carriage was then brought forward with horses from Mr Stiles' tavern in Saint-Jean ward, five or six flags were unfurled, the voters put on cockades which were also attached to the horses; and the horses started

prancing. After a few moments waiting, the drummers of the 98th Regiment arrived, the candidates got into the carriage, and the procession started off. About 100 steps from the poll, the horses refused to go further; they were unharnassed and men took their place. Young Gagné climbed on at the back of the carriage with a flag; some people wanted to force him to come down, but he stayed put, claiming he had as good a right as any to be there. The parade went up Saint Louis street to Mr Sewell's where it stopped; there were three runs on the drums and three cheers. It then went down the street to Mr Panet's and there were cheers there too. (Mr Ryland followed from behind). It then went on through several streets until it got to the lodgings of the Candidates. Then the taverns were thrown open for all who had followed the procession, everyone drinking (it is said) on the two candidates.

.   .   .   .

The voters from Saint-Jean Ward were well-behaved in general; if they voted as they did, it is because they were misled by the lies told them by Mr. Perrault, the instrument of Judge De Bonne who is himself someone else's tool. The disorders came from Mr. Perrault's bullies, among which was his own son. On passing in front of Mr Panet's, these ruffians intended to sing out: "*On le chasse poliment*" and some threatened to drag him in the mud under the carriage. One even wanted to disembowel one of Mr Panet's people. They made terrible noises, boasted they would beat up all opponents, and kept insulting everyone in sight. Ordinary, honest, straightforward people had to keep quiet and suffer this abuse for fear of worse trouble still. Besides, neither Mr. Dénéchaud nor the voters who elected him intended this commotion; they did not even know it was meant as support for themselves.

Document E–4

WOE TO THE CONQUERED, II

(From *Le Canadien*, 20 octobre, 1834; trans. Jacques Monet, S.J.)

We commented lately on how the elections in the City were marked by examples of the most noble independence, and on that occasion the *Mercury* did not lose the opportunity to answer with a description of the "magnanimity" and the "indulgence" of the British merchant bosses who would not deprive of their livelihood those men who freely exercised their rights as free members of the Electorate. We did not think then and we do not think now that the merchants deserved such high praise simply for abstaining from so serious a political crime as to interfere with the freedom of elections, or to not punish those among their employees who merely exercised their rights. Today, however, it appears that whatever small worth there is in allowing a man to exercise his rights, even this the British merchant class has lost, for many of the bosses have been discharging old and honest employees who voted contrary to their wishes. We shall collect all the necessary data to use it when need be.

PROBLEM 9

Balance and Stability: Nova Scotia Considers an Elective Legislative Chamber

K. G. PRYKE
University of Windsor

In 1851 J. W. Johnston, leader of the Conservative party in Nova Scotia, proposed that the Legislative Council of the province should be made an elective body. He offered this proposal in an effort to strengthen the position of the upper chamber in relation to the House of Assembly. For some time, the upper house had been losing prestige and power to the lower house, and in 1848 it was further diminished by the introduction of cabinet government. This political eclipse of the upper house occurred without any formal change in its powers or its composition. Perhaps the most galling aspect of the change was that all new members of the council would henceforth be appointed by the governor, acting on the advice of the cabinet, which was now constitutionally responsible to the assembly. For many politicians this was an intolerable situation. The appointive upper house was viewed as the primary safeguard of a class society; indeed as the rightful bastion of a governing élite.

Johnston's proposal to strengthen the upper house by abandoning the principle of appointment seemed to some observers to be so extreme as to raise doubts concerning his sincerity. In the minds of many politicians, elections were equated with "the people" and thus with American republicanism, whereas appointments were equated with the aristocracy, and with British society. But was there any real reason for this equation? Was there a possibility that since the utility of appointments was destroyed by the cabinet system, a true Conservative might fall back on the elective system as a means of ensuring class representation in the government? Johnston's proposal could be seen either as a rejection of basic Conservative thought or as an attempt to shift ground in order to preserve an essential principle of social order.

In raising the question of class representation, however, Johnston was at once faced with the problem of finding a social class which could be represented in the upper house. If such a class did exist, then there was the problem of finding some political device based on this class, such as a high property franchise for electors and for candidates, which would be acceptable to the Assembly. The Conservatives thus were forced to examine the applicability of their assumptions to Nova Scotian political life, as well as to examine critically the nature of their society. If their conclusions showed that there was no real basis for an upper house, would they have the courage to advocate the total abolition of the upper house?

After 1852 interest in the elective legislative council receded. However, in 1857, Johnston became premier and attorney general, a position that provided him with a fresh opportunity to reconsider the problem of the council. During the legislative session of 1858, he revived his earlier proposal. Instead of recommending the immediate abolition of the existing upper house, he now proposed that a gradual introduction of elected members be made into the council. His resolution passed the committee of the whole by only one vote, and he subsequently claimed that this scant majority was insufficient to justify proceeding any further. His refusal to fight for his own proposal was perhaps due to his own doubts concerning its merits or to the fear of antagonizing his own supporters.

The Conservative argument that the upper house had to be revitalized relied heavily on traditional British thought, which stressed the need for a balance between the Crown, the House of Lords, and the Commons. In replying to the Conservatives, some speakers countered that the true essence of the British constitution lay not so much in the principle of balance as in the principle of harmony, inherent in the cabinet system, which emphasized relations between the executive and the lower house, or assembly. Thus the proposal for an elective upper house involved the more basic question of the true nature of the constitution. If the upper house had only a minor role in the structure of the government, then there was no need to waste time in discussing any changes. Furthermore, unless there were a role for the upper house, there was actually no justification for retaining it.

Yet another basic issue was raised by the proposal for an elective upper house: to what extent could, or should, political thought and institutions be transported from England to Nova Scotia? Was it really possible, asked some Liberals, to apply British practices, in all details, to a society which differed so greatly from British society. If not, then why did most of the Nova Scotian politicians insist that their political institutions were British in nature? At what point did the variations in detail cease to be minor changes and to take on a character really different from British institutions? Was it possible to introduce a deliberate variation, such as an elective upper house, without producing yet further changes?

The proposal for an elective upper house was debated in all the colonies of British North America and was adopted in the Province of Canada and in Prince Edward Island. For one interpretation of the movement in the maritimes, see W. S. MacNutt, *The Atlantic Provinces* (1965) and also his work *New Brunswick A History: 1784–1867* (1963). For Nova Scotia consult J. M. Beck, *The Government of Nova Scotia* (1957) and for a neighboring colony examine F. Mackinnon, *The Government of Prince Edward Island* (1951). The recent work of J. M. S. Careless, *The Union of the Canada* (1967) provides information as to the movement in the Province of Canada. As far as primary materials are concerned, the debates of the legislature were printed in an edited form beginning in 1855. The debates of the assembly are rather scarce, and the debates of the upper house for this period, where in existence, are available only at the Public Archives of Nova Scotia, Halifax. The debates of the lower house, however, are printed in the *Nova Scotian*, and this paper is available on microfilm. The 1858 Assembly debates are also to be found in the Halifax *Evening Express*, which has also been microfilmed. Abbreviated debates of the upper house were printed in two Halifax newspapers, but neither have yet been microfilmed.

A. The Concept of the Elective Legislative Council, 1850-52

In 1850 J. W. Johnston, leader of the Conservative Opposition, proposed that the elective principle be applied to the upper house. The following resolution was reported out of the committee of the whole, with J. W. Johnston's resolution attached as an amendment. The main resolution was ultimately carried.

J. W. Johnston sat in the Legislature from 1838 until his resignation in 1843 to seek a seat in the lower house. He remained in the Assembly until his appointment as Equity Judge of the Supreme Court in 1864. He held government office longer than any other politician of his period and remained a respected and influential spokesman for the Conservatives throughout his lifetime. Despite his obvious contribution, there is no adequate biography of the man.

Document A–1
THE RESOLUTION OF J. W. JOHNSTON, 1850
(Nova Scotia House of Assembly, 1850, *Journals*, March 27–28, 1850 [Halifax, 1850], pp. 600–604.)

"*Whereas*, the forms of Government and modes of Administration which exist in this Province, have been established and adopted, after ten years' discussion and conflict, with the full knowledge and approval of the People of Nova Scotia, as expressed at the Hustings and with the sanction of their Sovereign, conveyed in the Despatches from the Right Honorable the Secretary of State.

"*And whereas*, the same system of Government, has, with equal deliberation, and after many sacrifices, been established by the people of Canada and New Brunswick, while it is eagerly sought by the Inhabitants of Prince Edward Island and Newfoundland.

"*And whereas*, it would be unwise, while designing men are seeking in other Colonies to unsettle the minds of Her Majesty's subjects and to renounce their allegiance, to afford to them the slightest countenance by applying at this moment for any fundamental change.

"*And whereas*, the Salary of the Lieutenant Governor was fixed in the Civil List Bill and formed part of a compromise, by which the Casual and Territorial Revenues of the Crown were transferred to this Province, and any breach of that compact would be dishonorable to the People and Legislature of Nova Scotia.

"*And whereas*, the Lieutenant Governor of Nova Scotia, [Sir John Harvey] venerable by his age, distinguished by his military achievements, and by the successful administration of affairs in three other neighboring Colonies, is possessed in the administration of our affairs in three other neighboring Colonies, is possessed in the administration of our Local government, of the same constitutional prerogatives and powers, that Her Gracious Majesty enjoys in England: *and whereas*, in obedience to the instructions of his Sovereign, and in accordance with the well understood wishes of the People, His Excellency has so governed this Province as to secure the confidence and esteem of its Inhabitants.

"1°. *Therefore resolved*, that having recorded its sentiments on these important topics, this Assembly does not deem it expedient to suggest any change in the Institutions of this Province."

"*And whereas*, the Legislative Council, as now constituted, has exercised its power in co-operation with this House, so as to secure our confidence, and the question of an Elective Council for a Colony having been recently suggested for the first time by the Ministers of the Crown in the House of Commons, and the views that may be ultimately sanctioned in the Imperial Parliament and the Home Government being as yet unknown—

"2°. *Therefore resolved*, that it would be premature in this House to express any opinion on so material a change in our Provincial Constitution, and that the sentiments of the People thereon ought to be first of all ascertained."

And the first Resolution having been again read—

The Hon. Mr. Johnston moved that the same be amended by leaving out all the words thereof after the first word "Whereas," and inserting instead thereof the following words after the said word "Whereas," viz:

"The self-Government extended to the British North American Provinces by the Secretary of State for the Colonies, having placed the Local affairs of the Province in the hands of the Executive Council unrestrained by any control on the part of the Lieutenant Governor or the Imperial Government, it is necessary to correct the anomalies and inconveniencies unavoidable in the application of Imperial usages to a Colony; and a common duty is created, irrespective of party interests, to cast the Institutions of the Province into such forms as may unite the freest operation of the public sentiment with the most efficient, upright and economical exercise of the Executive, Legislative and Municipal functions: nor is it less obligatory on this House to obtain more perfect stability and certainty for the principles of Provincial Government that can now be relied on—the present Secretary of State for the Colonies having, both in declarations and acts, shewn that a Minister of the Crown in the administration of Colonial affairs may hold himself free to disallow what a predecessor in the exercise of his official functions had established.

"*And whereas*, First: *As regards the Lieutenant Governor*—This officer while in theory possessed of the Executive authority has been in reality denuded of all power, and should he attempt to exercise an independent control over the affairs of the Province he would disturb the principle of responsibility under which the Executive Council are now called to administer the functions of Government.— Hence so long as the Lieutenant Governor shall continue to be viewed as the head of the Provincial administration, he must either sink into insignificance or become the instrument of Executive obstruction; in the one case the reverence due the Sovereign being insensibly diminished by the contempt engendered for the office of Her Representative; in the other the harmony of the Province being endangered by the violation of a principle which the British Government in the last two years has affirmed, and Earl Grey as Colonial Secretary has sealed by acts of unmistakeable significancy.

"*And whereas*, Secondly: *As regards the Legislative Council*—The construction of the Legislative Council is inconsistent with the harmonious working of the present mode of Government and its useful influence as a Legislative Body; With a majority created by the Government of the day for securing party measures, the Legislative Council is for most essential purposes but the subservient instrument of the Provincial Government. The same majority on a change of parties would make it an obstructive Body opposed to the existing Administration and the wishes of the people as expressed by their Representatives in this House.

"*Resolved therefore*, That to avert the evils of renewing questions of Government which, after years of agitation and uncertainty, have been established by Imperial authority, it is proper that the Lieutenant Governor of this Colony should be unquestionably recognized as an Imperial functionary, charged with the protection of National interests and as. the official organ of communication between the Parent State and the Colony, but holding no relation to Colonial affairs beyond the ceremonials of office; That to fix this character to the Office as is proper the Lieutenant Governor should be paid entirely by the Imperial Government; That if this Province shall be required to contribute any portion of the Lieutenant Governor's Salary the sum of £1000

would fully meet the just proportion of this Colony and the value of his services under the present system—this House deeming it unjust that so large a sum as £3000 Sterling should be now paid by the Province, and absurd that £250 Sterling, or any sum, should be granted for the Private Secretary of an Officer who himself has but to subscribe the documents that others are required to prepare.

"*And further*, that for the evils now existing in the constitution of the Legislative Council, the most efficient remedy is to be found in the Election of the Legislative Council by the people for a limited period—the Members going out by sections periodically: Thus the Body would be brought nearer to the feelings and would more perfectly reflect the opinions of the Country, while the periodical infusion of new Members would enable the people to correct the inconveniences that occasionally might arise from its composition, and would tend to weaken the influences that result in mere party adhesions."

Which proposed amendment being seconded and put, and the House dividing thereon, there appeared for the amendment fourteen; against it, twenty-six.

Document A—2

J. W. JOHNSTON ON THE UPPER HOUSE, 1851

(The *Nova Scotian*, March 3, 1851, pp. 69–70.)

In 1851 J. W. Johnston returned to the subject of the elective upper house. As the following selection indicates, his approach differed in tone from that of the previous year. He also dropped the direct link between the position of the governor and the elective principle. The absence of Joseph Howe, who was in England during the legislative session of 1851, may have been one reason why the government accepted the idea in principle.

Now, sir, I would meet the objection sometimes urged against the proposed

change that it is unbritish. But it must be remembered that we are not an integral portion of the British Empire. We have not nor can we have the exercise of the Sovereign power; nor have we a body holding its position by hereditary right—independent equally of the Crown and the people—preserving the balance between them and ready upon any exigency to oppose their intervening power between the arbitrary acts of either. The Lieutenant Governor cannot exercise the functions of the Sovereign in Britain—he exercises his functions by delegation, and is appointed by and responsible to the Crown and we have only to turn to the somewhat sharp despatches which Colonial Governors sometimes receive from Colonial Secretary's to understand the position they occupy—and to feel that their power is worth nothing if the person at the head of the Colonial Office chooses to school them to their duty and insist upon the pursuance of a particular line of conduct. A peer when once created, transmits his privileges by hereditary descent as I have before remarked, and thenceforth holds his title altogether independently of the Crown—while each English Councillor is a first creation and retains his seat at the will of the Queen. Thus, sir, there is no analogy between our Governor and Legislative Council and the Crown and second branch of the Mother Country. You might as well ask the West Indian planter to exchange the vestments that suit a tropical clime, for the furs that protect a Canadian from the rigors of his winter, or the Esquimaux to meet the Arctic frost in the lighter garment of the Hindoo, as to attempt to mould colonial institutions in strict accordance with imperial models, or to check all progress that harmonized not in close analogy with British precedents.

. . . .

The answer in each case is the same, "our conditions is [sic] different, and what imparts comfort or benefit to the one, would be destructive to the other.

Mr. Chairman—I am desirous that this question should be presented in the fairest manner to the committee, and therefore it is that I commence with suggestions that may be supposed inimical to my argument; and that I now proceed to make an admission which contains the strongest argument that can be opposed to the introduction of *Elective* Councils into Nova Scotia. On the principle I advance in the estimation of all writers who have studied the subject of mixed forms of government—the several branches of the Legislature should have a different origin in order to render efficient the control which each should exercise over the other; I may be told, therefore, that the same power which gives both an existence to this branch of the Legislature should exert no influence in the appointment of the other. I admit the difficulty— but it is unavoidable. Lord Brougham in his work upon Political Philosophy 3d. vol p. 143 states the principle in this language. "The desire of requiring two Legislative bodies to concur in making any law is efficacious in proportion to the diversity between those bodies. If both proceed from the people whose power and will the double consent is intended to temper and control, this never can be effected completely, however different the constitution of the two may be, at page 157 nothing but another origin or other duration or other materials can secure the required check."

This is the strongest argument which can be opposed to the proposition I have made to change the constitution and character of the second branch. But as his Lordship goes on to say that this objection may be urged against the system of government in the United States; I am in some measure relieved from apprehension when I find how successfully the constitution of the United States has worked since the establishment of the Union, notwithstanding the same objection in greater or less degree exists there. Still, however, the question may be put to me—"Why, with such an authority as Lord Brougham's in opposition, do you venture to propose the introduction of this change?" Because, sir, there is another principle involved in the subject yet more imperative; one upon the inviolability of which, depends the well working of every Legislative body. It is this—*that each branch should be independent of the other*; and it is because this principle does not exist in the case of our Legislative Council; and has been outraged and set at naught, that I deem the change necessary. On this point let me quote the same high author. At pages 146–7, Lord Brougham says: "Mixed government is that in which the supreme power is lodged in more than one functionary or body, each being *entirely independent of the other*, and each being both *irremovable and unaccountable* to any authority whatever." And again, at p. 148 he reiterates the same principle in these strong words—"The *foundation* of every form of mixed government is the *absolute independence* of each order in the State." So to quote another writer,—Stevens in his Commentaries. (and these works are on the shelves behind the hon. members) 1 vol. p. 33, says—"But the Constitutional Government of this Island is so admirably tempered that nothing can endanger or hurt it, but destroying the equilibrium of power between one branch of the Legislature and the rest. For if ever it should happen that the independence of any one of them should be lost, or that it should become subservient to the views of the other two, there would soon be an end of your constitution."

Now, sir, I have before shewn [*sic*] that the Lieut. Governor does not stand in the position of the Crown. He is not an independant officer, and yet has the power of appointing the Legislative Council; nor is the case altered if it be said he does not exercise this power of himself, but of his Executive—for they again are responsible to this house. If the origin of the Legislative Council be referred to the Imperial Government, then the first and second branches of our Legislature have the same origin; if it be referred to the Lieut. Governor, then the second branch is dependant on the first for its creation; if to the Executive Council, then it is made indirectly dependant on the third. Each way that fundamental principle—the independence of the several branches—is violated and destroyed. Nay, more sir, as the Legislative Council is in fact at present constituted, *both* of the principles to which I have alluded are violated; for the Governor being appointed by the Crown and the Council also virtually emanating from the same source, the first of these principles is infringed, and I have just proved that no one branch, with the exception of this house is independent of the other.

Document A—3

J. B. UNIACKE SPEAKS, 1851

(The *Nova Scotian*, March 10, 1851, p. 76.)

James Boyle Uniacke (M.L.A. 1830–54).
During his long legislative career he held several government positions. He was attorney general and premier of the province from 1848 until his resignation in 1854.

I am now, as I ever have been, in favour of the general principle; upon the journals of this house years ago, my name is recorded in its assertion; therefore I only now carry out that of which I approved when I was a young member of this house and in times far more exciting and stirring than the present. In these days of reform it appears the people will not sustain old institutions which hang around them crippling their liberties and retarding the onward progress of the times, but whilst they move forward steadily and firmly, great caution is necessary, lest in adopting any change they sanction and bring into operation, evils worse than those they seek to remove. And in dealing with the present question I ask this house to consider the subject as it is submitted now before them. To enquire when we have swept away the present Council—what we are to have in its stead; or shall we have a second branch at all? This is a grave question, requiring mature and deliberate action. If we decide as to the necessity of the second branch and that it shall be elective; what are to be its powers, what the qualifications of the electors, or the candidates for election? These are important inquiries;—but at every step questions arise equally grave—equally important—of the first magnitude as effecting the working of this change, and all demanding the strictest scrutiny and most guarded prudence. The hon. and learned member for Annapolis [J. W. Johnston], represented Nova Scotia as being in a peculiar position. "No chief magistrate,—no Peers—no Commons." Let us contrast the present with the past—let us see what this Council displaced, and the situation of that body in the olden time. Year after year this house chosen by the people, legislated to have the measures they passed rejected by a body legislating in secret—dealing with the rights and liberties of the people without responsibility uncontrolled and unrestricted—in fact, as they thought proper. Committee of our house were continually appointed to ascertain the fate of measures, by searching the musty confused journals of that body—and as resurrectionists examined the buried corpse, they delving brought to light the information; they sought who killed or buried the measure, but they could not discover, although the measure might, if passed, promote the liberties of the people.

Was this body allowed to obstruct? No, Sir, the people rose in their majesty, and by the force of public opinion and the popular voice, worked a great and important change in the constitution which had existed before in Nova Scotia. The doors were opened despite the strenuous and determed [sic] resistance—Legislative and Executive functions were separated and the people asserted and maintained their rights and privileges, and that Legislation should be conducted in public, under the scrutinising eye of a free people.

Other great changes in the first principles of our government were demanded —and the people sent to this House men pledged to carry out and perfect the responsible system, and they were resisted by a majority of the old party still remaining in the Upper Branch, determined to retard the changes sought by every means in their power; they were not successful,—they were beaten by constitutional means;—and now the hon. and learned member from Annapolis [J. W. Johnston] complains that the Upper Branch harmonises with and does not obstruct this popular branch. Sir, I congratulate this House and the Country that such is the case; that the efforts to stifle the voice of the people have failed, and that a system of government which commands their respect, while it ensures their liberty—and is based upon right principles, and founded on a stable and sure basis. The hon. and learned gentleman deprecates changes—all *free* governments have and do change and remodel their constitutions. But he says quoting Cromwell the Regicides opinion, "that good government is the supremacy of order, and not the mere realisation of the popular will." But I attest that it is the just representation of "the popular will," that maintains "the supremacy of order,"—when the will of the people is disregarded, despotism and tyranny, anarchy and confusion prevail.

Document A—4

GEORGE RENNY YOUNG SPEAKS, 1851

(The *Nova Scotian*, March 24, 1851, p. 72.)

Young was the son of John Young, who under the penname "Agricola" wrote a long series of articles on agriculture in the 1820's and who became active in politics as a Reformer. George Young, trained a lawyer, was also active as a journalist, founding the Nova Scotian *in 1824, and soon engaged in politics. He was a member of the first cabinet after the winning of responsible government in 1848 and resigned in 1851 in opposition to the decision to build government-owned railways.*

I have shewn the necessity and advantages of a second branch, independent, but sympathetic—a check but not an obstruction. I have shewn to what the present system leads—it holds the upper as a mere echo and reflex of the lower house. It gives its leaders and the majority the power of moulding the upper branch to carry any measure which they please,—it deprives the people of a direct influence in the selection of its members, over whom they ought to exercise a certain and useful control—that their structure has been condemned by the highest constitutional authority,—that the Crown has also condemned it, and is ready to concede the principle of election, if demanded, ought we to do so? That is now the question which is to be met. I frankly admit, that we are embarrassed in the consideration of it, by the bald and imperfect mode in which this question has been propounded by the learned member from Annapolis [J. W. Johnston]. I gave him warning at the first hour this session, when he laid his original resolution on the table, that he need not anticipate any opposition to the affirmance of the elective principle,—that the only difficulty or dispute would be on the details;—and I think, that after the delay of a year, and the ample opportunity afforded for reflection and inquiry, if sincere in pressing it, he ought to have brought down a perfect measure, matured in all its aspects. Had this been done, much time and fruitless debate might have been spared. We must deal with it as it is before us, and draw the best lights

we can obtain. Let not the idea prevail that the application of the Elective principle to the second branch, is a new and untried experiment. It is the beauty and perfection of the British Constitution, as it is the genius and excellence of the common law, that its principles are flexible, and can be moulded to meet new exigencies and changes as they arise. Although the power of the Lords is based upon primogeniture and hereditary rights, when the union with England and Scotland were effected, this principle was invaded, and the Peers of Ireland were made elective for life, while those of Scotland are elected every succeeding Parliament.

.   .   .   .

To remove the undue ascendency of Halifax alone, and to elevate the influences of the rural districts would be cheaply purchased by such a sacrifice. Sir, I believe this question to be settled. The boon has been offered to the people, and it will be accepted.—We will not occupy any inferior position to New Brunswick in this respect. The weight of constitutional argument is in favor of the change. At the next Election the will of the people will speak out, and if it be my fortune to come back, and be a member of the new Administration, I will correspond with the Queen's Representative, and be able to submit in the early part of the Session a scheme, matured and perfect, and presented for the acceptance of, and with the sanction of the Crown.

Document A—5

THE MEMORANDUM OF THE LEGISLATIVE COUNCIL, 1852

(C.O. 217/218, Microfilm, Public Archives of Canada.)

In 1852 the subject of the elective Legislative Council was again debated in both chambers of the Legislature. Taking advantage of a temporary majority, the Conservatives in the council authorized the following memorandum to be sent to the Colonial Office. The minority reply comprises part (b).

(a) The Island of Cape Breton comprising four counties and six populous counties to the westward have altogether but two members representing them in the Legislative Council and it has been a subject of regret with all parties that owing to existing circumstances gentlemen from the Country have declined accepting seats in this House and in consequence it has been found necessary to make the appointments to it principally from the City of Halifax and nearly one half of the members are now resident in the Capital which forms one of the grounds of objection to the present Legislative Council.

At present no collision takes place between the two branches of the Legislature because Majorities in both Houses usually vote with the Government but at the last change of administration on a new Government coming into office in order to carry out a Measure deliberately adopted by the people and their representatives an undesirable exercise of Your Majesty's prerogative became necessary to carry it through the Legislative Council and it cannot be doubted that a similar exercise of the Royal prerogative will be unavoidable whenever any material change in the administration of the Provincial Government takes place.

The last House of Assembly during the session of the year one thousand eight hundred and fifty one unanimously declared that the time had arrived when the Legislative Council ought to be elected by the people thus indicating that this sentiment was prevalent among the Inhabitants of this Province and the Members of the Legislative Council are of opinion that the application of the elective principle to the Constitution of the Council affords a salutary remedy for the evils complained of and they beg to assure Your Majesty that whenever Your Majesty shall think proper to sanction such a change no obstacle will be raised on their part to the carrying out of a measure which may be deemed necessary to the satisfactory conduct of public affairs in this province.

(b) Protest against the address of the Legislative Council of Nova Scotia to Her Majesty on the subject of the Constitution of the Legislative Council of 3rd April 1852. Dissentient.

Because they believe the Address does not express the well understood wishes of the People—the principles of an Elective Legislative Council having been negatived by their Representatives during the present Session when introduced into the House of Assembly by Bill.

Because a Legislative Council if elected by the same qualification as the House of Assembly would only be a second House of Assembly under a different name and if elected by a higher or materially different qualification would furnish no guarantee against that inharmonious action subversive of all Government professedly against which the Advocates of the Elective Principle affect to provide.

Because nine of the ten Honourable Gentlemen who in the third day of April voted for this Address and for the Resolutions upon which it is founded on the first day of April instant voted for a Bill materially to alter the Constitution of the Legislative Council having no reference to the Elective Principle brought in by one of their number which Bill recites that "whereas the principle of responsibility to the People so important to the preservation of their rights is at present limited and partial in its operation being confined to one Branch of the Legislature and it is just that the same Principle should be extended to both in order that the People may exercise over both the same wholesome control the Constitution now gives them over one and then enacts. That whenever members of the Legislative Council being also members of the Executive Council shall resign their Seats in or otherwise cease to be members of the Executive Council they shall also thereupon cease to be members of the Legislative Council."

Because the change now sought would destroy the analogy between the Constitution of this Country and that of the parent Government and is inconsistent with Responsible Government.

Because if the Legislative Council should become Elective the further introduction of the Elective Principle to the appointment of the Lieutenant Governor, the Judges and other Public Officers will probably in a short time necessarily follow and thus render the whole system Republican.

Because this Colony being an integral part of the British Empire and Dissentients being desirous that it should continue so they deprecate any movement having a tendency to dissolve that connection.

Because there are no Petitions upon the Table of this House requiring a change in its constitution.

B. The Revival of the Concept, 1858

Document B–1

JOHNSTON REINTRODUCES AN ELECTIVE COUNCIL, MARCH 2, 1858

(Nova Scotia, *House of Assembly, Debates*, 1858, pp. 103–5.)

I assume it as a proposition of unquestionable truth, that if we are to have two branches—and I hardly think any public man would venture to deny the necessity for two—it is essential that each should be independent of the other, and should move in an orbit of its own. Let me ask the house to consider if this is the case now. The Executive power is wielded by a body of men having the confidence of a majority of the people's representatives in this house. Appointments to the Upper Branch are made by the Executive, who, as a matter of course, select their own friends, so that this house, having, through the government it supports, the appointment, have also a controlling influence over members of the Legislative Council. Under the present system, therefore, the second Branch is dependent upon this house; and it is to restore independence to that body, to make it what the British constitution intended—to take away the anomalies and incongruities of our present system—that I have moved to make the Council Elective.

It has been said that the proposed change is altogether without precedent or example; that it is opposed to the system adopted in England—upon which our institutions have been modelled. Sir, there is no analogy between the Legislative Council in this Province, and the House of Lords. The Lords are not appointed by the Crown; but mainly hold their seats, through and by virtue of their own inherent hereditory rights, conferred by the Crown upon their ancestors for services rendered to the state. Once appointed the Lords hold their seats by right,—equally independant of the Crown and the Commons. A few peers out of that large body, it is true, are elected from the noblemen of Scotland and Ireland.

. . . .

Now, sir, it has been urged—and it is the only argument against this measure that has the slightest effect upon my mind —that by making the Upper Branch Elective, you give to both houses the same origin. But I do not feel that this objection should be allowed to have any weight with us. The change proposed should be considered in the light of expediency rather than a choice. Suppose we were now called on to frame, for the first time, a constitution for this country, would any man propose to create a body such as the Council, composed of its elements,—owing its existence to this Branch of the Legislature, and by consequence dependent, if not entirely impotent? Surely not, sir. I say, then, that the fact of both branches owing their existence to a common origin does not impress me against the proposed change. The members may be elected by different constituencies—and sit for a longer term—which will obviate the objection urged. But, sir, I contend that the anticipated disadvantages resulting from the proposed change will be more than counter-balanced by the beneficial effects that must ensue, and are far out-weighed by the anomalies of the present system. Let us consider for a moment the position in which we stand. Suppose the majority in this house were opposed by a hostile majority in the Council, how could any government carry on the administration of public affairs without creating a preponderance in the Council favorable to them by new appointments? It is obvious, sir, that they would be driven to adopt some such expedient.

It is now some seven or eight years since I first brought this subject to the notice of the house. I foresaw at that time the necessity for a change, and every succeeding discussion has tended to confirm me in the opinions I then entertained. I hold in my hand a very elaborate constitution for a colony, framed and introduced into the British House of Commons by the late Sir William Molesworth. I have also under my hand the debate upon this very New Zealand constitution, which took place in the house of Commons, in which Sir William Molesworth and Sir Frederick Peel participated. Both those gentlemen spoke strongly in favor of the Elective principle.

Document B–2

WILLIAM ANNAND OPPOSES ELECTION, MARCH 2, 1858

(Nova Scotia, *House of Assembly, Debates*, 1858, p. 108.)

William Annand was first elected to the Assembly in 1836. In 1867 he was appointed to the Legislative Council and was premier of the province from 1867 until 1875 when he retired from politics.

Mr. Annand said.—I have watched the discussions upon the Elective Council bill for some years past with much attention. I have always been opposed to the principle of the measure, for I felt that its introduction into our constitution would strike a fatal blow at the system of government which it cost us so much time and labor to attain. I listened with attention to the arguments urged in favor of the bill, and so far as I could perceive, but one of any weight or importance was used. It has been said that the Legislative Council should be independent; but hon. gentlemen seem to forget that although to secure independence of action in every branch of the Legislature may be thought necessary, that harmony is also essential. Pass this bill and the time must arrive when the harmony which now subsists between this branch and the Legislative Council will be destroyed, and we will not have the power to restore it. The bill provides for the continuance of the present members of Council, during their lifetime—and for the Election of certain other members; we all know the political predilictions of those who compose that body. Let us suppose that a change in the administration were to ensue, and a government adverse to the present, assumed the reins of power—is it not apparent to every reflecting mind that the two bodies would be placed instantly in collision, the one with the other. The Governor has no power to dissolve the Council;—this bill does not give him the power,—virtually it is admitted, the members of that body will hold their seats for life. Does it not follow then that the Legislative Council will denude this house of its legitimate power and become *par excellence* the people's house?

Sir, I hold that there is no country in the world possessed of a constitution superior to that of Nova Scotia; the people possess the power to exercise legitimately every privilege which freemen should enjoy. Does it not seem strange, then, that her Majesty's Attorney General, [J. W. Johnston] whose duty it should be to conserve the constitution,—to prevent injurious innovation, should seek to tamper with a system of government which has been found during the last ten years, by practical experience, to work admirably. Pass this bill, and you will find that there is nothing to prevent an artful minister from playing off one branch of the Legislature against the other. For these reasons, sir, I am opposed to the passage of this bill.

Document B–3

JOHN LOCKE PROPOSES ABOLITION

(Nova Scotia, *House of Assembly, Debates,* 1858, pp. 132–33.)

John Locke was a member of the Assembly from 1851 until 1867. Although an opponent of confederation, he was appointed to the Senate, where he sat until his death in 1873. He was also a member of two Liberal governments prior to union. In 1858 he proposed, as he had in 1852, that the upper house be totally abolished.

Mr. Locke said.—I rise, Mr. Chairman, for the purpose of moving the following resolution, which I hope will commend itself to the good sense of the house:—

"*Whereas*, It has been proposed by her Majesty's Attorney General to alter the constitution of this Province, by making the Legislative Council Elective;—a change which, while increasing the expense of that body, already amounting to upwards of £3000 per annum, would not ensure that harmony essential to the practical working of British representative institutions. *And Whereas*, One Branch of the Legislature is sufficient to transact all the business of this country,

"*Resolved therefore*, That a Legislative Council in this province is unnecessary, and that an humble address be presented to the Crown praying that the Legislative Council in Nova Scotia may be abolished."

It has been long in my opinion, that the exigencies of this country did not require two branches. I am still of that opinion; for I am at a loss to conceive what possible benefit can result to the public from the constitution of two branches, deriving their origin from the same source,—each being in fact but a reflex of the other. The annual cost to the province is considerable, and I do think that if abolished it would be to our advantage. . . .

Mr. Locke said—As the discussion on this bill progresses, I feel more and more impressed with the soundness of the principle which I some days since moved —to abolish the Legislative Council altogether. In effect it is of no practical benefit; its legislative action does not materially benefit the country—while the loss to the province amounts to some £3000 per annum, a sum which by the abolition of that body we would at once save to the country. Sir, I may have been called a chartist, and a sweeper—but at least it cannot be denied that my action has been uniform and consistent. In 1852 —when this question was first introduced, I made a motion similar in effect to that which I have now introduced; at that time one hon. member voted for my resolution, but has since taken his seat in the Legislative Council; the hon. member for Horton [Edward L. Brown] argued in favor of my resolution, but I think that timidity on his part prevented his voting for it. The same principle may induce him to oppose it now, although there is no doubt but he entertains a conscientious conviction of the soundness of the principle of my resolution.

I do not expect to carry this measure in a day; all reforms require time to effectuate them—but I have implicit faith in the principle and have no doubt but that in the end it will be adopted. The hon. member for Windsor [J. Howe]—when he attempted to remove that black spot—the old Council of 12, from the face of the constitution—was obliged to struggle for some time before he effectuated his object; I do not expect to be more fortunate, but I have no doubt but that the day will come when the bill I have introduced will be adopted by the unanimous action of this house. The Legislative Council as now constituted I hold to be of no practical utility; The house of Lords, in England, is the embodyment of the wisdom of the realm, is composed of the aristocracy—a body of which we have no prototype in this country,—most of the speakers in that body are, to say the least of them not inferior to those in the Commons— while from their training at the best collegiate institutions in the country, they are enabled to bring to bear on all questions submitted to them—the results of a matured experience and an intimate acquaintance with the necessities and requirements of the country. Does the Legislative Council in this country occupy that position?

I think not; this house may without flattery be said to possess as much of wisdom as the Upper Branch. There exists no disposition to entrench upon the constitutional action of the crown, deriving their origin from the people, but admitting and sustaining the Queen, this house in conjunction with the representative of majesty, is quite capable of conducting the business of the country.

For these reasons, sir, I believe that the Legislative Council is an unnecessary element in the constitution and should be abolished.

Document B–4

WILLIAM YOUNG AND JOHNSTON DEBATE

(Nova Scotia, *House of Assembly, Debates*, 1858, pp. 106–7.)

William Young, the brother of George Young (Document A–4), was first elected to the Assembly in 1832 and remained in the Assembly until his appointment as Chief Justice in 1860. He was twice attorney general and was also premier of the colony. Two points raised by Young in selection a. were answered by J. W. Johnston. Part of his reply is also included in selection (b).

(a) YOUNG'S COMMENTS

The measure now [establishing the elective upper house] submitted differs widely from the Canadian bill. There they have rejected the old county divisions, and defined 23 distinct townships or districts, for which members are to be elected. The hon. Attorney General [J. W. Johnston] proposes to introduce a county representation. We all know that the representation by counties in this province is unfair and unequal; in introducing a new measure one would have thought that the hon. Attorney General would not adhere to the anomalies and inconveniences of our present system. Is it fair that Pictou should have no larger representation in the upper branch, (which I will presently show you, will, under the proposed bill, be beyond all question the superior power in the constitution)—than a county with one half its population? What difficulty or impediment exists in the way of an equitable division, by laying out some 6 or 8 electorial districts, and giving to each its fair share so that the whole country may be equitably represented? I can see none.

Now, sir, I ask what is it that has given to the House of Commons their dignity and power, and enabled them to keep in check the enormous influence which the prestige, position, wealth and talent of the House of Lords give them? I answer, the right of initiating money votes. Let

20 or 21 gentlemen sit in the other end of this building, beyond the control of this house,—a body created by statute which the crown has no power to dissolve,—elected by the people, they would at once claim the right of moving what votes they pleased; and, sitting for life as they will until the present members die off, will gradually usurp the functions of this branch of the Legislature and denude this house of all real practical power. To introduce a bill of this kind, founded on county representation,—the members of Council being elected by constituencies whose right to vote involves the possession of a superior franchise, is to strike a death blow at the power of this house.

(b) REPLY OF J. W. JOHNSTON

He [W. Young] says the House of Commons have always zealously guarded the right they possess of initiating money votes. I agree with him, and the reason is self-evident. The right to dispose of monies collected from the people belongs to the people; the House of Lords is a hereditary body, non-elective, and therefore cannot share the right to exercise this privilege, but the moment you make the Council elective, the reasons which formerly existed for withholding from them its enjoyment are dissipated.

The hon. gentleman has moved in amendment to the first clause of this bill a clause introduced by me into the act of 1852, the effect of which was to disorganise and dissolve the present council, and compel the members who desired to continue in that body to seek constituencies. The answer to the action he has taken is clear: if it was possible to pass such a clause through the council it might be wise to move it, but when we know that the council would not assent to it—and that therefore even if sanctioned by this house our action would be nugatory and ineffectual—is it not worse than a waste of time to discuss it. Why should we be asked to pass a clause which would be inoperative. If the hon. member for Inverness is really desirous, as I am, of introducing the elective principle into the council, he will abandon this amendment and allow the bill to pass as introduced. It is a significant fact, which hon. members would do well to reflect on, that not a member of this house has ventured to oppose the principle of the bill.

Document B–5

COMMENTS OF STEWART CAMPBELL

(Nova Scotia, *House of Assembly, Debates,* 1858, pp. 109–11.)

Stewart Campbell sat in the Assembly from 1851 until 1867 and was a member of the Canadian House of Commons after confederation from 1867 until 1874. He was speaker of the Assembly from 1854 until 1861.

At our elections, we receive at the hands of our constituents, the sacred deposit of our present constitution. Pledged we all were, either expressly, or by implication, to guard and defend it; and when the day arrived for the surrender of our trust, to return it with its proportions undiminished, and its value unimpaired. Shall we do so if we pass this bill? As-suredly not. Sir, I have heard it asserted in this debate, and the declaration excited my astonishment, that the passage of this bill would tend to the augmentation of the power and liberties of the people.—Sir, I shall ever be ready to promote the welfare of the people in that respect, by any practical and effective measure; but at the same time, I shall ever oppose such speculative legislation as this, even though the name of our cherished friends, the people, be used in connexion with it. But, Mr. Chairman, this bill is not only speculative, but the argument by which it is sustained is delusive. It may hold promise to the ear, but mark me, t'will break it to the hope. Trumpet it forth as you may, that it is to give the people more power; depend upon it, it cannot add one tittle to the popular influence. The great, the inexorable power of the people is already here in this house, in all its plenitude. It is emphatically the people's house, and I trust the day will never arrive when by such legislation as this we weaken its legitimate and constitutional influence. We are told we shall have two people's houses. Sir, I reply that when a vessel is full, you may pour to all eternity, but you cannot add one drop to its contents. So with regard to this house, the power of the people through their representatives here is full and complete. You can make no addition to it by this bill. What, sir, have we seen with our own eyes? It is not many months since we saw on this very floor the power of the people exercised to the utmost extent which the most ardent imagination of the most devoted champion of popular rights could conceive. A majority here by a peaceful revolution, by a single paragraph, transferred the administration of our public affairs from the hands of the late to the hands of the present government. Had you two, or had you ten elective chambers, instead of one, could such a consummation have been more effectually achieved? What then, sir, do the people require, or rather what is required for them, beyond this, which is the very touchstone and essence of responsible government.

But, sir, I may be asked am I satisfied with the Legislative Council as it at present exists. I answer, no. It is one thing, however, to say that the city of Halifax, or any other part of the province, has too large a representation there, and another to say that that body should be Elective. My idea of what their organization should be is this—they should be nominated by the government of the day, and for that nomination it should be held strictly responsible to this house and the country. They should be taken from the several counties of the province, Halifax as the metropolis, receiving fair consideration, but nothing more. The qualification of its members should be such as would strikingly recommend them for such honorable distinction; and last, but not least, party considerations should be forgotten in their selection. They should be men above the influences of party—they should be of broad and liberal and enlightened views, moving among and sympathizing with the people; but at the same time regulating their public conduct by an intelligent recognition of that conservative principle which is the peculiar characteristic of a constitutional upper branch. Elevated and distinguished on such a basis as this, I feel assured that the Legislative Council would be worthy of the confidence of this people.

I know it may startle some to find me advocating so slender a regard for party considerations in the selections to that board. But, sir, in this particular I am influenced by a desire to maintain its similarity to its great original the house of Lords. We have been asked if the people of England would submit to the nomination and elevation of Peers by the government. Sir, the Crown, under the advice of its ministers, constantly exercise this right. We need not go back far in the history of the present state for very many examples on this point—the recent creation of Macaulay, Parke, and Denison, are but a few of the names that might be mentioned. Do these men owe their present proud position of peers of the realm to political or party considerations? No; talent and general worth, their value to the state, were their title to nobility no less palpable than the parchments on which their patents were engraved.

. . . .

Mr. Chairman, I love to think and to speak of Old England. I revere her institutions, and would wish to trace their spirit and their value here. Sir, I call upon the hon. and learned Attorney General, as the first crown officer of this country, to pause ere he takes that final and irrevocable step which is to throw into a foreign mould the constitution which modelled upon that of the parent country has now for many years existed here. In that interval our children have grown to manhood, they have become imbued with its spirit. Like ivy tendrils, they have clung around it amid the blast of the political tempest; in calm hours they have been embosomed in its branches, and beneath its peaceful shade they have held sweet converse on the hopeful future of their native land. A few short years, sir, and these places which now know us, will know us no more. The laudable aspirations of another generation will summon them to this arena to be the champions of their country's interests. They will then be the fathers, as they are now the sons, of Nova Scotia. Mr. Chairman, in their name, if not in our own, I protest against the present measure. This strain breaks upon my ear, and I know it comes from them. Will the hon. and learned leader of the government be deaf to its entreaty?

> "Woodman spare that tree,
> Touch not a single bough,
> In youth it sheltered me,
> And I'll protect it now."

Document B–6

REMARKS OF A. G. ARCHIBALD

(Nova Scotia, House of Assembly, Debates, 1858, pp. 111–13.)

A. G. Archibald was a conspicuous member of a prominent family. He sat in the Assembly from 1851 until 1867 and was a member of several Liberal governments. He was a Father of Confederation and sat in John A. Macdonald's cabinet until his appointment as Lieutenant Governor of Manitoba. He also served in the same position in Nova Scotia for 10 years.

I look on it as one of the great vices attaching to free institutions, that there is a prevailing disposition to tinker and to change them. It seems inherent in our nature, to be discovering apparent defects in such matters,—and to seek to escape by change. So much has this been considered the feeling of human nature, that the fathers of the American constitution, tried to provide, in their system of government, against the tendency,—by deciding that when once a constitution was established, it should not be changed by any sudden gust of feeling,—but that before alteration, the change should receive the two-third vote of Congress, and subsequent to ample time allowed, the assent of three fourths of the legislatures of the various states. This was ingrafted as one of the first principles of the government of the Republic,—and if that action were necessary there, is it not worth consideration whether we should not exhibit similar caution here? The Speaker of the house called attention, in his remarks just made, to the manner in which this question appears.—Has it been submitted to the people—has it been called for by any county, or any township, or any hamlet of the land? No; we are not called on by any public declaration of any kind, to legislate on the question. When the Atty. General [J. W. Johnston] was in opposition, he might have considered the state of the Legislative Council one of the abuses of our system of government, and have attacked it accordingly; but he is very differently situated now; and if government is particularly charged with any one function, it is to conserve the institutions placed in their care. If meddling with such matters be hardly pardonable in an opposition, it is worse than impudent in a government to come forward unnecessarily, with propositions for such changes.

It would appear as if on accession to office gentlemen opposite were willing to disarrange almost all that they found established. If such a bill to unsettle the upper branch, and another will soon be presented to unsettle this house, Where are those matters to end? Some years ago, to improve the constitution of the Assembly, which then rested on the forty shilling freehold, the rate-paying franchise was introduced. How long did that stage continue? Two or three years; and then followed a change greater than was anticipated at the commancement of the march of alterations, and we landed on universal suffrage. Whatever might be the sentiment then, are there ten men here now who would not say that it would be better for the dignity, the integrity of the country, to repose on the former franchise than on the present? The Attorney General claimed credit for that change; I hope he will not have the credit of placing the country step by step in republican institutions, such as we would be sorry ever to arrive at. Beginning with the Legislative Council, we may go on by degrees to elective judges and other officers, until we have republican institutions throughout. Is the country prepared for that? If not, I give it warning on the introduction of this, as I would on the introduction of the franchise changes if I were here. If you take this bill, you are so far pledged to go on, to elect all your officers, judges, governors, and all throughout the country.

C. Evaluation

Document C–1

THE POSITION OF THE *NOVA SCOTIAN*
(The *Nova Scotian*, March 3, 1851.)

The Nova Scotian *was owned by William Annand and was the most prominent Liberal newspaper in the colony. It was founded by G. R. Young, who sold it in 1828 to Joseph Howe, who remained as editor until 1856, although ownership of the paper passed to Annand in 1843. When this particular editorial was written, Howe was in England.*

As far as the principle of making the Legislative Council elective is involved, the vote of the House will probably be unanimous, but there is, notwithstanding, a great variety of opinions as to how the measure is to be carried into practical operation. If we were called upon to analyze the House we would divide Members into four classes:—

1st. Those who sincerely advocate the change but are not prepared to show how it can be safely introduced.

2nd. Those who countenance the movement because popular, who consider it as impracticable.

3rd. Those who hope that the agitation of the question will lead to entirely abolishing the second Branch of the Legislature, and substituting a Single for a Double Chamber.

4th. Those who look upon an Elective Legislative Council as an entering wedge which will ultimately rend asunder the existing political fabric, and lead to further organic changes in the Constitution.

The Hon. leader of the Opposition, or we are much mistaken, belongs to the latter class. Mr. Johnston spent the best energies of his mind, and some of the best years of his life in resisting the introduction of Responsible and Departmental Government. It was represented as inapplicable to our Colonial condition—as burthensome to the Revenue—as leading to the corruption of Heads of Departments, and collusion between the members of Administration and their supporters in the Legislative. Despite these ravings and predictions, the people gave in their adhesion to the Departmental system, which, after being tried in the balance was *not* found wanting. There it stands—a monument of the labours, perseverance, wisdom and patriotism of the old Liberal party, and there, too, it stands a significant record of the defeat and humiliation of the party who vainly endeavoured to prevent its erection.

Mr. Johnston has ever been the enemy of Departmental Government. He is so now. His purpose is still the same—to overturn the system perfected by his political adversaries. He cannot go back to his first love—his own party would desert him if he did. The game now is to advance, and, under the specious plea of increasing popular privileges, change the mode of appointing the second Branch of the Legislature. The hon. and learned member now seeks to introduce a new and untried element into our Constitution —to sap and undermine what he intends ultimately to destroy. Our readers would do well to mark the course of the learned Leader. For years and years previous to the introduction of the Departmental system, he steadily and unceasingly resisted the attempts of the Liberal party to extend the liberties of the people. Mr. Johnston was then the bold and uncompromising champion of the irresponsibles, and the defender of the constitution of the Legislative Council—the self-same Constitution he now so bitterly assails. Whence this change of sentiment? To what influence shall we ascribe the sudden conversion—too sudden to be sincere —of the learned member from Obstructive to ultra-liberal views? Men of Mr. Johnston's age and experience rarely change the entire current of their lives—or as a quaint old poet has it:

"By the time a man is turned of forty,
  His ruling passions grow so haughty,
  There is no clipping of his wings."

But Mr. Johnston has himself suggested the motive. His conversion dates from the time that the Government, after overcoming every obstruction offered by the leader of Opposition and his friends, carried the address in the Legislative Council which made the Departmental system part and parcel of the Institutions of the country. The system was now com-

plete, and then it was that Mr. Johnston commenced his agitation for changing the composition of a body which had harmonized with the Representatives of the People and frustrated all his plans. We do not believe he will succeed; although at the present moment both parties in the Assembly are ready to assent to the elective principle. The tried and sincere friends of the Departmental system will, or we are much mistaken, come to the conclusion that an Elective Legislative Council is incompatible with the harmonious working of British Representative Institutions, and that a change in the mode of appointing the upper Branch will lead to other changes:—to the Election of the Governor—the appointment of the Chiefs of Departments by that Functionary and their withdrawal from the Assembly—the right of the Governor to veto the acts of the Legislature—the election of Judges—the dismissal alike of principals and subordinates upon a change of administration, together with *all* and singular the peculiarities of the Republican system.

We may be wrong, but we would have our friends pause before committing themselves to a principle which may be fatal to the system we now have, and which since its introduction has worked well. The harmony between the several Branches of the Legislature during the last eight years—under Conservative and Liberal administrations, has been undisturbed: but where the security or even reasonable prospect, we ask, that there will be equal harmony for the next eight years if both Branches of the Legislature are elected? What security that there will not be Conservative Majorities in the one Branch and Liberal Majorities in the other? What Guarantee that the Administration will not have votes of want of confidence hurled at them in one Chamber while they are gallantly sustained in the other? that the whole business of Legislation will not be brought to a dead Lock and the Country plunged into most admired confusion. Then the question would arise whether the greater should yield to the lesser—the Assembly with its 51 members, to the Legislative Council with its 17, and under what circumstances the people should be appealed to, to reconcile difficulties or rebuke the excited and angry combatants.

And then, too, would probably come the question, whether a system without precedent—neither British nor American, could work without further changes which, if carried, would not leave a single trace of Monarchical Institutions behind. If the Country are prepared to adopt, and the Home Government to concede such a fundamental change in the Constitution, we have no objection; but if they are not, we would caution the Assembly to pause before they are committed too far to effect an honorable retreat, and to remind them, one and all, that—

"It is better far to bear the ills we have than fly to others that we know not of."

Document C–2

JOSEPH HOWE COMMENTS

(Nova Scotia, *House of Assembly, Debates,* 1858, pp. 105–6, 138–44.)

Joseph Howe, a longtime member of the Assembly, was first elected in 1836. During his legislative career he held several positions, and was premier from 1860 until 1863. He was prominently identified with the struggle for cabinet government. After confederation, which he fervently opposed, he entered the federal cabinet. Just prior to his death in 1873 he was appointed lieutenant governor of the province. His political prominence made it particularly important to determine how he answered the points of substance raised by the Conservatives and whether he spent much time in raising secondary issues.

I could not understand what he [J. W. Johnston] meant when he said,—"Here is the bill—regulate, alter, amend it as you please,—I am indifferent as to the details." Why, sir, does he not know that it is in these details that he will find the difficulty? He asks us to adopt a principle, yet he refuses to shew us how that principle can be carried out. My object is to ascertain what it is that the hon. gentleman really proposes, and therefore I am content that the bill should be sent to committee. The hon. gentleman tells us that the council is a body dependant upon this house, impotent and powerless. Is this the case? Let me try the soundness of this doctrine by a single illustration. The members of that body thought themselves entitled to be paid,—this house thought otherwise,—the issue was fairly raised, and we soon found that they had some power; they refused to sanction the payment of the members of this house until we agreed to pay them; and they succeeded in obtaining what they sought. How then can the hon. gentleman assert that the Legislative Council is dependant.

Now, sir, I believe that this tinkering with the constitution is out of place; that it is the duty of the Crown officers, to preserve the form of government, unless change appears absolutely essential, and not to impose on us such a ridiculous hybrid, mongrel sort of constitution, as we shall have if this bill pass. Think of the position we should occupy in this house if half the members were elected by the people, and half appointed by the government; the hon. member from Falmouth [Ezra Churchill], who sits opposite me—and myself, both have to run our elections, but suppose he had to go back to his constituency, and I had not. Would he not occupy an unfavorable position. Let us reflect then, how those hon. members who have to run their periodical elections for seats in the Council will feel when they see 18 or 20 gentlemen sitting perfectly unconcerned—stereotyped in their seats. The idea involves such an absolute absurdity, that I wonder how it can be seriously proposed. But, sir, as the bill is not fully understood—and the mode in which the details are to be regulated, has not been explained to us, I shall reserve any further remarks I may have to make, for the discussion in committee.

Let us look, Mr. Chairman, to the guards and checks which we have here. First, this house must go back to the people every four years; check the first meanwhile any member whose conduct is disapproved of by his constituency, may be called to resign; that is check the second. The Legislative Council, such as it exists, also exercises a controlling power, that is check the third. The Executive Council is responsible to this house and the people, check the fourth. And then the Lieutenant Governor, as a branch of the State, presents, by no means, a trifling check. It may be supposed that he is denuded of power under our present system; I differ from that view. To a large extent he exercises a controlling, guarding power, and a reasonable check, only used for good purposes generally. I ask the Solicitor General [M. I. Wilkins] have we not another check? He heard his colleague, in urging the Mining arrangement, ask again and again, what would the British government think of your propositions? That implies another check, and a powerful one. The house will not run wild on any question, without weighing the power of public opinion across the water; and an additional check of like character, is the power of public opinion in British North America. The Provinces are not united yet, but the power of public opinion runs over all, and is acknowledged in each.

·   ·   ·   ·   ·   ·   ·   ·   ·   ·   ·   ·

One argument does require an earnest answer. He says that the Sovereign of England has not power over the House of Lords, and does not influence it. I might give illustrations that the Sovereign does possess power to influence that house, and the opinions held there. Several of the offices of the household are in the House of Peers; and it includes many of the land holders and aristocracy, men looking to rank and station and likely to be influenced by the Sovereign of the kingdom. Fox's India Bill was a measure for transferring power, similar to that talked of in modern times. It has been sustained in the People's House, and a determination existed to press it through parliament. When it arrived at the Lords, George the Third determined to defeat the measure, and to turn out the ministry; and he did so by influence exercised on that house. That is an illustration that the Sovereign may exercise power there to a large extent. The general scope of the learned gentleman's argument I admit to be correct. That House may claim high political characteristic of independence and intelligence, which entitle it to the respect and confidence of Englishmen, down to the present day.

Document C–3

WHAT IS "RESPONSIBLE GOVERNMENT?"

(Nova Scotia, *House of Assembly, Debates,* 1858, pp. 133–34.)

One of the more intriguing figures in provincial politics, Martin I. Wilkins had the reputation of being the most intelligent man in provincial politics and also being the biggest fool. He sat in the Assembly from 1851 until his retirement in 1859 brought about by a dispute with his Conservative colleagues. His opposi-tion to confederation brought him back into the Assembly, and he was attorney general from 1867 until 1871.

Let me now examine the present system of miscalled responsible government. In describing it I shall do it no injustice. I shall speak of it as it is, and as the poet says, "in naught extenuate nor set down aught in malice." We have then sir, an Executive Council, created by, and holding their offices at the will of a majority of this house. The Legislative Council are created by, and hold their seats, at the will of, the Executive Council. This branch of the Legislature therefore are an entirely dependent body, existing at the will of the government. If therefore the Executive Council have an influence over the House of Assembly, and possess an absolute control over the Legislative Council, they are supreme, and we have all the blessings of an oligarchical despotism. If on the other hand, the majority in this house possess an actual influence over the Executive Council, and this Council holds the existence of the upper branch in its hands, then, sir, we possess the blessings of a democratic and party tyranny. The minority of the people are under the yoke of the majority.

The hon. and learned member for Colchester [A. G. Archibald] has challenged us to show anything in the world, like the system, we are desirous of producing, may I not ask him to produce, within the whole range of the civilized world, a constitution bearing the most distant analogy to that which it is the object of government to reform. The excellence of the British constitution has been lauded, in no measured terms, by several speakers in this debate; our system is intended to be the antitype of that, of which the people of England so proudly boast, and which is the envy of the surrounding nations. Let us contrast it with ours. The great beauty, and the admirably working properties, of the British constitution proceed from that balancing or checking power, which is inherent in a system, composed of three equally and co-ordinately independent branches of legislation. The Queen, the Lords, and Commons, each independent of the other, ready at all time to act together, and in perfect harmony, for the attainment of the general good, but able and prepared to check, and control, each other, on the least attempt to disturb the public wel-

fare.—The absolute independence of each of these branches, constitutes the most prominent excellence of this noble political fabric.—Each of these branches possesses its peculiar attributes, and no one of these bodies can trespass upon the rights of another, as the third is ever ready to interpose its weight, to keep the balance even. The house of Lords, with which our Legislative Council is intended to correspond, may be looked upon as the backbone of the British constitution; by throwing its weight either to one side, or the other, it is at all times able to keep the balance even:—Take away the Peers, and the contest would not be long between the people and the crown, for these two bodies can never balance each other, and if the crown prevailed over the people, we should have an autocrotic [sic] despotism, if the people prevailed over the crown, a democratic tyranny. It is the House of Lords, and its entire and absolute independence, that prevent the occurrence of either of these calamities to the people of England.

To be at all analogous to the Peers, the Legislative Council must possess the power, and independent authority, to check the action of the administration on the one hand and the violence of faction in this house on the other. The moment this independence of the upper branch is invaded there ends all resemblance between the constitution of this, and that of the mother country.

The governor of the province for the time being represents the legislative authority, the power and dignify of the Queen, and administers the government under the advice of a Council of nine drawn from the other branches of the Legislature. His Council are intended to be responsible to the people of the colony, to whom he is not responsible, being to that extent like the Sovereign, incapable of doing wrong. Unless the executive Council are sustained by a majority in this house they must resign.

That the Legislative Council have no independence, both the hon. and learned leader of the opposition [W. Young], and the hon. member for Windsor [J. Howe] well know. By the royal instructions, which they have often seen, the Governor is authorised to appoint 21 persons to seats in that Council, *during the will and pleasure of the Crown.* The Executive Council, therefore, are not only the manufacturers of the upper branch, but have the power to cut them off at a moment's warning.

. . . .

Nominally, the Executive Council are the responsible servants of the majority of the representatives of the people in this house. But what is the real state of the case? If the Executive are really the servants and the majority masters, there is something very like "high life below stairs" occasionally,—and the respective parties have a somewhat singular method of manifesting their relation to each other as master and servant. The servants, as is not usually the case, occasionally offer sumptuous entertainments to the masters. The servants are a good deal wiser and better informed than the master, who generally come to the city with their heads like cocoanuts, filled with milk rather than brains, which, by the influence of a few bottles of sparkling champagne, poured into them by their obsequious servants, becomes crddled like cheese, and it is not surprising that such an article should soon engender nothing but maggots and corruption.

As I before remarked, I have been charged with hostility to responsible government. If by responsible government is meant a system conferring upon the people, under due and defined limits, the control of their own affairs, I am by no means an enemy of rational liberty; but if

the system at present in operation is to be continued, I have no hesitation in repeating, what I have before remarked, that the inhabitants of this country were better governed when power was in the hands of the sachems, who, gathering around their fires, smoked the pipe, and tossing their tomahawks into the air, decided on the affairs of their nation, and declared war or peace with the surrounding tribes, according to the impulses which influenced them in matters affecting their national welfare. It cannot, sir, be denied that under the present constitution eight or nine artful men, by judicious combination, may effectually rule over the destinies of the country, set the people at defiance, and provide for their own interests at the expense of the province.

The hon. and learned Speaker [S. Campbell] dwelt, in glowing terms, on the excellency of this glorious tree of responsible government, and deprecated any interference with its majestic proportions:

"Woodman spare that tree," &c.

He well knows that, on high authority, we are taught that the tree is known by its fruit. Let us examine this tree then by this infallible test. What then does responsible government actually mean? In my apprehension it signifies a government deriving its authority from, and answerable for the use or abuse of that authority to, the people, according to their well understood wishes, as expressed by a majority of their free and independent representatives. If the government, as at present constituted, has operated in direct opposition to the will of the people, then this responsible government is a misnomer.

PROBLEM 10

The Mid-19th-Century Debate on the Future of the North West

LEWIS H. THOMAS
University of Alberta

In the 1850's, the Hudson's Bay Company's network of commercial activity spanned the northern half of North America, for the company was the residual legatee of all the earlier fur trade enterprises whose employees had penetrated the remotest corners of the Canadian wilderness since the days of Champlain. The Company of New France, the La Verendryes, the Pedlars from Montreal, and the North West and XY Companies had all passed from the scene, although not before each had contributed to the wealth of nations, to the transformation of aboriginal society, and to the mapmakers' store of topographical knowledge. The English company had participated in these achievements, and in addition had managed to survive through nearly two centuries of turbulent political and diplomatic changes and of cycles of prosperity and stress. Now at midpoint in the 19th century it was boldly maintaining its claim to the vast Hudson Bay drainage basin (Rupert's Land) based on its charter of 1670. Beyond Rupert's Land it held a license of exclusive trading privileges west of the Rockies and northward to the Arctic shores, and also since 1849 bore, by imperial command, the responsibility for colonizing Vancouver Island. The administrative organization which directed these widespread activities was a product of the genius of Sir George Simpson, Governor-in-Chief of Rupert's Land since 1839, supported by the faithful and laborious service of hundreds of post managers and other employees and by the astute business policies of the company's directorate in London.

Yet despite the prestige of nearly two centuries of corporate existence, and the immense geographical extent of its possessions and activities, the middle years of the 19th century saw the emergence of influences which by 1870 were to transform the business objectives of the Hudson's Bay Company and terminate its political prerogatives in Rupert's Land. The continuity of the fur trade as the exclusive economic interest in the region between the Great Lakes and the Pacific was dependent on the preservation of the area in splendid isolation from rival economic interests such as mineral prospecting and agricultural settlement. The first area to succumb to incursions by new forms of enterprise was the intermountain and coastal region, which was close to the burgeoning settlements in Washington, Oregon, and California, and with immediate access to ocean transport. Under company auspices, coal mining, lumbering, fishing, and agricultural activity commenced on Vancouver Island, and with the gold discoveries on the Fraser River, the crown colony of British Columbia was created in 1858.

It was in the interests of the Hudson's Bay Company as a fur trade concern to postpone for as long as possible the penetration of the region between Canada and British Columbia by competing forms of economic activity. But during the 1850's, this policy had to be maintained in the face of increasing criticism by British advocates of empire development such as James Edward Fitzgerald and Lord Lincoln (later the Duke of Newcastle), by liberal critics of monopolies such as William Ewart Gladstone, and by Canadian expansionists such as George Brown, William McDougall, and Alexander Morris.

The resulting debate is of importance to the student of Canadian history because it reveals the emergence and convergence of influences which ultimately were to cause the largest British possession in North America to be incorporated in Confederation in 1870. Detectable among these influences are political considerations, economic interests, and the impact of new scientific knowledge. So far as this last is concerned, the debate reveals the scanty public knowledge of the climate and resources of the North West at the beginning of the 1850's and the veritable "information explosion" produced by scientific investigations toward the end of the decade. These investigations thrust British North America into the new era in which the findings of scientists were increasingly important in the calculations of businessmen and politicians.

Although the debate involved much discussion of such questions as the legal validity of the Hudson's Bay Company's charter, the unsettled boundary between Rupert's Land and Canada, and the company's relations with the Indians, the documents selected for study are chiefly concerned with the image of the North West in the minds of Britons and Canadians, whose restless search for new economic opportunities was transforming large parts of the world in the 19th century. Since the Canadian contest with the wilderness still continues, the student will find parallels between this mid-19th-century debate on the future of the North West and the mid-20th-century discussions on the development of the Canadian North.

The critics of the Hudson's Bay Company contended that it was hostile to all forms of enterprise other than the fur trade and was standing in the way of progress by deliberately discouraging agricultural settlement. Company spokesmen denied these allegations, and asserted that the spread of settlement in the North West would always be inhibited by formidable climatic and geographic obstacles. Did corporate self-interest blind the company in this matter, or was it merely being realistic, in view of the state of agricultural science and technology at that time? Were the critics oversimplifying the problem of opening the North West?

For further study of the context of this problem, the student should consult J. S. Galbraith, *The Hudson's Bay Company as an Imperial Factor 1821–1869* (1957); W. L. Morton, *The West and Confederation 1857–1871* (Canadian Historical Association Booklet, 1958); and A. S. Morton, *A History of the*

Canadian West to 1870–71 (1939). Canadian interest in the North West in the 1850's is described by J. M. S. Careless in *Brown of the Globe, Vol. I: The Voice of Upper Canada 1818–1859* (1959). The threat of American expansion and the reactions which it produced in Canada and Britain are treated in A. C. Gluek, Jr., *Minnesota and the Manifest Destiny of the Canadian Northwest: A Study on Canadian-American Relations* (1965). For the origins and significance of the British and Canadian scientific expeditions of the late 1850's, see Irene M. Spry, "Captain John Palliser and the Exploration of Western Canada," *The Geographical Journal*, Vol. CXXV (1959), pp. 149–84, and Lewis H. Thomas, "The Hind and Dawson Expeditions 1857–58," *The Beaver*, Winter, 1958, pp. 39–45.

A. Estimates of Economic Prospects in 1849

The Hudson's Bay Company's territory, although a part of the British Empire, was never under the direct control of the Colonial Office; hence the British Government received no regular reports on its condition and prospects such as were supplied by governors and other colonial officials. This point was raised in the House of Commons in 1848 during the debate on the proposal to make the company the agent for colonizing Vancouver Island. The public interest in this debate prompted a prolific British writer on colonial affairs, Robert Montgomery Martin (1803?–68) to publish a book the following year which purported to describe the policies of the company and the conditions prevailing in its domain. A few months later he was answered by a critic of the company, James Edward Fitzgerald (1818–96), who had recently failed in an effort to organize a company for the colonization of Vancouver Island. The following selections from Gladstone's speech and from the books by Martin and Fitzgerald indicate the difficulties of designing a policy for the North West at this time. What contradictions are evident in the estimates of agricultural potential in this region? How adequate is the evidence presented? Would it have been reasonable to expect the company to have compiled and published statistics on the climate and resources of Rupert's Land?

Document A–1

THE INFORMATION GAP

(William Ewart Gladstone, *Parliamentary Debates*, 3d Series, Vol. CI, cols. 270, 272 [August 18, 1848].)

A land company had an interest in colonization, but a trading company compelled the colonists to compete with a powerful monopolizing body. Upon that ground, the Legislature had deprived the East India Company of its trading powers. The experiment of managing colonies by trading companies had been tried and failed in the old North American colonies; and he might particularly refer to the cases of Virginia and Massachussets. The objection to a trading company under such circumstances applied with tenfold force to the Hudson's Bay Company. There never was a case in which the evils of monopoly acquired a more rank development than in the instance of that Company. In the case of the Hudson's Bay Company the monopoly of land and trade was aggravated by absolutism in politics covered by the cloak of impenetrable secrecy. In the vast British empire all imperial concerns were made public, and particulars relating to all the Queen's subjects were placed upon the tables of both Houses of Parliament, for the information of their Members. But what did any of those whom he was now addressing know, by means of Parliamentary information, of the Hudson's Bay Company, and the condition of the country—as large as the continent of Europe—which they held under their rule? Absolutely nothing.

We knew that they had a charter, and a license to trade; but with respect to the government they had established, the power they exercised, the sanctions by which they enforced that power, the condition of the people, and the laws by which they were regulated—with respect to all these points we knew absolutely nothing. Those who wished to obtain information upon these interesting points, must hunt through the works published by travellers, American exploring expeditions, and missionaries: none could be had in an official shape. . . . What was the object which a fur-trading company had in view? Could it be their wish that the country in which they carried on their operations should be reclaimed and cultivated? On the contrary, it must be kept like a desert. They must, to be sure, cultivate a few spots in order to obtain corn for the support of their cattle and their agents—but as respected the country at large, their interest required that it should be kept just as nature had left it.

Document A—2

THE NORTHWEST "OF LITTLE VALUE FOR AGRICULTURE"

(Robert Montgomery Martin, *The Hudson's Bay Territories and Vancouver's Island, with an Exposition of the Chartered Rights, Conduct and Policy of the Honble. Hudson's Bay Corporation* [London, 1849], pp. 6, 14–15, 16–17.)

It is difficult to convey an idea of the territories belonging to, as well as those included in the trading licence of, the Hudson's Bay Company. A great portion of them, east of the Rocky Mountains, consists of inland seas, bays, lakes, rivers, swamps, treeless prairies, barren hills and hollows, 'tossed together in a wave-like form, as if the ocean had been suddenly petrified while heaving its huge billows in a tumultuous swell.'—(*T. Simpson's Life and Travels.*) La Hontan has not inaptly called the region north of Lake Superior, the 'fag end of the world.' There are, doubtless, several spots, such as the Red River, adapted in some respects for European settlements; but they are like oases in the desert, few and far between—and totally inapplicable for extended coloniza-

tion; indeed, at a great many of the posts, not only can no corn be grown, but even the potatoe and other crops are cut off by summer frosts, so that the rearing and preservation of a sufficient quantity of human food is an object of the most anxious solicitude throughout the country. By the concession of part of the Oregon country and the Columbia River to the United States in 1846, we gave up a fertile and temperate region, south of the 49th parallel, capable of yielding abundance of food; and the tract now left in the possession of the Hudson's Bay Company will require great care and industry, to render even the most promising spots productive.

. . . Changing the course from west to west south-west, the traveller reaches the immense prairies of the Saskatchewan River, of which entire tracts are frequently bared by fire to the very soil. The cold in these plains in winter, with the wind from the westward, is terrific; there is not a shrub or even a blade of grass to break the force of the blast, whose temperature is at least 40° below zero. The only exposed part of the traveller, the eye-lashes, becomes speedily covered with a heavy crop of icicles, which the half-frozen fingers have a difficulty in removing. These plains in summer are frequented by the Indians as hunting grounds. The heat in these wild plains is as unbearable in summer as is the cold in winter. Throughout this country, says Sir G. Simpson, every thing is in unparalleled extremes. Cold and excessive heat,—long droughts balanced by drenching rain and destructive hail (sometimes 5½ inches in circumference). At one period both whites and natives are living in wasteful abundance of venison, buffalo, fish, and game—at others reduced to the last degree of hunger, often passing several days without food. . . .

Mr. Robert Greenhow, in his History of California, Oregon, and other territories on the north-west coast of America [London, 1844], before referred to, speaking of the countries in the occupation of the Hudson's Bay Company with respect to colonization, says, p. 37:—'North of the 50° parallel, the climate is more moist; but its extreme coldness renders the country of *little value for agriculture*. The only part at which any settlement has been attempted, is that of the Red River, where, about 5000 persons, principally half-breeds and Indians, have been established by the Hudson's Bay Company; *but the success of the enterprise is yet doubtful.*' And, again, at page 397, the author says:—'With regard to colonization it has been already said, that a very small proportion of the Hudson Bay Company's territories is capable of being rendered productive by cultivation.' Mr. Greenhow then alludes to the Red River settlement, and the unfortunate results of the first attempts to colonize it, and adds:—'The land may be considered fertile when compared with other parts of the continent situate far to the north; it is, however, deficient in wood, and notwithstanding *all the advantages held out by the Hudson's Bay Company, there is no probability it will ever rise to importance in any way*, and, least of all, as a check to incursions from the United States, which seems to be one of the principal objects proposed by its founders.' [Italics by Martin.]

Document A—3

THE NORTHWEST "A MAGNIFICENT COUNTRY FOR COLONIZATION"

(James Edward Fitzgerald, An Examination of the Charter and Proceedings of the Hudson's Bay Company, with Reference to the Grant of Vancouver's Island [London, 1849], pp. 114–18; 120; 289–91.)

The Company know very well that as long as there is a general belief that the interior of the continent of America is of no value, so long they may feel secure in the possession of their privileges; and therefore the idea is circulated, that the whole country north of the 49th parallel of latitude, is a frozen wilderness, where human life can with difficulty be supported, and where the earth will not yield its accustomed fruits: and the same facts are assigned as the necessary and unavoidable cause of those awful and devastating famines, with all their fearful accompaniments of starvation and cannibalism, to which the miserable natives are periodically exposed.

The Company have a direct interest at this moment in keeping up this erroneous idea.

There is a good example of how the facts of the case may be distorted, for interested motives, in the representations made at first about the country in which the Red River settlement is situated. The North-West Company saw at once that the settlement was directed against, and would be fatal to, their trade; and so we have, in their efforts to cry it down, frequent assertions of the impossibility of founding a settlement in so remote and desolate a country. Yet experience has shewn that there is not a more favourable situation on the face of the earth for the employment of agricultural industry than the locality of the Red River. As far as the produce of the soil is concerned, the settlers revel in abundance.

In the work by Mr. M. Martin, to which we have, unfortunately, frequent occasion to allude, because it bears all the appearance of authority, it is confidently stated, that although "there are, doubtless, several spots, such as the Red River, adapted in some respects for European settlements, they are like oases in the desert, few and far between, and totally inapplicable for extended colonization" (p. 6); and again, that "the tract now left in the possession of the Hudson's Bay Company will require great care and industry to render even the most promising spots productive" (p. 6).

In order to shew how little truth there is in this statement, it will not be without utility or interest if we give a brief account of the physical features of this country.

The territories of the Hudson's Bay Company may be considered as containing three great districts, totally differing in their general aspect: these may be called, the *Woody* country, the *Prairie* country, and the *Barren* country.

· · · · · · · · · · · · ·

The woody country extends round the south of James' Bay, and the west of Hudson's Bay, from East Main, as far as North Lined Lake. The belt of wood is said to finish abruptly at this lake,—one side being a forest, and the other entirely open country. The breadth of the belt of wood may be considered to be pretty nearly the same throughout; being bounded, as has been said, towards the

north-east by James' and Hudson's Bay, and, towards the south and west, by a line stretching along the north of Lake Superior, from the frontiers of Canada, through the Lake of the Woods, Lake Winnipeg, Deer Lake, and Wollaston Lake.

It is not asserted that all the country within the boundaries here described is a forest, or that all the land in the other districts is barren, or open. The general features of each district are, however, such as those names indicate. Thus the general feature of the country in the broad horse-shoe belt here described is forest. A line from the shores of Hudson's Bay, through the north of North Lined Lake, Lake Athepescow, to Great Slave Lake, and down Mackenzie's River, will cut off all the country towards the north, which may be called the *Barren* district. And the country west and south of Lakes Winnipeg, Deer, Wollaston, and Athepescow, as far as the Rocky Mountains, may be denominated the plain, or Prairie district.

Now it may be quite true that only a small portion of the Hudson's Bay Company's territories is fit for colonization, and indeed for anything except the chase; but it may be, and *is* true, that that the small portion is a country sufficiently large and fertile to support all the population of Great Britain and all her dependencies.

In the first place, there is the neighbourhood of the Red River, which experience has shewn to be fertile in the extreme. Then there is the whole country, several hundred miles in extent, between the Red River and the frontiers of Canada, along the line of rivers and lakes which connect Lake Winnipeg with Lake Superior. It is needless to make any long references to authors to support this assertion—that this is a magnificent country for colonization. . . .

· · · · · · · · · · · · ·

The part of the possessions of the Hudson's Bay Company which is habitable and applicable for settlement, is the Prairie district—a broad belt stretching from Lake Superior, in a north-westerly direction, to the Rocky Mountains. It is a country of varied features: immense plains, hills, lakes, and woods, are chequered over its surface, abounding with every animal and fish which contribute to the support of man in his savage state, and which, therefore, render the advancement of civilized man into the wilderness a matter comparatively neither of difficulty nor of expense.

. . . .

When the whole world is asking, what is the best route across the continent, ought this country to neglect the opportunity of opening the highway through its own territories? It is said that there are the means of doing so. There can hardly be conceived a duty more incumbent upon a government, than that of ascertaining whether these reports are true: whether there is a possibility of opening a route across the continent from ocean to ocean. The first thing to be done is, to send out an expedition of competent persons to survey the country along the course of the Saskatchewan River. Such an expedition would commence with an examination of the line of rivers and lakes which unite Lake Superior to the Lake of the Woods—a magnificent country, which we know affords the most abundant facilities for settlement, inferior to none in the best parts of Canada. It could be readily ascertained by an Engineer, how far these waters could be made useful for the transit of merchandise. The expedition would then cross the Lake of the Woods, and ascend the Saskatchewan; report upon the best mode of surmounting the falls in the neighbourhood of Cumberland House; and proceed to survey the whole course of the river up to the Rocky Mountains,

taking notice of what spots are most favourable for the formation of villages and settlements along its banks; ascertaining how far its waters could be navigated by steam-vessels, and whether the coal, said to abound upon its banks, could be made available for the supply of steamers. Passing on from the head waters of the Saskatchewan, the expedition should ascertain the best route to the shores of the Pacific, through, and from, the Rocky Mountains. Upon all these points there is much need of accurate information. In case, then, it were found practicable to open this line of communication, the next thing would be, to direct the stream of colonization partly in this direction. At present, it would be requisite to carry food the greatest part of the journey, or to depend upon the chase. The formation of settlements and villages would obviate this necessity; food would be provided in abundance, along the whole course of the river. If this were accomplished, Vancouver's Island, and the country in its immediate vicinity on the main land, would become what the terminus of a railway station is in this country. To form any idea of its importance, and of the rapidity of its growth as a colony, it is sufficient to recollect how we have seen towns spring up in this country, where not a cottage stood a few years ago. For the same reason, Canada will feel the change. Canada would become the line of transit for emigrants, and for all the commerce which colonies in the interior would necessarily create, instead of being, as she now is, planted against an impenetrable wall of desert, two thousand miles thick.

B. Canada Covets the North West

Although George Brown was only one of many Canadians whose interest in the North West was aroused in the 1850's and who advocated Canadian westward expansion, his involvement in the debate was particularly important because of his leadership of the Reform party, and the great influence which his newspaper, the Toronto *Globe*, exerted on public opinion in the province. The first selection suggests that Brown was quick to grasp the significance of Fitzgerald's arguments for the future of Canada. Six years later, after the Northern Railway linking Toronto with Collingwood on Lake Huron was completed and the North Western Steamboat Company was organized, the discussion was revived in the columns of the Toronto *Globe*. From this time on, annexationist sentiment in Canada West became a political fact with which all politicians had to reckon. To which economic classes and interests do these editorials appeal? Is there any evidence of an increase in reliable knowledge of the North West between 1849 and 1856, or are the arguments still weighted with political rhetoric? Is there evidence that the annexation of the North West was more strongly favored by the Reform party than by the Liberal-Conservatives who controlled the government in 1856?

Document B–1

GEORGE BROWN ENTERS THE DEBATE

("Lake Superior and the Northern Country," The Globe [Toronto], November 12, 1850.)

It is a remarkable circumstance that so little attention has been paid in Canada to the immense tract of country lying to the north of our boundary line, and known as the Hudson Bay Company's Territory. There can be no question that the injurious and demoralizing sway of that Company, over a region of four millions of square miles, will ere long be brought to an end, and that the destinies of this immense country will be united with our own. The people of Upper Canada are the most interested in the controversy now going on between the people of Red River settlement and the Hudson's Bay Company, as to the validity of the Company's charter; and we think the time has nearly arrived when Canada should become a party to the demand from the Home Government for a stringent inquiry into the validity of the said charter. It is unpardonable that civilization should be excluded from half a continent, on at best but a doubtful right of ownership, for the benefit of 232 shareholders.

· · · · · · · · · · · · ·

Our present purpose is not, however, with the validity of the Hudson Bay Company's claim to the country north of the Canadian line,—but to call attention to the value of that region, and the vast commercial importance to the country, and especially to this section, which must, ere long, attach to it. The too-general impression entertained is, that the territory in question is a frozen wilderness, incapable of cultivation, and utterly unfit for European colonization. This impression was undoubtedly set afloat, and has been maintained by the Company for its own very evident purposes; so long as that opinion could be kept up, their charter was not likely to be disturbed. But light has been breaking in on the subject, in spite of their efforts to keep it out. Europeans unconnected with the Company, and servants of the Company with whom ruptures have occurred, have, from time to time, been dropping information on the capabilities of the soil, and we believe it is now established to the satisfaction of all who have studied the subject, that there is an immense tract of most valuable land immediately north of Upper Canada, which will, ere long yield a rich return to the hardy pioneer of the forest. In a recent work by Mr. James Edward Fitzgerald, it is stated that "there is not a more favourable situation on the face of the earth for the employment of agricultural industry than the locality of the Red River."

Document B–2

TORONTO'S METROPOLITAN AMBITIONS

("The Great North West," *The Daily Globe* [Toronto], August 28, 1856.)

While congratulating ourselves on the rapid growth of our city, it behoves us to consider well the circumstances that have produced that expansion, and to be sure that we take such measures as will ensure to her future a program commensurate with the past. As the commercial centre and outlet of a magnificent back country, and as the headquarters of many public institutions, including during many years the offices of the Provincial Government, Toronto has prospered in a manner that compares favourably with any city in America. But are these *helps* to prosperity sufficient for the future? Unlike the cities of Lake Michigan, our back country is comparatively limited, and unlike the cities on the south shore of Lake Erie, we have as yet no commerce with the distant states and territories of the United States to pour its riches into our lap. . . .

But Toronto has arrived at a magnitude —occupies a position among the cities of America—and has a prestige which it is a point of honour to preserve. Can that position be maintained by resting satisfied in being the local entrepot of a district, or with the dignity that attaches to a county town? Should we not rather look for progress in the extension of our commerce beyond the old Home district or the limits of the County of Simcoe, and by a judicious foresight secure a participation in the foreign trade of the great West, and in the domestic trade which must be developed on the shores of the great Northern Lakes. A highway to these formerly distant regions has been opened.

They are now within our reach. Shall Toronto take possession of her legitimate share in the traffic they can afford, or shall she sit down quietly as the chief city of the County of York, and erstwhile the political and commercial capital of Canada?

.   .   .   .

In considering the possibility of settling the vast territories northward of Lakes Huron and Superior, they have been commonly connected in our estimation with the frozen regions bordering the Arctic Ocean,—in fact nearly all we know relative to their topography has come to us *via* Hudson's Bay. Hence, though it is sometimes doubtfully conceded that they may represent some value in the products of their forests, and that their mineral wealth would be worthy our attention, could we find miners sufficiently hardy to endure the rigours of the climate, there are but few who look upon them as susceptible to cultivation, or as capable of supporting an agricultural population. This erroneous impression has arisen from our habit of considering climate and temperature as dependent on latitude, and of comparing the climate of the territory in question with that of places under the same parallels; . . .

.   .   .   .

The position of Toronto in relation to the north-west is such as can enable her citizens to reap a rich harvest by engaging in the promotion of enterprises in that direction. . . .

Document B–3

THE GLOBE CALLS FOR ACTION

("The Great North West," *The Daily Globe* [Toronto], December 10, 1856.)

The eagerness with which the Canadian public have taken up the question of

extending their sovereign claims over the territories of the Hudson's Bay Company, is sufficient to show that the full time has arrived for acting in the matter. So long as there was a wide extent of country lying between the Company's forts and the Canadian settlements, there was little desire to go far beyond, and to plunge into the wilderness in search of new territory. Now, however, that almost every acre south of Lake Huron is sold, and the head waters of the Ottawa River have been reached by the Government Surveyor, we are looking about for new worlds to conquer. The desire to trench upon the great North Western Territory would have been formed, undoubtedly, long ago, but for the means adopted by the Company to check it; and we might have had ere now a territory stretching as far west as that of the United States. In the progress of American settlement, the hunter goes first, the trader next, and afterwards follows the agriculturalist; but in the Hudson's Bay Territory, the hunter and the trader have been controlled completely by the Company, who have made it their business to prevent them giving such information as would induce the agriculturist to pursue their foot tracks, and the two pioneer classes have themselves been circumscribed in all their operations by the action of the trading monopoly.

. . . .

The question which presents itself to us in Canada relates to the best method of taking possession of the vast and fertile territory which is our birthright, and which no power on earth can prevent us occupying. In the adoption of our course of action, attempts will no doubt be made to influence us for the benefit of the monopoly. Members of the government and its organists in the press, who were a few days ago very warm in their support of this scheme, have changed their tone wonderfully within that time. The wily and wealthy Company which maintains military control over a great territory, and subordination amid thousands of employees, will not suffer anything to be done in Canada prejudicial to their in-

terests, if money or influence can affect the decisions of Ministers or members of the press. From the [Toronto] *Leader*, we learn that the monopolists are willing to give up a slice of territory for a consideration, but hope to retain their exclusive right of trading throughout the remaining portions. We are not informed how much they are willing to give, but that is of little importance. It is the duty of the Canadian public to have it established at once, that no part of this continent is to be considered closed to their enterprise, and that if they can establish a profitable trading connection with the Mackenzie River, or the Fraser River, or the Moose River, they are at liberty to do so. The *Leader* says that the Company exercises a control over the territory which the Province could not do; but we entirely dissent from the statement. We are quite as well able to preserve the peace of our borders against hostile Indians as the United States; and it will be strange, indeed, if the Aborigines were not better satisfied with our rule than that of the Company. . . . Let it never be forgotten in considering this subject, that through British territory lies the best route for the Atlantic and Pacific Railway, which has now become a necessity. In our latitude there is but one mountain range to cross; a little further south there are many, and proceeding still nearer the direct California route, there are found desert plains without water, and unfit for human occupation. The most northerly line through British territory, passes over the prairie to the very base of the great mountains, and possesses, moreover, an approach to the ocean unequalled on the whole coast. These are facts which the Americans themselves admit, and they appear to indicate, not only that the British American territory west of Lake Superior will be occupied speedily, but that it will inevitably become the greatest highway in the world. No friend of British institutions will counsel indifference to this aspect of the question under discussion. The American settlements now approach within a few miles of British territory, and it may be taken as a certainty that, if the settlements of the Red River are not extended westward, our American neighbours will soon occupy these magnificent prairies of which all travellers speak with admiration. Once in their possession, American statesmen will have little difficulty in making the boundary lines to suit them. They have had too much success in that way before, both in the east, and west, to permit them to fear failure in the center.

C. The British Parliamentary Inquiry of 1857

The British Government assumed a cautious attitude to any proposed change in the administration of the Hudson's Bay Company's territory. But the agitation which had developed in Canada, and the need to study the advisability of renewing the company's trading license west and north of Rupert's Land (first granted in 1821 and renewed in 1838) prompted the establishment of a House of Commons committee in 1857 to investigate the affairs of the company and the proposals of its critics. The evidence taken by the committee was voluminous. Its brief report was generally favorable to the company's record of administration, but on the other hand was also well disposed to any practical proposal for the promotion of agricultural settlement under Canadian auspices. Compare the views of the Canadian Government witness, W. H. Draper, with those of George Brown as expressed in the Toronto *Globe* articles. Considering the terms of the committee's report, how effective were Simpson, Ellis, and Draper as spokesmen for the interests which they represented?

Document C–1

THE COMPANY'S SPOKESMEN ON THE WITNESS STAND

(*Report from the Select Committee on the Hudson's Bay Company* [London, 1857], pp. 45, 86–87, 331–32.)

EVIDENCE OF SIR GEORGE SIMPSON

714. Of course, having administered the affairs of the Hudson's Bay Company during so long a period, you are well acquainted with every part of their territories?—I have travelled through the greater part of the country; I have not visited what are usually known as the Barren Grounds.

715. You are well acquainted with the western portion, as well as the eastern?—Yes; I have not been in Mackenzie's River, but I have been in nearly all the other parts of the country; my usual route in going up the country is from Montreal by Rainy Lake and Lake Winnipeg to Red River; I have crossed the Rocky Mountains at three different points to Oregon.

716. Will you have the goodness to give to the Committee an account of your impressions of the character of the territory of the Hudson's Bay Company in point of soil and climate, particularly with reference to its adaptation for the pur-

poses of cultivation and colonisation?—
I do not think that any part of the Hudson's Bay Company's territories is well adapted for settlement; the crops are very uncertain.

717. Do you mean that observation to apply only to Rupert's Land or to the entire of the territory now administered by the Hudson's Bay Company?—I mean it to apply to Rupert's Land.

718. How would you describe the limits of Rupert's Land to the west?—The Rocky Mountains to the west.

719. Would you apply that observation to the district of the Red River?—Yes.

720. And the country immediately behind it?—Yes.

721. Is it not actually settled?—I do not consider it well adapted for settlement.

722. Why so?—On account of the poverty of the soil, except on the banks of the river. The banks of the river are alluvial, and produce very fair crops of wheat; but these crops are frequently destroyed by early frosts; there is no certainty of the crops. We have been under the necessity of importing grain within these last ten years from the United States and from Canada, for the support of the establishment.

723. Have you an equally unfavourable opinion of the country on the Saskatchewan River?—Yes; the climate is more rigorous, and the crops are even less certain on that river; the scarcity of timber also is a great bar; there is little or no wood in the country. The present population of Red River have great difficulty in providing wood for their immediate wants.

724. Is there any part of the territory of Rupert's Land towards Lake Superior that you think adapted for cultivation?—Immediately upon the right bank of the Rainy Lake River cultivation might be carried on to advantage; but there is merely a slip of land adapted for cultivation; immediately behind are deep morasses which never thaw.

.   .   .   .

1635. *Chairman.* Supposing an arrangement was made by which any portion of the territory now administered by the Hudson's Bay Company, which might be supposed to be fit for the purposes of colonisation, was separated from that administration, such a district of country, for instance, as the Red River, and any land in the neighbourhood of the Red River, or of the frontier of Canada, or land on the extreme west coast in the neighbourhood of Vancouver's Island, would there be any difficulty in the Hudson's Bay Company continuing to conduct their affairs after that separation had taken place?—I think not, because I do not believe there would be any settlement for a great length of time; I do not believe there would be any migration into the country for ages to come.

EVIDENCE OF THE RT. HON. EDWARD ELLIS, M.P.

5844. Do not you think it is desirable that, by some mode or other, there should be a British colony established in the Red River and the adjacent country, which might be civilised and cultivated?—It is very easy to talk of its being desirable to have an English colony, but how are you to establish it? If this country will pay the expense of establishing it, or if Canada will pay the expense of establishing it, I can understand your establishing an English colony; but I know no circumstances at present connected with Red River which would give me the least idea that a prosperous colony could exist there without great assistance.

5845. Why do you think that it would be so very expensive?—In the first place, you must get people to establish themselves on the land; there are very few people there. It is a great mistake to suppose that that is a very inviting part of the country. I have more experience than most people of the mode of settlement in America. I have never known a settlement succeed which did not succeed in continuation of some settlement which almost reached it. I have known very adventurous Americans, whom we call squatters, the pioneers of civilisation, establish themselves in advance of settlement, in hopes of its overtaking them; but that forms no settlement to pay a government; it must be followed by a certain establishment of people, society sufficient to provide for its own wants, and to provide the means of taxation to carry on a government.

5846. The way in which the Americans govern a territory is very simple and inexpensive, is it not, before it becomes a State?—Yes; but their territories are in very different latitudes to this.

5847. Is the climate so very different between the Minnesota territory and that of the Red River, and the neighbouring country?—It is only different, inasmuch as the Red River is further north; but even the Minnesota territory is not a very hospitable country; and the most northern settlement in Minnesota nearest to the Red River Settlement, is five degrees to the south of it. You will recollect that a great part of this territory of the Red River is very barren, very marshy. Along the banks of the river, there is a quantity of good soil, which is to a certain extent productive. Then it is 1,000 feet above the level of the sea; it is in the latitude of 50 degrees; Quebec is in 46.50. It is three or four degrees further north than Quebec. The settlement of the Red River is 60 miles north of the line; it is in about 50 degrees; the line is 49 degrees by the Lake of the Woods. When you come to a latitude of 50 degrees and 1,000 feet above the level of the sea, the climate is not very favourable; so it has been found by the settlers at the Red River. Some gentlemen go there in the middle of the summer, and find a little land cultivated in two or three patches upon the banks of the river, where there is alluvial soil producing good crops; and they think that that is a state of things which may be calculated upon through the year; two or three times this colony has been very nearly starving. I am satisfied of this,

which I repeat again, that if the place is fit for settlement, and you can obtain the means of settling it, it ought to be settled, and it ought not to be occupied by a set of fur-hunters; but I do not see what settlement, either from Canada or from the United States (it is more likely from the United States), is likely to approach that settlement and to increase its numbers for years to come; then I must also state, that there is a still greater deficiency there than is found in those prairie countries in America, and that is becoming a very serious difficulty with them, namely, the deficiency of wood, both for fuel and for building, I believe that Minnesota will get a good deal of wood from the country to the southward of Lake Superior; the mining districts; but that is a difficulty which is becoming immense; the wood is diminishing, and coal is not found where people cannot exist in that hard climate without abundant fuel; at the Red River there is scarcely any; the same I may say about the Saskatchewan. I have heard that evidence has been given to this Committee that the Saskatchewan is a country capable of settlement; that may be when a second generation from this are in their graves, but it will only be because the population of America becomes so dense that they are forced into situations less fit for settlement than those which they occupy now. The Saskatchewan is higher up again; it is up at 53 degrees; the Athabasca Lake is in 60 degrees. I have no doubt that gentlemen who go out in the summer and look at the border of these rivers, and see the fine pastures which they find for the buffalo, say, "These will make admirable farms;" but they have not been there during the winter, and they have not considered the circumstances of the country with respect to fuel.

Document C–2

THE EVIDENCE OF A CANADIAN MODERATE

(Report from the Select Committee on the Hudson's Bay Company [London, 1857], pp. 211 ff.; 216.)

EVIDENCE OF THE HON. WILLIAM HENRY DRAPER, C.B.

4054. *Chairman.* Have you any personal knowledge of any portion of the territory belonging to the Hudson's Bay Company?—I have not; I have never been nearer to it than the eastern portion of Lake Superior.

4055. In what manner do you conceive that the inquiry before this Committee particularly affects the interests of Canada?—First, very materially with regard to what I conceive to be the true boundary of Canada. I may say, secondly, with regard to the deep interest that the people of Canada have, that that territory should be maintained as a British possession. I may say, thirdly, because the people of Canada look to it as a country into which they ought to be permitted to extend their settlements. Those three points I think would involve all that I could say upon that subject.

4056. Taking the points in the order in which you have mentioned them; first of all, with regard to the question of the limits of the province of Canada, are there any statements which you wish to lay before the Committee on that head?—I should say with regard to that point that the view which is taken, be it sound or unsound, is this: at present it is understood by us that the Hudson's Bay Company claim as a legal right all the land which is drained by any streams, no matter how remote their sources may be, which flow into either the Hudson's Bay Straits, or Hudson's Bay. We consider that that is an ill-founded claim, principally upon this ground, that it is a claim of which we can find no trace until a very modern period, and is quite inconsistent with the claims advanced by that Company for nearly a century and a half.

. . . .

4060. Will you favour us with your individual opinion of what it would be for the advantage of Canada to have as boundaries; how far you would extend them?—I should myself propose, if I were making a proposition upon a subject of that sort, that Canada should have in the first place a free right to explore and survey, in order to ascertain the capabilities of the country; in the second place, to open communication roads in the manner pursued in that country, by putting settlers on each side of them with free grants, which in the course of a comparatively short period of time, facilitates the intercourse with those portions of the country which hitherto have been inaccessible, or very difficult of access by persons going to settle; in the next place I should propose that Canada should be permitted to lay out townships, and that as fast as she did actually lay them out and settle them, those portions of the territory so settled should become incorporated with and form part of the province; I would limit it under all circumstances and at any distant period by the Rocky Mountains; I should never dream of pushing beyond them.

4061. Sir *John Pakington.* Would you claim that right of survey without any limit, except the Rocky Mountains?—Yes.

4062. *Chairman.* Do you think that at present Canada could conveniently or efficiently govern and manage the whole of that vast territory to the east of the Rocky Mountains which belongs to British North America?—If you say at this moment, I shall be obliged to answer in the negative, because at the present moment our communications are not opened; we have not yet established the prospect of opening them; and to undertake to govern a country which we do not know that we can get at, would be a rash and unwise step, which I think no one would ever think of taking. That is why I premise that we should desire to survey and explore before we do anything else. When we speak of governing the whole of that country it involves the consideration that, unless the country be put under an efficient government of some sort, we entertain (I speak for myself individually, but I believe I am speaking the sentiments of large numbers of the inhabitants of Canada) a very serious apprehension that if something is not done that territory will in some way or another cease to be British territory; and upon that point they feel an extreme anxiety. Any one looking at the map can see that the effect of that would be to cut off a portion of the British Empire from all possible communication with the Pacific; and therefore they look at it with extreme anxiety, and it is with the view of insuring, which they think they could more effectually do than any one else, the maintenance of British authority within those possessions, that they entertain the views which I have just stated, and which I myself entertain and advocate.

· · · · · · · · · · ·

4068. Do you believe that the fact of this territory being under the government of the Hudson's Bay Company has prevented any settlements from Canada that otherwise would have been made there?— It is difficult to answer that question,

except by assuming that people who have left Canada to go to the territory of Minesota, or who are about leaving it for that purpose, would have gone perhaps as readily to the valley of the Saskatchewan if it had been thrown open for settlement; it is an assumption; I cannot speak of it as a fact.

· · · · · · · · · · ·

4086. Without raising the question of legal right in the Hudson's Bay Company to leaving that in abeyance, as it now is, would you object to confining them within a territory considerably to the north of the line which they now have?—The only difficulty which I have in answering that question is, that in giving my own opinion I believe that I should express an opinion which is not shared in by a great many people in Canada, and I would wish that to be distinctly understood. My own opinion is, that for the purpose of preserving peace among the Indians, and preventing difficulties arising, it is of great importance, for some time at all events (I should say a limited time), that the Hudson's Bay Company should maintain those stations and that trade which they have hitherto carried on, which have kept the Indians at peace.

Document C–3

THE COMMITTEE'S CONCLUSIONS

(Report from the Select Committee on the Hudson's Bay Company [London, 1857], pp. iii–iv.)

1. THE near approach of the period when the license of exclusive trade, granted in 1838 for 21 years, to the Hudson's Bay Company over that northwestern portion of British America which goes by the name of the Indian Territory, must expire, would alone make it necessary that the condition of the whole of the vast regions which are under the administration of the Company should be carefully considered; but there are other circumstances which, in the opinion of Your Committee, would have rendered such a course the duty of the Parliament and Government of this country.

2. Among these, Your Committee would specially enumerate,—the growing desire of our Canadian fellow-subjects that the means of extension and regular settlement should be afforded to them over a portion of this territory; the necessity of providing suitably for the administration of the affairs of Vancouver's Island, and the present condition of the settlement which has been formed on the Red River.

· · · · · · · · · · ·

7. Among the various objects of imperial policy which it is important to attain, Your Committee consider that it is essential to meet the just and reason-

able wishes of Canada to be enabled to annex to her territory such portion of the land in her neighbourhood as may be available to her for the purposes of settlement, with which lands she is willing to open and maintain communications, and for which she will provide the means of local administration. Your Committee apprehend that the districts on the Red River and the Saskatchewan are among those likely to be desired for early occupation. It is of great importance that the peace and good order of those districts should be effectually secured. Your Committee trust that there will be no difficulty in effecting arrangements as between Her Majesty's Government and the Hudson's Bay Company by which these districts may be ceded to Canada on equitable principles, and within the districts thus annexed to her the authority of the Hudson's Bay Company would of course entirely cease.

. . . .

11. As to those extensive regions, whether in Rupert's Land or in the Indian Territory, in which, for the present at least, there can be no prospect of perma-

nent settlement, to any extent, by the European race for the purposes of colonisation, the opinion at which Your Committee have arrived is mainly founded on the following considerations: 1°. The great importance to the more peopled portions of British North America that law and order should, as far as possible, be maintained in these territories; 2°. The fatal effects which they believe would infallibly result to the Indian population from a system of open competition in the fur trade, and the consequent introduction of spirits in a far greater degree than is the case at present; and 3°. The probability of the indiscriminate destruction of the more valuable fur-bearing animals in the course of a few years.

12. For these reasons Your Committee are of opinion that whatever may be the validity or otherwise of the rights claimed by the Hudson's Bay Company, under the Charter, it is desirable that they should continue to enjoy the privilege of exclusive trade, which they now possess, except so far as those privileges are limited by the foregoing recommendations.

D. The First Scientific Assessment of the Resources of the North West

Prior to 1857, the possibility of profitable development of natural resources other than furs in the North West was discussed without the benefit of a body of reliable scientific knowledge; as the student will have observed from the preceding documents, the debaters indulged in sweeping generalizations and much wishful thinking. Although the naturalist-explorer Sir John Richardson (1787–1865) published some crop production data from Hudson's Bay Company posts (*Arctic Searching Expedition: A Journal of a Boat-Voyage Through Rupert's Land and the Arctic Sea . . .* [London, 1851]), he did not attempt a systematic survey of the agricultural potential of the North West. But the pioneer American climatologist Lorin Blodget (1823–1901), basing his inductions in part on Richardson's data, confidently predicted that the British North West would be found capable of supporting a large agricultural population. In the same year (1857) as the publication of Blodget's work, the Canadian and British governments each sponsored scientific expeditions to survey the natural resources, climate, and transportation routes of the North West. The Canadian expedition, with Trinity College (Toronto) professor Henry Youle Hind (1823–1908) and civil engineer Simon James Dawson (1820–1902), concentrated on the area between the Red and South Saskatchewan rivers during two seasons of activity. The larger British expedition directed by Captain John Palliser (1807–87), included several scientists and spent three years in the West. It traversed the route recommended by Fitzgerald in 1849, and also examined the semiarid plains region north of the international boundary. To what extent do the observations of Hind and Palliser contradict or confirm Blodget's calculations? Hind's 11,100,000 acres of arable land include the present farming area of Manitoba and a good part of south-central Saskatchewan; was he conservative in his calculation, considering the present-day acreage of improved land in Manitoba? Were Palliser's conclusions regarding the most practical transportation system for the North West accepted after 1870?

Document D–1

A CLIMATOLOGIST APPRAISES THE NORTH WEST

(Lorin Blodget, *Climatology of the United States, and of the Temperate Latitudes of the North American Continent* . . . [Philadelphia, 1857], pp. 529–32.)

The great practical interest now felt in the northwestern areas of this continent requires that some distinct reference to their climate should be made, . . .

The assertion may at first appear unwarranted, but it is demonstrable that an area, not inferior in size to the whole United States east of the Mississippi, now almost wholly unoccupied, lies west of the 98th meridian and above the 43d parallel, which is perfectly adapted to the fullest occupation by cultivated nations. The west and north of Europe are there reproduced, with the exceptions caused by vertical configuration only; and important as this feature of configuration is in giving us a lofty mountain boundary on the west, we may charge much of disadvantage to that account and still leave all that is here claimed—an immense and yet unmeasured capacity for occupation and expansion. By reference to the illustration of the distribution of heat we see that the cold at the north of the great lakes does not represent the same latitude farther west, and that beyond them the thermal lines rise as high in latitude, in most cases, as at the west of Europe. . . .

The parallel in regard to the advancement of American States here may be drawn with the period of the earliest trans-Alpine Roman expansion, when Gaul, Scandinavia, and Britain were regarded as inhospitable regions, fit only for barbarian occupation. The enlightened nations then occupied the latitudes near the Mediterranean, and the richer northern and western countries were unopened and unknown. Climate is indisputably the decisive condition, and when we find the isothermal of 60° for the summer rising on the interior American plains to the 61st parallel, or fully as high as its average position for Europe, it is impossible to doubt the existence of favorable climates over vast areas now unoccupied. This favorable comparison may be traced for the winter also, and in the averages for the year. . . .

. . . .

The quantity of rain is not less important than the measure of heat to all the purposes of occupation, and for the plains east of the Rocky Mountains there may reasonably be some doubt as to the sufficiency; and doubts on the point whether the desert belt of lower latitudes is prolonged to the northern limit of the plains. If the lower deserts are due to the altitude and mass of the mountains simply, it would be natural to infer their existence along the whole line where the Rocky Mountains run parallel and retain their altitude; but the dry areas are evidently due to other causes primarily, and they are not found above the 47th parallel in fact. It is decisive of the general question of sufficiency of rain to find the entire surface of the upper plains either well grassed or well wooded, and recent information on these points almost warrants the assertion that there are *no* barren tracts of consequence after we pass the Bad Lands, and the *Coteaus* of the Missouri. Many portions of these plains are known to be peculiarly rich in grasses, and probably the finest tracts lie along the eastern base of the mountains, in positions corresponding to the most desert-like of the plains at the south. The higher latitudes certainly differ widely from the plains which stretch from the Platte southward to the Llano Estacado of Texas, and none of the references made to them by residents or travellers indicate desert characteristics. Buffalo are far more abundant on the northern plains, and they remain through the winter at their extreme border, taking shelter in the belts of woodland on the upper Athabasca and Peace rivers. Grassy savannas like these necessarily imply an adequate supply of rain, and there can be no doubt that the correspondence with the European plains in like geographical position—those of eastern Germany and Russia—is quite complete in this respect. If a difference exists it is in favor of the American plains, which have a greater proportion of surface waters, both as lakes and rivers.

Document D-2

PROFESSOR HIND'S CALCULATIONS

(Henry Youle Hind, *Reports of Progress; Together with a Preliminary and General Report on the Assiniboine and Saskatchewan Exploring Expedition* . . . [Toronto, 1859], pp. 32, 124, 131.)

The arid region, or Great Plain, west of the 101st degree of longitude receives a very small amount of precipitation from the humid south winds coming up the valley of the Mississippi from the Gulf of Mexico. It is too far south to be much affected by north-east winds, or the westerly winds from the Pacific. This vast treeless prairie forms in fact the northern limit of the great arid region of the eastern flank of the Rocky Mountains; but still its humidity is greater than the plains south of the Missouri, in consequence of its high northern latitude.

. . . .

Very great misapprehension has prevailed with regard to the region west of the Mississippi, as well as of the valley drained by the Saskatchewan. Sanguine enthusiasts have laid out new States and Territories on the broad map of the Federation, and peopled them in imagination with bustling, industrious, and wealthy communities. Other visionaries have converted the four hundred thousand square miles drained by the Saskatchewan into a region of unbounded fertility and inexhaustible resources. Whereas, a proper appreciation and use of facts will convince the most sanguine, that the larger portion of this area is, in its present state, unfit for the permanent habitation of man both on account of climate, soil and absence of fuel.

. . . It will at once occur to the reader that a knowledge of these facts gives great additional value to the truly fertile valleys of Red River, the Assiniboine, part of the Qu'Appelle, and portions of the South and North Branch of the Saskatchewan. It determines also the direction in which efforts should be made to people this great wilderness, and guide the progress of settlement in such a manner as will render the country available for that South Branch of the Saskatchewan will be continent.

. . . .

If we assume that the prairies of Red River and the Assiniboine east of Prairie Portage, contain an available area of 1,500,000 acres of fertile soil, the total quantity of arable land included between Red River and the Moose Woods on the South Branch of the Saskatchewan will be as follows:

	Acres
Red River and the Assiniboine Prairies east of Prairie Portage	1,500,000
Eastern water-shed of the Assiniboine and La Rivière Salè	3,500,000
Long Creek and the Forks of the Saskatchewan	600,000
Between Carrot River and the Main Saskatchewan	3,000,000
The Touchwood Hill range, the Moose Woods, &c., &c.	500,000
Mouse River, Qu'Appelle River, White Sand River	1,000,000
The region about the head-waters of the Assiniboine, including the valley of Swan River	1,000,000
Total area of arable land of first quality	11,100,000

or eleven million, one hundred thousand acres.

Of land fit for grazing purposes, the area is much more considerable, and may with propriety be assumed as fully equal in extent to the above estimate of the area of arable land.

Document D–3

PALLISER'S CONCLUSIONS

(Journals, Detailed Reports, and Observations Relative to the Exploration, by Captain Palliser . . . [London, 1863], pp. 7, 10, 11, 16–17, 18.)

The existence of a general law regulating the distribution of the woods in this portion of the continent suggested itself to us during our first summer's explorations, and subsequent experience during the seasons of 1858–9 fully confirmed it.

The fertile savannahs and valuable woodlands of the Atlantic United States are succeeded, as has been previously alluded to, on the west by a more or less arid desert, occupying a region on both sides of the Rocky Mountains, which presents a barrier to the continuous growth of settlements between the Mississippi Valley and the States on the Pacific coast. This central desert extends, however, but a short way into the British territory, forming a triangle, having for its base the 49th parallel from longitude 100° to 114° W., with its apex reaching to the 52nd parallel of latitude.

The northern forests, which in former times descended more nearly to the frontier of this central desert, have been greatly encroached upon and, as it were,

pushed backwards to the north through the effect of frequent fires.

Thus a large portion of fertile country, denuded of timber, separates the arid region from the forest lands to the north, and the habit which the Indian tribes have of burning the vegetation has, in fact, gradually improved the country for the purpose of settlement by clearing off the heavy timber, to remove which is generally the first and most arduous labour of the colonist.

. . . .

The richness of the natural pasture in many places on the prairies of the second level along the North Saskatchewan and its tributary, Battle River, can hardly be exaggerated. Its value does not consist in its being rank or in great quantity, but from its fine quality, comprising nutritious species of grasses and carices, along with natural vetches in great variety, which remain throughout the winter sound, juicy, and fit for the nourishment of stock.

Almost everywhere along the course of the North Saskatchewan are to be found eligible situations for agricultural settlement, a sufficiency of good soil is everywhere to be found, nor are these advantages merely confined to the neighbourhood of the river; in several districts, such as N.W. of Carlton, we traversed fine land fit for all purposes, both of pasture and tillage, extending towards the thickwood hills, and also to be found in the region of the lakes between Forts Pitt and Edmonton.

In almost every direction round Edmonton the land is fine, excepting only the hilly country at the higher level, such as the Beaver Hills. Even there, however, there is nothing like sterility, only the surface is too much broken to be occupied while more level country can be obtained. The places which have been chosen for mission stations are all at a distance from the river, a preference having naturally been given to the borders of the large lakes which lie along the base of the hilly country for the sake of the fine fish which these yield in abundance. . . .

In the upper part of the Saskatchewan country coal of fair quality occurs abundantly, and may hereafter be found very useful; it is quite fit to be employed in the smelting of iron from the ores of that metal, which also occurs in large quantities in the same strata. Building stone is wholly absent until quite close to the Rocky Mountains, but brick earth and potter's clay may be obtained in many parts of the country. The climate is more irregular than that of Red River, and partial thaws often occur long before the actual coming of spring and do great harm to the vegetation. The winter is much the same in its duration, but the amount of snow that falls decreases rapidly as we approach the mountains.

The North Saskatchewan freezes generally about the 12th November, and breaks up from the 17th to the 20th of April. During the winter season of five months the means of travelling and transport are greatly facilitated by the snow, the ordinary depth of which is sufficient for the use of sleighs, without at the same time being too great to impede horses. If proper roads were formed this facility would be greatly increased, and as a result there would be no season during which the country could be said to be closed for traffic.

Between Carlton and Edmonton there is no valuable timber to be found south of the river, the only trees growing there being small aspen poplars. To the north, however, and along the river above and below these points, the spruce, fir, pine, and birch occur abundantly. . . .

. . . .

The connexion . . . of the Saskatchewan plains, east of the Rocky Mountains, with a known route through British Columbia, has been effected by the Expedition under my command, without our having been under the necessity of passing through any portion of United States Territory. Still the knowledge of the country on the whole would never lead me to advocate a line of communication from Canada across the continent to the Pacific, exclusively through British territory. The time has now for ever gone by for effecting such an object, and the unfortunate choice of an astronomical boundary line has completely isolated the Central American possessions of Great Britain from Canada in the east, and also almost debarred them from any eligible access from the Pacific coast on the west.

The settler, who will always adopt the shortest and least expensive route, will undoubtedly follow the line of traverse indicated by the formation of the country.

He will travel by steamer along the Canadian Lakes through Sault Ste. Marie to Superior City, situated at the extremity of the "Fond du Lac" or most western extremity of Lake Superior; and he will then be only 70 or 80 miles distant from Crow Wing, on the high road between Saint Pauls and the Red River Settlement.

American squatters and lumberers are rapidly settling up Red River, and the railway communication (now nearly complete to Saint Pauls), will soon be completed to Pembina, in which case the establishment of a branch line to Superior "Fond du Lac" would be a positive certainty, thus easy and rapid communication would be established between Lake Superior and the frontier of Red River Settlement.

In the event of railway communication being extended as far as Pembina, it would not be unreasonable then to entertain the prospect that the Imperial Government might feel justified in encouraging the extension of such railway on the British side of the line to the northward and westward, through the southern portion of "the fertile belt" to the Rocky Mountains; at all events as soon as the country showed symptoms of becoming sufficiently populated to warrant such an effort.

. . . .

We do not apprehend that the Indians along the North Saskatchewan are likely to cause any serious difficulties to the settlement of the "fertile belt." The Salteans, Crees, and Thickwood Assineboines have been for many years on the best terms not only with the members and servants of the Hudson Bay Com-

pany, but with all the free traders, missionaries, visitors, &c., that have visited their country; this may be in some measure accounted for by the justice and good faith which characterize all the dealings of the Hudson Bay Company with them, and also by the number of the company's servants who have adopted their women, and have established with them relationships of which they feel proud.

If white men, or indeed if half-breeds were to settle as agriculturists in the country, I do not say that they would never have serious cause of complaint with the Indians of the North Saskatchewan; quarrels doubtless would arise sometimes out of horse stealing, at other times out of their harmless mischief; but I do not think that any organized system of aggression would be attempted against the settlers, and I even think that many Indians, provided they could obtain farming implements, would follow the examples they saw before them, and begin to till the soil themselves.

E. A New Company Policy for Rupert's Land

Although Sir George Simpson and other spokesmen for the Hudson's Bay Company emphasized the difficulties which would be encountered in any expansion of agricultural settlement beyond Red River, they were well aware that ultimately the company would have to relinquish its control of the prairie region. Hence they were prepared to dispose of part or all of Rupert's Land if suitable compensation could be arranged. Since the British Government was unprepared to buy the land and create a crown colony, and since the Canadian government had neither the funds nor the inclination to pay for what it regarded as nonexistent property rights, a new decade opened with no indication of an early practical test of the findings of the scientists who had surveyed the resource potential of the North West. This impasse continued until 1863, when an aggressive group of British railway and general investment promoters, with Edward Watkin as the chief negotiator, arranged the purchase of a controlling interest in the Hudson's Bay Company. A new board of directors was appointed, committed to a policy of developing all the available resources of Rupert's Land, while continuing to carry on the customary trade in furs wherever this proved to be practical. Selections from the prospectus issued in 1863 by the new directors in connection with an increase in the company's share capital appear below. The plans described in the prospectus were never implemented, but their very existence revealed that a great era in Canadian history was drawing to a close and that the fur traders would soon be displaced as the lords of the plains and forests of the North West.

What evidence is there in the prospectus of the effects of the findings of Blodget, Hind, and Palliser? Was it realistic to plan the opening of the North West under Hudson's Bay Company auspices? What actions by government would be required before the exploitation of the agricultural and other resources could be successful?

Document E–1

A PLAN FOR OPENING THE NORTH WEST

(Prospectus issued by the International Financial Society, Ltd., July, 1863, for the sale of new capital stock of the Hudson's Bay Company, Canada and British Columbia: Return to an Address of the Honourable The House of Commons . . . [London, 1863], pp. 17–19.)

The capital of the Hudson's Bay Company has been duly fixed at 2,000,000*l*., of which amount the International Financial Society, Limited, have obtained, and are prepared to offer to the public, 1,930,000*l*.

.   .   .   .

The Hudson's Bay Company were incorporated, under a Royal Charter granted by King Charles II. in 1670, by the name of "The Governor and Company of Adventurers of England trading into Hudson's Bay," and, by the Charter, a vast tract of territory was vested in the Company, together with the sole right of trade and commerce, and all "mines royal," as well then discovered as not discovered, within the said territory.

The operations of the Company, which, with slight exceptions, have been hitherto exclusively of a trading character, have been prosecuted from the date of the Charter to the present day.

It has become evident that the time has arrived when those operations must be extended, and the immense resources of the Company's territory, lying as it does between Canada and British Columbia, should be developed, in accordance with the industrial spirit of the age and

the rapid advancement which colonisation has made in the countries adjacent to the Hudson's Bay territories.

.   .   .   .

The Company's territory embraces an estimated area of more than 1,400,000 square miles, or eight hundred and ninety-six millions of acres, of which a large area, on the Southern frontier, is well adapted for European colonization. The soil of this portion of the territory is fertile, producing in abundance wheat and other cereal crops, and is capable of sustaining a numerous population. It contains 1,400 miles of navigable lakes and rivers, running for the greater part east and west, which constitute an important feature in plans for establishing the means of communication between the Atlantic and Pacific Oceans, across the continent of British North America, as well as for immediate settlement in the intervening country. The territory is, moreover, rich in mineral wealth, including coal, lead, and iron.

.   .   .   .

The trading operations of the Company are chiefly carried on in the fur-bearing and northern portion of the territory, where the climate is too severe for European colonization. These trading operations will be actively continued, and as far as possible extended, whilst the management will be judiciously economized.

Consistently with these objects, the outlying estates and valuable farms will be realized where the land is not required for the use of the Company. The southern district will be opened to European colonization, under a liberal and systematic scheme of land settlement. Possessing a staff of factors and officers who are distributed in small centres of civilization over the territory, the Company can, without creating new and costly establishments, inaugurate the new policy of colonization, and at the same time dispose of mining grants.

PROBLEM 11

The National Awakening: Canada at Mid-Century

A. W. RASPORICH
University of Calgary

Nationalism had been the favorite pastime and even obsession of European politicians and intellectuals since the outbreak of the French Revolution. The peak of national frenzy was reached at mid-century with the outbreak of a pan-European revolution dedicated to the cause of self-determination. In North America, the American Revolution had spawned a federal structure which soon became dedicated to the pursuit of national goals in the early 19th century. Canada, too, had had its revolution in 1837, and within three decades made claim to self-determination. Yet, Canadians have somehow never felt the pleasure of Americans, Frenchmen, Germans, or Italians in seizing their own birthright by violence. National status came only by negotiation which dragged out over decades, coming to fruition in a relatively inglorious legal statement, the Statute of Westminster. Even the first Father of Confederation, John A. Macdonald, must be considered benign by comparison to Bismarck or Cavour in his use of *realpolitik* in welding a new nation together. It has now even become fashionable to view Canada's first patriots, Mackenzie and Papineau, not as magnificent failures of the stature of Kossuth or Mazzini, but merely as neurotic impotents.

Despite these seeming deficiencies of means in the formative phase of Canadian nationality, a distinctive national character was emerging in central Canada. Technology was perhaps the most important catalyst in creating the self-image that must accompany such character formation. First, there was a rapid increase in journalistic activity to keep pace with the sharp upswing in literacy. By Confederation it was estimated that the total periodical output from daily newspapers to magazines was three hundred. Second, telegraphic communication was also introduced into Canada by this time, so that by 1850 all major centres in Canada and the Maritimes were interconnected, and it was not long before they would also be able to plug into direct communications with Europe via transatlantic cable.

Directly linked to the communications revolution was the boom in transportation and public improvements. All told, this small provincial society had by 1867 about one quarter of the total trackage of sophisticated European economies like England and Germany. The direct effect was to give immediate power to the forces of metropolitanism. More than ever Toronto and Montreal became the arbiters of Canadian spiritual and material tastes. Yet, was it possible, given the influence of New York and London in both of these areas, for Toronto and Montreal to give a distinctly native cast to Canadian life?

The question most often arises in literature, since colonialism had long been the accepted literary genre in English Canada. Wistful letters from the frozen bush of Upper Canada had in fact become the favorite pastime of displaced Englishmen and Englishwomen. The new poets of the 1850's like Charles Sangster, Alexander MacLachlan, and Alexander Glendinning lamented less their enforced exile from the mainstream of European culture, and wrote, if sometimes badly, upon local history, geography, and native toil. When Charles Sangster wrote his *St. Lawrence and the Saguenay* in 1856, he was immediately acclaimed by William Lyon Mackenzie as "a Canadian poet, whose poems are far above mediocrity—whose songs are of Canada—her mountains, her maidens, manners, morals, lakes, rivers, valleys, seasons, woods, forests, and aborigines, her faith and hope." But if these same authors consciously imitated the style of the Scottish and English romantics, could they really be said to be forging a distinctly Canadian literary tradition?

It was freely admitted by even English Canadians that French Canadians were further ahead in the promotion of a national literature. But they also emulated the French romantic tradition of Hugo, Lamartine, and Michelet by their intimate involvement of their literary activity with politics. They also imitated the general romantic tradition in searching their dim historical past or their contemporary folk patterns for a unique national style. Historians such as François-Xavier Garneau, and the Abbés Casgrain and Ferland sought evidence to clarify the former, and writers like Crémazie, Gérin-Lajoie, and de Gaspé constructed folk myths from the latter.

The question of literary distinctiveness in French Canada seems almost secondary to the utilitarian value of that literature as a tool of national survival. If socialist realism in Russian art, literature, and music must be condemned for its frankly propagandistic tone, must not French-Canadian literature and whatever English-Canadian literature which falls into this category be condemned on the same grounds?

From a political standpoint mid-Victorian Canada poses some interesting problems because of its fluid ideological state. If nationalism be accepted as an emergent cultural phenomenon, what was happening to the traditional allegiances of English and French Canadians? Did nationalism mean that the former could no longer feel a part of the British Empire? How far would they go either in assuming their own defence or in supporting the Mother Country in foreign and imperial wars? What happened to French-Canadian dependence upon the Crown as a source of national security as responsible government became a greater reality?

The place of anti-Americanism in the formation of a conservative national character also underwent some significant mutations by mid-century. The War of 1812, the Hunter movement of 1838, and the Oregon Crisis of 1846 had left a deep conviction in English Canada and part of French Canada that invasion was an imminent reality. The blight of the slave problem in the 1850's and in the

Civil War also deepened the conviction that British liberty was far superior to American democracy. Yet, could they really maintain the vigour of these prejudices when the Reciprocity Treaty of 1854 dictated that a great portion of Canadian trade should now flow from north to south? Furthermore, could they dismiss the American federal Constitution as a potential source of resolution for their own sectional problems? In short, could Canadians indefinitely maintain their counter-revolutionary character in spite of these growing inconsistencies?

Lastly, there is the significance of nationalism as it relates to the development of Confederation in 1867. The mere admission that one or two national characters had already begun to take shape in the 1850's throws an entirely different light upon that later pact. Did Canadians share enough conscious or unconscious values to make that event more believable than as a mere product of the bargaining table? On the other hand, was the agreement entered in 1867 any more viable for central Canadians than the Act of Union? Did it not merely serve to complicate the already difficult problems of dualism by importing another immune strain of Maritime regionalism? If there has been some success in merging these divergent nationalisms since 1867, in what areas have they lain? Finally, how has Canadian nationalism altered since the 1850's?

For those interested in further examination of this complex problem both on a contemporary and historical plane, the best studies are: Peter Russell (ed.), *Nationalism in Canada*, (1966); Mason Wade, *The French Canadians* (rev. ed.; 1968); J. M. S. Careless, *The Union of the Canadas, 1841–57* (1967); S. F. Wise and R. C. Brown, *Canada Views the United States* (1967); W. L. Morton (ed.), *The Shield of Achilles* (1968). On the development of literary nationalism, see: C. F. Klinck (ed.), *The Literary History of Canada* (1965); E. H. Dewart (ed.), *Selection from Canadian Poets* (1864); A. J. M. Smith (ed.), *The Book of Canadian Poetry* (1957); S. Marion, *Lettres Canadiennes d'Autrefois* (1944–54); E. Chartier, "La Vie d'Esprit au Canada Français: L'Histoire et L'Idée Nationale," *Mémoires de la Société Royale du Canada* (1934); A. J. M. Smith, "Colonialism and Nationalism in Canadian Poetry before Confederation," *Canadian Historical Association Annual Report* (1944). Other articles and monographs on the relation of religion and nationalism, and economics and nationalism are: J. S. Moir, "The Canadianization of the Protestant Churches," *CHAAR* (1966); J. Monet, "French Canadian Nationalism and the Challenge of Ultramontanism," *CHAAR* (1966); and R. B. Burns, "D'Arcy McGee and the Economic Aspects of the New Nationality," *CHAAR* (1967).

A. Political Nationality

The words *patriotism* and *race* inevitably recur in any discussion of nationalism. How did the concepts of *patrie* and race differ for French and English Canadians? How in turn did these special sets of priorities affect the ultimate political form those aspirations should take? Some argued that they should retain the political structure of the Union, others that it should be dissolved into its component parts, and yet others that a new federal or legislative union should be recast out of old and new political elements. Given the fundamentally different direction of national aspirations in each section of the province, were these legal and political constructs meaningful solutions or merely political self-interest?

Document A—1

CANADIAN PATRIOTISM
(Montreal Pilot, April 6, 1850.)

"Such is the Patriot's boast, where'er we roam,
His first, best country is ever his home."

We heard it remarked, a short time since, by an eloquent and powerful Christian orator, that one of the most serious impediments, if not the greatest hindrance to Canadian advancement, was the absence of a *true Canadian feeling*—a feeling of what might be termed *Canadian nationality*, in contradistinction to a feeling of mere colonial or annexation vassalage. The orator stated, that he did not like the term "British Canadian feeling." It should be Canada first for the people of Canada, and Canada British, either by civil connexion or national alliance. It was in the depth, vigour, and energy of this feeling, the speaker maintained that the hope and life of Canadian prosperity and greatness are bound up.

This subject demands the consideration of every man who claims Canada as his native or *adopted* country. Where a man emigrates to Canada, his home, his interest, and his hopes are no longer English, or Scotch, or Irish, or French, or German, but Canadian. He has left his fatherland and joined himself to Canada, as a "man leaves his father and mother and joins himself to his wife, and they twain become one flesh." He respects, he venerates, he loves, he sympathizes with his parentage; but his cares, his interests, his heart, himself, his future, his all, are blended and identified with other objects and with another home. The well-being of home is the first object of his natural and doubtful solicitude. What is true in respect to an individual family and home, is equally true in regard to a people and a country. An injury done to the credit

and security of a country is an injury done to each inhabitant of it, except those who speculate in their country's misfortune, and rise by its depressions, like ship-wreckers and free-booters.

It was the first duty and the true interest of the earliest settlers in Canada to make the most of their adopted country— to look at home as much as possible, and to look abroad as little as possible—to devise every plan and employ every energy to create a supply in Canada for the inhabitants of Canada—to rely upon themselves for the management of their country, as well as of their farms and shops, and not upon foreign management in the one case any more than in the other. This is clearly the pervading spirit of the Colonial Policy propounded on the part of Her Majesty's Government by Lord John Russell, in his late speech in the House of Commons; and it is the spirit which should actuate every colonist. Some of the ancient Greek and Phoenician Colonies soon equalled their parent States, with which they ever maintained, with scarcely exception, a filial friendship and intimate alliance; yet they looked to the territories they colonized as their homes, and relied upon themselves as the architects of their own fortune, and the founders of their countries' prosperity and greatness.

It cannot be too strongly impressed upon every mind that it is on Canadian energy, Canadian ambition, Canadian self-reliance, skill and enterprise,—in a word, on Canadian patriotism,—that depends Canadian prosperity, elevation and happiness. The fact that some men, by honest and intelligent industry, as tradesmen, mechanics, farmers, merchants, and professional men, have risen from poverty to comfort, and even affluence, shows what others might have done by equal honesty, intelligence and industry. In agricultural productiveness, Canada is superior to New York; in waterpower and hydraulic privileges it is equal to any of the New England States; in lumber it is a contributor to both American and English markets; its mineral resources are ample to supply its own implements and industry, as its cattle and flocks are equal to its wants for labor, food, and clothing. Its sky is as clear as that of Italy, and its climate as healthy as that of Germany; its institutions are even freer than those of England, and its administration of justice confessedly more independent and impartial than that of the United States. The social and material advancement in Canada in former years was confessedly slow; but compare its progress for the last ten years in any and every respect with any of the neighbouring states from Maine to Michigan, apart from the advantages some of them possess as being the sea-ports and thoroughfares for other States, and the results will be honorable to Canada. Compare everything progressive in those States which is not adventitious, but which depends upon home industry and enterprise, and Canada, with all its faults and shortcomings, has much more reason to be proud than to be ashamed.

Document A-2

A NEW BRITAIN BLESSED BY PROVIDENCE

(Cited in A. M. Morris, Nova Britannia, 1858 [Toronto, 1884], pp. 49–51.)

But, having thus directed your attention to matters that concern you all very closely, I shall only add that, while we are thus together conjecturing as to the future of this new Britannia, this rising power on the American Continent, I cannot refrain from a passing allusion to the paramount necessity of the right development and formation of the national character of this infant people. Nations, like individuals, have their peculiar characteristics. The British people, so firmly combined and yet so singularly distinct, present in proud pre-eminence a high-toned national character, a fit model for our imitation. Inheriting, as we do, all the characteristics of the British people, combining therewith the chivalrous feeling and impulsiveness of France, and fusing other nationalities which mingle here with these, into one, as I trust, harmonious whole—rendered the more vigorous by our northern position, and enterprising by our situation in this vast country which owns us as its masters—the British American people have duties and responsibilities of no light character imposed upon them by Providence. Enjoying self-government in political matters—bringing home, through the municipal system, the art of government, and consequent respect for it, to the whole people—let a high ensample of national character be kept steadily in view, and let every effort be directed by our statesmen and by our whole people to its formation. A widespread dissemination of a sound education—a steady maintenance of civil and religious liberty, and of freedom of speech and thought, in the possession and enjoyment of all classes of the community—a becoming national respect and reverence for the behests of the Great Ruler of events, and the teachings of his Word—truthfulness and a high-toned commercial honour—unswerving and unfaltering rectitude, as a people, in the strict observance of all the liabilities of the Province towards its creditors, and in all its relations towards all connected with it—a becoming respect for the powers that be, and a large and liberal appreciation of the plain and evident responsibilities of our position—should be pre-eminent characteristics of the British American people; and so act-ing, they will not fail to win the respect, as they will command the notice, of the world.

But in all this do not think that you have no share; for in the formation of that character there is none so humble that he has not a part to play. Society is a complex whole. All its members are so fitly combined—each so acts and reacts on the other—circles of influence are ever so meeting, contending, and extending, that thus the whole derives its characters from the natures and features of its com-ponent parts. In this view, then, each individual among us is exercising an in-fluence, more or less widely diffused, upon the society in which we mingle. And a people is, after all, but an aggregation of individual influences. Let each, then, adopt and firmly act up to high views of the social, moral, and religious duties we owe to ourselves and to society, and so the well-being of the whole will be pro-moted.

And to those young British Americans who are within my hearing, I would say: Be no loiterers or laggards by the way. Here, you have a princely heritage before you. Here, steady industry and unflinching integrity will secure the rise of any man. Here, there is no keen competition, no overwrought crowding of the masses; but there is the widest scope for the exercise of every species of calling. And be your position what it may, recollect that your own conduct may dignify and elevate it. You live in a country before which there lies a dazzling and brilliant future. Be equal to the emergencies of your position, and recollect that you will have some greater or smaller influence in the shaping of its destinies. Be true, then, to your-selves, and you cannot help rising with your country. Take a deeper interest in its affairs, watch the course of events, and be ready to adopt an intelligent opinion on the requirements of daily occurrences. Cherish and promote by all means the spread of national sentiment. Familiarise yourself with all the interests of your country; and henceforth feel, if you have never felt before, that you have a country of which any people might well be proud.

And now, in conclusion, if anything that I have urged shall cause the pure flame of patriotism to burn more brightly in the breasts of any of my hearers, I shall feel that this endeavour to contribute my mite towards extending somewhat more widely a knowledge of the capabili-ties of British North America has been amply rewarded.

Document A—3

D. M. ARMSTRONG TO WILLIAM LYON MACKENZIE (NOVEMBER 22, 1852) ON COMPACTS AND RACISM IN CANADA

(Mss., Ontario Archives.)

You cannot succeed in Quebec, or I may say in any part of Lower Canada *just now*, in establishing a paying radical newspaper: the only publication which might succeed would be a thoroughly Irish Roman Catholic paper; but I am satisfied you would be the last man to raise a National or Religious war among us.

In Upper Canada you are differently situated as regards your Political and Social compact—You have a Family Com-pact, however sickly they still have life, & a Church which is striving to become a part of the State—all those who do not belong to the Compact or to the Church are considered Radicals—Republicans, Levellers—and in fact every other im-aginary name calculated to throw a shade of doubt on the loyalty of such dissenters; but this [. . .] body which now inhabit Upper Canada are a religious people;

and loyal too! to every other power of the State except that assumed heretofore by the compact and Mother Church. Here in Lower Canada the British population have had no Family Compact nor dominant Church,—or at least such elements have been disregarded because another ball has constandling [sic] bowling among the population.—Nationality, mixed with some little Relgious gealousy [sic] seems to keep the People divided; hence the heretofore complete success of the Minority governing the Majority & this is still felt notwithstanding our present form of Government—A measure introduced and Carried on by (or designated as such for party purposes)—What is called the English party must be orthodox—the same measure handled by the Franco Canadians would be denounced as Anti Loyal:—in a word those who signed the Anexation [sic] Manifesto of 1849 have never ceased to be considered loyal,—except by the bye the few Franco Canadians who did so,—they were Rebels and will for ever be considered as disaffected,—and many by this time might have been in Exile if they had not been shielded by the English names linked along with their own.

There are very few English (I mean by English, also Irish and Scotch) reformers in Lower Canada in the sense you would have them to be. They have been nursed up with the Idea that they are a Superior Race to the Franco Canadians, and on all occasions put forth their pretentions:—on the other hand the Franco-Canadians are the mass, and are by no means behind hand in upholding the principles of La Belle France "un Francais avan toutes" [sic] and yet I am, and many others might be cited as a proof that they do not carry their principles to such a length as the English portion of the Community.—In a perfectly French Constituency I have been three times sent to Parliament—but neither in the Townships in Lower Canada nor in Sandwich in Upper Canada has a Franco Canadian ever had any chance of being elected. . . .

Document A—4

PATRIOTISM IN FRENCH CANADA
(La Minerve, June 23, 1857.)

There is a sentiment in man which forms the most noble and the most essential part of his existence. A delicate fibre, a strong nerve, it exists in the heart of a Frenchman as in that of a Chinese; it fills the heart of the farmer as that of the diplomat; it gives birth to glory, it creates immortality: it is patriotism.

It is said of patriotism that it was a grand word, that is to say void of meaning. Yes, it is true. Insurrections, revolutions, and demagogues have at all times used this sublime word to sustain their crimes and follies; they have thrown it to the multitude, as the signature of their horrible mandate, and nations have thrown themselves in pursuit of it. But as many times as there was a deviation from the path and a falling into an abyss by this cry of Syrene, nations have not hesitated to reject a word made low and dirty by the mouths of the infamous. But because the hand of the traitor and of the murderer have been visited upon this monarch of societies is this to say that it is necessary to ignore them? The greater the sacrilege, the greater the necessity of promptitude and zeal in the purification.

God, in creating man and inflicting upon him life after his sin, put in his heart a tie which bound him to all who had witnessed his birth, growth, and fortification. Reduced to the family circle, this divine chain first took the name of filial love. Little by little the family grew; soon it formed a community, then the society. It is at this time that patriotism was born. The love of a country, such was the first offspring of the love of family.

Divinely given, it must fructify, as all things of celestial origin. In fact, dig to the bottom of all the triumphs in history; what do you find? Patriotism. It is the rock on which nations, as the heroes of all centuries have based their name and their noble deeds; it is the rock against which brutality, tyranny and injustice have struck in hopeless ranting. Show me a patriotic people and I will give you a great nation, illustrious, and immortal. Name one which does not know or rejects this virtue of society: in a little time, I will have you hear the rasp of its agony. . . .

Document A—5

NATIONALITY VERSUS THE UNION, 1848

(Louis-Joseph Papineau, in *Montreal L'Avenir;* cited in the *Elgin-Grey Papers,* Vol. I, pp. 152–54 [Ottawa, 1937].)

THE UNION AND NATIONALITY.

For a long time repressed, stifled in the name of the public interest, the attachment to our nationality, by which we are characterised, would appear destined to become one of those prejudices, which the heart may still cherish, but which reason proscribes as a weakness, an error in sentiment. No one dares to protest in its name, for the sake of a position, into which we have been led by a train of unhappy events; a position considered advantageous to us, whilst all the benefits which can result from it, can only be obtained on the one condition of giving no signs of our existence as a nation. That was avowedly considered as an obstacle to our obtaining political rights; we must denude ourselves of our nationality; we must cease to consider ourselves *French Canadians,* if we desire to have any importance or weight in this system of social organization; and thus, under the pretence of amalgamation, our nationality will be absorbed in liberalism. The principle of nationality ceasing to be respected, as it is repudiated from interest, must become fable, lose its moral force, and soon end in being completely destroyed. So, during nearly ten years, we have seen its very name forgotten, and its slumber so profound, that it almost appeared dead.

So long as this state of things has existed, the people of Lower Canada would appear to have been seized with a general numbness, which paralized their public spirit. This torpor would continue to prevail, but for the awakening cry happily raised by some generous men, friends of their country and devoted to their nationality.—They have dared to break the silence, in spite of its profoundness, to raise their voices and recall the remembrance of that nationality, in preaching a doctrine which leads directly to its preservation. Why have they not done so sooner—why? because there existed interests which, with a menacing gesture, imposed silence upon them; because the expectation of a political welfare, always uncertain, renders us timid, under the feigned name of prudent; because the Union, the inconveniences and bad consequences of which it would be tiresome to relate, promising us in its results certain advantages, demanded the death of our nationality, in exchange for that constitutional liberty which we have so dearly, paid for. The Union has caused incalculable evils to us, it weighs down our existence.—Seduced, amused in some sort with its details, we have for a long time lost sight of the object of that measure, which, however, is every day recalled to our recollection by that invasion of ideas and institutions, foreign to our ideas and institutions, which renders each day the most desirable, in the midst of that confusion of institutions, that perfect labyrinth of laws, of manners and of language, which imposes upon us a double nationality, so as to render the one necessary, the other useless, that is to say, to make us lose ours and submit to the other. Such in effect was the success of that machiavelian work. The Union was made for the purpose of destroying us! it will evidently destroy us.

Document A—6

NATIONALITY AND THE UNION, 1848

(L. H. La Fontaine, in *Revue Canadienne*; cited in the *Elgin-Grey Papers*, Vol. I, pp. 155–59.)

UNION AND NATIONALITY

We have read with the greatest astonishment in the last number of *L'Avenir*, an editorial article under the above title, which seems to us of a nature to produce the most mischievous consequences if public opinion be not enlightened as to its tendencies and if good citizens do not unite hand in hand to prevent its pernicious effects.

At a time when the entire Country is contented and satisfied, when the Imperial Government has expressed its well considered determination to render justice to her colonies, to decline interference in their local affairs; and to accord them Responsible Government in all its fullness, when a new era is opening before us, when confidence is returning, when power is in the hands of the majority of the people, when this majority through the Parliament has accepted with joy the new order of things, and has testified its determination to set to work, in order to make it work for the general good—by what right, and in whose name, does *L'Avenir*, at such a time, advance with a cry of reprobation of every thing that exists. By what right, and in whose name does it display the flag of agitation, of trouble and of discord? By what right and in whose name does it attempt to throw distrust into the public mind—disorder and discontent into our ranks.

L'Avenir, a journal published in the interest of our youth, edited by a committee of youthful co-adjutors, takes on itself to raise a war cry in the midst of profound peace—takes on itself to condemn without exception the existing order of things, the long and arduous labours, the sacrifice, the devotion of those, who have struggled during ten years for the cause of the country, for our nationality, our institutions, our religion, our language, and our laws. From whence comes this strange abuse of words and ideas—this fatal aberration of an intellect calculated for disorganizations, destructive and wicked? How! Dare you tell us that for a long time attachment to our nationality has been pressed down, stifled by public interest; that no one has dared to advance claims in its name; that it has been an avowed obstacle to the attainment of our political rights, and that for ten years it has been nearly forgotten? It is an infamous lie: it is an unworthy calumny against all the efforts, all the acts of our public men, who have led us to the magnificent position we now occupy? Is it not for our institutions, and our nationality that our chiefs have fought for ten years past? And if after the unhappy events of which you speak, they have followed a calm, peaceable, moderate course of politics, is it because this course has been crowned with success that you are emboldened to-day to cast injury and outrage in their faces as recompense, of what they have done for us?—Where were you, then, when during all this epoch of ten years our present chiefs claimed in the name of the country her part in political rights, protested against the invasion of these same rights, and strove courageously for the preservation of our institutions, our language, and all our national interests? Have you not heard them since the Union in and out of Parliament exclaim energetically against those acts of injustice of which we were the victims, and defend foot by foot that precious heritage of our ancestors which has risen from the contest greater and more glorious than it was before? Whence come you, then, that you have not seen them opposed to an unjust, corrupt, and corrupting power, to a Governor so forgetful of his dignity as to descend into the arena and take personal part in the strife, yet maintaining that proud and firm bearing which has given the last blow to the reign of arbitrary power in Canada? Was it to forget our national for individual interests, or as you say again, with malignant perfidy, to *prefer the fusion, the death of this nationality in order to have the pleasure of reviving and being resuscitated in a foreign nationality*, that the chiefs of our party resigned in 1843, that they engaged in an obstinate combat with Lord Metcalfe, and that they repeatedly rejected the offers made them to enter the Cabinet to revive and be resuscitated because these offers were unworthy of our nationality and insufficient? Was it this often repeated refusal which sacrificed our national interests, or was it not rather the most eloquent manifestation of our public men of attachment to these same interests? Tell us gentlemen of *L'Avenir*, who weep so much over the ruins of the passed, and over imaginary evils—tell us at what period of our history the French Canadian nationality has been more brilliant, more honored, more respected, or has occupied a higher position than that which it occupies this day? Was it as you, with shameful self will, tell us an avowed obstacle to the attainment of our political rights? Or has it not rather been thanks to the ability, the tact, the firmness and the patience of its representatives so strong, that it has gained more in a few years, than it had done before in a half century of combats? . . .

But tell us ye young and fiery apostles of the Franco-Canadian nationality, what do you mean by the principle of nationality applied to the management of public affairs? Is it, that the principle at present in operation, personified in the Executive Council, in the magistrature, in all orders of society, protected by Executive power, and more than ever sheltered from insult, is not the thing? Is it, *par hazard*, that famous principle of public action which has excited the French lately to drive from France, all workmen of English or foreign origin? If it be a principle so advanced as that, which you wish to implant on the Canadian soil—and your article has very much the air of pretending to that you lose your time and pains. It is not after our party has recruited its ranks with men of all origins when our friends, the liberals of Upper Canada, and those of Lower Canada of foreign origin, have made prodigious efforts to carry the elections, and that altogether we have gained the most signal victory—it is not now that your appeal to prejudices and passions will have the least echo in the country. The people will laugh at your beards, and it will have reason.

Document A–7

FEDERATION—A FRENCH-CANADIAN VIEW

(J. C. Taché, *Des Provinces de L'Amerique du Nord et D'une Union Fédérale* [Québec, 1858], pp. 139–42 [translation].)

In declaring ourselves in favour of a confederation of the British North American provinces, in pleading the cause of the establishment of several separate but confederated governments, we do not in the least pretend to announce a new proposition; still less do we pretend that this form of organization is the best for the states. We are doing only one thing, studying a question which thrusts itself forward and in its solution considering the exceptional circumstances which we cannot avoid.

In order to create a state of affairs which is both desireable and durable and based on the principle of unity, it would be necessary to unite homogeneous elements, the nation, the people, and the state; these do not exist here. The nation is formed of people reaching back to a common origin and living with the same aspirations; the people is composed of collections of individuals united among themselves, by the constant and vital contacts between close neighbours and by sharing absolutely identical interests; the state consists of the administered capable in all of living under, and supporting the same homogeneous laws, and answering to the uniform demands of a government without danger to themselves.

We have said that these elements are not present here, and that the work of assimilation capable of producing unity can only be the work of time and genius. How much work, care, and struggle did French unity cost; begun under the reign of Philippe-le-Bel, continued by Louis XI and the Cardinal de Richelieu; however, in this work the people, united to the kings, only had to struggle against the great feudal interests; even so the unity of France has not taken such deep root that the question of federalism was not present at the heart of the republic of 1793, this in spite of the new centralized organization adopted by the national assembly in '91.

All the diverse elements which join in these provinces the vast extent of territory, the recruitment of population by immigration, the flow of which has varied and may vary again at the point of departure, imposes on us, as similar circumstances in several respects imposed upon the German confederation, on Switzerland, on the United States, the federative principle, whether it is or is not the best form of government in the abstract.

A short time ago a publicist wrote:

"The constitution of a people is not only the guarantee of its rights, the result of its civilisation, the expression of its customs, it is also the entire mechanism of government and its working parts. After the legislator has organized the powers, regulated their features, deduced the means by which they are related, and marked the limits which separate them, it is the rigorous precision of each of these powers operating within the general function, that determines the order, action and unity of the administration and direction of public affairs.

"This vital precision which alone can give to a government its effectiveness, is not attained immediately in the operation of a new constitution; there are inveterate traditions which resist both the most ingenious principles that condemn them and the necessities which transform them. Progress in all things, is never the victory of a single day; it is only the slow laborious conquest realized by perseverance and time. No matter how close a constitution may conform to the customs and interests of a country where it is law, no matter how evident the truth of its principles, the new powers which are created involuntarily embody something of the former powers which they have replaced."

Little do the forms and names which one adopts matter to us; we are not among those who to be right in the defence of certain theories are always ready to put difficulties out of view; and who like the cat in the fable looked at all which flattered its ideas or desires through the small end of the glass and all which represented an obstacle to its projects through the big end.

Document A—8

UNION OF THE BRITISH NORTH AMERICAN PROVINCES

(*The Daily Globe* [Toronto], October 25, 1853.)

The lower provinces have lately given to us various rumours and suggestions relating to a union between all the colonies of British North America. The subject appears to be intermingled by them in some way with Lord Elgin's visit to England. There has certainly been no overt act of his Excellency to indicate that he intends any movement with the Imperial authorities towards a federation, but he is said always to have been favourable to the project, and his taking the difficult land route through New Brunswick on his journey homewards, has probably induced the Blue-noses to suppose that an active movement is proposed.

There is a very evident feeling among Canadians, as well as among their brethren of the lower provinces, that destiny points to these colonies being united under one government. Derived from the same source, owing allegiance to the same empire, inhabitants of lands identical in position and climate, grown up to manhood under the same institutions, it appears natural and proper that the people of Canada, of New Brunswick, of Nova Scotia, of Prince Edward Island, even of Newfoundland, should endeavour to draw closer than before the connecting ties, and unite themselves under one government. It is very striking indeed to observe how much ressemblance there is between the people of Nova Scotia and Canada, for example, the inhabitants of which rarely see each other, and in reality know little of each other's affairs. The Nova Scotian who visits Upper Canada finds himself as thoroughly at home, as if he had not left his native country. He understands without an effort our local politics and the feelings which move us both in public and private affairs, for they are kindred to his own. There is as sturdy a spirit of freedom and independence in the elector of Queen's county, on the Atlantic shore, as in the freeholder of Kent on the waters of the St. Clair, there is as great a desire for progress, moral and material in Halifax as there is in Hamilton. We have the same rough climate as New Brunswick to harden the frame, and awaken the intellect, the same great forests from which to hew out our subsistence, the same toils, the same dangers, the same pleasures. It is said that we in Upper Canada, with the same fertile soil, have somewhat gone beyond our Eastern neighbours, that we are more wealthy, more advanced in the means of education. There is no saying, however, how long this may continue. It is not the country of the greatest natural resources which ultimately reaches the highest point in civilization. Men are developed by the difficulties of their position. The soil of Scotland has produced the best gardeners of the world because the utmost exertion is required to overcome its poverty, and to withstand its climate, and so the Nova Scotian and New Brunswicker, being somewhat deficient in the natural riches which we have in such abundance, may, in the future, produced the most ingenious mechanics, the most skilful farmers, the most enterprising merchants, simply because their position demands the exercise of economy and the utmost exertion of which they are capable.

It is not only, however, because we are of one mind, that we should come together, there are other reasons to be given for a union of the British American Provinces.

Canada contains two millions of inhabitants, and the lower Provinces about seven hundred and fifty thousand. Ten years from hence, the whole will embrace a population of five millions, and twenty years ten millions. The question of their future destiny will begin to force itself on the mind of the people, as their numbers increase. Aspirations after a national name, a national position, a national literature will grow up in their bosoms, as soon as wealth and consequent independence reach every quarter of the country, through which they are now making giant strides. There will be a demand for the acquisition of new territory, a longing after a wider field, for the nation as it will then exist. The natural outlet for this feeling will be in the union of the Provinces, and in the absorption of the territory which now rightfully belongs to them—we mean that of the Hudson's Bay Company. A magnificent state would grow from such a confederation under British protection, having all the life and activity of the American continent, yet retaining more of the virtues of the parent state than the neighbouring union, and avoid many of the evils which afflict that Republic. Such a power is absolutely required on this continent.

B. America, Fair or Foul?

Then as now, Canadians derived a sense of political and social uniqueness by comparing themselves to Americans. Although they apparently admired what was yet English in American culture, they generally rejected the post-Revolutionary political tradition. Overall there was a deep admiration for American material progress, but also an equally firm conviction that Canadian society was a more civilized, albeit humbler, alternative. For many Canadians the violent eruption of the slave question was simply the just visitation of providence upon a society steeped in corruption. Yet even on this question there was dissent ranging from admiration of southern planterdom to denunciation of northern philanthropy.

How accurately are these ambivalent attitudes reflected in contemporary Canadian thought on American culture? Indeed, what sustenance have they given to Canadian nationalism for the past century?

Document B–1

EIGHT YEARS IN THE UNITED STATES

(AMICUS—*Anglo-American Magazine* [Toronto, 1852], Vol. I, pp. 412–90 *passim*.)

At a time when many well-informed and candid individuals in the United States entertain doubts as to the result of the problem which has yet to be solved in that country, with reference to the effect of republican institutions upon the moral, social, and political conditions of the people: the popular mind is impressed with the conviction of its actual success, and views all other forms of government, whether of absolute or constitutional monarchy, as neither more nor less than positive and insufferable despotisms; under which a prosperous national condition cannot be attained, nor individual liberty secured. But it has yet to be determined whether the American revolution will be productive of permanent advantage or injury, to the cause of human freedom.

The immense advance in commercial importance, which the United States has made, their vast increase in population, the extensive establishment of manufactories, and the corresponding accumulation of wealth, would seem to sanction popular delusion,—particularly when these effects are viewed, as is generally the case, without comparison with other countries. Still, the same energy of character, that formerly enabled the colonists successfully to contend against the Parent State, and the extraordinary position of the world, during the first fifteen or twenty years after their independence was acknowledged—and of which that event was the cause, would have accomplished the same results, under a different form of government.

The troops of France, who served in America during the revolution, carried back with them the seeds of a popular movement there, and produced the long and momentous war, in which England found herself compelled to engage for upwards of twenty years, during which the French mercantile marine was swept from the ocean, and a field was opened up for American enterprise, of which the people of the United States were not slow to avail themselves, and of which they did not fail to profit. . . .

Whoever has conversed freely with persons in the better walks of life, in the United States, and particularly those who have visited England, and there seen the workings of constitutional monarchy, must be satisfied that there is a wide-spread dissatisfaction prevailing among that class of Americans, who perceive that a mere popular government has neither the stability nor the security for life, person, or property, which exists under the better regulated government of Great Britain. . . .

Nor with reference to the choice of State Governors, do the people of the United States possess any advantage over those of the Provinces. Having occupied a rather prominent position in three of the Colonies, I have had ample opportunities for forming a correct judgement upon the subject; and, with very rare exception, have found those who have been appointed to administer the government where I resided, to be men who understood the interests of the communities over which they presided,—whose minds were free from local prejudices,—who could be actuated by no sinister motives, who could have no selfish purpose to accomplish; and who being selected from the highest walks of life, and most of them distinguished for their military services, were guided by a high sense of honour; and would, had they been properly supported by those whose duties it was, have introduced, improvements, the beneficial effects of which would have been felt, long after they had ceased to govern,—or perhaps to exist.

A good deal has been said about what is popularly considered the exorbitant salaries that are paid the Colonial Governors, which were fixed at the time the Provinces deliberately agreed to defray the civil expenses of the Government, in return for the surrender of the Crown lands, which, particularly in Canada, have been an abundant source of revenue; and which, after all, are not extravagant, when we consider the dignity of the office,—the position its incumbents occupy, and which they must retain in society,—the hospitalities they are called upon profusely to extend, and the numerous applications that are continually and successfully made for their aid in the promotion of objects of charity, benevolence, or usefulness.

Document B–2

AMERICAN SOCIETY AND POLITICS, THE DARKER SIDE

(Toronto Leader, June 30, 1858.)

A dark chapter might be written on the personalities of American politics. On this continent, politics are perpetually merging into personalities. In this respect, things are very different here from what we find them in Europe. There are several reasons why this could be the case. The struggle for political power, in this country, is too often also, one for personal advancement, in a pecuniary sense. Where so much is at stake, the struggle becomes intensified and embittered to an extent that would otherwise be impossible. Something too must be set down to the account of education and the influence of society, and the prevailing state of manners, among different classes of the population. The license of language and the scandals of personal altercation and personal encounter, at Washington, have been turned, on the continent of Europe, into an argument against Democratic Government and constitutional systems, in every shape. In the Federal capital of the United States the Senators go armed. The bowie knife or the revolver is the constant companion of a large number of them. The national Legislature is every now and then the scene of personal violence. The streets, the hotels and the public offices witness death-struggle between persons who ought to be patterns of society. Insults for the purpose of provocation are not infrequently given; in any case, they provoke retaliation. Personal encounters, violence and bloodshed are the inevitable results. It is true we have not reached a like condition of things here; but the experience of the last few days admonishes us that we are fast drifting towards it. The license of language, the grossness of insult, the swell of the bully, the large number of informal challenges, show that in everything but physical courage we fully match the Americans. In nothing else are we behind.

It would be improper to make this statement without adding that this quality is not absent from Canadian society. But there are some among our legislators, who imagine they have a right to the most unbounded license of language; to give the lie, to brand as tools the independent supporters of the government, to resort to every epithet of vilification which the English language affords: they fancy they have a right to do all this; that it is perfectly parliamentary, and that they are free from the burden of all personal responsibility, with regard to their conduct. But everywhere the same causes produced the same effects; and if this sort of license is to continue its inevitable concomitants cannot be long in presenting themselves. The worst of the offenders, such as Mr. Brown, are not duellists, and for this they would deserve commendation, provided they were careful never to give offence. But what we object to is the assumption that because they are not, they can offer insults as a matter of right and with every assurance of impunity. This mistaken feeling of abandoned responsibility is the prime cause of the whole mischief, and threatens soon to turn Canadian politics into a mere contest of physical strength. If the results which come of resenting insults are to be avoided, the use of insulting language must cease; they must observe, as Mr. Powell said on Friday night, decency of behaviour, if gentlemanly conduct is impossible to them. If not, Toronto must soon be a second Washington. The revolver will become a familiar companion, and the arbiter of disputes which propriety of conduct would have prevented.

Document B–3

THE UNITED STATES AND CANADA—A PARALLEL

(*The Daily Globe* [Toronto], August 28, 1855.)

The United States are governed by a section of their population, situated in the least improving portion of their territory, and both in numbers and intelligence inferior to those over whom they rule. We of course refer to the South as the governing, and the north and west as the governed. By union of action and devotion to one great object, the minority of slave-holders manage to control Congress and the executive, and to cause legislation to retrograde towards despotism and barbarism, rather than progress to freedom and civilization. They hold the keys of office and gain northern support, by unlocking for their worshippers the doors of the bureau.—As the United States has a ruling South, so Canada has a governing east, likewise containing a minority of the people, likewise ruling on retrogressive principles, and likewise by mercenary inducements offered to the representatives of the majority. The parallel is perfect, and in the minor details there is also a singular similarity. So long as the south remained on the defensive, or contented herself merely with a demand for the delivery of escaped slaves—she found individuals at the north who could take her money and yet preserve a measure of influence among their neighbours. Her position was insecure however, she needed more than defence to preserve her position. The growth of the north was more rapid than her own, and she would soon be overwhelmed, did she not succeed in subjecting thoroughly to slave influence

a portion of territory above Mason and Dixon's line. Hence arose that measure of invasion on Northern rights, the Kansas-Nebraska bill, and thence followed the almost unanimous outburst of indignation from the free states, which threaten to destroy forever the influence of the slave power in the Union. In Canada the Roman Catholic hierarchy is the slave power. It holds its subjects in bondage as slavish as the southern taskmaster. It has used influence with western politicians to strengthen its power in its own territory and to extend it in a milder form to Upper Canada. The earlier Sectarian School bills might be likened to the U.S. Compromise Acts of 1850; the latter gave the slaveholder a foothold on free soil to recapture his bondsmen, the former gave the priest a similar foothold to prevent his spiritual servitor being enlightened by a system of free education. Like the slaveholder the priest was not content with this; education must not only be kept from the Roman Catholic, but it must be destroyed by the breaking up of the whole national school system. It was this design which produced the School Act of last Session—our Kansas-Nebraska bill.

Document B-4

REMARKS ON THE SOUTHERN STATES AND THEIR INSTITUTIONS BY A CANADIAN

(Anglo-American Magazine [Toronto, 1854], Vol. V, pp. 129-38.)

The chief attraction of Norfolk is its refined and agreeable society. The inhabitants, principally natives of the place, are mostly of English or Scottish descent, and are entirely free from any of those peculiarities of appearance and accent, which Canadians instinctively associate with their idea of all Americans or "Yankees" as they are almost universally though erroneously termed. Making just allowances for the difference of their sentiments and views on political subjects —the natural effects of the form of Government under which they live, and the

"peculiar Institution" which prevails among them, the Virginians, as a whole, present, to my mind a truer type of the "old countryman," than even we Canadians can, though it is our glory and boast that we are still bound by ties of loyalty and affection to the "Fatherland." They are extremely hospitable to strangers; and, if I may judge from my own experience, visitors to the South, possessing the proper means of introduction, may rely upon being received and treated with every attention. . . .

I must confess that the prejudices

which I always entertained against slavery, have not been much strengthened by my experience. We hear but of the evils and abuses of the system here: and, before passing sentence upon it, justice demands that both sides should, at least, be heard. It is true, that the master has an almost uncontrolled *legal* power over the liberty and even the life of his slave; that he can, and will, sever the ties which bind the slave to all that he has hitherto held dear—from his children and his partner—I can hardly, in strictness, call her *wife*, as I believe that the marriage ceremony is seldom if ever performed among them. It is also true that the principles of learning are carefully and strictly denied to the coloured race. Still, although there are so many things in the social condition of the slave and in the uncertain tenure with which he holds his liberty and all family ties, and are abhorrent to our British ideas of right, it is but justice to the Slaveholders to say, that the evils of the system alone, are held up to view, and these generally much exaggerated. The slaves are with little exception, well treated, well fed and comfortably clothed; and seldom, if ever, are any of these scenes of cruelty, so forcibly portrayed in *Uncle Tom's Cabin,* perpetrated in real life. Neither are they by any means overworked. A good farm servant in Canada would be required and expected to do twice the amount of labour that is exacted from a slave. I am also bound to say, that in many sales and auctions of slaves that I witnessed, (which perhaps present one of the most abhorrent features of the system), I observed every anxiety displayed to effect the sale in such a way to prevent, if possible, the separation of husband and wife, and mothers from their young children. Again the slaves themselves appear universally happy and contented with their lot, and generally attached to their masters. I have myself conversed with some of them, and particularly I remember, with one—almost completely white, and with little of the appearance of the negro about him—who possessed a greater degree of intelligence than the majority. He told me he was well-treated and happy, in answer to some observation of mine, said that as long as he remained in his present position he would prefer slavery to freedom. . . .

C. Economic Nationalism

A sense of material success has often accompanied the growth of political nationalism. The prosperous 1850's gave Canadians much cause for self-satisfaction because of the rapid growth in population, transportation, and industry. With this growth there came the inevitable demand for protection of native mercantile and manufacturing interests, all of whom spoke in the name of Canadian nationalism. The French Canadian differed in his approach to economics from the Anglo-Saxon mercantile interests of Montreal and Toronto. He stressed instead the defensive mission of French Canadians to preserve his patrimony and his national integrity by enterprise in both spheres of politics and economics. The question then arises, was the metropolitan drive of Toronto and Montreal during the Union genuinely "national" in outlook, or was it a mask for more sinister objective of economic imperialism within Canada and the new regions to the West? Did the French Canadians interpret this rapid metropolitan expansion as an attempt to fulfil Lord Durham's prophecy of cultural extermination in 1839?

Document C—1

CANADA'S MATERIAL DESTINY

(Cited in J. S. Hogan, *Canada: An Essay* [awarded first prize by the Paris Exhibition Committee of Canada], [Montreal, 1855], pp. 9—11.)

In England, or France, or any of the States of Europe, if upwards of a million of the working classes had, within a short space of time, and by means hitherto unknown or unthought of, raised themselves to comparative affluence and independence, their example would be alike a matter of wonder and of instruction. To the poor, who are struggling against becoming poorer; to those who, though they may be able to steer clear of actual want themselves, have the painful picture constantly presented to their minds, of their offspring being otherwise circumstanced; to the mere "hewers of wood and drawers of water," who are too low to dream even of comforts or respectability, how deeply interesting should be the knowledge, not only that a million and a-half of people like themselves had been able to cast their poverty behind them, but that many millions more could "go and do likewise." Nor to the statesman, who gathers from such examples the knowledge of how to make nations great, and to become great himself; or to those who are engaged in the humane task of endeavouring to mitigate the evils of redundant population, should such a fact be less interesting or valuable. And this, without exaggeration, is the lesson that may be learned from the industrial history of Canada, but especially of the Upper Province.

In 1829 the population of Western Canada—for that Province, having exhibited greater progress in population and wealth, I shall at present allude to—had but one hundred and ninety-six thousand inhabitants. Its assessable property, being the real and personal estate of its people, was estimated, and I think with sufficient liberality, at £2,500,000. Its population in 1854 had increased to 1,237,600; and its assessed and assessable property, not including its public lands, the timber on them, or its minerals, is set down, in round numbers, at fifty million pounds. This sum is over the assessors' returns, but when it is considered that the assessments were based upon the people's estimates of their own property, and that these are proverbially made with a view to avoiding taxation rather than to appearing rich, and that bonds and mortgages and other valuable effects were not included in the assessments, the addition of fifteen per cent.—being that made—is by no means an error on the side of exaggeration. The Marshalls appointed to correct similar returns in the United States make a much larger addition, although the property I have named, as exempted in Canada, is all assessed in the States.

Thus then the remaining inhabitants of 1829, and the descendants of those who have died, together with the settlers who have come into the Province since, divide between them fifty million pounds worth of property, being £200 4s. 2d. to each family of five, and £40 0s. 2d. to each man, woman and child,—a degree of prosperity it would be difficult to credit, were it not established by proofs wholly incontrovertible.

And who and what are the people who divide among them this magnificent property? And how have they acquired it? Did they come in as conquerors, and appropriate to themselves the wealth of others?—They came in but to subdue a wilderness, and have reversed the laws of conquest; for plenty, good neighbourhood, and civilization mark their footsteps. Or did capitalists accompany them, to reproduce their wealth by applying it to the enterprises and improvements of a new country? No;—for capitalists wait till their pioneer, industry, first makes his report, and it is but now that they are studying the interesting one from Canada.

Or did the generosity of European Princes, or European wealth or benevolence provide them with such outfits as secured their success? On the contrary, the wrongs of Princes, and the poverty of Nations, have been the chief causes of the settlement of America. Her prosperity is the offspring of European hopelessness. Her high position in the world is the result of the sublime efforts of despair. And he who would learn who they are who divide among them the splendid property created in Canada has but to go to the quays of Liverpool, of Dublin, of Glasgow, and of Hamburg, and see emigrants there embarking, who knew neither progress nor hopes where they were born, to satisfy himself to the fullest.

It is the object of this Essay to describe the country, its soil, its climate, and its resources, in which these people have prospered; to trace their advancement and its causes; to describe the public works and improvements they possess; to show how they govern themselves, and what are their institutions—religious, educational and municipal; to exhibit, in short, what may guide industry in search of a place wherein to better its condition, and capital in quest of fields for profitable investment.

Document C–2

FAIR PLAY FOR NATIVE INDUSTRY

(D'Arcy McGee in *New Era*, April 1, 1858.)

The word *protection*, used in relation to industry, has become odious in England. It was the selfish cry of a class already highly privileged—the landed aristocracy of England;—and therefore it became hateful to the masses, who really wanted to be protected against the monopolists of the corn market. But protection is a good word, and expresses more than any other the true nature and end of a good government.

What we demand for native industry in Canada is not protection—at least not exploded English protection—but fair play. We demand that our workmen shall not be swamped, through the culpable remissness of our Legislature, in our own market. We demand that the reciprocity treaty shall establish a real reciprocity; and that if our markets continue to open to the mother country, our manufactures —be the same more or less—shall be as free to enter her ports. In short, we ask a Canadian tariff, in the interests of Canadian industry, and not of a few commission agents for foreign houses.

This is a question of employment and population, as well as of capital and currency. It is a question for farmers as for mechanics. The operation of such alterations in the tariff would be to encourage manufactures in Canada, and to sustain a large manufacturing population. That population is to be fed, and the money earned in the mill must find its way to the field. To create a domestic trade between the different classes of the same community, has been the first object of all national legislation. Diversity of pursuits and diffusion of wealth are the inevitable consequences of a well-balanced system, combining both artificial, and agricultural employments. It is the immediate interest of the farmer on the Thames and Trent that the mill in his neighbourhood should be steadily at work: it directly affects him if it employs a hundred hands, fewer or more;—it therefore directly concerns him that the present tariff should not continue to allow into Canada the manufactures of other countries at from 5 to 15 per cent, while our manufactures in the United States and in England are mulcted at from 15 to 30 per cent.

The common fallacy is, that if you raise

the duties on any given article, you make it dearer to the consumer. This would be the effect on articles which we could not, by any possibility, produce; for example, higher duties on teas and coffees would of course, enhance their price—the very thing we don't want to do. But to impose the same duties on certain descriptions of woollens, cottons, hardware, glass, furniture, leather, paper, books, &c, does not necessarily increase the price to the purchaser. The effect of a judicious system would be, *not to make them dear, but to make them here.*

Document C–3

SOIL AND FRENCH-CANADIAN NATIONALITY

(George-Etienne Cartier, a speech delivered at the funeral of Ludger Duvernay, the editor of *La Minerve* and a founder of the St. Jean Baptiste Society; October 21, 1855, *La Minerve* [translation].)

Population does not suffice to constitute a nationality; a territorial element is also necessary. Race, language, education, and customs form what I call a personal national force. But this force must perish if it is not accompanied by the territorial element. Experience shows that for a nation to maintain and preserve itself an intimate and indissoluble union of the individual with the soil is necessary.

French Canadians, do not forget; if we wish to assure our national existence, it is necessary that we hold fast to the land. It is necessary that each of us do everything in his power to conserve his patrimonial territory. Those who do not have any land must use the fruits of their labour to acquire a piece of our land no matter how small that portion may be. For it is necessary to bequeath to our children not only the blood and language of our ancestors but in addition a hold on the land. If later our nationality is attacked, what strength for this struggle will French Canadians draw from their roots in the soil? The giant Antée knew greater strength each time he touched the earth; it will be the same with us.

Only a century ago we were hardly 60,000 scattered on the banks of our beautiful St. Lawrence; today we number more than 600,000 and are owners of three quarters of the fertile fields we cultivate. I do not see the eventuality of a death blow being given to our nationality, as long as we have full possession of the land. Let us constantly remember, compatriots, that our nationality can be maintained only on this condition.

Turn your glance to France, that dear fatherland of our ancestors. Why do we see there the national spirit so strong and vigorous? It is because the Frenchman is united with the land he inhabits by his proprietorship. One writer in a delirious moment dared to proclaim that property is theft. . . . A blasphemous and deleterious maxim! A maxim destructive to the work in all nations! In fact, would work be possible, if there was not property to serve as a goal and a means of payment? And without property, could a nationality and fatherland exist? Notice that the necessity of holding titles of ownership to the land exists for members of other national sister societies just as it does for us. The struggle which must arise between us and the members of these societies for the possession of the soil, must be a struggle of work, economy, industry, intelligence, and good conduct; and not a racial struggle of prejudice and envy. Canada has space; there is room for them; there is room for us; there is room for all. Our horizons are without limits.

Document C—4

VIRTUES AND NECESSITIES OF POLITICAL ECONOMY

(Etienne Parent, *Importance de l'Etude de l'Economie Politique. Lecture Prononcé Devant L'Institut Canadien*, November 19, 1846 [Montreal, 1846], [translation].)

It is no longer possible for our public figures to sustain honourably and successfully the struggle simply by courage, devotion, eloquence, and a broad knowledge of natural, political, and constitutional law. Nor is it still possible, by numbers alone, to hold in check the social and political forces opposed to us in a struggle on the very principles of government itself. The machinery of our government is now regularly organized, that is, the principles which regulate the functioning are set forth and recognized; this is not to say, however, that all is for the best in the present political arrangement.

But the struggle is not finished, and will never finish under our system of government; it has only shifted ground. Abstract governmental theories have given way to questions of material interest, which for the mass of the people are often of greater importance than the first. For half a century we have struggled with each other on the form which communal life must take; and now that this question is regulated, each sets to work in his own way to occupy the best place he can. The million and one diverse interests which fill a society work to make the position of each better and better, or at least less and less difficult.

And in this new struggle, no less talent and enlightenment is required than in the other; only one will need a somewhat different order of talents than were required in the earlier struggle; it is necessary to acquire them quickly, for in the new arena as in the old, even more perhaps, victory will go to the most able; still as much more than formerly, it will be necessary that we be right twice, and that we be capable of demonstrating it twice. Thus did Providence, which has thrown us into this corner of the globe, wish that we live among foreign people from whom we can not expect much sympathy. Do not protest however; for who can fathom the secrets of Providence? Who will say to us that she does not have designs for us, and that the tests to which she puts our adolescence is not a preparation for some glorious destiny on this continent? Furthermore, whatever may be the fate which the future reserves for us, let us know how to be worthy of it if it is good, and if it is bad let us in breaking away from it show that we did not merit it. Such is the duty of each generation, of each individual. And this duty, we will fulfil in bearing in our hearts the sacred fire of a noble imitation which will make us maintain in all, at all times an equality with the people who surround us.

In speaking a moment ago of the lively political struggle which continued until 1840, and from which derived the present governmental arrangements, I believe I have said enough to indicate that it was scarcely possible that our public figures, before the present time, could give themselves to long and diligent studies of political economy. To the young generation I say that since '91 your predecessors have had to struggle for political liberty, for the practical consequences of representative government which until recently we had in name only. They have created, developed, and organized popular power and have acquired for it the degree of influence and action which it exercises today in government; this action and influence is such compared to what they experienced earlier under the former order of things that the change constituted a veritable revolution in our political position. That you know is the achievement of hard and incessant work, work which must have consumed all the moral and intellectual force of your elders. How then could one have studied a science which requires much time and even more a tranquil spirit to be understood thoroughly? And was one able to think of ordinary occupations and had the time to study them, one lacked the stability in the state necessary to apply the principles which political economy teaches. Furthermore, the action of the economists was much more narrow when the mother country reserved for herself the regulation of our commerce: here then is another motive, another excuse for past generations not to occupy themselves especially with economic studies.

Thus, gentlemen of the young generation, no reproaches; be indulgent, be just. By the sacrifice of the long and hard work of your elders, you are here entering the promised land; they have done their task, now it is up to you to do yours. They have sacrificed their time, their energy, their intelligence to the great conquest, it is now up to you to profit from it. They may have been the tribunes, you be the Statesmen, enlightened economists.

D. Literary Nationalism

The *literati* played a most significant ideological role in the promotion of a national spirit before Confederation. Conscious of the deficiencies of national spirit, English-Canadian writers consciously set out to break the colonial mentality which had previously characterized Canadian literature. Yet, could they legitimately cast off that vassalage by imitating popular themes current in Europe and the United States (nature poetry, racism, self-help, and frontierism)? French-Canadian writers sought national themes more in historical situations which were either set in the French régime or in later events which compromised English Canadians. Since both forms of nationalism in Canada East and West were so heavily colonial in theme or technique, can there be said to be anything beyond a confused and vague desire for national literary distinctiveness by Confederation?

Document D-1

WHO READS A CANADIAN BOOK?

(D'Arcy McGee in *New Era*, July 25, 1857.)

The New York *Daily News* favors us with a friendly essay on the dearth of Provincial literature, which essay, in part we transfer for the public good, to the *New Era*. We are sorry to say, the reproach implied in the question quoted, is but too true. And wherefore? Not because there are not men of ability in this country; but because in part, we have been overreached in the Reciprocity Treaty with the United States, so far as the *materiel* of literature is concerned. In the articles of paper, ink, and type; and in the whole book trade, the reciprocity

is all on one side. The Americans have an advantage in this market, of from 15 to 20 percent over the resident capitalists who might be disposed to embark or who are embarked, in their production. The consequence is that Montreal and Toronto houses are mere agencies for New York publishers, having no literary wares to exchange with Harper, or Putnam, or the Sadliers, or Appleton. Economically, this is an evil; intellectually, it is treason to ourselves. If the design is to Massachusettize the Canadian mind, this is the very way to effect that end: if, on the other hand, we desire to see a Canadian nationality freely developed, borrowing energy from the American, grace from the Frenchman, and power from the Briton, we cannot too soon begin to construct a Grand Trunk of thought, which will be as a backbone to the system we desire to inaugurate.

Every literature would seem to begin with poetry, and no region of the New World is fitter for the habitation of Muse, than the wide and wondrous North—

> "stern and wild,
> Meet Nurse for a poetic child"

The Northmen of the Old World have struck the harp with a skill that rings through the heart of Time. From the Niebelungen to the "Lay of the last Minstrel"—from the first scald to Bishop Tegner and Thomas Moore—what glorious gushes of song have sprung from the isles and fissures of the North? And why not *our* North, as well as theirs? Why not, if we crave the renown of song, and seek it sincerely, why should it not come? And in the train of song, all the grave and stately company of the Muses,—the Olympian procession which the Greek colonies could boast, when they were even younger than these Provinces now are. To human intellect and human will, no height which man has once scaled is inaccessible.

The Canadian public must do its part. The Reciprocity Treaty must be overhauled. Where it works equally let it stand, by all means; where it favors only one side, let it be modified. Either give us full and free trade in the *materiel* of literature, or reciprocal protection. The interests of the few must yield to the wants of the many, and Canada has not, to-day, a greater want, than that of a home-made literature.

Document D–2

CHARLES SANGSTER AND THE ST. LAWRENCE

(Cited in C. Sangster, *St. Lawrence and the Saguenay and Other Poems* [Kingston, 1856], pp. 33–37.)

xlix.

Th' inconstant moon has passed behind a
  cloud,
CAPE DIAMOND shows its sombre-colored
  bust,
As if the mournful Night had thrown a
  shroud
Over this pillar to a hero's dust.
Well may she weep; hers is no trivial trust;
His cenotaph may crumble on the plain,
Here stands a pile that dares the rebel's
  lust
For spoliation: one that will remain—
A granite seal—brave Wolfe! set upon
    Victory's Fane.

l.

QUEBEC! how regally it crowns the height,
Like a tanned giant on a solid throne!
Unmindful of the sanguinary fight,
The roar of cannon mingling with the
  moan
Of mutilated soldiers years agone,
That gave the place a glory and a name
Among the nations. France was heard to
  groan;
England rejoiced, but checked the proud
  acclaim—
A brave young chief had fall'n to vindicate
  her fame.

li.

WOLFE and MONTCALM! two nobler names
  ne'er graced
The page of history, or the hostile plain;
No braver souls the storm of battle faced,
Regardless of the danger or the pain.
They pass'd unto their rest without a stain
Upon their nature or their generous hearts.
One graceful column to the noble twain
Speaks of a nation's gratitude, and starts
The tear that Valor claims, and Feeling's self
  imparts.

lii.

Far up the Golden Ladder of the Morn
Had climbed the sun, upon the Autumn
  day

That led me to these battlements. The corn
Upon the distant fields was ripe. Away
To the far left the swelling highlands lay;
The quiet cove, the river, bright and still;
The gallant ships that made the harbor
    gay;
And, like a Thought swayed by a potent
    Will,
POINT LEVI, seated at the foot of the Old Hill:

liii.

What were the Gardens and the Terraces,
The stately dwellings, and the monuments
Upreared to human fame, compared to
    these?
Those ancient hills stood proudly ere the
    tents
Of the first Voyageurs—swart visitants
From the fair, sunny Loire—were pitched
    upon
Wild Stadacona's height. The armaments
Whose mighty thunder clove the solid
    stone,
Defaced yon granite cape, that answered
    groan for groan.

liv.

Down the rough slope Montmorenci's
    torrent pours,
We cannot view it by this feeble ray,
But, hark! its thunders leap along the
    shores,
Thrilling the cliffs that guard the
    beauteous bay;
And now the moon shines on our
    downward way,

Showing fair Orleans' enchanting Isle,
Its fields of grain, and meadows sweet
    with hay;
Along the fertile shores fresh landscapes
    smile,
Cheering the watchful eye for many a
    pleasant mile.

lv.

It seems like passing by some Fairy-realm.
The cottages are whiter than the snow.
Joy at the prow, and true love at the helm,
Both heaven and earth smile on us as we
    go.
Surely they never feel the breath of woe,
The dwellers on this Isle. Spire after spire
Points to the heav'n whose presence seems
    to glow
Within their happy bosoms who aspire
To naught beyond their hearths, their own
    dear household fire.

lvi.

Peace to their cheerful homes! where
    bless'd Content
Reigns paramount throughout the circling
    year.
A courteous, gentle race, as ever blent
Religion with Simplicity. The cheer
That greets the stranger who may wander
    here
Glows with the zeal of hospitality.
Peace to their quiet homes! where
    blanching fear
Ne'er enters, nursed by jealous rivalry.
From the world's bitter strife the Habitant is
    free.

Document D–3

NORTHERN LATITUDES AND MAPLE LEAVES— CANADIAN NATURE POETRY

(E. H. Dewart [ed.] *Selections From Canadian Poets* [Montreal, 1864], pp. 112–14, 164–65.)

I'VE WANDERED IN THE SUNNY SOUTH.

National Song.

John F. M'Donnell.

I've wandered in the sunny South,
    Beneath its purple skies;
And roamed through many a far-off land,
    Where cloudless beauty lies:
I've breathed the balm of tropic eves,
    Upon the Southern sea;
And watched the glorious sunset pour
    Its radiance far and free.

But give me still my Northern home,—
    Her islands and her lakes;
And her forests old, where not a sound
    The tomb-like silence breaks.
More lovely in her snowy dress,
    Or in her vesture green,
Than all the pride of Europe's lands,
    Or Asia's glittering sheen.

I've basked beneath Italian suns,
    When flowers were in their bloom;
And I've wandered o'er the hills of Greece,
    By ruined shrine and tomb;—

Oh sweet it was to gaze upon
    The Arno's silver tide—
And dearer still, the ruins grey
    Of Athen's fallen pride.

But dearer unto me that land
    Which the mighty waters lave,
Where the spreading maple's glorious hues
    Are mirrored in the wave:—
Where music from the dark old woods
    Ascends to heaven's dome—
Like angel hymns of peace and love—
    Around my Northern home.

THE MAPLE.

Rev. H. F. Darnell, M.A.

All hail to the broad-leaved Maple!
    With its fair and changeful dress—
A type of our youthful country
    In its pride and loveliness;
Whether in Spring or Summer,
    Or in the dreary Fall,
'Mid Nature's forest children,
    She's fairest of them all.

Down sunny slopes and valleys
    Her graceful form is seen,
Her wide, umbrageous branches
    The sun-burnt reaper screen;

'Mid the dark-browed firs and cedars
    Her livelier colors shine,
Like the dawn of a brighter future
    On the settler's hut of pine.

She crowns the pleasant hill top,
    Whispers on breezy downs,
And casts refreshing shadows
    O'er the streets of our busy towns;
She gladdens the aching eye-ball,
    Shelters the weary head,
And scatters her crimson glories
    On the graves of the silent dead.

When Winter's frosts are yielding
    To the sun's returning sway,
And merry groups are speeding
    To sugar-woods away,
The sweet and welling juices,
    Which form their welcome spoil,
Tell of the teeming plenty
    Which here waits honest toil.

When sweet-voiced Spring, soft-breathing,
    Breaks Nature's icy sleep,
And the forest boughs are swaying
    Like the green waves of the deep;
    In her fair and budding beauty,
        A fitting emblem she
    Of this our land of promise,
        Of hope, of liberty.

Document D-4

LITERATURE AND NATIONALITY

(Octave Crémazie, cited in O. Crémazie, Oeuvres Completes [Montreal, 1882], pp. 40–43 [translation].)

The more I reflect upon the destiny of Canadian literature, the fewer chances I would give it to leave a mark upon history. What Canada misses most is having a language of her own. If we spoke Iroquois or Huron, our literature would live. Unfortunately we speak and write, in a sufficiently pitiful manner, it is true, the language of Bossuet and Racine. Say or do what we will, we shall always remain a simple colony from a literary viewpoint; and even if Canada became independent and thrust her flag forth into the sunlight of nations, we should remain nonetheless literary colonials. Look at Belgium, which speaks the same language we do. Is there a Belgian literature? Unable to compete with France in her beauty of form, Canada might have conquered a place among the literatures of the old world, if there were among her native sons a writer capable of introducing Europe, before Fenimore Cooper, to the greatness of our forests and to the legendary exploits of our trappers and voyageurs. . . . I repeat, if we spoke Huron or Iroquois, the works of our writers would attract the attention of the old world. This acutely masculine language, born in the forests of America would have the primitive poetry which delights the foreigner. One would be overwhelmed by a novel or a poem translated from the Iroquois, while one does not take the trouble to read a book written in French by a native of Quebec or Montreal. For the last twenty years there have been published annually in France translations of Russian, Scandinavian, and Roumanian novels. Suppose these same books were written in French, they wouldn't have found fifty readers. . . .

But what does it matter, after all, if the works of Canadian authors are destined not to cross the Atlantic? Are we not a million Frenchmen forgotten by the mother country on the shores of the St. Lawrence? Is it not sufficient to encourage all those who write to know that this little people will flourish, and that it will always cherish and protect the name and memory of those who have assisted it in conserving intact the most precious of all of its treasures, the tongue of its fathers?

When the father of a family, after a tiring day, tells his many children about the adventures and accidents of his long life, provided that those gathered around him get pleasure and instruction from listening to what he tells them, he does not worry about whether or not the rich owner of the manor knows the simple and delightful tales which adorn his home. His children like to listen to him and that is all that matters.

This is how it must be for the Canadian writer. Renouncing without regret the fine dreams of resounding fame, he should consider himself amply rewarded for his labours if he can instruct and delight his countrymen, if he can contribute to the preservation of the old French nationality on the young soil of America.

Document D–5

HISTORY AND NATIONALISM IN THE WAR OF 1812

(From François-Xavier Garneau, *History of Canada*, trans. from the French by A. Bell [Montreal, 1862], Vol. II, pp. 319–21.)

Such was the first permanent effect of the war. A second result, not less important, was that the Northern States, which wished for separation in 1814, are become, since then, the natural rivals of Britain, because it is in New England, mostly, that American manufacturing industry, on a large scale, is located; its people, therefore, being concerned to secure for themselves a home market throughout the Union, are now the least likely to move for breaking up the confederation. Accordingly, there is no reason for its enemies to calculate on a separation of the north-eastern from the central or south-western States, through clashing commercial interests; as, every day, new ties are forming to bind its parts more closely together than ever.

On the other hand, it is not likely that the Americans will attempt to acquire the Canadas without the consent of their inhabitants. In their eyes, colonial dependence is neither a natural nor durable state for a people; and the manifest tendencies of metropolitan governments themselves give a plain enough indication that they have a similar feeling as to the future. Such an eventuality [independence?] pre-occupies the attention of the politicians and historians of Britain; but neither her historians nor her statesmen, it seems, can rid themselves of their old-world prejudices, so as to form an imperial judgment of what ought to be done, in order to maintain the integrity of the British empire. Under whatever aspect we view this question, a solution of it appears difficult; for the mother country cannot allow to colonists the like controlling influence over its own immediate government, that the people of the Three Kingdoms demand and exert; nor can she invite the people of her remote dependencies to send representatives to the imperial parliament in proportion to the population they contain: for there may (and probably will) come a time, when the collective population of the Canadas, New Brunswick, Nova Scotia, &c., will exceed that of insular Britain; and thus, metropolitan supremacy passing out of her hands, the United Kingdom will become a dependency of a *greater* Britain, and derive thence its final destinies. This necessary consequence shows the force of the obstacles which colonial rule has to encounter as it becomes decrepit, and population arise under its sway. Separation of the parties at last appears to be inevitable, however adverse one or other, or both, at first, may be to its taking place. All that polity can do in the case, is to postpone the consummation as long as possible, and make the disjunction with the least detriment to both when the time for it arrives. But foresight, almost always, is wanting to the protecting party, when the protected become strong enough, as well as inclined, to go their own ways. Meanwhile, as fear restrains the compression of the governing, so does hesitation signalise the resistance of a majority of the governed; while a younger or more ardent minority among the latter, is ever chafing at the constraint its bent is put under.

Nations owning colonies are often blind to the real causes of their revolts. For Britain to assure for herself the continued possession of her North American colonies, says Alison, she ought, above all things, to win the attachment of their inhabitants, and make sure of their support. "Although we must deplore the effects of the culpable acts and criminal ambition of those revolutionists of Canada, who alienated from us the affections of a simple and industrious people, formerly so loyal and so devoted, the evil is not irremediable: if it be dealt with in a right spirit, there may grow out of temporary evil, abiding good. Those events, attracting attention among ourselves, have become means for disclosing to public view many abuses, which, but for them, would have remained in the shade; thus have they shown us the necessity there was for reforming them." But abuse of power is the canker-worm at the root of *all* colonial government. Those who, in the mother country, seem to be most ardent for reform at home, are the very men who are the least reserved opponents of colonial reforms. The insurrections which took place in the two Canadas in 1837, were but the natural consequence of the bad administration of those provinces; and of the obstinacy of the depositaries of power, who ever turned a deaf ear to the earnest remonstrances of the people's representatives, during a long series of years. Prejudice is so difficult to remove, that the historian cited above, while proposing his remedy for the evils of those times, virtually justifies the movers in the Upper Canadian revolts he denounces; but he merely meant to do so out of respect to malcontents of British birth or descent: whereas, in regard to the Lower Canadian outbreak, he takes the freedom to stigmatize its leaders and promoters as rebels outright. The discrimination he makes, in the case, is simply this: the Upper Canadians were misled into resistance by instigators of too active tempers and over energetic minds, (signs these of a superiority of race!) while the unreasonably rebellious conduct laid to the charge of the Lower Canadians he ascribes to selfish ambition in their leaders, and ignorance in themselves: in brief, what is denounced as a crime in a Gallo-Canadian shall pass for public virtue in a Brito-Canadian.

Document D–6

THE POETRY AND PROSE OF NEOCOLONIALISM IN FRENCH CANADA, I

(O. Crémazie, "Le Canada [1859]," cited in L'Abbé Nantel [ed.], *Les Fleurs de la Poésie Canadienne* [Montreal, 1887], pp. 71–72 [translation].)

Greetings, O Heaven of my fatherland!
Greetings, O noble St. Lawrence!
In my softened soul your name
Flows as an intoxicating perfume.
O Canada, you son of France,
Who covered you with her blessings
You our love, our hope,
Who will ever forget you?

On the shores of the new world
Like the shining beacons
Which guide on the deep sea
The bold navigator,
You radiate the light
Of your glorious memories
And tell to the world
The great deeds of our forbears.

In your verdant fields,
Where true happiness lies
The Canadian has for companions
The most blessed virtues of the heart.

Faithful to the worship of their fathers,
From their example he follows the law,
And fleeing foreign ways
He maintains his language and his faith.

Ah! if only this sacred union
Which made our ancestors so great,
Would never suffer
By the crimes of your children.
And if ever for your defence
The great day of combat should sound,
They as their ancestors would know how to seize
The sword of the conquering soldier.

Happy is he who devotes his life
To the glory of serving you,
Under your beautiful skies, O my fatherland!
To be able to say with his dying breath
O Canada! son of France,
You who cover me with blessings
You, my love, my hope,
Who will ever be able to forget you?

Document D–7

THE POETRY AND PROSE OF NEOCOLONIALISM IN FRENCH CANADA, II

(J. G. Barthe, *Le Canada Reconquis par la France* [Paris, 1885], pp. 291–93 [translation].)

Lower Canada being a French country, and the free navigation of the St. Lawrence having been granted to all the ships of the world, it seems to me that France cannot close her eyes to the evidence of her dearest interest, not to mention the profit which she could draw from a country attached to her by the memory of so many objects. Our valleys, newly opened to agricultural exploitation, invite the children of French Canada to unite in common labour with their brethren overseas to clear this promised land: the Saguenay, for example, destined to out-shine the St. Lawrence by the brilliance of its future prosperity and the extent of its fertile zone. Nowhere does Algeria offer more resources of all kinds than this northern region, where, by a singular combination of meteorological laws, variations in atmosphere and sudden, sharp transitions of climate are felt less than at points further south in the lower valley of the St. Lawrence.

But if your emigrants are looking for a more advanced area or one already developed, they have only to follow the course of the great river, crossing the inhabited plain which it irrigates and fertilizes, or to follow its tributaries which traverse the interior towns and limitless farms. This is all they must do to set foot in settled areas which will remind them of those areas they have left. All those who settled and established the future of their families in Quebec or Montreal have not left these cities if they brought with them those attributes of industry and morality which are everywhere the basis of individual prosperity.

The French who live in Montreal are so convinced of the happy resource which their adopted country offers to their compatriots, that they have in one of their assemblies seriously considered the convenience for France, more opportune now than ever, of establishing a consul in their midst. Will their wish be heard? I flatter myself that it will because of a common interest; and if my feeble voice can be of some weight in the balance, it will not hesitate to support those interested in this project.

The Anglo-French alliance is well suited, it seems to me, to lead to this result and contribute to its permanency. Before the need to effect the common good and promote universal prosperity, the prejudices of race and the distinctions of origin are fading more quickly than ever between the English and French of America, just as between the English and French of Europe. It seems natural to me that the cordial understanding between Albion and France may extend further, and that the harmony of their relations may be fused and enlarged for the honour of their flags and the tranquil co-existence of their races on the other continent.

PROBLEM 12

D'Arcy McGee: A Father of Confederation

ROBIN B. BURNS
Sir George William University

In many ways, the Fathers of Confederation intended the federal union of British North America to be a solution to the major problems which faced Canadians in the middle of the 19th century. The Act of Union had terminated in deadlock and crisis; Confederation would concede representation by population to Canada West, while securing a degree of provincial autonomy for French-Canadian and Maritime particularism. By the 1860's, most of the arable land had been taken up, and the new generation of farmers was beginning to leave for the western United States. Confederation would bring a new Canadian west. Canadian merchants had lost their special position in the British market at the end of the 1840's, and were soon to lose a similar position in the American market with the end of the Reciprocity Treaty. The people in the Maritime provinces and the new pioneers out west might become a market which would be a substitute for those losses. A more united British North America might also mean a greater immunity from an American threat, and allow the withdrawal of British troops.

Confederation was supposed to be something more than a complicated solution to a complexity of problems. When the Governor-General, Lord Monk, introduced the Quebec Resolutions to the Canadian Legislature, he said, ". . . the general position of British North America induced the conviction that the circumstances of the times afforded the opportunity not merely for the settlement of a question of Provincial politics, but also for the simultaneous creation of a new nationality." Confederation was also designed to inaugurate a new nation.

When historians have looked back at the 1860's, they note that the enthusiasm for a new nation was perhaps the most popular force encouraging British-American union. They also conclude that no one really knew what the creation of a new nationality involved. This seems to be borne out when one examines the debates in the Canadian Legislature on the subject of Confederation. There were opponents of the scheme who looked at the idea of a Canadian nation, and reasoned that to be a nation, Canada would have to be sovereign. Sovereignty, in its turn, would mean separation from the Empire and eventual annexation to the United States. Not at all, assured the defenders of the Resolutions, Canada was to be a nation, and not a colony; but it was to continue to be a part of the Empire. There were some French Canadians who looked at the idea and concluded that a new nationality would mean that all Canadians would have to submerge themselves into a common Canadianism. French Canada would be assimilated. Once again the Fathers assured those who were suspicious that the Canadian nation was to be peculiar. It was going to be a multi-national nationality, providing for the survival of distinct cultural groups. Moreover the realization of a new nationality was far into the future and was not an immediate problem. The discussion of a new nationality was characterized by a vague assertion of platitudes. And judging from the controversies in Canada's history since Confederation, many of the questions raised in 1865 have become perennial Canadian questions—a search for a Canadian identity.

One of the most enthusiastic Canadian nationalists in the 1860's was the M.P.P. from Montreal West, D'Arcy McGee. McGee had been the first to use the phrase "new nationality," and he had been an early advocate of the federal union of British North America. Historians of Confederation have called him "the prophet of the new nationality." There are several other aspects to McGee which make his ideas worth some attention. First, there was his unusual background. Most of the Fathers of Confederation had spent their adult years in Canada. McGee had been born and raised in Ireland. He emigrated to the United States as a teen-ager, and became the editor of a Boston newspaper. At 20 years of age, he returned to Ireland and participated in the Irish nationalist movement known as Young Ireland. When the rebellion against British rule failed in 1848, he had to flee back to the United States. He spent another 10 years there, before coming to Canada in 1857. His experiences in Europe and in the United States gave him a unique point of view with which to approach the Canadian situation. Moreover, McGee was an English-speaking Catholic at a time when language and religion combined to make them a principal source of English-French difficulties. Thus, he occupied a kind of middle position between the two groups who are identified with the bicultural character of the Canadian experience. A close examination of some of McGee's ideas will give one a different approach to the Confederation years. The study will yield a series of changing thoughts on some of Canada's perennial questions. Are Canadians really different from their North American neighbors to the South? Does Canada's membership in the Empire or Commonwealth compromise her nationality? What is the relationship between the Canadian nation and different minority groups? Are there two nations in Canada? Hopefully the following selections will also raise other questions.

For those who wish to pursue the topic, P. B. Waite's, *The Life and Times of Confederation* (1962) is the most satisfactory study. It combines a good survey of the Confederation years, with an excellent analysis of the general opinion of leading spokesmen in the different regions. W. L. Morton's *The Critical Years* (1964), examines the various regions associated with Confederation over a longer period of time; and D. G. Creighton's *The Road to Confederation* (1964) focuses on the Conferences and devotes more attention to personalities.

The Canadian Centennial Commission and the Canadian Historical Association have published a series of historical booklets which serve as a good introduction to the subject. R. Cook has edited an excellent collection of interpretive articles in *Confederation* (1967). For those who would like to take the biographical approach, almost all the leading Fathers of Confederation have good biographies. The best are D. G. Creighton's *John A. Macdonald* (1956) and J. M. S. Careless's *Brown of the Globe* (1959). There have been several biographies of D'Arcy McGee. Isabel Skelton's *The Life of Thomas D'Arcy McGee* and Alexander Brady's *Thomas D'Arcy McGee* are good biographies. Robin Burns has looked at other features of McGee's career and ideas in "D'Arcy McGee and the Economic Aspects of New Nationality," *Canadian Historical Association Annual Report* (1967); "D'Arcy McGee and Fenianism, A Study of the Interaction between Irish Nationalism and the American Environment," *University Review* (Dublin, 1967); and "French Canada and the New Nationality: D'Arcy McGee's View," *Revue du Centre d'Etude du Quebec* (1967).

If one would like to examine the debates on Confederation for himself, the Queens Printer has reprinted *The Confederation Debates*. P. B. Waite has edited a more abbreviated version of the *Debates* (1963) with a good introduction.

There have not been many studies on the subject of Canadian nationalism. F. H. Underhill has many insights on the subject in *The Image of Confederation* (1964) and *In Search of Canadian Liberalism* (1960). One might want to look at W. L. Morton's *The Canadian Identity* (1961). There is also a good collection of essays edited by P. Russell entitled *Nationalism in Canada* (1966).

A. McGee and Irish Nationalism

When McGee returned to Ireland in 1845, he began to participate in an Irish nationalist movement. The movement grew out of Daniel O'Connell's campaign to repeal the Act of Union between England and Ireland. O'Connell's efforts to secure a domestic legislature for Ireland corresponded to the Canadian reformers trying to obtain a government responsible to the Canadian legislature. In fact, both groups referred to each other's cause in their respective campaigns. O'Connell's agitation, and popular nationalism in Europe, inspired a group of young men who worked through popular literature to try and instill a sense of nationalism among the Irish. They emphasized a distinct Irish history that was being threatened by English assimilation. They also stressed the requirement for Irish Protestants and Catholics to subordinate their religious differences to an Irish nationality.

Under British pressure, O'Connell suspended his agitation and sought to work for better government through an alliance with the Whig government at Westminster. The young men criticized O'Connell for compromising the cause. When they refused to accept O'Connell's principle of peaceful agitation and to disavow the use of force, they left his organization and founded the Irish Confederation.

D'Arcy McGee was one of those young men. At 20 years of age, he acted as the Secretary to the Confederation and was responsible for organizing Rifle Clubs throughout the country. He helped to edit *The Nation*, the principal newspaper in the nationalist movement. When revolution broke out in France in February 1848, he participated in the preparations to resist British rule. By July the British government suspended habeas corpus and passed a Coercion Bill authorizing the seizure of arms. As the resistance collapsed, McGee escaped to the United States. Upon his arrival in Philadelphia, he published a public letter. If one were to attach a political label to McGee in 1848, what would one call him? Why?

Document A—1

THE REBELLION IN IRELAND

(Boston Pilot, October 21, 1848.)

In February last, the Irish parties who sought a change of Government, were two—the "Moral force Repealers," and Young Ireland. These parties originated in July, 1846, when Young Ireland seceded from the Repeal Association on the object of the lawfullness of shedding blood to achieve political rights. Before that event, Daniel O'Connell was as absolutely the ruler of Ireland, as Nicholas Romanov is of Russia. The old honoured him for his cautious tactics, the young because England feared and hated him; many Protestants sincerely cooperated with him for his liberality, the Catholics revered him as a man who rebuilt their altars, and loosed the tongues and arms of their priesthood. Two thousand Catholic clergymen quartered in every hamlet and at every cross-road were his captains and his magistracy. His word was the only law in the land, and children were baptized with his name, as with the name of a Saint.

This man, so powerful and so well beloved taught in his last days the doctrine that no amount of liberty was worth the spilling of one drop of human blood and the great majority of the clergymen and the people adopted it implicitly. But there was an undergrowth of a new generation in Ireland, who desired self-government, and who thought it a cause worth fighting

for—who indeed wished to fight for it, provided it could not otherwise be had. O'Connell introduced, in July 1846, his test of membership in the Repeal Association, known as the "peace resolutions,"— and young Ireland, believing that such a course would be fatal to success against such an enemy seceded in January, '47, they formed the "Irish Confederation" out of which the heat of Continental events proved this late attempt at insurrection.

In 1847, Young Ireland was busy gaining over the inhabitants of the towns from "moral force" and with the examples of Pious the Ninth and the revolutions of last Spring, we succeeded. At any time during the last six months the towns people of Ireland were, in terms, committed to attempt a forceable expulsion of the British power.

. . . .

But the Confederate principles did not pervade the rural populations up to the last hour. For this there are many causes. The famine of '46 and '47 had left a lassitude after it like that which follows fever. The Peasantry could not retain the heat that Mitchel and Meagher would infuse into them. They felt the electricity as—shock—and it passed through them.

The government saw—it was a potent fact—that we had converted and organized the towns, but had not reached the heart of the country. They knew that the club system, formidable where population was grouped, was unsuited to the districts. They, therefore, opposed the Insurrection with two weapons, they concentrated their forces on the towns, and used every art to prevent the junction of the Catholic clergy with the Revolutionary leaders.

. . . .

Anyone who knows Ireland, socially, will know how indispensable the Priesthood are to discipline and movement in the rural parts. In many parishes the priest is the only educated man; in nearly all he is the only one who feels and toils for the people. Ireland has no middle class, and it would be well for her if she had no gentry. But the priesthood is everywhere and revered everywhere. And this reverence had been the reward of unchanging devotion. Through the entire seventeenth century, the Priests and People fought side by side. Bishops commanded armies, and Friars conducted sieges. In the penal eighteenth century, the flock upon the mountains stood sentinel for the shepherds, and many a bloody corpse bolted the paths by which they escaped. I am satisfied that if the Church had been involved, even ever so little in 1848, we would have beaten the English. But the Bishops and dignitaries opposed the movement, or what had just the same effect, prophecied its failure, and argued its ruin. The secondary Clergy and the Curates who were more favourable to it, in submission to their order, were silent.

. . . .

The conclusion I draw, from all I know of this attempt, is this—that the clergy of the people made a grave political mistake —and that that mistake was fatal to the insurrection in its incipient stages. It would be unfair and false to say that they cannot allege strong grounds for their course; but I am, for one, fully convinced, that if they had headed the peasantry, we would have renewed the miracle of St. Patrick. I know there would be slaughter,

but Fever and Famine, now under the protection of the British flag in Ireland, will destroy more lives and with worse weapons, than the 60,000 armed men could have killed. And then compare the two results!

I left Ireland at the beginning of September, despairing of any immediate National movement. But I do not, and never shall despair of the country. The people are not to blame, that there has not been any revolution. Next time they must trust in local leaders, like the Rapparees and Catalonian chiefs, fierce men and blunt, without too many ties binding them to the Peace. They must choose, too, the favourable concurrence of a foreign war, an event which is likely to precede the settlement of the newly awakened races of the Continent. The extermination of the Irish people is not to be apprehended: they cling to the soil like grass, and while they cling, they hate England. The numerous emigrations of them make scarcely any sensible diminuation of the parent stock. Their two strongest political feelings, are hatred to England and a sanguine hope in Ireland.

. . . .

Freedom's battle once begun,
Bequeaths from bleeding sire to son,
Though battled oft' is ever won.

That it will be won in Ireland, and sooner than many, even among her friends, dare hope, I believe. The vice of loyalty is gone at the root, and it but needs a little more of Time's teaching to make a Democratic Revolution, which will wait for no leadership to strike to make Ireland as free as the freest—even as free as this parent land of Liberty itself.

Requesting your indulgence for this too long letter, I remain my dear Sir,

Yours very truly,

Thomas D'Arcy McGee

(*A traitor to the British Government*)

B. The American Experience

When McGee first emigrated to the United States, there was a growing popular reaction against the Irish immigrants among native Protestant Americans. Native Americans blamed the immigrants for current social ills, and condemned them for their ignorance, intemperance, and living conditions. Many Americans believed that the Catholic faith would undermine democratic institutions. The movement also drew popular support from native workers who feared the competition from cheap immigrant labour. The form of reaction ranged from political action to restrict immigrant rights, to the sacking of Catholic religious institutions.

Initially, McGee was much more preoccupied with the situation in Ireland than with conditions in the United States. He began to publish his own newspaper, the New York *Nation*, in which he continued to campaign for Irish revolution and against the Catholic clergy. McGee, in turn, was denounced by the Archbishop of New York, who spoke out against his newspaper. The journal soon failed. At first he thought of returning to Ireland, but he learned that the order for his arrest was still in effect. He moved to Boston and began another newspaper, the *American Celt*. As the name suggested, McGee became more concerned with the situation of the Irish immigrant in the United States.

How could this American situation affect McGee's attitude toward his assumptions of 1848?

Document B–1

THE IRISH IMMIGRANT

(T. D. McGee, *A History of the Irish Settlers in North America* [Boston, 1855], p. 235.)

Suddenly thrust out of the bottom of an ancient society, by political pressure, Irish men and women awake, and find themselves in America. The cry of "land" calls them all on deck. Land! what land is this? Its parti-colored forest trees, its shining new houses, its steaming harbors, its busy trading-people, with pale, care-knit brows, and lips compressed like oyster-shells,—how strange, how wonderful is all this to the man who whistled to his wooden plough along an Irish field, or the girl accustomed to gather her cows behind the hawthorn, and fill the evening air with "*Ma colleen d'has cruitha n'ma bho!*" while she filled her pail with milk!

The wonder wears away, and knowledge comes painfully, and in bits, through experience. It is a hard school, this school of emigrant experience. It may be likened to a crowded corridor, in which there is no turning back. From the front to the back door, from manhood to death, there is no pause, no return. The vanishing backs of our predecessors before us, the eager faces of our contemporaries round us, are all we see, or can see. Some in this crowd may have their pockets picked, or their ribs broken, or their corns trampled; but on they must go, with ribs broken or whole, pockets full or empty. The rich and poor, the weak and strong, the native and the stranger, are all thrown mercilessly upon themselves, in the common school of American experience.

But for the inexperienced emigrant large allowance should be made by all the rest. He starts with no stock of native traditions. He was not reared in the neighborhood. His knowledge, such as it is, being suited only to a totally different latitude, is rather a burden than a benefit to him. An East Indian suddenly left on a cape of Labrador would not pass more visibly from one condition of being to another, than the Irish immigrant who finds himself new landed in America.

Document B–2

AMERICAN CONDITIONS

(T. D. McGee, *The Irish Position in British and Republican North America* [Montreal, 1866], pp. 7–11.)

Causes, some natural and justifiable enough—such as ready employment for their labor on landing,—detained them at the great seaports, or drew them to the factory and railway centres. Never in the world's history, were a purely agricultural population so suddenly and unpreparedly converted into mere town laborers. They did not, indeed, exchange agriculture for artificial pursuits, for you cannot well call mere loading and unloading ships, or porterage, or digging drains, or domestic service, works of art. But the tens of thousands of this class who were peasants in Ireland in the Spring, and town laborers in America the same Summer, threw up to the surface, by the natural law of their numbers, a small fry of demagogues and overseers [or "bosses"] whose interest it never was that they should look to dock and suburb labor only as a temporary condition, but to the acquisition and ownership of land as their ultimate object. Hence this strangely contradictory result, that a people who hungered and thirsted for land in Ireland, who struggled for conacre and cabin even to the shedding of blood, that this same people, when they reached a new world, in which a day's wages saved would purchase an acre of wild land in fee, wilfully concurred, under the lead of bad advisers, to sink into the condition of a miserable town tenantry, to whose squalor even European seaports can hardly present a parallel.

. . . .

. . . the tenement house population of the Fourth and Sixth Wards of that city [New York], chiefly inhabited by our broken down poor people, are thus described. The *Tribune* says:

The places are chiefly in cellars, with naked stone or brick walls, damp and decayed floors, without beds or bedding fit for human beings. They are mainly un-ventilated or lighted, except through the entrance door. In condition they are filthy and disgusting beyond description, overflowing with vermin and infested by rats.

Into these hideous places are packed nightly an average of ten persons to each place, or six hundred in the aggregate.

In violation of the laws of decency and morality, men, women and children, white and black, with no regard to the family relation, sleep promiscuously together, exhibiting less of the impulses of decency than the brute creation.

From the character of these apartments, their owners and occupants, and the manner of their use, cleanliness is impossible, and hideous diseases of various classes and types are engendered and propagated.

While thus occupied they cannot be made decent or healthy, and those who frequent them are beyond the reach of reform, except through the strong arm of the law.

Horrible details are then given of these general statements, and as showing the relation which your unhappy countrymen and women who have fallen into such hopeless servitude to the devil and his agents in the American seaports, bear to the proprietary class—the landlord class—in such cities as New York, I quote the *Tribune's* next statement, founded on the same Annual Report, which is in these words:

It will be noticed, too, that many of these hideous dens are owned by "respectable citizens," officers in banks and the like, and are let out probably by agents—these citizens never taking the trouble to look at their property, and utterly regardless whether their tenants are poisoned or debauched, or in what way their houses affect the health and morals of the city. Surely, if any one sin needs preaching against by the clergy, it is this cruel neglect *by rich men of their tenantry, and their indifference to the condition of their dependents.*

.   .   .   .

There *is* an Ireland enslaved; there *is* a battle for Ireland to be fought in the New World; there *is* a glorious, redeeming work to be done for her here; it is to be fought and wrought in the Fourth and Sixth Wards of New York, and in every large city south of the line, where our laboring population have suddenly been centralized, with all their old peasant habits stripped rudely off, and no new habits of discipline and self-government, as yet, substituted in their stead.

C. A Canadian Contrast

Besides answering nativist charges, McGee also hoped to influence a change among the Irish immigrants. To McGee, the Irish had exchanged one kind of misery in Ireland for another in the United States. At first he worked for minor changes. He participated in the first organization of night schools, and he tried to establish social clubs to encourage self-help. Before long, he came to the conclusion that a more basic change would have to be effected. He now began to urge the immigrants to leave the slums in the East and to return to the land in the American West.

McGee carried his pleas for immigrant reform and his criticism of American society through the editorials of his newspaper, and on his many lecture tours. On several of these tours he visited the Province of Canada. Canada in general, and the Canadian Irish in particular, seemed to conform more to his ideas than those with whom he had laboured. After 10 years of trying to influence opinion in the United States, he accepted an invitation from the Irish in Canada, and moved to Montreal in 1857. What was there about Canada which McGee preferred to the United States? Was McGee's analysis of Canadian and American society accurate? Were the reasons he gave for the differences valid? What political label would one attach to McGee now? Why?

Document C-1

THE IRISH IN CANADA

(T. D. McGee, *The Irish in Republican and British North America* [Montreal, 1866], pp. 11–15.)

Here, fortunately for themselves and for society at large, this perverted peasantry have not been concentrated so suddenly, or in such dense masses as in New York, Boston, and Philadelphia.

Here, too, the leaders [for our race, like all others, will have leaders] have generally been gentlemen. In every British Province the foremost Irishmen have been among the first people in the Judiciary, in politics, in commerce and in society. This high standing has kept up the standard of the class, while, happily for us Catholics, the Church in these Provinces has always been sufficiently up with the people to preserve its legitimate control of their faith and morals. . . . I have great faith, for my part, in our steadily doing our duty by our own government, by our fellow-subjects, and by one another as Irishmen. I feel that we, at all events, have achieved a home and have a position to guard; I feel that we are in the right path; if we can go on steadily in that path, good must come of it, for us and for all.

·   ·   ·   ·   ·   ·   ·   ·   ·   ·   ·

Our rural numbers bear an almost inverse ratio to the urban, to what the same classes do to each other in the United States. I speak now of Canada. If not quite three-fourths, certainly the large majority of our emigrants in this Province now, live by land, and own land. There are at least thirty counties in Canada where the Irish Catholic vote ranges from a fifth to a third of the whole constituency, and in most of these, if the Irish Protestant and Catholic were taken altogether, they would form a clear majority of the whole.

·   ·   ·   ·   ·   ·   ·   ·   ·   ·   ·

. . . the great healthful mass of the Irish farmers of Canada—men breathing pure air and living pure lives—are untouched by the infection, thanks to their own sound sense, to the inevitable conservatism which springs from property,

and thanks too, whenever it is required, to the timely warnings of their loyal clergy!

The ignorance as to the United States in Ireland is only equalled by the ignorance as to Canada in the United States. There again the great obstacle to the reception of truth lies in preconceived opinions. The demagogical Irish leaders also, many of whom are glad to send their own sons and daughters to be educated in our higher moral atmosphere, have not the moral courage, or rather the common honesty, to tell the truth publicly as to this country. They know, right well they know, from personal observation, that the Irish *status* here is vastly higher than ever it was with them. But they find it more profitable to trade upon impulsive ignorance than to impart unpalatable instruction. They prefer to let their poor deluded followers believe of Canada what they have all along taught them, that neither freedom, nor justice, nor good government can exist under the British flag. Right well they know *we* have no State Church, no irresponsible territorial aristocracy, no proselytizing schools or colleges; but they suffer their dupes to believe that Canada endures all the ills of which Ireland complains. Blinded by such falsehoods they would dash their reckless, homeless masses against this peaceful Province, which has done them no wrong, but where alone, in North America, their race has always had the fullest recognition.

Document C–2

THE SUPERIORITY OF CONSTITUTIONAL MONARCHY

(T. D. McGee, "A Plea for British American Nationality," *British American Magazine*, Vol. I [1863], pp. 342–43.)

The republic of Washington was, in truth, a work of virtue and genius well calculated to excite the hopes and admiration of mankind. It was not the creation of an empirical or presumptuous

spirit. All the first fathers would gladly have retained their English connexion, if Lord North and George III. had permitted them. Slowly and unwillingly, and with many misgivings, they sundered the last ties that bound them to the parent state. With awe-struck solemnity they laid the foundations of their new order, among the only materials they had left—the colonial democracy, with a feeble and almost unfelt infusion of the remains of the old colonial aristocracy. The crown and the connexion were gone; but the founders of the new system invoked the blessings of religion, and the bright examples of the remotest ages, to consecrate and dignify their work. Still, the best and most thoughtful of those men—Hamilton, Madison, Jay, Jefferson himself, Adams, and Washington, above all,—though with very various degrees of confidence in the result, never looked upon their new State as other than "a great experiment." For fourteen years that experiment was tried as a loose league; for seventy years it has been tried as a close-knit confederacy: it is in no spirit of presumption, from no irreverent disregard of those great men and their motives, that, reasoning after the fact, we conclude their experiment to have failed, and recommend the avoidance of a similar error to our own colonial statesmen. It failed in that which the banished Kent saw and desired to serve in the face of the discrowned king— *authority*. It failed in the authority of the president over his cabinet; in the authority of the supreme court over the country; in the authority of the Congress over the States; in the authority of the commander-in-chief over the forces, naval and military, supposed to be under his orders.

The modern age seems more and more to want, and the new spirit of the new world to exact, a wider degree of individual liberty and equality than is consistent wtih stability or longevity in the State, unless the principle of authority shall be as strongly fortified in the constitution as the love of liberty is among the people. Not that authority and liberty are at all incompatible; not that, rightly considered, they are even separable; but that liberty is active, exigent, perennial, and self-asserting; while authority, in our times, must be early introduced into the system of the State, widely known and felt over the land, carefully protected in its prerogatives, and recommended by word and example to the veneration of all the people. With us, liberty has nothing to fear except from the unworthiness of the people's own representatives; while should authority, endangered and dishonoured, perish out of our State system, it would soon be found, as it was found of old and of late, that the rent, large enough to permit the removal of that palladium, is also large enough to permit the triumphal entry of a dictator.

Hitherto, the whole experience of mankind has known but one system of government which combines, in fair and harmonious proportions, authority with liberty, and that is, the limited monarchy, of which England furnishes the oldest and Italy the latest model. For this desired form of government—the fond reflected image of a free people—Prussia is now contending with a despotic prince; Poland is in arms; Hungary in agitation; and the first minds in France and Spain in renewed expectancy. Constitutional monarchy has its defects, for it is human; its tendencies to abuse, for it is the favourite theatre of party; its assailable point, in hereditary succession; its anxieties, in the nice preservation of the domestic balance of powers; yet whether we compare its great names, and its great capacity for endurance, with the names and the permanency, of elective governments like Venice, Holland, Poland, or the United States, on the one hand; or of despotic powers like Russia, Turkey, and Morocco, on the other,—we shall find no reason to doubt that both the rulers and the ruled have enjoyed much more security than those who existed under a despotism,— with much more freedom than those who lived under any elective form of state sovereignty.

D. A Canadian Nationalist

McGee began a third newspaper in Montreal, called the *New Era*. While once again it was designed to serve the interests of the Irish immigrant, its editorials were also filled with a great variety of projects for the creation of a Canadian nationality. The newspaper was published until 1858, when McGee found the duties as a Member of the Provincial Parliament too time-consuming. What was happening in Canada in 1857 and 1858 to cause such reflections? Who else was proposing the kind of ideas that McGee was putting forward in the *New Era*?

Document D–1

A UNION OF THE PROVINCES

(The *New Era*, August 4, 1857.)

At fitful intervals here and in England, the political union of the provinces is discussed. Just at present Judge Haliburton's Glasgow address, an article in *Blackwood's Magazine* for July, and the uncertainty of the Seat of Government, have given an unusual degree of interest to the subject.—Not to beat around the bush, the whole discussion seems to us to resolve itself into one inquiry,—have the several Provinces any great interest, which they can protect and control more advantageously by being politically united?

No sensible man can deny that there are interests which such a union would vastly provide. For example, the *fisheries* ought to be the richest resource of these Provinces. The Yankees have their cotton-carrying trade, their manufactories, and their *West*; to the Gulf Provinces united, the riches of the ocean ought to be a sacred inheritance. Their fishing-fleet ought to outnumber all others combined; it ought to react on our ship-building interest, and lay the foundations of a great reciprocal commerce. The Parliament of the United Provinces would be wholly unworthy of its great trust, or wholly incompetent to discharge it, if it could not and would not so provide, as to draw into the net of this country the wealth with which the northern Atlantic annually swarms.

Again, as to *internal public works*, there can be no second opinion, that united legislative superintendence would greatly promote them. Our railroads can never be considered complete until they abut on the Atlantic. This obvious necessity drove the Grand Trunk Company to lease the Atlantic and St. Lawrence line, because it had an ocean harbor for its terminus. Why should not the harbors of St. John and Halifax have the preference of Canadian trade and travels, if they can compete with Portland? We know all that is usually urged about allowing trade to choose its own channels; but we can never believe that the laws of trade, rightly understood, can conflict with the higher laws of self-preservation. The future political being of Canada is bound up most intimately with that of the maritime provinces. None of us can afford to let the United States encroach a league upon that coast. The Grand Meenan [*sic*], rightly considered, is as vital to Canada as the Island of Montreal itself. For the new Nation that does not advance, but gives way on the first trial, on any of its outposts, has no surety for the citadel itself. Considerations of trade, suggested by the great truths of political science, all recommend the Union of the Provinces, for the promotion of a uniform system of internal communication.—No interest would be better served by such Union than our *postal* arrangements. At present one is much more certain of his letters from San Francisco than from St. John. Our general post office, with one capable Postmaster General, controlling and overseeing a uniform system, would in three years draw the Provinces closer together in feeling, than they ever can become under their present isolated conditions.

We purposely refrain from the consideration of the advantage to be derived from a uniform currency, from one widespread banking and credit system, from the establishment of courts of last resort for all the Provinces. Each of the innovations would require a treatise, but every one of them would bring its special benefits in its train.

Not last nor least is the consideration of the enlarged sphere which would be afforded the public view of the several colonies,—the generous emulation,—the higher responsibilities,—the deeper studies,—the nobler undertaking which would inevitably follow. Great common interests would beget a love of the common weal; in the largeness of the receiver the little tributaries of faction would be lost. Happily for our hopes for these countries, they rest upon a geographical basis as unalterable as the globe. Mutual interests, mutual selfishness, may do much: political and military reasons have their weight but the strongest bond of their future amity is the river and Gulf of St. Lawrence. In its free navigation, the youngest settlement on Lake Huron has an interest as direct as the oldest as Gaspe. A shallow in Lake St. Peters, or a rock below Quebec, necessarily impedes the population of the back country. The only sole Strait between the Lakes and the Atlantic, it is equally valuable to the fisherman of the farthest seaward Cape, as to the lumberers of the remotest interior forest.

Document D—2

FRENCH CANADIAN SURVIVAL

(The *New Era*, October 22, 1857.)

Whether that union shall involve separation from the British Crown or not, depends very much on the crown itself. As an inhabitant of Canada,—seeing that Canada has all reasonable power over her own affairs,—I cherish no unfriendly sentiment towards the connection. If I cannot be enthusiastic in its praise, I can cheerfully give credit for the magnaminous concessions of the Home Government. The hostility I inherited towards it, on my natal soil, has no business here. In discussing a Canadian question, I first of all ask myself what is best for Canada, and I honestly try to carry out the conclusions formed in that spirit. One of these conclusions is in favour of a Federal Union; but this innovation should include the reservation of local rights as well as the equality of territorial representation in the upper house of Parliament. To this last requirement I see but one practical difficulty, a foregone determination on the part of the British portion of the West, socially to subjugate and incorporate the French-Canadians of the east. Supposing such an arrangement as I have subscribed, I humbly conceive the autonomy of Lower Canada ought to be cheerfully conceded by the English-speaking Provinces. . . . Our river system dictates our union, railroads and canals will strengthen these natural bonds, but complete *one-ness* of political life must still be wanting to sea-beaten Newfoundland, and the wheat-bearing West. The commercial exchanges may supply a Federal basis, but they cannot create a London or a Paris on so vast a map as this. Each Province must retain its local Parliaments for local purposes, conceding to the Federal authority such powers only as are necessary for the general progress and safety—for the superintendence of commerce, the sanction of international acts, the constitution of the higher courts of justice, and for other common and supreme concerns. In short, these Provinces, if ever united, will necessarily copy the American system. Modify where you will, but still you must copy. That system was not born of Jefferson's brain, was not fed to strengths by Franklin's providence; it existed in the *circumstances* of the Thirteen United Colonies south of the St. Lawrence and St. John, just as it exists at this moment in the circumstances of the six disunited colonies which will still acknowledge Queen Victoria's sovereignty.

. . . .

The descendants of the original occupants of the region over which we have cast our eyes, do not then claim too much, in my humble opinion, when they ask Lower Canada as an heir-loom. Their pride is radicated in the soil, and they are, as yet, the only race in Canada who can justly boast that patriotic past. They have a Canadian History, which we who speak English may well envy, or better still, try to imitate. Their ancestors held this soil as sovereigns two hundred years before Wolfe landed at Quebec. They reverence the intrepid Cartier, the devout Champlain, the lion-hearted Frontenac, and LaSalle, the Columbus of our inland

waters. To them *Canadian* is a sacred name, and so long as that is respected, their allegiance to our free institutions can never be disturbed. For two centuries they held the valley against the Puritans, the Hollanders, and the Iroquois; for the greater part of another century—until "responsible government" was conceded—they preserved their language, their religion, and their social life, against all attempts at Anglican assimiliation, and they will not, now that they are above a million, yield what they so well defended when scarcely fifty thousand strong. Though first planted by France, they owe their present position rather to themselves than to France. Their experience has been a peculiar one, and it has left its trace deep in all their characteristics. Neglected by France, mistrusted by England, they have been—for their own good, perhaps—remorselessly driven in upon themselves. —We must remember their experience before we pronounce them too exclusive. We must take them as we find them, and while professing to consider them fellow-citizens and fellow subjects, we must not dishonourably seek to undermine that which they hold dearer than life itself—their social life, their historical rank, their language, their religion, and their nationality.

Suppose a Federal compact, entered into between the Provinces, what a career would then commence for us all!

Document D–3

CANADIAN NATIONALITY AND THE QUESTION OF SOVEREIGNTY

(The *New Era*, January 19, 1858.)

What should be the main object—let us ask—of a patriotic representative entering Canadian public life for the first time, in the year of our Lord 1858? We answer, —overlooking all generalities,—the speedy and secure establishment of the Canadian Nationality. We are convinced the time has come to proclaim the Colony of age; to declare that its period of dependence ought now, of right, to cease. Does this imply any revolutionary revolt on the

part of the inhabitants of Canada? By no means. We think we can prove that the new *regime* may be proclaimed to the world, not only without the hostility, but with the approval and cooperation of the Imperial Government. Nor is the discussion of this subject premature or uncalled for at this moment; since admitting, as most men do, in one vague sense or other, a Canadian Nationality to be desirable. It is clearly the duty of statesmen to render practicable that which is so very generally desired.

The consideration of a new nationality raises at the outset high and difficult questions of sovereignty. A nationality cannot be established apart from local sovereignty. Nationality includes sovereignty, and lives or dies with it. We speak indeed of the nationality of Scotland, and the nationality of Ireland—because the remains of their ancient estates can still be traced in Ireland and Scotland. . . . Scotland, and even Ireland may assimilate and be assimilated with England, but the northern regions of America, divided by three thousand miles of sea, and entering on the world stage two thousand years after England's historic birth, cannot be so assimilated. Yet Haliburton's plan of binding the colonies by a federal connection to the Mother country sounds to us altogether impracticable. Dependence for longer terms may be practicable, independence may be practicable; but the middle course, in this dilemma, seems simply impossible.

How then are we to establish amongst us a Canadian sovereignty?—since that is "the previous question" to Canadian Nationality. Our neighbours, the Americans, solved this difficulty for themselves in 1776 by declaring "the people" of their thirteen united colonies the sole sovereigns of the same.—The temper of that time was favourable to revolutionary measures. Two men of genius, Thomas Jefferson and Thomas Paine, wrote the Democratic theory into vogue; two men of wisdom, Benjamin Franklin and George Washington, mitigated its excesses and encased it in a constitutional system.—But with all our admiration for that wise and gifted generation—the Fathers of the first American Republic—we do not advocate copying after their pattern. Their democratic federal republic is still a magnificent experiment, in its administrative and moral results, so far, whether in its oldest states or newest territories are not altogether to be envied. The colonial conditions of American society still continue—half the country is still to be settled—vast members of the population are still in motion from East to West—the limits of change have not been reached—the period of solidity is still remote—the experiment is incomplete, and the example is imperfect.

The Canadas and the Maritime Provinces which, it is to be hoped, are destined to enter into and give breadth and force to our future nationality, are now as far advanced in population as the original "thirteen United States" were, when they declared themselves sovereign. But our present relations to the parent state are very different from those against which our southern neighbours openly revolted. We have not one of the causes of complaint against Queen Victoria which they pleaded against George III in justification of their "Declaration of Independence." These colonies could not, except from a perverse and wanton ingratitude, set up such complaints as causes of separation. We possess a reduced model of the English Constitution, and we rather seek to develop than to destroy the system she has given us. Let us ask a plain question: —Are we content to copy the Constitution of England? Let us give a plain answer to this question:—For our personal part, we cannot but think the outline of the English Constitution, which has excited so much admiration from so many illustrious politicians of various nations, a model not to be likely rejected . . . at the same time, there enters into the field of our Canadian affairs, a host of uncouth, aboriginal circumstances not be repelled. They have to be accommodated, or nothing is established. A forest-covered country; a five months winter, an unhomogenous people, an over-shadowing neighbour, a distinct patron, a lengthy, exposed, half-quarter settled frontier, these are some of the circumstances which must mold our Canadian Constitution, whether we will it or not.

. . . If Canada—that is, British North America—is to attain to political sovereignty in our time, it is most natural she should look for the founder of her destiny in the Royal Family of England. Besides the Prince of Wales, there are two princes, children of Her Majesty—the one in his thirteenth, the other in his tenth year. It is not a very violent hypothesis to suppose that, within ten years from this date, either of these young princes might be found capable of fullfilling all Royal Offices in a new kingdom upon the St. Lawrence. . . . For our part, as a safe guard against assimilation, absorption and subjection to and by Americanism—and as a guarantee, focus, a standard of Canadian Nationality—we should gladly greet the settlement of such a permanent responsible ruler to these shores.

In entering into public life in this province, we do so with the strongest desire to preserve the individuality of the British North American colonies, until they ripen into a new Northern nationality. We shall judge of all proposed changes, not only by their own merits, but by their applicability to this end. Representation by population—the maintenance of the union of Upper and Lower Canada—a union under proper conditions with the Maritime Provinces and Bermuda—the annexation of Hudson Bay territory—the education, employment, and civil equality of all classes of people—in fact, every important topic that can arise ought to be viewed by the light, and decided by the requirements of Canadian Nationality.

E. Some New Questions

Every generation has new problems to solve, just as every new generation of historians has a different set of questions to ask the past. The years after Confederation would see a host of new problems. The Riel rebellions, the struggle between English and French Canada over the West, and the revival of imperialism would present new questions for Canadian nationalists. But the man who had been the first to use the phrase "new nationality" was assassinated in 1868.

The 1860's saw the advent of the American Civil War. Confrontation between England and the United States would threaten Canadian security. How was Canada to guard her frontiers against one of the largest land armies in the world? If she required the Empire as never before, how was this to affect her aspirations for nationality and sovereignty? Moreover, the Civil War seemed to demonstrate the futility of federations. Was it not absurd for the British-American provinces to begin negotiating a federal union after the American experience? Just as important, if Canadians rejected a loose federation, what was French Canada's fate to be? Without an autonomous province in a larger union, how was French Canada to survive?

Document E–1

THE IMPERIAL CONNECTION

(T. D. McGee, "A Further Plea for British American Nationality," *British American Magazine,* Vol. I [1863], pp. 561–62, 565–67.)

If ever a people of the New World were called to prove their capacity for self-examination and self-guidance, it is the British Americans of our day. All men who think at all, admit that we have entered into a veritable new era—that we are hereafter to dwell in a New America, to feel the pressure upon us of new forces, and the necessity of finding, if we do not intend to succumb to that pressure, adequate means of resistance. The sudden overcasting of our whole firmament has almost baffled the speed of thought. No natural storm ever spread over a fair prospect with more awful rapidity. Like the lightning that cometh out of the east, it appeared even unto the west; the evening went down calm and silent, but the morning woke dark and menacing. There, upon our visible horizon, the elements of aggression, are gathered together apparent to every observant eye; there they hang and blacken, ready to pour out their deluge upon our fields and cities, at the first shifting of the wind to the northward; in which hour the cry of the land will be for those prompt measures of defence, which can never be improvised, on the spur of momentary necessity.

.   .   .   .

All these changes which we advocate, internal and external, we may be told, tend to one result—separation from the Empire. We would be altogether misunderstood if any reader was left under that impression. That which we advocate we do most sincerely believe to be the only means to perpetuate a future connection between Great Britain and the transoceanic Provinces of the Empire, which connection is the interest of these Provinces; and of civilization itself we hold to be beyond all price desirable. What we advocate is to substitute for the present provincial connection of dissociated provinces, belonging *to* rather than being *of* the Empire, a new explicit relation, more suited to our actual wants, dangers, and dimensions, in other words, a modification of the Federal principle, reduced to the conditions of a compact equally intelligible to the central and the outlying administrations.

.   .   .   .

. . . That they should advance to sovereignty is as natural as that youth should grow to manhood; but there is no inevitable inference to be drawn, either from the nature of the case, or from past experience, that sovereignty should include separation. The two ideas, we know, are popularly identical. But a very limited acquaintance with the varieties of Imperial constitutions which have existed and do even still exist in the world, will show sovereignty in the members of an Empire, to be entirely compatible with the unity of the whole body. It is true that where the separate courts and legislatures approached each other too narrowly in space, or where the united or allied kingdom pushed to its last result its latent independence, or where the central power flagrantly disregarded the charters and customs of the associated state, very serious discontents and insurrections have followed. But the American and Australian Provinces of Great Britain, have both moral and national guarantees against these evil contingencies. In the spirit of the age, in their own internal resources, and above all, in their safe and salutary distance, from the great vortex of over-centralization, they have every desirable safeguard for their local independence.

Our greatest dangers lie in the opposite direction from centralization. Divided by vast oceans from the metropolis and arsenal of the Empire, divided from one another, even here in North America, by long tracts of roadless wilderness, we are vulnerable in our separated resources, and dis-united means. We cease to be secure, when we cease to be formidable, and we cease to be formidable because our enemies know that we are not now crown colonies, to be thought for, and fought for, by the crown, neither are we allied states, claiming protection under any well understood compact with our own sovereign. We have passed out of the stage of pupilage, and we have not emerged into the stage of partnership. We are retained in the Empire under a temporary engagement, terminable at a month's notice, because we have not shown ourselves truly desirous of understanding or acting upon the duties of another more intimate and more responsible relationship.

Document E–2

CANADIAN FEDERALISM

(T. D. McGee, *Speeches and Addresses Chiefly on the Subject of British American Union* [London: 1865], pp. 129–31, 133–35.)

Mr. Chairman,—You will probably like me to define that particular adaptation of the federal system which has lately found such high favour in the eyes of our leading colonial politicians. Well, this definition has been, I think, pretty accurately given in the published text—or what professes to be the text—of the results arrived at at Quebec. Don't be alarmed: I am not going to read you the whole seventy-two propositions: it will be quite sufficient for my purpose to give you, both by contrast and comparison, a broad, general view of what is and what is not included in our proposed constitutional charter. In the first place, I may say, gentlemen, to take the most familiar comparison, that we proceeded in almost an inverse ratio to the course taken in the United States at the formation of their constitution. We began by dutifully acknowledging the sovereignty of the Crown, as they did by boldly declaring their total separation from their former Sovereign. Unlike our neighbours, we have had no question of sovereignty to raise. We have been saved from all embarrassment on the subject of sovereignty, by simply recognising it as it already exists, in the Queen of Great Britain and Ireland. There, for us, the sovereign powers of peace and war, life and death, receiving and sending ambassadors, still reside so long as Her Majesty and her descendants retain the allegiance of the people of these Provinces. No doubt, some inconvenience may arise from the habitual personal absence of the Sovereign; but even this difficulty, now that the Atlantic is an eight-day ferry, is not insuperable. Next, we made the general, the supreme government, and the local derivative; while the Americans did just the reverse.

As to the merits and the consequences of this fundamental difference, I must observe this, that merely to differ from another, and a sometime-established system, is, of course, no merit in itself; but yet, if we are to be a distinct people from our republican neighbours, we can only be so and remain so by the assertion of distinct principles of government—a far better boundary than the River St. Lawrence, or the Ashburton line. But suppose their fundamental politics to be right, would we then, for the sake of distinction, erect a falsehood at the North, to enable us to contend against a truth at the South? Would we establish monarchy merely out of a spirit of antagonism? No! gentlemen, God forbid! I of course hold not only that our plan of government is politic in itself, but also that it is better than the American. I am prepared to maintain this at all times—against all comers: for if I had not myself faith in our work, I should scorn to inculcate its obligations on the public. We build, as I said the other day at Montreal, on the old foundations, though the result of our deliberations is popularly called "the new constitution." I deny that the principles on which we proceeded are novel or untried principles. These principles all exist, and for ages have existed, in the British Constitution. Some of the contrivances and adaptations of principles are new; but the Royal authority, Ministerial responsibility, a nominative Upper House, the full and free representation of the Commons, and the independence of the Judges, are not inventions of our making. We offer you no political patent medicine warranted to cure everything, nor do we pretend that our work is a perfect work; but if we cannot make it perfect, we have at least left it capable of revision, by the concurrence of the parties to the present settlement, and the consent of the same supreme authority from which we seek the original sanction of our plan. Still it is to be hoped that the necessity for any revision will seldom occur, for I am quite sure the people of these Provinces will never wish to have it said of their constitution, what the French bookseller of the last century said so wittily, on being asked for the French Constitution, that he did not deal in periodical publications. We build on the old foundations, and I trust I may say, in the spirit of the ancient founders, as well. The groundwork of the monarchical form of government is humility, self-denial, obedience, and holy fear. I know these are not nineteenth-century virtues, neither are they plants indigenous to the soil of the New World. Because it is a new world, as yet undisciplined, pride and self-assertion, and pretension, are more common than the great family of humble virtues whose names I have named. Pure democracy is very like pride—it is the "good-as-you" feeling carried into politics. Pure democracy asserts an unreal equality between youth and age, subject and magistrate, the weak and the strong, the vicious and the virtuous. But the same virtues which feed and nourish filial affection and conjugal peace in private life, are essential to uphold civil authority; and these are the virtues on which the monarchical form of government alone can be maintained.

. . . .

We have also solved, so far as the late Conferences could do so for these Provinces, the relation of the Crown to the people, the powers of the prerogative, and the sphere of the suffrage. We have preserved every British principle now in use among us, and we have recovered one or two that were well-nigh lost; we have been especially careful not to trench on the prerogative of the Crown, as to the rights, or rank, or income of its future representative on this continent; as to the dignity of the office, or the style and title of the future kingdom or viceroyalty, or by whatever other name it may be Her Majesty's pleasure to designate hereafter her dominions on this continent. Next to the United States, we have the most extended suffrage in the world; some think quite too far extended; but in our state of society, I do not see how that is to be avoided, in the selection at least, of the tax-imposing House of Parliament. We have, besides, restored to the Crown one of its essential attributes when, as the fountain of honour, we leave to the Sovereign the confirmation of the second and Conservative Chamber; and we preserve for the Crown its other great attribute, as the fountain of justice, by retaining its right to appoint the Judges, of course upon the advice of the Constitutional Councillors of the Queen in this country, who are in turn responsible to Parliament and the people for their advice and appointments. We have provided also, in our new arrangements, that the tenure of all offices shall be good behaviour, in contradistinction to the "spoils principle" of our next neighbours. In all these respects we have built on the old foundations, in the spirit of the old wisdom, and we have faith, therefore, that our work will stand.

Naturally, gentlemen, we cannot expect that our course will be all plain sailing. We must have our difficulties, as all states, new and old, have had; and this brings me to refer to the apprehensions excited as to the local legislatures. The difference of language between the majority of Lower Canada, and the majority of the whole union is a difficulty; but it is a difficulty which almost every other nation has had and has solved: in Belgium they have at least two languages, in Switzerland they have three chief languages—German, French, and Italian; the Federal form of Government, the compromise between great states and small, seems peculiarly adapted to conciliate difficulties of this description, and to keep politically together men of different origins and languages. I confess I have less anxiety on this score than I have on another—the proper protection of the minorities, as to religion in Upper and Lower Canada respectively. On this point there is no doubt a good deal of natural anxiety felt in these Townships, as there is among my own constituents in Montreal, and I dare say you would like me to enlarge upon it as the point most immediately interesting to yourselves.

I am, as you are, interested in the due protection of the rights of the minority, not only as an English-speaking member in Lower Canada, but as interested naturally and reasonably for my co-religionists, who form a minority in Upper Canada. I am persuaded as regards both minorities, that they can have abundant guarantees—sacred beyond the reach of sectarian or sectional domination—for all their rights, civil and religious. If we had failed to secure every possible constitutional guarantee for our minorities, east and west, I am sure the gentleman who may be considered your special representative at the Conference—(Hon. Mr. Galt)—and I am equally sure that I myself could have been no party to the conclusions of the late Conference. But we both believed—and all our Canadian colleagues went with us in this belief—that in securing the power of disallowance, under circumstances which might warrant it, to the General Government, in giving the appointment of Judges and Local Governors to the General Government, and in expressly providing in the Constitution for the educational rights of the minority, we had taken every possible guarantee, legislative, judicial, and educational against the oppression of a sectional minority by a sectional majority. You will have for your guarantee the Queen's name,—which I think the case of Ottawa has shown is not without power in Canada; you will have the subordination of the local to the general authority, provided in the constitutional charter itself, and you will have, besides, the great material guarantee, that in the General Government you will be two-thirds of the whole told by language,

and a clear majority counted by creed; and if with these odds you cannot protect your own interests, it will be the first time you ever failed to do so. The Protestant minority in Lower Canada and the Catholic minority in Upper Canada may depend upon it the General Government will never see them oppressed—even if there were any disposition to oppress them—which I hope there is not in Upper Canada; which I am quite sure there is not in Lower Canada. No General Government could stand for a single session under the new arrangements without Catholic as well as Protestant support; in fact, one great good to be expected from the larger interests with which that Government will have to deal will be, that local prejudices, and all other prejudices, will fall more and more into contempt, while our statesmen will rise more and more superior to such low and pitiful politics. What would be the effect of any set of men, in any subdivision of the Union, attempting, for example, the religious ascendency of any race or creed? Why the direct effect would be to condemn themselves and their principles to insignificance in the General Government. Neither you here, nor the Catholic minority in Upper Canada, will owe your local rights and liberties to the forbearance or goodwill of the neighbouring majority; neither of you will tolerate being tolerated; but all your special institutions, religious and educational, as well as all your general and common franchises and rights, will be secured under the broad seal of the Empire, which the strong arm of the General Government will suffer no bigot to break, and no province to lay its finger on, should any one be foolish enough to attempt it.

This is the frame of government we have to offer you, and to this system, when fully understood, I am certain you will give a cheerful and hearty adherence.

Document E–3

FRENCH CANADA AND THE NEW NATIONALITY

(T. D. McGee, "The New Nation and the Old Empire," Montreal *Gazette*, December 9, 1865.)

. . . English and French Canada remain, socially, if not politically distinct. English Canada is mainly Protestant, progressive and utilitarian; French Canada is mainly Catholic, conservative, and content with its present condition. Formerly there was a fierce and envenomed struggle for superiority between these great social divisions of a common country; wrongs and insults were inflicted and resented; but when under the act of union of the two Canadas, the equality of races and religions was established by law and custom, there was needed only the healing influence of time to remove the traces of ancient animosities, and to constitute ourselves, if not in all things, certainly in most things, one people. I never have concealed from myself nor from others the fact that the bilingual line which divides us socially is one of the difficulties of the government of this country. But though a difficulty, it is by no means a serious danger, unless it were to be aggravated by a sense of injustice, inflicted either by the local French majority on the English minority, or by the English majority on the French minority. So long as we respect in Canada the rights of minorities, told either by tongue or creed, we are safe, for so long it will be possible for us to be united; but when we cease to respect those rights, we will be in the full tide towards that madness which the ancients considered the gods sent those whom they wished to destroy.

. . . The diverse elements of our population, in language and creed, in Canada, make it a difficult country to govern. If every element of the population is to be represented in the government—if it is to be a microcosm, on a small scale of the whole population, then the twelve Councillors of the Queen's Representative must bring into the Council Chamber as many diverse views and opinions as there are in the country itself and, though it is one of the misfortunes of our position in some respects, still, on the whole, if the men who go there discharge their duty honestly to the Executive Chief Magistrate of this country, they cannot go far wrong, or justly offend the susceptabilities of any class of our people, whether English or French, or whether they kneel at one altar or another. The people of Canada, having the leadership of British North America, need, above all things, some general common principle that will lift them out of the shell of their narrow sectional and provincial politics.

. . . About ten years ago, when I first began to observe and travel through the various provinces of British North America, I made a careful observation of the public and private tendencies of the various classes of our society, to shape my course as far as I could in relation to what I found, the existing state of the public mind and intelligence in those colonies, and not only to govern myself thereupon but also to create new convictions, if it were in my power to do so, and to lead public sentiment in a direction towards the rational union of those several dissevered provinces. I have been blamed for using the phrase—"creating a new nation in the North," a phrase that has since acquired a great deal more significance than I ever could have given it, as it has been used in several offical documents, and employed in relation to the Maritime Provinces. The motives that govern me in the choice of that phrase— for it was not one hazarded at random— I will state. I believe then, and still believe, that we want an inspiration beyond the local, sectional and sectarian feelings that divided and yet separate us. I believe that, in relation to Upper Canada, for example, the only way to enlarge its views and liberalize them, was to show

the people there was a great future in store for the inhabitants of all British North America; that, instead of looking commercially, and to some extent politically, across lake Ontario and lake Erie, they ought to look down the St. Lawrence and among their fellow subjects on the sea-board. And when I went to the sea-board I held similar language to the people there, telling them they should look westward—not by way of the United States—but through their own country, to land under the same flag as that which floated over themselves. I saw that Canada was their natural avenue to the great west, and that the Atlantic Provinces were our natural and proper outlet to the ocean.

. . . To the British people here, who sometimes complain of more than their share of patronage being given to the French Canadian, I say, is there a country in the world where, on the whole, you have been better treated than in Canada. To the American citizen who boasts of greater liberty in the States, I say that a man can state his private, social, political and religious opinions with more freedom here than in New York or New England. There is, besides, far more liberty and toleration enjoyed by minorities in Canada than in the United States. I would rather be a serf of a Russian Boyar than of that many-headed monster, public opinion, that will not permit me to have my own private opinions on subjects social, religious, national and political.

Document E—4

THE BOUNDARIES OF FRENCH CANADA

(T. D. McGee, *Speeches and Addresses* . . . [London: 1865]. pp. 288, 290, 301–2.)

. . . Now, Sir, I wish to say a few words in reference to what I call the social relations which I think ought to exist and are likely to spring up between the people of the Lower Provinces and ourselves if there is a closer communication established between us, and also in reference to the social fitness to each of the parties to this proposed union. And first, I will make a remark to some of the French Canadian gentlemen who are said to be opposed to our project, on French Canadian grounds only. I will remind them, I hope not improperly, that every one of the colonies we now propose to re-unite under one rule—in which they shall have a potential voice—were once before united as New France. (Cheers.) Newfoundland, the uttermost, was theirs, and one large section of its coast is still known as "the French shore;" Cape Breton was theirs till the final fall of Louisburgh; Prince Edward Island was their Island of St. Jean; Charlottetown was their Port Joli; and Fredericton, the present capital of New Brunswick, their St. Anne's; in the heart of Nova Scotia was that fair Arcadian land, where the roll of Longfellow's noble hexameters may be heard in every wave that breaks upon the base of Cape Blomedon. (Cheers.) In the northern counties of New Brunswick, from the Miramachi to the Matapediae, they had their forts and farms, their churches and their festivals, before the English speech had ever once been heard between those rivers. . . .

. . . .

. . . Well, gentlemen of French origin, we propose to restore these long-lost compatriots to your protection: in the Federal Union, which will recognise equally both languages, they will naturally look to you; their petitions will come to you, and their representatives will naturally be found allied with you. Suppose those four New Brunswick counties are influenced by the French vote, and say two in Nova Scotia, you will, should you need them, have them as sure allies to

your own compact body, to aid your legitimate influence in the Federal Councils.

. . . .

—I beg to offer a few observations *apropos* of my own position as an English-speaking member for Lower Canada. I venture, in the first place, to observe that there seems to be a good deal of exaggeration on the subject of race, occasionally introduced, both on the one side and the other, in this section of the country. I congratulate my honourable friend the Attorney-General for this section on his freedom from such prejudices in general, though I still think in matters of patronage and the like he always looks first to his own compatriots—(laughter)—for which neither do I blame him. But this theory of race is sometimes carried to an anti-christian and unphilosophical excess. Whose words are these—"God hath made of one blood all nations that dwell on the face of the earth?" Is not that the true theory of race? For my part, I am not afraid of the French Canadian majority in the future local Government doing injustice, except accidentally; not because I am of the same religion as themselves; for origin and language are barriers stronger to divide men in this world than is religion to unite them. Neither do I believe that my Protestant compatriots need have any such fear. The French Canadians have never been an intolerant people; it is not in their temper, unless they had been persecuted, perhaps, and then it might have been as it has been with other races of all religions. Perhaps, on this subject, the House will allow me to read a very striking illustration of the tolerance of French Canadian character from a book I hold in my hand, the "Digest of the Synod Minutes of the Presbyterian Church of Canada," by my worthy friend, the Rev. Mr. Kemp, of the Free Church of Montreal. The passage is on page seven of the Introduction:—

"About the year 1790 the Presbyterians of Montreal of all denominations, both British and American, organised themselves into a Church, and in the following year secured the services of the Rev. John Young. At this time they met in the Récollet Roman Catholic Church, but in the year following they erected the edifice which is now known as St. Gabriel Street Church—the oldest Protestant Church in the Province. In their early Minutes we find them, in acknowledgment of the kindness of the Récollet Fathers, presenting them with 'One box of candles, 56lbs., at 8*d*., and one hogshead of Spanish wine at 6*l*. 5*s*.' "

(Laughter.) I beg my hon. friends, who may have different notions of Christian intercourse at this time of day, just to fancy doings of that sort. (Hear, hear.) Here, on the one hand, are the Récollet Fathers giving up one of their own churches to the disciples of John Knox to enable them to worship God after their own manner, and perhaps to have a gird at Popery in the meantime—(laughter)—and here, on the other hand, are the grateful Presbyterians presenting to these same Seminary priests Presbyterian wine and Presbyterian wax tapers in acknowledgment of the use of their church for Presbyterian service. Certainly a more characteristic instance of tolerance on both sides can hardly be found in the history of any other country.